M

RUNNING MATES

RUNNING MATES

The Making of
a First Lady

Ann Grimes

WILLIAM MORROW AND COMPANY, INC.
New York

...ather,
...imes,
with love

Library of Congress Cataloging-in-Publication Data

Grimes, Ann.
    Running mates : the making of a first lady / Ann Grimes.
        p.   cm.
    ISBN 0-688-08532-6
    1. Presidents—United States—Election—1988. 2. Presidents—
United States—Wives. 3. Women in politics—United States.
4. Bush, Barbara, 1925- . 5. Dukakis, Kitty. I. Title.
E880.G75 1990
973.928'092—dc20   89-78542
                                                                        CIP

Printed in the United States of America

First Edition

1 2 3 4 5 6 7 8 9 10

BOOK DESIGN BY PAUL CHEVANNES

CONTENTS

ACKNOWLEDGMENTS

Writing a book, like running for president, is in its own way a marathon. It can't be done alone. There are many people whose time, patience, and insight helped shape this project. I am grateful for the cooperation of nearly two hundred individuals who were interviewed for this book, some at length several times over two years. I want especially to thank Barbara Bush, who talked with me frequently during the 1988 campaign, and took time from her White House schedule to share her thoughts. I also want to thank all of the Bush children, Nancy Bush Ellis, and members of Mrs. Bush's White House staff: Susan Porter Rose, Anna Perez, Jean Becker, and Sondra Haley.

I am also grateful to Kitty Dukakis who shared her thoughts with me both during the campaign and after the 1988 election. John, Andrea, and Kara Dukakis also shared their personal reflections with me on several occasions. Paul Costello, Bonnie Shershow, and John Keller of Mrs. Dukakis's campaign staff were extremely helpful.

I also want to thank Hattie Babbitt, B. A. Bentsen, Elizabeth Dole, Tipper Gore, Jane Gephardt, Jackie Jackson, Marilyn Quayle, and Jeanne Simon with whom I spent time on and off the campaign trail.

My agent, David Black, who got the project going, has been a good-natured friend throughout. I am indebted to Lisa Drew, my editor at William Morrow, who helped me enormously in shaping the book and making the leap to book writing. I also want to thank Bob Shuman and Joan Amico of Morrow for their enduring patience and help in getting the manuscript done.

Several colleagues read the manuscript and gave invaluable input. Patrick Clinton of Northwestern's Medill School of Journalism provided unparalleled support and painstaking commentary on the manuscript from start to finish. Two long-time veterans of the Washington political scene read the manuscript before publication. Tom Oliphant of *The Boston Globe* made several helpful suggestions. Columnist Jules Witcover of the *Baltimore Sun* provided both suggestions and encouragement at key points along the way.

Bonnie Booth, Mike DeMar, Liz Villere, and Ariane Sweeney helped at various points with research and tape transcription.

I want to thank Roy Larson of *The Chicago Reporter* for extending me a leave of absence to complete the project and the *Reporter* staff for bearing with an editor who disappeared.

Finally, I want to extend personal thanks to my parents and family—Paul, Tom, Peter, Merilee, and Serge—and thank several people who give new meaning to the word *friendship*. Bill Stamets helped in countless ways: from tracking candidates' ever-changing schedules to turning his quirky filmmaker's eye to the manuscript time and again. Cathy Altman of TLK advertising in Chicago came up with the title. Cindy Hoffman, George Booz, Dolores Wilber, Ben Goldhagen, Connie McKenna, Pat Schulman, Susan Chaplinsky, Vicki Barker, and Pam Janis read portions of the manuscript, put me up during my cross-country travels, and most important, provided me with emotional support throughout the writing of this book.

CHAPTER ONE

A Loss and a Win

The Presidency is much more than an institution.
It is a focus of feelings.

—JAMES DAVID BARBER,
Presidential Character

On the afternoon of March 9, 1989, dozens of reporters gathered in the the lower-level conference room of Boston's Park Plaza Hotel. As they waited for noon to arrive, the air grew warm, the atmosphere collegial. The room steadily filled with members of the media, some of whom hadn't seen each other in Boston since the night of Mike Dukakis's defeat. That evening, they had waited for the election returns to trickle in. Now, four months later, they waited to hear Kitty Dukakis explain why she had spent the last twenty-eight days in a Rhode Island alcoholic-treatment center.

Sitting around the dusky-pink Art Deco Terrace Room few talked of the governor's wife. Reporters swapped information on flights and departure times that would return them to New York, Washington, and other news hubs. It seemed a bit like a reunion of grown-up campers from the campaign trail. The governor's aides scurried about. Massachusetts statehouse people mixed with those who had toiled on the failed election effort. Old names and faces now were matched with new jobs. Colleagues who hadn't seen each other in months embraced, caught up, swapping news of former associates.

As 12:30 approached, and the hubbub grew to the noisy pitch of a party, a handful of photographers gathered near a side door. "Awwww, here she comes," murmured Kitty's old friend Anne Harney as the door began to open. Suddenly, cameras clicked into action and Kitty stepped into a blaze of paparazzi light.

Under the glare of the minicams, the conference room suddenly turned into that stratum of theater called news. Isolated on stage, Kitty nervously surveyed the room. Dressed in bright red, her favorite campaign color, she looked drawn, thinner than she had on the campaign trail. Then, her liquid brown eyes had flashed invitingly at cameramen across the country. Now, they gleamed stonily into the lights.

The governor looked ashen, grim. As his wife spoke, he stared blankly up at her from a seat at her side. He barely moved as Kitty gave brief introductory remarks, then began to read a poem given to her by another patient from Edgehill-Newport, the center where she had been treated and released just two days before.

> "Don't be fooled by me,
> Don't be fooled by the face I wear,
> For I wear a thousand masks,
> Masks that I'm afraid to take off,
> And none of them are me. . . ."

As she read, her father, retired Boston Pops conductor Harry Ellis Dickson, eighty years old at the time, looked on impassively from the front row, his arms folded across his chest. In another row sat Kitty's former trio of aides, on hand to lend moral support. They watched in sorrow as this woman they'd been so close to reviewed and detailed an emotional trauma they said they knew little of until just the month before. Nattily attired Paul Costello, her press secretary, was up for the day from Washington at the governor's bidding. As Kitty spoke, Costello took care to survey the room, trying to read reporters' reactions. Bonnie Shershow, Kitty's diminutive campaign traveling aide, sat next to him, dwarfed by Kitty's former speechwriter, John Keller. When the press conference was done, the three were scheduled to join Kitty for lunch.

". . . I give the impression that I am secure,
That all is sunny with me,
That confidence is my name
And coolness my game.
That the water's calm,
And I'm in command,
And that I need no one,
And don't believe me please. . . ."

Behind the press pack, the governor's top confidants—Jack Corrigan, his deputy chief of staff, and John Sasso, who had served as his campaign manager—wanly looked on. Reporters shifted uncomfortably in their seats. One usually tenacious newsmagazine writer decided he would not be asking questions, and listlessly scratched at his notebook with his pen. Others listened quietly, sorry to have to witness this raw display of private despair, especially from a woman who had become a favorite during the grueling election year.

After months on the campaign trail, this is what it had come to for Kitty. After all the "Meet 'n' Greets" in Iowa, Illinois, New York. The highs of the primary wins. And the devastating lows of the November defeat. After months of being so many things to so many people, some reporters wondered privately how she could not feel as if she were wearing a mask. After months of ricocheting across the country, rarely being home, after fighting such an embattled, bitter campaign, was this really unexpected?

"People are less interested in you as a person than as an image they want to see. And whether you like it or not, if you're campaigning all the time, you fulfill that image" is how Kitty's daughter Andrea, twenty-three years old at the time, tried to explain her mother's postelection condition.

"I think you retain your sense of self, but it gets blurred with the fact that you're expected to go out and make these appearances. Constantly. And not for yourself, but for your spouse. So your identity becomes wrapped up in being an image for your spouse. Or you're not sure if you're projecting 'you' or your spouse. And whether that projection is really 'you,' or something that you're expected to project."

Compounding identity questions was a cruel history of depression that no one dared talk about on the campaign trail, or even that day in March. Then, her eyes glistening, her voice trembling with emotion, Kitty reached the end of her poem and described her problems this way:

> ". . . Do not pass me by,
> Please, do not pass me by,
> Who am I? You may wonder,
> I am someone you know very well,
> For I am every alcoholic man or woman
> You know."

Kitty paused and swiftly answered a few reporters' questions. Then she and the governor, trailed by a coterie of aides, left the hotel. And Kitty joined her former aides for lunch.

The same week Kitty Dukakis retreated to Rhode Island, Barbara Bush undertook her first foreign trip as first lady—to Ottawa, Canada. Then she got her first weekend "off" at the Bush family estate in Kennebunkport, Maine.

Traveling to Canada with the national press corps on February 10 must have seemed like a new round of campaigning to the new president and his wife. There were the nonstop schedule of public events, the carefully worded statements, the artfully arranged photo opportunities. Reporters engaged in the familiar scramble for seats on the press bus as a convoy of limousines carried off the principal players. For the winners of the presidential sweepstakes, it seemed, the whirlwind pace of the past long months would not end at all.

After the day spent with Canadian Prime Minister Brian Mulroney and his perky wife, Mila, during which both Bushes were pelted with questions about acid rain, it was close to midnight when the presidential party flew into the airport at Portland, Maine. While the Bushes were helicoptered to Walker's Point, reporters quickly picked up rental cars and followed neatly typed directions that would get them within range of the new vacation White House.

It was just three weeks since the inauguration and the first chance Mrs. Bush had to relax, lace up some sneakers, sport a pair of jeans in public, and make more "news" with her husband. This time, it was a "spontaneous" Saturday morning stroll from the Bushes' compound at Walker's Point to downtown Kennebunkport on a chilly Saturday morning: an excursion on which the couple's every move down what residents call the Shore Road, and every exchange of pleasantries with shopkeepers and neighbors was chronicled by the national press who followed in their wake like pushy puppies.

The next day, after attending Sunday morning services at a postcard-perfect New England church, George met for a closed-door policy give-and-take with specialists in Soviet affairs assembled from across the country. Barbara—"Bar," as her husband and friends call her—headed out of the main house to a nearby converted gardener's cottage where George Bush has an office—waiting for the men to leave so she could take a hot bath. Wearing a turquoise-and-green-striped turtleneck underneath a clashing tutti-frutti-striped sweater, large pearl earrings, and blue jeans, she propped her black Reeboks up on the president's desk and gabbed at length about Kitty Dukakis, the White House, and her new station in life.

Back in D.C., Bar had watched the news when the Massachusetts governor, in a manner that many viewers thought chillingly dispassionate, told the country that his wife would undergo treatment for alcoholism. When she heard the news, Mrs. Bush said she was "devastated." She released a public statement of sympathy, and like thousands of people across the country, dashed off an empathetic personal note.

Ever mindful of the two worlds of Washington, D.C.—the world of "off-the-record," or unvarnished truth, and the world of "on-the-record," or carefully chosen words bandied about for public consumption—Bar said her views about Kitty and Mike were to stay "off-the-record." She did note, however, that Kitty had joined a sad casualty list of political wives and former first ladies whose problems with drugs and alcohol testify to the tremendous pressures of political life on the political wife.

Then talk turned to *her* new life.

Mrs. Bush described how *she* had managed to steel herself against the pitfalls of a possible loss. It was by keeping an emotional distance and a dry Yankee wit, she figured. By never actually believing her husband was going to win. "I always thought we were going to lose," she confided, as a young, casually dressed aide brought out hot tea and freshly baked but slightly burned cookies. With her muddied spaniel, Millie, bounding around the room, Mrs. Bush said she certainly didn't want George to win the presidency for her sake. "I haven't really wanted this for so long. At all. I couldn't have cared *less*, really, as far as for myself, honestly," she insisted.

Pausing between sips of tea, she looked around the room, with its large flagstone fireplace, oil painting of the sea, and ocean view. "I would have liked it if we hadn't [won]," she admitted, though it is difficult to imagine the busy Bushes, compulsive socializers that they are, ensconced alone for long periods of time in the eleven-acre compound at Walker's Point. Owned by the Bush family since 1902, the rocky peninsula jutting into the Atlantic is the only place where the two have planted emotional roots during their nomadic married life. Looking at the expansive house with its breathtaking view of the sea—now interrupted by crisscrossing Coast Guard patrols—Bar insisted she would have "loved to have come back here and cleared out all this junk and had our own life back. . . ."

What would she have done, had her husband lost? She thought a second, laughed cavalierly, and imagined a trip with him down the Inland Waterway. Or a barge trip through the French wine country. Or fishing in Baja.

"But now that I'm in the White House," she said, energy infusing her voice, "I'm liking it."

Despite what she said, one sensed ambivalence in Barbara Bush that winter day in Maine. It was hard to know whether that came from uncertainty about the expectations ahead, anxiety over having to carve a niche of her own for the first time in her life, or awareness of the rigors of White House life, having had a close-up view for the last eight years. After all that time of being George Bush's wife, for the first time ever, Barbara Bush had a position much more of her own. One certainly tied to, but separate from, her husband's. Asked about the expectations of the public, she replied, "They're laying an enormous load on me, if you want to know the truth. I think that is fair to say."

★ ★ ★

There is nothing in public life to compare with the rigors of a presidential campaign.

"In order to begin to understand what a White House aspirant puts into his reach for power, and what it takes out of him, it is necessary to accept that running for President is no one-year crash effort, but a way of life extending over a number of years," Jules Witcover wrote in *Marathon*, his book on the 1976 Ford-Carter race. "The exercise is no romantic odyssey, at the end of which the winner emerges bright and shining and ennobled by the experience. It is a grueling, debilitating, and often dehumanizing ordeal that exacts an extravagant price not only for winning but also the mere running and losing."

What Witcover says of candidates is true. Certainly the losing candidate pays a very high price for this run. Not far behind him are his wife and family, whose price is less public and whose stories usually don't make it to the history books.

Politics as practiced in this country is a family business. In the 1988 presidential race family became a bigger part of the packaging of the presidency. In an effort to reach out to voters' emotions, family members were cast in key roles in America's election pageant. Large and telegenic, George Bush's family became useful for campaign commercials. The image of the family—even in a fifteen-second video clip or sound bite—carries what candidates, especially presidential contenders, like to think is a potent message about themselves.

During a presidential race children of candidates often put their lives on hold to make endless campaign appearances. Such appearances testify to their father's humanity, even if a political career has in fact kept this man far away from home, and his constituents know him better than his own flesh and blood do. Children frequently organize on his behalf; they appear at events where his schedule precludes him. In the 1988 election George Bush, Jr., and John Dukakis, the candidates' eldest children, functioned as political operatives, bridging the potentially troublesome gap between family and staff. Each in his own way acted as a watchdog in an arena where political consultants "treat their candidates like red meat," to quote the youngest of Bush's four sons, Marvin, thirty-two years old in 1989.

Candidates' wives, too, have a job. Usually an unpaid job that has grown in visibility as American politicians and their handlers try to add an intimate sense of character to the political equation. Wives provide a window on to the candidate's character. Our president and his spouse are a kind of Mr. and Mrs. America. Desperate to distinguish increasingly similar candidates, voters in their search for answers look at them on the campaign trail, and ask, "What does this couple's life have to do with ours?" Voters wonder, "Does this candidate tie his personal life to his vision of leadership, and what he can do for the country?" And perhaps most important, "Can he convince us that because he cares about his own family, he will care about ours, too?"

Wives, giving yeoman service, help candidates deal with those important questions which the voters and the media seem insistent on having answers to, even though the campaign-arranged answers they receive may not mean much.

Going under the microscope, wives present themselves for inspection. That act is more important than anything they can say. But some speak on the issues and try to provide persuasive responses to queries about marriage that probably no one could answer confidently. The wife is not a candidate—her name never appears on a ballot—but she often performs like one. She is seen and heard, but not too loudly.

Conventional wisdom has it that these wives must support their husbands and families and endure the strain of separation, while appearing to love every minute of a life where chaos becomes the norm. When things are going well out on the stump, the wife experiences the same rush of adrenaline and ego boosting as the candidate—she may be speaking on her husband's behalf, but the applause is for her. Like her husband she gains celebrity status. Exposure. Confidence.

When times get tough, she becomes a cheerleader rallying demoralized staffers. Like a den mother urging unhappy campers to put up tents in the rain, she perseveres even in races everyone knows are shot. When she is in trouble, she can't—or doesn't—retreat into the privacy of her bedroom and quietly sing the blues. When her husband loses, she too is abruptly forgotten. When he wins, she takes on what *Time* magazine once called an "ill-defined, unpaid job," one that forces her to dance and dodge "the many conflicting notions Americans hold about women as mothers, wives, lovers, friends, colleagues."

And leaders.

★   ★   ★

On November 11, 1988, just three days after her husband was defeated in his campaign to become president of the United States,

Kitty Dukakis met with reporters for a three-hour session of wrap-up, postmortem interviews in her modest home in Brookline, Massachusetts. One reporter asked: "In the face of obvious disappointment, Mike Dukakis goes back to work. He has a structure. He has tons of aides around him. It's not quite that simple or set up for you. What will you do?"

Still numb, exhaustion etched on her carefully made-up face, she sat upright in a straight-backed dining-room chair. Next to her, the polished table was strewn with campaign memorabilia—posters, snapshots, an odd can of Hawaiian potato chips. The reporter's question was already more than hypothetical. Governor Dukakis was back at work, taking the Green Line to his office each morning to battle with a state budget gone awry in his long absence. Following a tearful farewell lunch, Kitty's personal staff had departed for new jobs, new opportunities. Even the closest of her aides had declined to stay on.

What would she do? In answer to the reporter's question, Kitty talked of returning to direct a design program at Harvard. She would keep up on issues that interested her: homelessness and refugee resettlement. She spoke mechanically, with at best a dutiful enthusiasm, of plans to start an AIDS nutrition program. The readjustment would, she said, "take some real challenge and opportunity."

It would take more than she had.

Three months after his election defeat, on February 7, 1989, Mike Dukakis announced to the press that his wife had entered a $271-a-day treatment program for alcoholism. "Unfortunately, a combination of physical exhaustion, the stress of the campaign effort and the postelection letdown all combined to create a situation in which, on a limited number of occasions while at home, she has used alcohol in excessive quantities," he said.

Dukakis's announcement was cold and off-putting, marked by the same difficulty at expressing emotion that had hurt him so much in the campaign.

While Barbara Bush spent the weeks following the election busily preparing to make her twenty-ninth move in forty-four years, Kitty Dukakis described her days in the modest Brookline duplex she and the governor have shared since 1972 as "terribly painful and lonely."

Indeed, the picture friends sketched of that period was a grim one—a time of unreturned phone calls, of listlessness, of despair escaped via unhappy avenues of antidepressants and vodka. Already a "dependent" person (five years before the election she had kicked a twenty-six-year addiction to amphetamines), Kitty was scared enough by her new alliance with a liquor bottle to seek new treatment. Although in the early Iowa phase of the campaign reporters occasionally saw her drinking with campaign staff in hotel bars, and she later confessed to binging sometime before the New York primary, no one, including her own top aides, admitted to seeing her drink to excess during the more demanding general-election campaign. Just two days after Bush's victory, Kitty said, she began to drink. Only her closest friend touched on the real root of Kitty's reaction.

"This last bout was massive depression, that's really what it was," her old friend and confidante Sandy Bakalar said some months later. "I think it is fair to say that it's the loss, the sense of loss that brought about the depression. And it was a loss of everything. Absolutely everything."

Everything: A life-style. An identity. A future.

Four years before, when Dukakis was contemplating his bid for the White House, top aides told him he had nothing to lose by seeking the presidency. Kitty backed him all the way. In hindsight, a senior aide said shortly after Dukakis decided not to seek reelection as governor, they didn't know what they were getting into. Look at what happened, the aide said. "The wife's in wherever. The state's in the toilet. He's unemployed. And everyone thinks he's a jerk."

"There was nothing they didn't lose," Sandy Bakalar added, talking over coffee in the living room of her Chestnut Hill home. "It's the feeling 'If I'm so good, and I worked so hard, how come I couldn't make a difference?'"

Bakalar, a wispy attractive former social worker now married to a retired industrialist, said she watched her friend Kitty sacrifice all control over her life. "I think that when you lose that kind of control over your life you become in some ways very dependent and you become very protected. You are going to have a hard time when they take it all away."

There was also the embarrassment of letting so many people down. Disappointing all the people who supported them. Who worked for nothing. Gave up their law practices. Risked marriages and sacrificed a normal home life. "I am thinking about what

Kitty was feeling," Bakalar said slowly. "You feel so guilty about everything that everybody has done for you that you just don't want to look at any of them. You just cut yourself off. It is just too much to deal with. . . . 'Think of all the money that we spent.' 'Think of all the time.' 'Think of everything and look what we did.' It's like 'I am so embarrassed, I can't face anybody.'

"There you are, November eighth, looking great and wonderful on TV. And on November ninth you have to go to the super-market," Bakalar recalled. "It isn't as though you lose your job, it is much bigger than that. It's much more like an artist who paints a picture and everybody says 'That's lousy' while the artist is standing there. And let me tell you that is devastating. Because basically they are saying that *you* are lousy."

The perks of celebrity status—the private planes, the lim-ousines, the nonstop attention that Kitty's friends say she loved—all of these vanished overnight. "She was flying thirty thousand feet high," said another friend, "and then BAM." He slammed his fist into his palm—hard—to show just how quickly dreams can end.

During the campaign there were moments when Kitty longed for some time alone. When it was over, that was all she had.

But there was more to what Kitty Dukakis went through than mere exhilaration and disappointment brought on by her own medical history and the pressures of the campaign loss. In a year when the role of first lady seemed in the process of a sea change, no one pushed harder than Kitty Dukakis to create a new model for candidates' wives. She took on one of the most basic ideas about practical politics, the role of women in their husbands' ca-reers, and even public life itself, and invited recognition that she was more than just Mike's wife. She sought and won a place of achievement for herself. Over the two-year span of the 1988 race she tested conventions that had bound political wives in the past. In the end, her efforts didn't bring about the desired result for her husband, herself, or for women on the political stage. Indeed, in 1988 the political system still rewarded what it always had—a con-ventional public wife: the antithesis of the notion that women can actively create an independent place for themselves. In 1988 that was not what American women got at all.

Like Kitty Dukakis, when the campaign was over Barbara Bush found herself alone—but in quite a different way. She found herself in a spot her best friend, Mary Ann Stewart, unexpectedly described as "a very lonely place."

On January 20, 1989, Barbara Bush was catapulted to a standing that made her potentially the most powerful woman in politics in America. For this she will undoubtedly earn a place on next year's *Good Housekeeping* list of most admired women, a pedestal few American women have achieved by votes instead of vows. At a time when women are still underrepresented in the U.S. Senate and House of Representatives, the first lady continues to have power, though she gains it the old-fashioned way: by marrying it.

Not elected, but bound to love, honor, obey, and follow the nation's highest elected public servant, Barbara Bush found herself faced with enormous demands and duties.

"In a job as responsible as first lady," Mrs. Stewart said, "you're totally dependent upon yourself."

Mrs. Stewart, known as Andy, is a slight perky woman—the kind who drops grocery bags on the floor of her helter-skelter kitchen, then forages through them for cookies she never finds. Sitting in her home in the posh Palisades quarter of Washington one rainy afternoon, looking out at a gnarled, blooming cherry tree, she reflected on the road ahead for her dear friend, a woman she has known for over twenty years.

She saw Barbara's new path to the Rose Garden as thorny. "It's a hard role, and I think you have to be ready for it, and to have had enough experience so that it isn't depressing, or lonely, or too tough."

Mrs. Stewart, widow of U.S. Supreme Court Associate Justice Potter Stewart, pointed to the element of physical danger facing the president. She pointed to the lack of privacy. "You either have too much of it, or too little. Not being able to be outside all the time as much as you want. . . . Not being able to drop in on people." There are the public expectations. The first lady is expected to do her bit yet not stray from a cautious norm lest she damage her husband.

All that comes alongside the grand perks: Meeting the world's most fascinating people. Acquiring a national forum for your deepest concerns. Being able to stand for things that you feel are worthwhile. "It is awesome," Mrs. Stewart marveled. "[But] anybody in a high position, when the decision is theirs entirely as to what to do, and how to handle it"—she paused—"I mean, people can advise you all you want, but the buck stops with you. That's the duty of a first lady, too."

★   ★   ★

In Washington some pundits argue that since the Carter White House, when Americans elect a president, they inceasingly elect a team.

"As Nancy Reagan's influence has been chronicled and criticized, press and public have been educated about what White House intimates have always known: You can't dismiss the influence of the person who shares the bed of the President of the United States," *The Washington Post* commented in July of 1987.

Nearly a year before the election, political analysts such as Norman Ornstein at the American Enterprise Institute, a conservative Washington think tank, pointed to Nancy Reagan and Rosalynn Carter as important transitional figures in shaping the public's expectations of presidential wives. "The experience of both . . . has sensitized people to the fact that you elect a team, not just president and vice-president," he said.

Six years into her husband's tenure Nancy Reagan was credited with—and criticized for—elevating her post to a kind of "associate presidency." During the 1988 campaign political operatives began to recognize the candidate's spouse as the one adviser certain to accompany a president-elect to the White House. Apparently voters noticed too. "The total package is important," fifty-six-year-old Twila Awanek, a Des Moines voter, told a reporter fourteen months before election day.

Walking with her infant son from a Brookline, Massachusetts, voting booth, another voter, thirty-one-year-old cancer epidemiologist Abby Janov, agreed. "If I'd been asked that eight years ago, I'd have said no," she responded. "But Nancy Reagan made it very clear that a spouse really, whether female or male, can play an important role. So it's important to see and know about the spouse."

Other analysts say voters don't want to elect a team or co-president. They say a wife can't help a candidate but can hurt one. They point out that if Bush's controversial choice of Dan Quayle as vice-president didn't derail the GOP ticket, a spouse, even if seen as a liability, certainly couldn't hurt that much.

"I think that people are voting for the individual," said Linda DiVall, president of American Viewpoint, a Republican polling and research group. "There is some evidence, in 1976, for example, that Betty Ford was certainly an asset to Gerry Ford. You try to take advantage of that by the way you put the campaign together. But people in this country are voting for the chief executive and that is one individual."

On June 3, 1989, Nancy Reagan returned to Washington to plug her own Washington insider "kiss-and-tell" book, a tome with all the depth of an upscale shopping trip. Stopping by the Library of Congress for a panel discussion on the first lady's role, she took on her critics and shared her decidedly mixed feelings about the "job."

She said living in the White House "was not a sacrifice to be endured, but an honorable opportunity to serve. I wouldn't trade our time in the White House for even extra years added to my life." But, she observed, "I found the life of a first lady is sometimes difficult to explain to those who haven't been through it. One thing most people don't realize—and I certainly didn't realize it until I'd gotten a few bumps and scrapes—is this: You just don't move into the White House, you must learn how to live there. Life in that mansion is different."

Her personal insecurities aside, Mrs. Reagan sounded like first ladies of the past when she said she sometimes felt as if she had been "kidnapped and kept up in an attic" at the White House. She described it as a place where "the highs are higher and the lows lower" than anywhere else.

Like other women who have held the position Nancy Reagan pointed to the pressure she felt against openly speaking her mind as one of the biggest drawbacks for the president's wife. "Ironically, in some ways a first lady loses her freedom of speech," she told the friendly gathering in the Coolidge Auditorium. Seeing screaming headlines she felt powerless to respond to—the *New York Post*'s ASTROLOGER RULED WHITE HOUSE or *Time* magazine's WHY MRS. REAGAN STILL LOOKS LIKE A MILLION—she recalled, "There were things I longed to say over those eight years but I couldn't. At times it wasn't appropriate. At other times it would have further complicated my husband's life. I don't mind telling you it was frus-tra-ting," she said, gritting her teeth to the group's sympathetic laughter.

Six months earlier, just a few days before she and her husband moved back to California, Mrs. Reagan had discussed her role with Mike Wallace in a *60 Minutes* interview.

"Nobody understands what it's like to be here until you're here," she told him. "Nobody understands all the pressures—I've never worked harder in my life. All the people see is the glamour of it, the state dinners, the meeting people. . . . But they don't—they have no conception of what the other part is."

When the 1988 presidential race began, thirteen women thought they were ready to find out.

CHAPTER TWO

~~~

The Competition Lines Up

Campaigning in America is done with wives,
wives are on public display; the code calls for
their participation, however unrealistic this code
may be.

—THEODORE WHITE,
The Making of the President, 1964

It was the first time anyone could remember a First Ladies Forum,
an occasion that more than any other over the next long months of
the 1988 race resembled a beauty contest. Indeed, when each of
the women—dressed in a photogenic spectrum of "Nancy" reds,
polite pinks, businesslike navys, and summery whites—got up to
speak for her allotted five minutes and tell Iowa and the world
what she would do as first lady, the format reminded a veteran
Washington Post reporter of "the Big Question at the end of the
Miss America competition, the one that's supposed to reveal the
I.Q. above the bathing suit."

And this was supposed to be the Year-of-the-Spouse.

In some ways of course it was. From the start, as the Polk
County, Iowa, Democrats' First Ladies Forum indicated on July
26, 1987, more than fifteen months before 91,584,820 voters (out of
182,628,000 voting-age Americans) would select Ronald Reagan's
replacement, there was an unprecedented—and serious—focus on
the candidates' spouses as full partners in the political process.

Headlines signaled the trend: POLITICAL WIVES A POTENT

FORCE IN RACE TO D.C. *(New Orleans Times-Picayune)*. POLITI-
CIANS IN THEIR OWN RIGHT: CANDIDATES WIVES STEP INTO
NEW ROLES *(Chicago Sun-Times)*. POLITICAL HELPMATES WITH
AGENDAS OF THEIR OWN: CANDIDATES' WIVES STAND BY THEIR
MEN—AND ON THEIR OWN . . . *(New York Newsday)*. Grand-
motherly Barbara Bush showing off her puppies in the White
House, or Kitty Dukakis nursing her emotional scars, was not
what political pundits had in mind when the "spin" on the wives
started up back in the summer of '87. That wasn't the way the
political operatives saw it. For them, wives were an invaluable
campaign commodity—conveyers of such messages as "Workplace
Democracy" and "Good Jobs at Good Wages."

"In Iowa," one of Dick Gephardt's canvassers said, watching
the candidate's wife, Jane, greet diners in an Iowa City mall restaurant—the kind that doesn't know what a vegetable is—"people
make decisions on character. The spouse and kids tell a lot. People
want to have an opportunity to meet her," he insisted. "They
make their decision by getting to meet her."

Workers in all campaigns took that dogma to heart. Everyone
assumed that in order to reach voters, surrogates, especially wives,
were indispensable members of the supporting cast. For the first
time since 1960 no incumbent ruled the race. Wives could help the
baffled voter winnow the field. If successful, she could help
staffers keep their jobs for a few months more at least.

Wives could also help narrow the so-called "gender gap." They
could reach out to the ten million female voters who were expected
to make the difference in this election. Operatives hoped candidates' wives with their own professions could boost their husbands' images as sympathetic to women's concerns. Working
wives of candidates sharing their own juggling acts—kids, job,
home and husband, plus campaign—wives with jobs talking
"pocketbook" issues, wives talking day care, parental leave, pay
equity—would reach at least half of the many two-income couples
out there. The sisterhood of wives touting their spouses' records of
hiring women couldn't hurt. Nor could wives with panache. Celebrity status. And old-fashioned good looks. On the front line of
visibility the wife of a presidential contender became a role model.
Before her stood a whole community of American women. Women
would watch what she did. Men would watch, too. Wives would
help, operatives calculated.

★

For the candidates and their wives that edict translated into accommodating the seemingly endless whims of Iowa voters. And so on July 26, 1987, the "fabulous dwarfettes," as Hattie Babbitt dubbed the sorority of spouses, got up on stage at Drake University.

Reporters watching the event that day saw some of the six women nervously smooch the air behind each other's ears in greeting. Over fifty reporters, including a TV news crew from Germany, had turned up. So did nearly three hundred Iowans who paid ten dollars apiece to get a seat in the school auditorium. The women milled around the foyer, trailed by minicams. Only one was trailed by a candidate. Senator Joseph Biden of Delaware followed his thirty-six-year-old wife, Jill, telling the press, "I'm just carrying her bags today. She comes where I go. Why shouldn't I come where she goes?" Protests aside, a parade of minicams lit his path, not hers.

Once they were at the podium things calmed down thanks to Hattie, wife of former Arizona Governor Bruce Babbitt, who opened with a joke: "It's a real honor to be here when I think of women who did so much as first lady. People with names like Eleanor Roosevelt, Jacqueline Kennedy, Rosalynn Carter.

"And then I look at us—people with names like 'Hattie,' 'Kitty,' 'Tipper.'" As the crowd erupted into laughter she deadpanned: "One of us here will join that illustrious group. And the rest of us will go on to look through life for regular adult names."

After Babbitt, Tipper Gore, a thirty-eight-year-old mother of four, promoted her new book, *Raising PG Kids in an X-Rated Society*, a tome defending her crusade against violent rock-music lyrics. Former Illinois legislator Jeanne Simon, gray-haired and bespectacled, said the first thing she would do as first lady was get rid of the title. "'Jeanne Simon, the president's wife' will do just nicely," she quipped.

That corner of the electoral universe called Iowa is actually a small one. Only 200,000 to 225,000 people, or about 15 percent of eligible voters, show up on caucus night. It's those voters—sophisticated and demanding, some say spoiled—whom the candidates and their wives wooed like fickle lovers. Some argue that Iowa misleads the nation. Too few voters get too much say in the nomination process.

Conventional wisdom aside, Iowa, the first two-party contest for delegates, is the most morally satisfying chapter of the presidential race. Iowa forces candidates to emerge from the statehouse, the Senate, the House—and meet ordinary people, shake their hands, and even hike through farmyards full of mud and cow dung to talk, really talk to voters.

And not just any voters, these. For the candidates and their wives Iowa meant talking to uncommonly informed citizens primed to debate any would-be president. Iowa meant courting people like Elaine Baxter, the Hawkeyes' secretary of state. "Presidential candidates call me," she boasted to Fred Barnes of *The New Republic* early in the race: "They visit me. They send members of their family. I've had breakfast with Kitty Dukakis. I've had lunch with Hattie Babbitt. Lee Hart was in to see me. I've met with key staff people for Dukakis, Gephardt, Biden. I get phone calls from Gephardt and Biden. We talk about how they're doing."

For the candidates' wives Iowa meant following Rosalynn Carter's path. In 1976 she broke new ground with a solo itinerary, stumping alone for Jimmy in 105 communities in Iowa's ninety-nine counties. "It was a job, a very demanding job, with pressures and deadlines. . . ." she wrote after she had left the White House. "A job that required constant studying and cramming to stay current and being able to stay cool under fire; and it was a traveling job. . . . It was not a vocation I would want to pursue for life." But it did set the pace for wives of later contenders.

Out on the Iowa trail one day, Jane Gephardt remembered the advice Rosalynn Carter gave Jane and her husband when they visited the Carters in Plains. "One of the things Rosalynn said to me, I'll never forget," Jane recalled. "She said, 'Go into those small towns. Just drive in. Go to the local newspaper. Introduce yourself. Be sure to take in a bumper sticker, because if they want to take your picture, you stand out in front of the newspaper and hold up the bumper sticker. Then go down Main Street and introduce yourself to the people on Main Street.' She told me they would go out campaigning all week and come home every weekend to be together as a family. That sounded like an excellent idea to me. However, it never really worked for us."

Together, the Carters set new rules for the primaries: Work the state long and deep. Come to Iowa—early and often.

Iowa also meant keeping voters aware of who was winning the candidates' in-state-days scoreboard. By early May of that year, the Democratic contenders had already spent nearly two hundred days in in a state that has only 58 Democratic delegates out of 4,161 total. When it was all over, between January 1985 and caucus night, Dick Gephardt led the pack with 148 days, all the while ostensibly representing the citizens of Missouri in Congress.

Keeping in that spirit, when Kitty Dukakis got up before the First Ladies Forum that hot July day at Drake, in her husky smoker's voice and New England accent, she carefully chronicled her own faithful courtship of Iowa voters. "I've been here seven times in the past three months." She smiled at a constituency who until recently couldn't pronounce her husband's name. But, she went on, "as I stand here today, after three months of campaigning with innumerable breakfasts, lunches, drop-ins, drop-bys, receptions, county fairs, photo opportunities, press availabilities, dinners, and cups of coffee under my belt, I still feel that same sense of welcome whenever I come to this great state." She dolloped out her flattery, acknowledging coyly, "You are the first to vote."

Tipper Gore, the saucy, blond wife of Senator Al Gore of Tennessee, also appealed to local vanity. She was impressed by the seriousness with which Iowa voters claimed their duty in giving candidates a head start toward New Hampshire. She promised, even though this was her first trip on her own to the state, that "the entire Gore family is going to commit an enormous amount of time and energy here in Iowa." Never mind that her husband, unable to muster much support, would soon decide to virtually skip the state and throw his resources to the twenty mostly Southern Super Tuesday states voting on March 8.

Part surrogate, part vote-getter, the would-be first ladies assured the audience that day at Drake that they were not only supportive wives and devoted mothers but independent women as well. The Drake forum got them, voters, and the media thinking early on about who they were and what their role in the campaign ahead would be.

The only wife to call herself a feminist, Hattie Babbitt jokingly told the audience she would have loved to see Colorado Congress-woman Pat Schroeder in the presidential race. "It would be nice to have a spouses' forum," she said. "But I understand James Schroeder won't be with us today. He couldn't decide what to wear." The crowd loved it.

★ ★ ★

Ironically, it was an early casualty in the campaign, Gary Hart, who intensified scrutiny of the candidates' wives. And it wasn't an eighties-style issue or the women's professional status that caught the nation's attention, but an old one: fidelity.

Newsweek magazine targeted May 6, 1987, as the date that press attention turned toward spouses and the focus on character—*the* issue of the 1988 race—sharpened. On that day in New Hampshire, Gary Hart dodged reporters' questions about a *Miami Herald* exposé of his dalliance with twenty-nine-year-old Miami model Donna Rice. Three days later, after a second newspaper threatened to expose yet another, reportedly long-standing, relationship with a Washington woman, a publicly humiliated Lee Hart stood in a generic Denver hotel ballroom as her husband withdrew from the race.

Lee Hart's face could only be described as gelatinous the day she emerged from a place near her home, unhappily but aptly named Troublesome Gulch, to stand stoically by the man she had married years before. Her humiliation, coupled with her subsequent participation in her husband's so-called "People's Campaign" when he reentered the race seven months later on December 15, earned Lee Hart a long-sought-after place in history. Not on her terms, unfortunately, but on Donna Rice's. By the time her husband had dropped out of the race for good Lee Hart had joined the ranks of Joan Kennedy, Margaret Papandreou (American-born wife of Greece's prime minister), and other long-suffering political wives blindsided by younger women. She also made a place for herself alongside other women not in the headlines or history books, women who have quietly lost themselves—as so many women are wont to do—to their men's egos and enterprises.

One had to wonder: Was Lee Hart a victim or willing accomplice? Her conduct was questioned by many and countenanced by few. One who empathized was Jeanne Simon, sixty-five-year-old wife of Illinois Senator Paul Simon. "I tried to put myself in Lee Hart's place," she told *The Washington Post*. "I could see myself doing that, standing by my man. . . . But the younger women got very upset, saying, 'She doesn't have to take that.'"

Indeed, not many women were as accepting. Lee Hart puzzled the press, which reacted with consternation and sympathy in editorials, cartoons, and gossip. Her faithfulness in the face of infidelity, and her husband's hollow words—"She's always believed in me, and she has a remarkable ability to detach her relationship to me as my wife from my roles as a candidate for the Senate or President"—hit women especially in the gut and generated a flurry of commentary.

Gary Hart had his defenders. The media speculated at length about the consequences of 1988 standards depriving history of the leadership of such reported womanizers as John Kennedy, Lyndon Johnson, and even Wendell Willkie. "Would any of the Presidential giants of the past have survived today's nomination gauntlet?" wondered Dennis Farney, a *Wall Street Journal* reporter. In an essay appearing before the Iowa caucuses he raised his eyebrows and hypothesized, "Just think about Thomas Jefferson. No way. (Allegations of an affair with a slave girl . . .)"

Such press reports were countered by arguments from feminists. Chicago writer S. L. Wisenberg spoke for many women in a notably thoughtful essay published in a small literary magazine, *The Sun*. Titling it "For Lee Hart, Standing By," Wisenberg raised a host of questions about the role of political wives and how their behavior reflected on the behavior of women at large. She asked:

> Should we be angry, angry at Lee, at Joan and Jackie and Eleanor, for being dupes, for being stoics, for standing silently beside fireplaces, for turning their backs to the flame, for not looking the embers in the eye, for turning away, for turning to something else, some worthwhile endeavor, for turning? Angry at their weakness, their foolishness, their acceptance of themselves as dray horses, as back-up, as stage crew, art crew, prompter, makeup artist and costumer all in one? Angry at our mothers for taking it, day after day, at our grandmothers, for years of inherited deference? Angry at them for doing as they were told because—the reasons are obvious. The choice was obvious, there was no choice.
>
> Anger at the system—shall we rail at [it] . . . because Lee Hart is not Geraldine Ferraro, she is not Ellie Smeal, she is not Jeane Kirkpatrick or even Elizabeth Dole? She is not Sen. Nancy Landon Kassebaum, born into politics. She also is not the immorally extravagant Mrs. Marcos or the flirtatiously Western yet scholarly Mrs.

Gorbachev. We didn't know until now who she was. And now all we know is that she is not a twenty-nine-year-old Miami model-actress with streaks in her hair and a penchant for dangerous travel.

Should we rail at the system because Lee Hart is part Fawn Hall, part Pat Nixon—dupe, colluder, less than second-in-command—because she was not the Hart running for President?

In another essay, this one published in *Newsweek*, journalist Susannah Lessard argued that Gary Hart's escapade actually revealed the country's deep, hitherto unnoticed concern for the status of women. "A feminist sensibility has seeped into the public consciousness sufficiently to make philandering appear to many at best unattractive, maybe unacceptable and possibly even alarming where the candidate's emotions and psychology are concerned. Viewed from this perspective," Lessard insisted, "the real issue in the Hart controversy was not 'Hart's judgment' as some have argued, but the question of womanizing. It is the awareness of the dignity and equality of women."

That "dignity and equality" were scarcely evident a few months later in the summer of 1987 when the news was full of Rice and her sister bimbos Jessica Hahn and Fawn Hall—a trio of young women, each of whom in her own way brought down a "powerful" man. Mercifully, the homage paid Rice in terms of tell-all interviews, screen tests, and a single advertising contract for blue jeans ("I make no excuses, I only wear them") lasted just a few weeks.

Albeit inadvertently, Lee Hart did contribute to the 1988 race by injecting a heightened awareness that the perfect families brought out for campaign appearances were often little more than facades used for political advancement. Ironically, her husband's alleged transgressions put Lee Hart in a very powerful position, if only momentarily. As a presidential contender, Gary Hart needed credibility as a family man. Key to her husband's comeback, Lee Hart's claim "I've always believed in Gary" and her constant, supportive presence shielded Hart from hostile questioning once he reentered the race. Few had the nerve to ask Hart about his womanizing with his wife always around.

Despite her brave performance, Lee Hart was unable to recreate the image of the happy Harts at home. The panic darting in

her eyes when reporters moved in with questions after Gary returned for a final debate in Des Moines was that of a colt tethered
to a flaming tree. Her own daughter, Andrea, told reporters about
her mother's reluctance to reenter the race. Lee herself fueled the
flames of disbelief when, riding in a van in New Hampshire with a
Time magazine reporter, she said, her eyes welling with tears, "I
don't want Gary to be President—that's *his* wish. But I don't want
to be in the way. I couldn't live with that."

Hart's own view of the sacrifice he expected his wife to make for
his attempted comeback was appalling. Using the same magazine
as a confessional he said: "It got down to how much abuse she was
willing to take." And abuse rained down. Not only from her husband, but the nation. An open target, Lee Hart endured unwanted
commentary and advice. "I'd have told her to leave the jerk," a
Texas feminist told a national newsweekly. "Is she any different
from the wife who is forever beaten and berated by a husband who
is always coming back and asking forgiveness?" an Illinois man
wrote his local daily. For once, the boys at *Esquire* echoed feminist
sentiments when, in their yearly roundup of notable women, they
put Lee down as "One Woman We Just Plain Don't Understand."

Somehow, Lee Hart made her own private peace.

★   ★   ★

After Gary Hart's affair became public, the game plan for con-
ducting the presidential sweepstakes changed for both the press
and the pols. Old rules were erased and new ones penciled in.
"For the press, sex is no longer something you titter at among
yourselves, because it's proven to be a critical issue. For candidates, it suggests you better be who you parade yourself to be,"
said the late Howard Simons, at the time head of Harvard's
Nieman Foundation for Journalism.

Many months later, newspeople were still debating just how far
to go. Bill Kovach, then editor of the *Atlanta Journal and Constitution* (and subsequently head of the Nieman Foundation), addressed
his colleagues at an American Press Institute seminar in September
1987 about the "A-question"—adultery. "I had a reporter go out
to Iowa and one of the candidates' wives said, 'Are you going to
ask me the A-question?'" Kovach related. "My reporter had no
intention of asking the A-question, but, after it was invited, he
asked it, and then asked it about all the other candidates, too."

Indeed, when the reporter from Kovach's newspaper put the question to Tipper Gore, the normally outspoken "rock critic" and mother of four was speechless. "It really threw me for a loop," she later told *Newsweek*. "I thought [Al] would get the question—but not me."

More than any other wife, Jackie Jackson stymied pursuit of the A-question. Jackie made her most visible and lasting contribution to her husband's campaign when she preempted a media strike into her husband's alleged womanizing by telling reporters: "I don't believe in examining sheets. If my husband has committed adultery, he better not tell me. And you better not go digging into it, because I'm trying to raise a family and I won't let you be the one to destroy my family."

The press backed off.

A bubbly, energetic woman who stands a foot shorter than her husband, Jackie Jackson beams a broad smile and a warm, husky laugh. She favors stiletto heels, colorful coats, big brassy earrings, and long sweaters that streamline her full figure. After dining in a Manhattan pasta restaurant prior to the New York primary, Jesse's wife told a reporter she empathized with Lee Hart and was horrified by the media's hounding.

After the Hart episode, Jackie steered clear of reporters. It took weeks for writers to get interviews. Staffers, including her own scheduler, never were sure where she was or what she would do. One reporter for a national women's magazine desperately sought information on Jackson's wife after she canceled and refused to reschedule an interview for which the magazine had hired a photographer and rented a New York City hotel room.

"She decides what she wants to do," said Kathleen McShea, an aide who coordinated Jackson's Iowa press schedule. Jackie put it another way: "I have a great deal of control."

Jackson campaign adviser Ron Brown, now chairman of the Democratic National Committee, said after the election that Jackie was acting on her own in responding to the press. ". . . my own assessment is that it was probably her decision. . . ." Brown told a group of reporters and political operatives who gathered at Harvard for three days in December 1988 to discuss the race. "I think an attack on her husband at that point was an attack on her. She was defending herself as well as him. . . . I would not put Jackie's response in the category of some profound strategic decision. My belief is it was a visceral response."

Strategic or not, Jackie's remarks earned her a reputation among the press as the invisible wife of the unelectable candidate. Her reputation as a "character cop" policing her own privacy, earned her kudos with her husband's constituency.

One night in February 1988 well-heeled members of Chicago's black establishment gathered for a fund-raiser at Seagulls, an upscale eatery on South Michigan Avenue. After dinner and drinks, speaker after speaker stepped to a dais fronted by Jackie's flower-flanked photo to sing her praises.

South Side Congressman Gus Savage, who after four terms in Congress has earned himself a bad rap as one of the Hill's worst legislators and ladies' men, drew chuckles when he teased that he'd wanted to marry Jackie when he first spotted her—but she preferred, and found, a more successful man.

Helen Argin, godmother to the Jacksons' youngest daughter, caught the audience's ear when she told them that Jesse never promised Jackie their road would be easy, but he did promise he would never leave her. "Every day has not been a cakewalk for Jacqueline Jackson," Argin said. "Nevertheless, she has remained faithful. And she makes presidents because of her faithfulness."

But it was Jackie's old acquaintance Jorga Palmer who brought down the house by repeating Jackie's widely reported remark to the press. Palmer relayed her own rendition of how Jackie stopped the press from potentially derailing her husband's campaign. "She met the media onslaught head on. She said, 'If you know anything about my husband, I don't even want you to tell me.'" Then pausing for effect, and stage-whispering a secret she confided softly, slowly: "And every black woman empathized, related, and understood *exactly* where this black sapphire was coming from!"

The sisters in silks and sequins broke into hoots and hollers. Laughter mixed with applause, for what seemed like a long, long time.

★   ★   ★

After the Hart fiasco every presidential contender became skittish about where reporters might uncover news. Candidates and their spouses began disclosing potentially embarrassing sides of their lives before they were even asked. Deeds and details that in another era would have remained under the rug were put on the front step. Who smoked marijuana when? Al and Tipper and Bruce Babbitt, too. All came clean and confessed to experimenting with the drug during the 1960s.

Early polls showed the public felt the press went overboard in rummaging around Hart's personal life and rehashing the news that television evangelist Pat Robertson's first child was conceived out of wedlock. Yet only a few politicians made feeble objections to the new "confessional politics." Most, like Michael Dukakis, couched whatever he did say within the context of the public's right to know everything about the one who would hold the highest office in the land.

"Our lives are open books and so are those of our families," Dukakis told reporters. "I personally think there is a line that candidates can and should draw between their own lives and those of their loved ones. But people ask questions at a time like this and I think the best policy is to be as straightforward as possible."

Naturally Hart saw things differently. "My very strong wife was close to tears because she can't even get into her own house at night without being harassed. . . . I refuse to submit my family, my friends and innocent people and myself to further rumors and gossip. It's simply an intolerable situation," he said at the time. In his withdrawal from the race for the first time he said that the system humiliates candidates and their families. He failed to mention that spouses and children are free to stay away from the circuslike atmosphere of a presidential campaign. Or that, in his case at least, he exacerbated the situation by inviting reporters to follow him around.

Political operatives, like Dukakis's senior strategist Kirk O'Donnell, talked about the increasing role television played in making politicians' private lives visible. "The candidates themselves use commercials to offer the public a positive view of their relationships with their wives and children," O'Donnell told *The New York Times*. The flip side for these same politicians, one that O'Donnell overlooked, was that TV could turn against them with negative revelations. Moreover, confessional politics was nothing new. Richard Nixon got that started in 1952 when, as a vice-presidential candidate, he delivered his famous "Checkers" speech and used his wife, two young daughters, and dog as character witnesses to defend himself against charges that he had misspent campaign funds.

"In a few refreshing instances," as *The New Republic* editorialized shortly after Hart first left the race, "[family members] have refused to submit and have retained their own identities rather than become appendages of campaigns beyond human scale. This independence of family members has never disadvantaged any contender. It is not the populace that insists on the happy family portrait, it is the candidate."

Most of the candidates did object to unveiling details of their private lives and refused to respond to a questionnaire submitted to them by *The New York Times* asking for very detailed information about their backgrounds. But they didn't refuse to bring family members into the political arena to play very public roles. In the post-Hart atmosphere, wives took on even more active roles in publicly exploiting emotions surrounding family crises that normally would be kept private: the death of a child (Bush, Dukakis); a child's critical illness (Gephardt); a crippling war injury (Dole). Candidates without personal tragedy almost seemed to be disadvantaged.

And spousal trauma, once a minus, in 1988 followed the script outlined by political pundit Jeff Greenfield in his 1980 book, *Playing to Win.* "Offering up a troubled family member to the press is a first-rate form of political inoculation," Greenfield wrote. "By acknowledging that a spouse, or child, is going through a difficult period, you ensure (a) that the press will treat that family member sympathetically and (b) that the problem of your family member will help insulate you from frontal attack. Even if it is your fault that your wife has turned to drink or your child to controlled substances, there is something potent about a politician publicly grappling with a private crisis. . . . A family crisis can help, and it cannot possibly hurt, in the effort to let the press unconsciously serve you."

Thus the stage was readied, two months after Hart excused himself from the race, for Kitty Dukakis to disclose her twenty-six-year addiction to amphetamines.

At the dedication of a substance-abuse treatment center near Boston in July of 1987, Kitty Dukakis announced to the press that she had abused diet pills since before her first marriage. "It was 1956. I was nineteen years old. I wasn't fat but, like many women then and now, I worried about my weight," she said then. "I went to a doctor who prescribed amphetamines. Other doctors continued to prescribe them over the years. Twice I tried to quit."

Kitty explained that her husband didn't know she was taking the pills because she began taking them before they met. "Pills are easy to hide and I hid them. But above all, I didn't tell my husband because I knew if I did, I would have to confront my dependency. I would have to stop, I was afraid I couldn't stop."

Later she said she simply liked, and came to rely on, the kick the pills gave her. With the highs, though, came lows. She struggled with doubts about her inner strength—doubts that would re-emerge on the presidential campaign trail and afterward.

After the election, Dukakis's manager, Susan Estrich, said the campaign decided it would be best for Kitty to disclose her addiction before the press discovered it. "My view is, you can deal with almost anything as long as you know about it and can control the story rather than having the story control you," Estrich said after the campaign, back in her office at the Harvard Law School. "On the drug issue, Kitty wanted to be up front about it. She didn't want to, in a sense, be lying about her past or be less than honest."

She continued, "My experience is that everything comes out in a presidential campaign. There is no privacy. The real question is whether you bring it out in a positive way, in a way that you can manage and control in the best sense of the word. Or whether it nips at your heels and catches you.

"I think our handling of her drug history was an example of the fact that she wanted to be up front and tell people. From the campaign's perspective, that is far preferable than on the eve of the Iowa caucus, somebody who was in Hazelden with her saying, 'Wait a second, I recognize her,' or something like that."

Which was the other pressing reason for disclosure. During her husband's tough 1982 gubernatorial rematch against Edward King, Kitty had entered Hazelden, a Minnesota alcohol and drug dependency treatment center. At the time, the Dukakis campaign put out official disinformation, announcing that Mrs. Dukakis was hospitalized with "a bout of hepatitis" and was "recouping with a friend in Michigan." Her absence during the gubernatorial campaign had prompted speculation that her marriage was in trouble. In the rumor-laden atmosphere of the presidential campaign, those rumors resurfaced. The only way to quash them, Kitty said at the time, was to go public about her treatment.

Was it hard to be so public about her dependency? In interviews Kitty would brush aside the question with a shrug. "It comes with the turf." Instead, she preferred to note that by talking about her drug problem she could help others.

But the disclosure was tougher for Kitty than she let on. It was only a few days after her husband had decided to enter the race, in mid-March 1987, and before he announced his intention, that Kitty informed John Sasso of her medical history. It was not until later that Kitty, the governor, Sasso, and other aides decided how to bring the story to light.

Patricia O'Brien, who initially ran Dukakis's press operation, recalled the apprehension the governor and Kitty felt as they grappled with how to disclose her dependency. "I felt she was uneasy about something and I asked her, 'Kitty, is there something you want to tell me?'" O'Brien remembered. When they found out what the problem was, both O'Brien and Estrich, who frequently differed on issues, reacted in the same way.

O'Brien remembered the governor's hesitation about his wife's undergoing such public scrutiny. "Kitty had to convince him that she could handle it. He definitely didn't want her to have to go through with it," O'Brien said one afternoon in her office at Columbia's Gannett Center for Media Studies, where she went after leaving the campaign in the fall of 1987. She recalled: "The governor, John, and Kitty and I had a meeting on a Sunday morning over at their house. We just sat down to talk about it. I had pressed for that because I thought we had to talk about it. Kitty was definitely all in favor of getting this out, or I would never have subjected her to that kind of approach. I still would have felt that it had to come out, but it helped immeasurably to have her strong desire to get it out herself.

"So we sat there, and the governor . . . I can't remember who talked first . . . John talked about what this had to do with the presidential campaign. 'We have to really think this through. Is this a necessary thing to do? Then, if it is, how best to do it.'

"Kitty said, 'I want the story out. I will feel much more comfortable going into this campaign if we have the story out.'

"The governor said, 'It's something that happened in the past; I'm not totally convinced it's necessary.'

"Then I gave my pitch," O'Brien continued, "which was, it *is* necessary. It's irrelevant that it's in the past. It will become a big story. We are in charge of the story if we get it out. Then it becomes a non-story because there's nothing to plumb for."

Then, O'Brien recalled, as Dukakis came back with more objections, Sasso interrupted him. "'Michael, we have to do it,' he said."

At that, the governor stopped.

"It was really a rather poignant moment," O'Brien recalled. "The governor got up. He stared at John for a second. Then he went around to the other side of the table, and he kissed Kitty on the cheek and said, 'Honey, I hope you can take this. I hope you can handle it.'

"She took his arm, and she squeezed it, and she said, 'Michael, I can. I know I can.'"

But making the disclosure was extremely difficult. Kitty's friends say that although she very much wanted to do it, she was embarrassed and worried it might be politically damaging. "The actual act of standing up and revealing this was incredibly hard," Anne Hawley, former executive director of the Massachusetts Council on the Arts and Humanities and a longtime friend of Kitty's, said after the election. "She was really agitated the whole week that led up to it."

Finally, when Kitty disclosed her problem at a formal press conference in Boston, her husband wept before live cameras and microphones. Even though he said at the time, "I don't think what Kitty has done today will hurt or help," his emotional response to her disclosure momentarily improved his cool, unfeeling image. It also gave Kitty an issue to call her own on the campaign trail. "She felt she was in a position to help people," Estrich said.

★   ★   ★

Not every wife played the post-Rice script in the same way. Beyond offering up details and responding to queries about their personal lives, most felt compelled to grapple with the model of what David Broder, *The Washington Post*'s senior political columnist, called "the new breed spouses." These weren't old-fashioned political wives. They couldn't be made to look that way. As the campaign progressed, that raised sticky questions.

In an early column entitled "Women in the Race," Broder predicted the wives of the candidates would "begin to redefine the concept of the candidate's wife in 1988 and the First Lady in 1989." As Broder put it:

When marriages are partnerships of independent, able and co-equal people and one of them seeks the presidency, new issues are created for voters, for reporters and for both spouses.

It would be fatuous to suppose that women with years of experience in government and/or clear views on public policy will be of no importance in governments their husbands head. It would be sexist to suggest that they might not be qualified to play some formal or informal role in the administration. But the Constitution did not envisage the presidency as a dual office, and it is not clear what standards or methods are appropriate for ensuring accountability in the unelected half of these modern marriages. . . . As [Ruth] Mandel, [director of the Center for the American Woman and Politics at Rutgers University's Eagleton Institute], said, "We may be electing an individual, but we've always been interested in his relationships. In earlier days, the press always worried about what first ladies wore. Now, the relevant question is, 'What does she think?'"

Lee Hart, the apparent victim, and Nancy Reagan, doe-eyed power behind the throne, ended the era of the silent political helpmate. The issue at hand was which model would take her place. The women involved didn't know themselves.

During the Iowa season, Hattie Babbitt said she was unsure what her role in the campaign should be. Like the others, she grappled with projecting the proper image and finding words to strike fire. "It is difficult because it's just so new to all of us and when I say all of us, I mean all of us—I don't just mean new to the candidates' wives and the candidates. I mean the press and the people who are watching us. Nobody knows quite what the standard is. It's hard to tell whether they're going over a line when you have a roomful of people who can't even define where the line is."

Early in the campaign, Kitty Dukakis shared that uncertainty. "There's a schizophrenia out there. We're not sure where we're going," she said.

Jane Gephardt, a Nebraska-raised homemaker, said she wasn't clear how to play her role either. The day before the Iowa caucuses, a day when Des Moines was swarming with over two thousand reporters—from network luminaries to small-town stringers—she set out with her kids to appear in Iowa Falls and Nevada (pronounced Ne-*vay*-da in those parts).

No media pack followed her. No one was around to notice her elegant two-piece white wool suit. No one was interested in reporting on her popping open the car trunk, loading up suitcases, settling down her three children, donning mirrored sunglasses, and roaring off at 70 miles per hour in search of last-minute votes in two tiny towns. On that day, she said her role was to be "somebody who is supportive of my husband. Who's out there trying to explain who he is. What he's about." Her image, she said, was "hopefully caring. Because Dick is a very caring person. I'm an extension of that."

But when the 1988 campaign was history, she confessed, "We were feeling our way. We really didn't know. There was so much press saying, 'This is the new age of the presidential candidates' wives. It's not the way it was before.' We didn't have any idea of what the role was. The stories were different this time. You thought, 'Gee whiz, how visible am I? How far do I go? This is the new age, yet I don't know what the new age or the new role is.'"

Giving speeches at first made Jane so nervous her teenage daughter Christine revealed, "She gets big red splotches all over her face." A shy woman, who gave up an advertising career for marriage, Gephardt remembered being intimidated by the competitive arena of the summer's First Ladies Forum at Drake. Sitting beside two lawyers, a teacher, an author, and a Harvard program director, she felt inhibited. Defensively reaching out to more progressive voters, at the time she implored: "I reject the right-wing dogma where wife and mother plays only one role. Women don't come in one shape and one size."

Months after the election, she recalled dreading the forum. "Coming from a homemaker background, I felt they were making me feel ashamed, like somehow I'd failed. It was hard to know what to say. Finally, as I got more comfortable, I decided to be what I am and say what I felt."

Tipper Gore later likened the forum to "wrestlemania." Indeed, despite their good-natured show of congeniality, the forum only stirred up latent competition. After the campaign, several wives took exception to the impression of a sisterhood of spouses bound by a common role and concerns. Though they sometimes confessed to sharing frustrations in holding rooms and hallways, all were constantly eyeing and sizing up one another. "It's hard when your husbands are running against one another," Kitty Dukakis said back in her office at the Massachusetts statehouse after her husband's defeat.

Other spouses felt the Drake forum put too much focus on wives rather than their husbands. But only Jackie Jackson refused to show up.

"Some of the candidates and their wives will step off the plane together for a picture. I don't think my husband's candidacy has those needs," she said one awfully cold day in Jackson's Chicago campaign headquarters after his successful Super Tuesday showing. "I don't believe in a wife coattailing her way to the White House today. It sets a poor image."

Looking back, she dismissed the First Ladies Forum as "a show." Nothing more.

In hindsight, it's difficult to fault her judgment—her appearance at that event was indeed unnecessary. That week in early July, Jackson, though not even an announced candidate, was leading the pack of Democrats. Fourteen percent of likely caucus-goers supported him, the local party reported at the time. Dukakis trailed, with 8 percent of the vote. Following him were Gore (7 percent), Simon (6 percent), Schroeder (5 percent), Biden (4 percent), and Gephardt and Babbitt (both 3 percent).

Unlike the other spouses, for Jackie there was no rush to help set her husband apart from the pack. The only black candidate, Jackson was unique. The other spouses knew that if their husbands didn't do well in Iowa, contributions would dry up along with any shot for the nomination, but Jackie said her husband's was "a poor campaign with a rich message." That message would disprove the conventional wisdom of the so-called Iowa bounce: "If you don't bounce, it's a splat."

Despite their discreetly hidden uncertainties, each woman claimed that summer day at Drake to have a vision of what she would do as first lady. Each sounded out her version of "the cause." All seemed to follow a similar strategy. No one rocked the boat. None of their ideas was noticeably different from what first ladies have served up on White House china in the last twenty-five years.

Typically tame, the list of issues proposed by "the new breed spouses"—education, children, family, homelessness, and adult illiteracy—was similar to those of their predecessors. Domestic, in the full sense of the word. Issues that directly touched people's lives. Areas often shortchanged by the president. Nobody mentioned foreign policy, civil rights, defense hardware, minimum wage, or the deficit.

As far as setting precedents, only Jill Biden, the youngest of the six, said that should her husband be elected, she would keep her job teaching disturbed adolescents in a Wilmington, Delaware, psychiatric hospital. Remarkably, just one woman, Kitty Dukakis, advocated bringing back the ERA. And no one—as Marilyn Quayle would do later—selected for her one allotted "cause" anything as unexpected as international disaster relief.

They did, however, address what might be called "the impossible question." Just how much could a first-lady-wife influence her-husband-the-next-president?

Sounding as though she were speaking both from the heart and from experience, Tipper Gore said she thought Americans expected "the activist tradition" around the role of first lady to continue. She saw the position as one used to bring issues not normally emphasized by government to greater national attention.

Then she floated a trial balloon and mused, "Yet at the same time, people won't tolerate the unelected representatives running government policy from either the White House dinner table or the White House basement." The Des Moines crowd burst into applause. It was the answer they wanted to hear.

Jeanne Simon, herself formerly a successful Illinois politician, disagreed. She would actively and openly lobby the president on certain issues, she said. "Americans understand there is no un-elected office called first lady. They also understand no person is closer to the president. No person speaks with more knowledge on the president's thoughts and beliefs than the first lady. Whatever the public may think about the president and his policies, they understand that a first lady is a partner to her husband and they respect her for that."

In closing the forum, Simon added that she was grateful the spouses weren't asked "to wear white orchids, pour tea, or give our husbands' favorite recipes" that day. She told the gathering: "You have accorded the candidate's wife a respect and worth as women who can fulfill the demanding and difficult role of president's wife. We've come a long way."

Although no spouse modeled a swimsuit that day at Drake, as the campaign unfolded it became clear that some wives had traveled a longer way than others.

CHAPTER THREE

<del>∾</del>

Republican Rivals:
Issues or Recipes

A political wife can't have opinions, but she must possess attitude. What this requires is a vague, passive pleasantness alternating with a jaunty, sunny optimism.

—SUSAN RILEY,
Political Wives

"Mrs. Bush doesn't talk on issues," Perry Liles explained. "She talks on literacy, on volunteerism, and on the family. She doesn't talk about the deficit. For her, speaking on the issues is not her thing. She doesn't want to be misquoted."

Perry Liles was a twenty-four-year-old former travel agent from North Carolina. In the months preceding the February 8 caucuses, she coordinated Barbara Bush's Iowa schedule. Like so many others, Republican or Democrat, who signed up for the voluntary campaign draft, Liles was a believer, a company gal. She, like hundreds in the yuppie labor pool staffing House, Senate, and presidential campaigns, gave up a paying job to work amid the flags and posters of Bush headquarters, toiling inside the downtown Des Moines strip known as Campaign Row, where outside, the temperature regularly fell below freezing. In just two days, Iowans would drive to town from frozen, financially struggling farms to begin the nine-month process of winnowing a field of thirteen candidates down to one president.

Liles's modulated Southern drawl was a bit out of place in Iowa.

As was her stylishly snipped blond hair. Her preppy clothes. As she talked at a table in a room of vending machines adjacent to Bush headquarters, campaign workers scurried to and fro fetching soft drinks, serious intent etched lightly on their youthful faces.

Since George Bush announced his candidacy in Iowa on October 12, Mrs. Bush had visited forty-two of Iowa's ninety-nine counties, Liles reported. "She by no means confuses their roles. He is the vice-president and candidate. Her role is the supporter." Liles enunciated each syllable slowly, liltingly. "Sup-por-ter," drawing the word out. "She doesn't bang away on issues."

Liles continued: "She'll tell what's prepared him for the job. She'll say he believes in the family. That he's very warm and caring. She tells you why he's the most experienced man for the job. She runs the household and is the disciplinarian," Liles added, perhaps forgetting for the moment that at the time the Bushes' five children ranged in age from twenty-eight to forty-one and that all had homes and kids of their own.

There was a rote quality to Liles's remarks, as though she were reading a prepared text. Indeed, Liles said that before coming to Iowa she was intensively groomed by Barbara Bush's professional staff, housed in the Old Executive Office Building next to the White House. Mrs. Bush's office stressed, "The thing about Mrs. Bush is she's very much a lady. We have to be precise about who she's meeting." Since coming to Iowa, Liles conceded, the campaign had had to be a little more accommodating about events set up in rural locales.

Where the Democrats were creating something new for political wives, Barbara Bush was busy maintaining the status quo, publicly keeping a "hands off" attitude toward the unseemly side of politics. Her goal, as she put it at the time, was to "show that his wife loves him and has enormous respect for him, which I do." She also hoped to shed light on the human side of the candidate. To persuade voters to see what she saw: a man who was "presidential."

To help her boost the vice-president to the presidency, Mrs. Bush traveled during the primary season with a slide show. The color transparencies "cover everything," Liles boasted, "and give people a good idea of her role as the wife of the vice-president."

Indeed, the presentation, complete with a script her aides said Mrs. Bush wrote and learned by heart, functioned as her standard stump speech. It purported to display what it was like to be married to America's vice-president. The dozens of slides certainly did show how the Bushes lived during the Reagan years. There were photos of the vice-president's official Washington residence and the "new antique" furniture the Second Couple picked out. There was Bush with heads of state—all living. There were pleasing shots of the Bush family, twenty-two strong.

As much as a campaign tool to show voters that George Bush was already only a heartbeat away from the presidency, the show was also a testimony to what the country would come to regard as the Bush style.

When slides of the 1893 Victorian house on the sprawling Naval Observatory grounds went up, Mrs. Bush told her audiences: "We entertain a lot at our house. We have lunches, teas, coffees, breakfasts, dinners, and receptions, receptions, receptions. . . .

She would continue, "With private funding and the generosity of many dear friends we have furnished the vice-president's house with antiques, rugs, and very comfortable furniture. And all of that will remain there long after George Bush and I have gone," she would say.

(She wouldn't mention the cost of the tax-deductible redecoration: $124,000. She wouldn't mention that the redecoration was done only six years after the Rockefellers refurbished the Observatory. She wouldn't mention—as the Associated Press did—that only hours after reports about her redecoration fund surfaced, she announced that no more money would be solicited. Nor did she remind the audience that her announcement came just a week after the controversial disclosure that Nancy Reagan had spent more than $200,000 to buy new White House china.)

Pressing on, Mrs. Bush would say: "We've seen beautiful places and met fascinating people. The pyramids in Egypt. The tombs in the Valley of the Kings. Margaret Thatcher both in America and in England. One of the most exciting things we did was, we spent a very quiet and relaxed weekend with Denis and Margaret Thatcher at Checquers, which was very exciting."

It was a catalog of world leaders, snapped stiff and smiling like distant kin at a family wedding. That was how they sounded in Bar's recitation: bland, nice, uninteresting.

"And here is former prime minister and Mrs. Sharak at our embassy in Paris. The king and queen of Belgium. We stayed with King Hussein and his beautiful American wife, Queen Noor, in his guesthouses both in Acadia and in Amman. We played and swam with their beautiful children. We met with Prime Minister Shamir or Prime Minister Peres of Israel—depending on the season."

Israel. Poland. North Yemen. China. Japan. India. You name it. The Bushes have entertained or been entertained there. As Bar told it, they were all "just folks." Her tone was the same tone heard from Perry Liles. From all Bar's people, in fact. The tone of an aristocrat who never admits that her life at its core is different from others' in anything but a few details. It wasn't quite intimate, not quite the tactical jockeying of an experienced small-town society hostess. But it came close.

Putting her husband and friends on display, Mrs. Bush was elusive, invisible, the way cartoonist Garry Trudeau would portray her husband in weeks to come. And this was the context in which she placed her main pitch.

"You didn't think I was going to come here and not mention the best man, did you?" she asked her audiences, sometimes several times a day. "A man who has worked for his country, a man who has experience, a man who has worked with the private sector, run a business, met a payroll and paid taxes and has dealt with governmental regulation. A man who has negotiated with all world leaders, a good guy, a strong man, a church man, a man of principles with strong values . . ."

As much as a Kodachrome review of her husband's résumé, Bar's slides were a splendid demonstration of her own keenly cultivated country-club style and the self-deprecating humor she has developed to cope with public life in official Washington. Guiding listeners through a Who's Who among the Bush elite, Bar would say: "I know what some of you are thinking— Now, this woman has to be the biggest name-dropper in the whole wide world!"

Not missing a beat, she'd move on to tell the story about a party given in Washington for her and George by Swedish Prime Minister Ingvar Carlsson, his wife, and four hundred and twenty of their "closest" friends. "American friends."

She'd recall people coming upon her one night in the receiving line, who stopped, looked amazed, and said, "Well, who are you?"

She'd remember the someone who held her hand, peered into her face, and as recognition rushed over theirs, said, "Well, hello, Mrs. Shultz!"

And she'd mention her favorite encounter with the individual who "looked at me lovingly and warmly said, 'Welcome to our country.'"

Bar underlined her "just plain folks" common touch each and every time. The coda to her well-planned slide show was a lovely view of the Bushes' Maine estate, obscured by their plentiful brood sprawled across their expansive lawn. "Well, here we are, all twenty-two of us," she'd comment brightly. "And every single person in this picture is dedicated to electing this man president."

What Bar wouldn't say, and didn't have to, others picked up on. A twenty-nine-year-old White House public-liaison officer eagerly talked up the Bush family one sweltering day in August during the Republican Convention in New Orleans, in a hotel room packed with Republican women telling the press why the GOP was good for their gender. "*Really*," she said, "they are just your basic all-American kids. . . . They are married and all of them have kids. They like to come home and they have jobs. None of them have really exotic occupations. The Reagan kids were exotic kids. Ron Reagan was a dancer, and that was exotic—he was talented, that was clear. Patti Davis was an actress and she wanted to make it on her own—and she basically took herself out. You don't have any of that with the Bush kids. They are so into it and they want to be a part of it and they want to contribute to the family thing.

"Those kids are really the secret weapon of the campaign," she theorized. "I hate to use this term, but think about it. Every single one of them is"—she paused for a second—"well, *normal*."

Bar's slide show worked effectively as a routine made for mainstream America. It was designed to underline her common touch. Voters listening closely would see that Bar tried to have it both ways—she lorded her life over her listeners and laughed at the very idea. It was, in the words of one reporter, "a kinder, gentler snobbery." Warm and cold, ambiguous, uncommitted to either side of any issue, politically manipulative, evoking feelings of inferiority and snobbery at the same time. Dripping with noblesse oblige. Take the whole package together, the trappings of power, the oddly banal materialism of the slides, the pieties, the covert class war, and the pitch, and you had a definitive artifact of our time. But what did it mean at heart? How were voters supposed to use it in making their important choice?

Through her low-key slide show Mrs. Bush tried hard to provide voters with a much-desired, much-called-for glimpse of the private side of one of the most carefully guarded, demographically modulated, media-managed presidential candidates. In a race where voters had a hard time knowing just "who" George Bush was—and what "the vision thing," as George Bush called it, was all about—Bar tried to negotiate the fine line between her candidate's private life and public self. Voters looked to *her* to learn what *he* was really *"like."*

Across Iowa, New Hampshire, New York, and California, Bar also tried to tell people about the one asset her husband cherished the most: his experience. But at the time it was hard to know just how much leadership experience George Bush had garnered from all this ceremonial travel she showed off. As one New Hampshire voter remarked to a newsmagazine reporter: "So he's met a lot of world leaders. So what?"

While the race was still centered in Iowa, commentators like Norman Sherman, a former aide to Vice-President Hubert Humphrey, were saying: "A vice-president goes as a messenger wherever he goes, trappings of derivative power substituting for the real thing. . . . So what shall we make of George Bush's claims? Not much, I'm afraid." It was all there in Bar's show. But during the primaries, the Democrats never paid attention to it. Watching this polite, white-linen routine, in hindsight it was hard to believe Lee Atwater *et al.* let it out of Bar's closet. Ironically, it furnished more ammo for Democratic charges that Bush was running on his résumé—a résumé that looked more like a royal bed-and-breakfast itinerary than a menu of policy initiatives.

Watching her on the campaign trail doing her "act," as Barbara called it, watching her engage in wife's work to the nth degree—routinely pleading her husband's case—one had to wonder just what voters really learned about the values of George Bush. Or even about his marriage and family.

Bar's slide show, while intending to convey the Good Dad side of Mr. Bush, didn't provide a complete picture. There is more to a political campaign than smiling children and good-natured ribbing. As she made the rounds exhibiting handshakes and august occasions, the media were showing some less polite goings-on in the unseemly frictions unfolding between her husband and Bob Dole. While Bar was on the road pushing her packaged nostalgia trip the week of January 18, her husband was challenging Dole and the other Republican candidates to make public their income-tax returns. The thinking on the Bush side was that Bob and Liddy's joint salary—about $600,000 in 1986—mocked the senator's claim that he was a Main Street kind of guy. Dole answered Bush, pointing out that most of his personal wealth was his wife's. The Doles, the senator said, had been more generous in making charitable contributions than the Bushes. Besides, Dole maintained, the issue was where they started, not where they ended up.

Bar never updated her presentation to include that story or the one that surfaced in a Kansas newspaper, *The Hutchinson News,* that was passed around by the Bush camp, alleging that Elizabeth Dole's blind trust was not quite legally blind. Or that a furious Dole flew to Washington the first week in February and in the midst of a Contra-aid debate on the Senate floor, confronted Bush "man to man," defending *his* wife's honor in a vituperative tirade.

Or that she was so worried about her husband's chances after an early straw poll taken in Ames, Iowa, that she did some micromanaging of the campaign and ordered her husband's national field director, Rich Bond, who had paid his dues in political trenches, to virtually move to Iowa and kick the campaign into high gear.

None of that was in Bar's slide show. Nor did her medium reflect the message put out in the January 25 edition of *U.S. News & World Report.* That week, the magazine ran large color photographs of Barbara Bush and Elizabeth Dole side by side. Stylishly dressed, Liddy was shown pressing the flesh, leaning toward a potential Dole supporter, clasping his hand in hers, and warmly patting his with her other hand. It pictured a substantive politician. Barbara, on the other hand, was pictured in a black suit popping with white polka dots, waving cheerily, public-relations style, at smiling navy officers in full dress. Beneath the bold-faced caption STYLE AND SUBSTANCE the magazine opined: "The race is so tight that points are won or lost in such areas as spousal campaign ability. Elizabeth Dole is among her husband's biggest assets— more in demand than Barbara Bush."

The unarticulated assumption in the magazine's analysis was that the candidate's wife should be interesting and visible, innovative and challenging. Liddy-like. That substance, not style, was a good thing. That voters would be comforted rather than distressed by the idea that the leader of the free world shared his bed with a woman at least the man he was.

George Bush's people may have understood the situation better than anyone in the opposition. True to the gentlemanly portrait his wife painted of him in her slide show, Bush defended his wife against the magazine's assumptions and slights. Bar was actually his "secret weapon," he insisted, even though her greatest campaign skill, it seemed, was in publicly remaining outside the fray and letting Liddy Dole take the bumps.

Before the Iowa upset, with polls showing Dole outdistancing Bush, and Robertson edging upward, the rivalry between the GOP front-runners naturally tainted each camp's perceptions of the candidate and his strategies but extended to the men's wives as well. In a personal drama that offered a subplot to the Republican primary, the tensions between the candidates infected their respective staffs.

"Dole hangs his wife out there on a limb to answer the press," Barbara's Iowa staffer Liles had said back in Des Moines. "The vice-president would never do that.

"Some people who support Bob Dole really support Liddy Dole," Liles argued. "They are looking for her to play an active role in the government when he gets to the White House. I'm bothered by a woman who is that powerful and wants to play an active role. I don't want to elect a president who'll have his wife playing an active role unless it's already established that that's the way it's supposed to be."

As Liles saw it, neither did the general public want such "interference" from a first lady. They wanted someone like Barbara Bush. "Through her experience as the vice-president's wife, she will continue to be the supportive wife and gracious hostess," Liles said. "I don't think she'll get into policy making." No Nancy Reagan or Rosalynn Carter, she.

"It's like seeing Mom and Dad," Liles suggested brightly, summing up the Bushes' campaign style.

More than any other spouse during the primaries, Barbara Bush had a fully managed image. Just the right mix of Yankee patrician manners and a down-home Texas touch. In the company of her husband the vice-president, she traveled with the same accoutrements of high government office that brought her just so close but kept her just so far away from voters. While in the early stages of the primaries other spouses traipsed around in rental cars and vans and on commercial flights, Bar often supplemented her commercial travel with limousine service and *Air Force Two*.

"This campaign was much easier than the last," she conceded one day during a chat after the White House became her home. "When we did it in 1979, [my aide] and I carried suitcases through airports. We would be gone eleven days and you carried eleven days of clothes with you. We carried boots and irons. We looked like packhorses. . . . That [campaign] was a different thing, much more stressful than this one. Because this one, I was the wife of the vice-president."

As a result, Mrs. Bush, with her husband, was the only spouse in the early months of the campaign to usher the press of Iowa and New Hampshire into receptions for carefully orchestrated "photo opportunities," very much in the manner of meticulously planned White House events. With the help of a professional staff she was the only spouse to issue and autograph campaign literature with a family portrait beside a recipe for "Four Dozen Oatmeal Lace Cookies." Like Nancy Reagan, she had her one major cause: literacy. She had other professional public-relations material. She wrote a short book, *C. Fred's Story*, ostensibly penned by the family's late pet. Like the slide show, it told how great life was for the Bushes.

But the longer the national campaign continued, the harder it was for Mrs. Bush to escape contact with reporters, and in the wear and tear of those interchanges more of Barbara Bush's personality showed through. Burned in 1984 with her oft-quoted remark about Geraldine Ferraro as the "four-million-dollar—I can't say it but it rhymes with rich," Bar was gunshy of the national media and sometimes touchy with local reporters. On the trail she was alternately amused, annoyed, and patronizing to the press, keeping them at arm's length by refusing to discuss issues or appear to be anything other than her husband's cheerleader.

On the road Mrs. Bush was sometimes known to tell interviewers what her interviews would be about. Shuttling from Iowa to New Hampshire the day after the February 8 caucuses, CBS White House correspondent Lesley Stahl related this tale:

"Hattie Babbitt just told me an extraordinary story. She was interviewed by a small newspaper in Iowa and Barbara Bush had just been there—they were doing the candidates' wives—and the reporter turned to Hattie and said, 'Well, what do you want me to ask you?'

"Hattie said, 'What do you mean? What do *you* want to ask *me*? You know, that's an extraordinary question. Why did you ask me that?'

"The reporter said, 'Well, Barbara Bush was just here and she said I couldn't ask her anything outside of her own projects. I couldn't ask her about issues on the campaign. I couldn't ask her about her husband. Only her own personal issues.'"

Stahl concluded: "Here's Hattie Babbitt saying, 'Ask me about my husband's position. I want to talk about that. I want to tell you why his ideas are good.' Barbara Bush will not talk. Mrs. Bush is a very intelligent woman. A very strong woman. I don't know if it's political calculation or if Mrs. Bush is still uncomfortable out there. . . . It's fascinating, though. Because she's smart."

Which may be just the reason why she wouldn't talk.

* * *

Traveling the country and learning about regional differences and issues—presidential campaigns can be seen as a school for would-be first ladies. The experience is broadening. Hard work. One that readies candidates and their spouses for the rigors of the White House. But that was not quite how Barbara Bush saw the way to the White House, at least during the primary season leading up to the 1988 race.

"I'll tell you in one sentence how you train to be first lady," Barbara Bush quipped in the early summer of 1987 when she was still living in the vice-president's mansion. "You marry well. That's all you need to know."

As is her way, Barbara Bush was only half joking when she let that formula slip tartly off her tongue. She repeated this bit of advice to other reporters later on the campaign trail.

"Marry well." It was a response that stung some interviewers' ears. Barbara Bush's philosophy of women's advancement—one she carried into the White House—seemed to be the opposite of the hard-won belief that women can actively create their own place and identity. That they can mesh families and careers with their personal ambitions. At times Barbara Bush seemed to measure success for women in a very old-fashioned way.

Barbara Pierce Bush has spent her adult life entirely devoted to her husband's career. She has adapted to that role with the industry of any working woman. "I really think she is the perfect political wife," her sister-in-law, Nancy Ellis, said one day. "She is equal but she is totally loving and looking out for him. The first thing in life for her is George Bush and then she takes it from there."

A woman of a generation enjoying few options, Bar saw that her marriage was in itself a career. Over the years, she carved a comfortable identity for herself as "the wife of." One of the few revealing comments she made in the otherwise superficial campaign diaries she and Kitty Dukakis each published in *USA Today* during the general election was an entry written upon her return to her hometown of Rye, New York. There, a week before the election, she joined old friends for a rally on the quaint town square, writing gleefully: "In the crowd at the village green were two girls—now women of course—I grew up with: Dr. June Biedler, a renowned researcher at Memorial Sloan-Kettering Cancer Center, and Kate Siedle, director of Osborn Memorial Home in Rye. And, of course, me—the wife of the vice-president of the United States!" All three had jobs, but one only by virtue of her wedding vow.

Bar grew up in an era when women were first defined by their fathers and then by their husbands. Since then opportunities for women have opened up and changed, but it took time for Barbara Bush to assert her independence. "She has sublimated her own personal ambitions, more than probably would be considered socially acceptable for women of the next generation," her son Jeb said.

The daughter of *McCall's Magazine* publisher Marvin Pierce, Barbara Bush grew up with three siblings in a substantial, but by no means ostentatious, red-brick house on Onondaga Street in Rye, where she lived until she went off for her junior year at Ashley Hall, an exclusive girls' boarding school in Charleston, South Carolina. Bar was a tall girl, who stood five feet eight at 148 pounds by the age of twelve. Her mother, Pauline Robinson—to whom she was not close and who has been described as very much concerned with appearances—hoped a stint at Ashley Hall would turn Barbara into a marriageable young woman, as it had done for her elder sister, Martha. While she was at home on Christmas vacation from Ashley Hall, Bar met George, "the first boy she ever kissed." This was the man she married.

Even among her group, one who knew her back then described Bar as a traditionalist. "I think she, perhaps more than the rest of us, was willing to sacrifice a college education to marrying the man she fell in love with. Obviously she did, because she never went back and got that degree or finished by getting her degree somewhere else," remembered Fran Welles, who knew Mrs. Bush at Smith College, where she studied for two years until dropping out to get married. Since she got into the White House, Mrs. Bush has said she never regretted that decision. Yet she stressed the value of a college education to her daughter. "She always wished she had," Doro told the *Chicago Tribune* in August 1988. Bar admitted as much in an earlier interview with the same newspaper. "The truth is, I just didn't want to do it. Now I am sorry I don't have that in my background."

After marrying, the Bushes headed to Yale and after George's graduation moved to Texas with their infant son. During the campaign much was made of those early days when George Bush launched a successful oil company, Zapata Petroleum Corporation. Bar said the experience enabled the young couple to get out from under the wings of two domineering women—their mothers. "I think going to West Texas was the best thing we ever did. When you don't live next door to your mother or mother-in-law, you're very much a different person. You have to make your own decisions—some of them are bad, but they are yours," Mrs. Bush told reporters during the campaign. Bar also painted a picture of herself as "a passive, sheltered girl" overwhelmed by these two strong women and her older sister, Martha. In a preconvention interview Mrs. Bush told the *Los Angeles Times*, "My mother and sister bought everything and told me, 'This would be nice for you.' After I was married, I went off and bought a tweed suit, brought it home to show my mother and Mrs. Bush my first purchase, and they both said, 'Well, no hem, dear. And the color—so drab' and whatever, 'It's cheap dear.'"

The move to Texas thus allowed both Bushes to grow up. Taking them away from family and friends, life in Texas wasn't as risky as campaign lore has made it out to be. "It wasn't like we were going to a foreign country. We could have come home," Mrs. Bush allowed during one interview. "George and I never thought we were poor. We knew if something terrible happened to us, we had family."

In 1949, when she was twenty-four, something terrible did happen. Bar's mother, Pauline, died in a freak car accident. While driving with his wife early one morning, Marvin Pierce lurched to grab a cup of coffee spilling on his wife and lost control of the car. Bar's mother was killed instantly. Barbara was seven months pregnant; she didn't go back east for the funeral. "I talked to [my father]. He said, 'Don't come home. I couldn't stand another loss.' Contrary to popular belief, it would have been an enormous strain," she told a reporter during the fall campaign. "My father would have had to pay for my trip. But he would have."

Despite the move to Texas, Bar's mother-in-law, Mrs. Prescott Bush, became a strong influence in her life. "Bar patterned herself in many ways on Mrs. Bush, in that she sought some of the same skills very early on," her friend Janet Steiger noticed. "I think she would tell you that Mrs. Bush was a very good and great influence in her early life as a young woman and young mother and that she learned a great deal from her."

Some have written that Barbara Bush has inherited the role Mrs. Bush filled as what was called "the backbone" and "conscience" of her husband's family. Others have described Bar as the "smart one" in the couple, a comment that caused Steiger, chairman of the Federal Trade Commission, to hoot with laughter. "Well, he's got the Phi Beta Kappa," the ordinarily reserved Steiger chuckled. "But Bar's a bright woman. There are different kinds of intellect. Bar's is a very practical nature. George is more cerebral."

Mrs. Bush has said that her husband let her know that he would speak his mind and not let disagreements build up. "Of course, I'd double up in hurt feelings," she told reporters. "But the truth is, that's what makes our marriage work—being able to talk. That and the fact he's so funny."

But the times in Texas were not all laughs. The towns of Odessa and Midland, where the Bushes settled, were a far cry from the sophisticated Northeast. In one of the few mentions he gave his wife in *Looking Forward,* the autobiography he published for the campaign, George Bush credited Bar with being a compassionate wife. "If you're married with a young family, you also need an understanding wife," he wrote. "In the early days, social life was limited."

Having worked only one summer during high school, it was in Texas that Bar took her first steps out of the privileged cocoon of her girlhood. In an interview for a profile of George Bush for *Vanity Fair,* Gail Sheehy quoted Mrs. Bush: "'Don't you think it was a shock for us to see their homes?' says Mrs. Bush about the mind-boggling six months she and George spent traveling across the country as a navy couple, staying in people's basements. But it was the destruction of her entire trousseau of silk lingerie that really got to her. A woman they were staying with showed Barbara how to use the washing machine, then marched upstairs to crow over the telephone, 'I wish you could have seen her; she put all those handmade beautiful things into the machine and ruined them, every one!'"

The story went that in those early days in west Texas, the Bushes lived next door to a prostitute. "Honey, we shared the same bathroom," she quipped to a reporter.

It was also in Texas that the Bushes' second child died from leukemia at the age of four. The story of how the couple coped with Robin's death was one they told time and again out on the campaign trail.

During those early years George was often away on business, Mrs. Bush said. Despite her many friends, with whom she still has close relationships, she often found herself alone. Doro said her mother—the wife of an active businessman and congressman—was virtually a single parent in those early years. "I think she

didn't like it all the time. I think it really was hard," Doro said.
"When I would tell her about problems with my kids, I remember
Mom saying she spent so many lonely, lonely hours with us kids.
She'd say stuff like 'You all weren't *that* fascinating at age two.' I
can understand how she felt. She did it all. She brought us up.
Not to say that my dad wasn't there some, but definitely she did
all the disciplining and she was at every game with my brothers
and all of that."

★　★　★

Ultimately, some pundits argued, Barbara Bush's traditional role
was just another part of the pragmatic, "make no mistakes" strategy of the Bush campaign. Her natural image helped soften the
harsh image engendered by the negative tone of the 1988 campaign. Together with her slide show, Barbara Bush's strong maternal, white-haired presence, television ads featuring George Bush
and his grandchildren, speechwriter Peggy Noonan's "kinder,
gentler" rhetoric, coupled with Dukakis's fumbling campaign and
failure to reach out to women voters, all helped close what aides
once called "the gender canyon." Bar's more maternal, grandmotherly role had broad appeal in the Republican party, aides like
Sheila Tate, Bush's campaign press secretary, claimed. "I think
there is an [expectation] of a more activist role on the part of Democratic women . . . there's a general feeling like that."

But before Barbara Bush was widely embraced as the "Silver
Fox" her personal history drew barbs and ridicule as "George's
mother." Like her husband, who was burdened with the "wimp"
image, Bar's traditional ways and biting tongue initially drew bad
press. "Her numbers originally were as bad as his," attorney Deborah Steelman, who advised George Bush on domestic-policy issues, said after the election. "It had to do with the bitch statement
about Ferraro."

Early in the campaign, news accounts leaked that some of
Bush's aides would have preferred a more glamorous and visible
wife. In the past, aides and some family members had even urged
her to dye her shock of snowy white hair—her most striking feature.

For much of the '88 campaign Barbara Bush was the butt of
jokes.

"In some ways, she's a dinosaur," sniffed *Chicago Tribune*

writer Cheryl Lavin in a profile published before the Republican Convention. "She may be the last wife of a presidential candidate who gives interviews discussing how she likes her sheets (pressed) and her petit fours (coated in pastel frosting) and how she feels about doilies and tablecloths at tea parties (doilies, yes; tablecloths, no). She has spent her life as a homemaker making twenty-eight homes in seventeen cities during forty-three years while her husband kept switching jobs: businessman, congressman, ambassador to the U.N., chairman of the Republican National Committee, envoy to China, head of the Central Intelligence Agency and vice-president of the United States. She has devoted her life to the care and comfort of her husband and five children and has few regrets."

SHOULD BARBARA BUSH GET WITH IT? a headline also in the *Chicago Tribune* asked on July 27, 1988, above a center spread of mock-ups of Barbara Bush makeovers. "You say silver-haired Barbara Bush looks a tad too frumpy—even for Washington? Consider the Alternatives." Readers turned the page to see Bar's weathered face pasted atop the bodies of Cher, Nancy Reagan, Cybill Shepherd, and even a gyrating Tina Turner.

"We were making fun of those people who were making fun of her," explained a *Trib* feature editor who worked on the spoof, which got mixed reviews from *Tribune* readers. "Because these people are public personalities their elements of personal style can give an indication of what kind of people they are. We've had several first ladies who put great stock in various kinds of appearances—whether the 'furnished-living-room-look' of Nancy Reagan or the 'much more easy and less studied naturalness' of Rosalynn Carter—two indicators of how they present themselves and act in public can be indicators of who they really are," he said.

Although age insults were aimed her way, and had been even eight years earlier, during her husband's first run for the presidency, Barbara Bush gamely fought back with humor. In 1980 when George Bush was running against Ronald Reagan, a *Los Angeles Times* reporter observed Bar in action in Madison, Wisconsin: "Mrs. Bush, white haired and lined beyond her years, tried to make women laugh by telling them how, after her husband's speeches, women often came up to her and said, 'I enjoyed your son's speech!'

"Some quiet gasps and cries rippled throughout the room.

"Jovially, Barbara Bush rushed on," the reporter noted, "stressing that she was 'one year younger than George Bush if anybody asks you. One woman in an audience recently was trying like mad to read my wrinkles.' Mrs. Bush laughed heartily, and her audience laughed too."

Sensing in Mrs. Bush some insecurity over her looks, the reporter described the audience as "understanding." Then she perceptively noted, ". . . Perhaps, that was what Barbara Bush needed very much for them to do."

"She is fairly easily hurt," a top campaign aide said after the election. "She makes fun of things when she feels vulnerable or embarrassed or inadequate. She uses humor to deal with it, very effectively."

In the 1988 race, with so many professional women on the stump for their husbands and her husband the GOP front-runner, scrutiny and sarcasm escalated. One of the most stinging episodes occurred on February 20, 1988, just after the New Hampshire primary, when *Saturday Night Live* broadcast a spoof featuring comedian Phil Hartman dressed frumpily in drag as Barbara Bush and Jan Hooks as Elizabeth Dole. They appeared on the "Pat Stevens" talk show. "Stevens," glib and smartly dressed, welcomed the "Republican first lady hopefuls running neck and neck." She virtually ignored "Barbara Bush," while encouraging a vivacious "Liddy Dole" to talk on and on and on about her stellar career.

When she did turn to "Bar" she began: "I'd like to congratulate George on his startling victory in New Hampshire. He's doing well in the South. He's had a wonderful reign as vice-president. Tell me, are you proud of your son?" As the audience laughed the dowdy sensibly shod "Barbara Bush" mumbled, "Pat, he is not my son. He's my husband!"

"Stevens" countered, to much laughter from the audience, "Well, she looks so much older. I hardly think it's *my* faux pas."

Then turning to "Liddy," she asked her to talk about the "remarkable book" she and her husband wrote for the campaign.

"It's entitled *The Doles: Unlimited Partners*. Because that's what we are," "Liddy" gushed. "It's about our lives and how we've dealt with being a dual career couple." "Liddy" then launched into a lengthy rendition of her résumé and capped it off brightly with, "Now, I'm just helping my husband campaign."

"Do they ever call you 'Wonder Woman'?" the hostess gushed.

After "Liddy's" résumé, "Pat" turned back to "Mrs. Bush." "Now, Barbara, I understand *you* have written a book about the family's cocker spaniel and are working on a rug?" she asked in a staccato voice.

"Bar" said yes, she had done those things. "I've also raised five children," she added.

"That's enough to turn anybody's hair gray!" "Stevens" snorted.

"Stevens" then urged an ever-chatty "Elizabeth" to read at length from her book, and offer other two-career couples advice like "Have as many Special Times as you can," and "Don't allow work to crowd out the really important things." She advised couples to "leave little notes around the house" as a means of communicating with spouses you never see. "Talk on the phone."

Appearing hopelessly out of date, "Bar" was then left out of the conversation.

Saturday Night Live simulated early-morning reality when during an interview *Today* show host Jane Pauley once asked Mrs. Bush bluntly: "Your husband is a man of the eighties and you're a woman of the forties—what do you say to that?"

"She's lucky I didn't burst into sobbing tears," Mrs. Bush recalled later. Her daughter, Dorothy LeBlond, nicknamed Doro by her family, said, "I hated that [criticism] of her."

In August at the Republican Convention in New Orleans, Doro, at the time a Maine housewife, again complained about her mother's negative press. "I think it is unfair. Why would anyone want to criticize her for the color of her hair?" she asked plaintively. "The criticism makes me mad because it is not fair to do that to somebody as good as she is. She works hard for my dad and to have them tear her down like that . . ." Doro continued, "It's one thing if she were outspoken and said to have some opinion that would merit discussion. But it is nothing like that. It is the way she looks that people talk about. Her critics, whoever they are. It hurts my feelings. To hear people tear her down like that is cruel."

With so many women talking hard-core issues, Barbara Bush was often not taken seriously by the press. "No one talks about her literacy programs," Doro went on defensively. "She's a potential first lady. A lot of first ladies didn't come with programs or interests. But she's been working on her literacy programs for a long, long time. Yet what do the press talk about? Her hair. Just as my father is giving his life to the country, my mother has done the same thing. Her schedule is packed with helping-out causes."

Though the press might have been unfair to Barbara Bush, Doro's complaint wasn't quite on the mark. The Bushes were playing a game of images: oatmeal cookies and crowned heads, normal children and dogs. Her hair really was never the issue. It was the symbol of the issue—a real one even in Jane Pauley's direct, simplistic phrasing: Wasn't Barbara Bush, or her image at least, hopelessly out of touch with the times, and by implication with her husband and American women?

Phrased more politely, the question turned out to be a topic Barbara Bush was surprisingly forthright about.

In December 1975, when George Bush was named CIA director and the Bushes came back from fourteen months in China, Bar faced an empty house and a husband who, she said, "couldn't share . . . couldn't tell me secrets." As a result Barbara Bush went through a period where, she says, she seriously questioned her self-worth and fell into a depression to such an extent that her husband urged her to seek professional counsel. She calls 1976 her "wasted year."

"It was the first time I'd ever been faced with nobody at home," she said over lunch one day on a campaign flight back to Washington, D.C. "I'd been such an active mother. And then such an active wife in China. Then suddenly, although George tried to include me at the CIA there wasn't much I could be included in on. And I saw all these people out working in the man's world and suddenly thought, 'Well gee, I should have done that.'

"I was so dumb. I didn't realize it was the empty nest syndrome. But then I got very actively interested in . . . I had a slide program on China and I went around the country raising thousands of dollars for charity. George encouraged me to do it and I felt more all right again.

"But for about a year, or a little less . . . and [George] was marvelous, I must say. I wept a little and just was depressed. And he sort of understood and tried to help me, and did urge me to . . . go talk to someone about it. But I felt that was weird. Someone who had everything in the world that I had—a loving family, a husband I adored more than life. I mean I could go play tennis every day if I wanted. Why would I ever need anyone to talk to?

"I later mentioned it to a doctor friend and he said, 'Well, why didn't you come for help?' I said, 'I wouldn't have thought of that.'

"And he said, 'That's so dumb.'

"It's not as bad as I'm making it out," she continued. "But I did spend sort of a painful year. It all worked out, once I got going."

When asked what she thought had caused her depression, she replied quickly, in a voice full of certainty, "The women's movement I believe caused it. I mean, that was the women's movement at sort of its height. I believe it made me feel that I was inadequate. I'm not quite sure how. I mean, every movement does good and bad. I think a lot of American women felt the same way. You were made to feel demeaned a little bit. Well, I got over it, shortly."

The year in China was a watershed for her, she said, and so she felt the letdown all the more. "I really feel in China that I developed much more intellectual curiosity than I had before, and I think partially because my children weren't home. It was learning a whole new society together. We took Chinese lessons together. We did a lot together that we hadn't done before."

But when that was over, George "went off to this very exciting secret job and I was left feeling slightly . . . let down. I mean, I missed him and the children, although he was there. . . . It was very hard for him to understand. . . . He was so sweet. . . . Many a time when he probably should have been asleep, he was holding me in his arms while I wept away. It was childish. It didn't last long. But I'm very sympathetic to people who have a depression now. It's a physical pain."

* * *

On the day before Iowans voted, Barbara Bush visited the Greenwood School, a public elementary school in West Des Moines. It was the kind of event Barbara Bush would attend hundreds of times over the election year, her way of getting votes and generating publicity for her husband. Joined by Doro and a contingent of Secret Service agents, Mrs. Bush was escorted to a first-row seat in a class of surprisingly articulate fourth and fifth graders, who put on a make-believe Republican caucus, followed by a pretend press conference.

Mrs. Bush listened attentively as the kids calmly simulated the crazy caucus scenario. She nodded approvingly as her husband's achievements were recited. She registered mock disapproval when some kids sang Dole's and Robertson's praises. Despite a few close calls, none of the kids, cute and funny, seriously botched a line. Not surprisingly, the caucus winner was George Bush.

Bar seemed entertained by the children, but her husband was nerve-rackingly behind in the polls. So when the kids were finished there was work for her to do: Parents, all potential caucusgoers, lined the schoolroom's back wall. Each kid was worth at least two votes and there were at least thirty kids in the room. When it was Mrs. Bush's turn to get up and say a few words, she started: "How many of your mothers and fathers are going to go vote in the caucuses tomorrow?"

A couple of hands went up.

Not enough evidently. "That's terrible," she chided them. Then she launched into a get-out-the-vote lecture, hurtling her words over the kids to their parents at the back of the room. "You ought to go home and scold your parents and say, 'I don't care if Republican or Democrat, you ought to go to your caucuses.' And if you ever hear them complain later, you say, 'You didn't vote,'" she directed them.

When it was time for a press conference, fifth-grade style, Mrs. Bush looked down at the kids sitting at her feet. "Any questions?" she asked.

Surprisingly, the kids got answers out of Mrs. Bush that eluded their grown-up counterparts in the national media. Gunshy of the real thing, Mrs. Bush opened up to the children who asked some of the same questions she regularly ducked from the national press. Contrary to the public stance she would adopt once in the White House, Mrs. Bush was well versed in her husband's positions and expressed a range of opinions of her own, and her husband's, on nuclear war, the solution to the homeless problem, negative campaign ads, the role of first lady—even her dog.

"If your husband gets to the White House, what issues will you be personally involved in?" a youngster wearing a handmade ABC PRESS badge started.

No surprise here. "I will continue to be interested in literacy," she answered. "And from ABC you ought to know that, because ABC has joined with public broadcasting and has Project Literacy U.S. [Plus] that's doing a wonderful job." As she launched into her area of expertise, statistics tumbled out of Mrs. Bush. She explained: "Nationally, almost twenty percent of our students who start ninth grade don't finish high school. The one thing you ought to say to yourself now is, I am going to finish high school. And I'm going to finish it well."

"If your husband is elected president, what does he plan to do about the homeless?" another four-footer asked. Talking over the kids' heads, Mrs. Bush again ran through a statistical analysis of the problem. Of the thousands who are homeless, she said, "I think thirty percent of them have jobs. They just can't afford homes. So I would put affordable housing on the very top priority. That's what my husband would do. That's very important. Because if you have got a job and you've got a family and you're not being paid enough to live in the houses in your neighborhood or where your job is, there's something wrong with that. So affordable housing would be a top priority."

She continued, "Twenty percent of the people, I believe, who are homeless are women with children. Now something has to be done about the fathers of those children if they have been married and deserted, and we have got to take care of those women with children. We've got to see that they are trained for jobs, they have day care, help so they can do their jobs. And then, of course, we have to have shelters for . . . others."

"What is your husband's position on nuclear arms?" another interjected. "Well, you know, my husband was the very first and until recently the only Republican candidate who was for the INF treaty, and that's, as you know, lowering a whole generation of nuclear weapons. Now, I'm sixty-two years old and this is the first time in my lifetime that we have suggested doing away with a whole type of weapon instead of escalating it up. So my husband is on record for doing away with not only this generation of nuclear weapons but others, too. Making a verifiable treaty with the Russians. He also wants to . . . put on the table that all chemical weapons should be outlawed. So he's for lowering. I don't think anyone's *for* nuclear weapons."

She talked on AIDS education, calling her husband's views on it "just right." She told the kids and their parents. "We must educate our students and ourselves about AIDS and we must put a lot of money into research; it's very, very important." She viewed the money for Social Security as "absolutely sacred. Nothing should be taken away from Social Security. . . . I wouldn't want to change his mind on that."

Another youngster, identifying himself as a CBS reporter, wanted to know about her dog, C. Fred. "You know, I suspected when CBS got up here that you were going to clobber me because they've been so mean to George and vice versa," she said, referring to her husband's explosive interview with Dan Rather, whom she nonetheless identified as "a friend."

Though Bar would not speak out on reproductive rights for women, she did speak about the reproductive future of her pooch. "Next year at this time," Bar planned, "no matter what happens . . . whether George Bush is president or not, Millie is going to get married and in April, I'm going to have puppies. . . . I've always wanted to have puppies and next year I'm going to have them."

Then Bar went on to describe her newest pet, Millie, in a way that no doubt would amuse the wags at *Washingtonian Magazine.* After the First Pooch gave birth to the First Puppies in July 1988, the magazine voted Millie the ugliest pup in the nation's capital. "Let's face it," they wrote, "this is a very homely springer spaniel." The White House responded rather huffily to that. But this cold day in Iowa Mrs. Bush couldn't have agreed more. She explained to the kids that C. Fred was dead and she now owned "a dog named Mildred Kerr Bush. Who is the most wonderful little dog, a springer spaniel. And she is really ugly. She's got yellow eyes, a pig's nose. They call her 'liver and white' color. Imagine a dog named liver. She's bow-legged. . . ." The *Washingtonian* editors couldn't have said it better.

As the program drew to a close, topics became weightier. One kid elicited Mrs. Bush's views on 1988 campaign practices and stumped her with: "Who would you vote for if you didn't vote for Bush?"

"I really hadn't thought of that," she said slowly. "It's very hard in a campaign when your opponents all are running negative ads about your husband to be for one of them. I know it would be a Republican. . . . I would be hard pressed to answer that. I don't think I will." As the parents laughed, Mrs. Bush conceded, "I'm sorry. That's not very fair of me."

Finally, one little Iowan wanted to know what it was like to be the vice-president's wife. Mrs. Bush warmed to this topic. "I love my life. It's the best job in the world," the unsalaried woman told the class. "I've been to sixty-seven countries with my husband. Some of them many times. I've gotten to know many world leaders. I've been to all fifty states in the U.S. I get to do all sorts of exciting things with my husband. You know, I'm the one who gets to put the star on the top of the national Christmas tree in a cherry picker. And I do some sad things, too. I've gone to more funerals. Some very sad ones.

"I felt I've made a difference, honestly, in trying to make America more literate," she went on, running down her résumé. "I'm very interested in boys' and girls' clubs. I'm the head of the Leukemia Society. I'm on a black-college board, the Morehouse School of Medicine. I'm very interested in that. I've raised thousands of dollars for charities I'm interested in. I entertain a lot. I obviously eat well."

Then, disarmingly, she gave an indication of her feelings about what might lie ahead. "So I think it's the best job in the world. Better than being the president's wife 'cause you've got all of the fun and none of the agonies."

Once the program wrapped up, Mrs. Bush visited a few more classrooms, then moved outside to a waiting black limousine surrounded by Secret Service agents. Her daughter was at her side. A mother of two toddlers, Doro was on her own trip in Iowa helping out in her father's campaign; the school event gave her a rare opportunity to spend some time with her mother. The Bushes' youngest child and only daughter, Doro traveled frequently away from Cape Elizabeth, Maine, where she lived with her husband, a builder from whom she has since separated. Pretty and surprisingly wide-eyed even at twenty-nine years, Doro aptly described herself as someone who "cries at just about anything."

Looking back at her own childhood, she said she grew up sharing her parents with lots of people. "By the time I came along, my parents were pretty much ensconced in public life. My mom and dad were away a lot when I was growing up." She said she learned to share her parents with "all the different, outside people," something she accepted as a fact of life. Her parents were so busy when she was growing up that Doro called the family's housekeeper, Paula Rendon, her "second mother."

"I learned Spanish before I learned English, from Paula," she said.

As Doro's "first" mother headed out the door of the Greenwood School, a reporter asked Mrs. Bush how she felt about her husband's chances. Did she expect to win?

"Not Iowa. I think we're going to do better than expected, which is all we need to do." In New Hampshire, she predicted a win. Then, sounding a lot like her husband, who frequently referred to "the vision thing," she said she was "nervous about 'this unknown thing.' Not the undecideds, but the Robertson vote. I don't quite understand it. They are very well organized. He spent way more money in this state than anyone else. I am nervous about that."

Then turning abruptly, she kissed Doro good-bye, cast her a wistful look, and said, "Call us."

As Doro made her own way toward a campaign staff car, her mother slipped alone into the waiting limo. Once she was securely inside, an agent slammed the door. Doro waved but couldn't see through the darkly tinted windows, not knowing if her mother waved back when the car pulled away.

CHAPTER FOUR

~~~

Her Career/His Campaign

"This is the first time so many women have to spend time actually rethinking their roles. It's a difficult position for a woman who has probably poured more than fifty percent of herself into her career to all of a sudden have to say, 'My husband's career is more important.'"

—JOANNE KEMP

The day after the Iowa vote the campaign shifted from the flat, frozen farmland of Iowa to the rolling hills and dark pines of New Hampshire. It wasn't just the landscape that was different. After more than a year of wooing Iowans almost one on one, the candidates and their moving media montage now spread out to Everywhere-USA. Transient campaign headquarters dotted the New Hampshire map. Appearances, rallies, and factory tours were scheduled in Manchester, Concord, Nashua, and other picturesque and not-so-picturesque towns statewide.

The candidates had just eight short days before the New Hampshire primary to build on whatever momentum they had gained in Iowa on February 8. The Democrats, bowing to the regional popularity of Mike Dukakis, were fighting for second place—and for some important individual goals. For Missouran Dick Gephardt, who squeaked ahead of Simon and Dukakis in Iowa, the issue was whether or not his populist-protectionist message—"It's Your Fight, Too!"—would go over in a more economically robust Yankee state. Paul Simon had to make a good showing just to keep his head above water. His tactic this week was to unleash a salvo of television ads challenging Gephardt for flipflopping on the issues.

On the Republican side Bush was fighting for his political life. Beaten in Iowa by the Kansan Dole, Bush was downright humiliated by television evangelist Pat Robertson. The vice-president hightailed to New Hampshire before the caucus results were counted, leaving three grim-faced Bush children to concede his defeat: George junior, Neil, and Doro made the obligatory appearances before the media, then headed to a hotel ballroom to thank discouraged supporters.

Unlike Iowa, whose depressed agricultural economy became a refrain the candidates heard incessantly for months and months, the citizens of New Hampshire were enjoying a high-tech boom. The state's population tripled in the last fifteen years. While many winners of the Iowa caucuses never became president, no one has been elected president who has lost the New Hampshire primary.

The national horse race rounded its second turn.

★   ★   ★

Bob Dole, as sour as his wife was sweet, desperately needed all the chances he could get to make his case—and preferably not in person. And so at noon on February 11, a cold overcast day, Elizabeth Dole and two aides made their way to a "coffee" at the Carriage House, a community center in Concord, New Hampshire, to meet fifty or so well-dressed men and women brought together by a bipartisan get-out-the-vote group called "Team '88." The noontime gathering hovered around a central table in the rehabbed brick stable, decorously tucking tea sandwiches into paper napkins. To one side a violinist embellished the atmosphere with light classical music. Anticipation, the sort that builds when a celebrity is about to arrive, hung in the air.

It broke when Liddy Dole entered. Though it was freezing outside she arrived sans coat, scarf, gloves, or purse. She wore a stylish deep-purple suit and low-heeled pumps; her dark-brown hair was recently styled and her face newly made up. She was "on" and primed to immediately start working the room. Moving from the doorway to the dais, she greeted potential supporters, her hazel eyes lighting up over and over again.

"Thank *you* for coming," she beamed, then moved on to clasp yet another outstretched hand. Her fingernails, ordinarily red-lacquered, were bare.

"It's a *pleasure* to share this time with you," she cooed in a tone calculated to make every person she met feel like the only person in the room. After several minutes of "meet 'n' greet," Liddy was officially introduced. As always the recitation of her résumé under-scored Liddy's status among the firsts: first female student-body president at Duke (1953), first simultaneous Phi Beta Kappa *and* May Queen, one of the first women graduated from Harvard Law School (1965), first woman chief of DOT (1983). "Thank you for your kind words of introduction. That was *so* nice," she crooned. "I almost didn't recognize *who* you were introducing. I don't think I deserve that. But I appreciate it all the same. . . . In fact, I'd *love* it if you could just travel with me and make that statement over and over again." As Liddy moved into the pitch for her husband, the hostess was left grinning in sheepish gratitude.

Unlike Barbara Bush in Iowa, Liddy talked tough on issues at that gentle coffee klatch in Concord. She went into the complex-ities of her husband's proposal to attack the federal deficit through a temporary budget freeze, though she didn't neglect to discuss her husband's compassion, a legacy, she said, of a war wound that rendered his right arm useless.

But a good portion of her standard stump speech that day, and every day until her husband quit the race on March 29, consisted of an accounting of why in the fall of 1987 she resigned her job as the sole female Cabinet member of the Reagan administration in order to work for Senator Dole. Wittingly or not, in 1988 Eliz-abeth Dole was not just selling Bob Dole—she was also selling herself.

She chalked up her estimable achievements at DOT. "You go into an area that is almost totally male-dominated and try to open it up for women," she began. She mentioned that under her guid-ance the department opened a child-care center. She noted that under her administration the number of women in the work-force jumped from 18.5 percent to 23 percent—after a twenty-year period where there had been *no* increase in women workers.

"Let me say that when I left the Department of Transportation, I had been there longer than anyone had ever held that job, almost five years," she said. "I loved it because it gave me a lot of oppor-tunities to make a difference for people and that's what counts, I'm convinced.

"As I left the DOT, I felt I was putting aside one cause which I believed very strongly in to take up another," she explained to the attentive room. "As I said at the time, I wanted to be by my husband's side, if not literally, then figuratively."

At the core of her presentation was a story she told at almost every campaign appearance.

"You know, Bob and I were back in Washington not long ago and while we were browsing across the headlines of the Sunday papers, he suddenly spotted one headline that stated Dole's position on a particular issue.

"He said, 'Elizabeth, what in the world is this? I never said this at all. This is not my position.'

"And I glanced over and said, 'No, Bob. That's not your position. It's mine.' "

She paused a beat while the audience tittered; then she let go with her punch line: "And you know, we may be the only two lawyers in Washington who trust each other!"

She laughed uproariously, as though the joke had just occurred to her. Her glee was infectious; for a minute she appeared to be a girl in pigtails telling stories out of school, or the naughty knowing wife. But the unstated message Elizabeth Dole transmitted to her audience was clear: She was on an equal footing with her husband. She knew it, and despite his patronizing tone when he talked about the issue—"Senator, what do you dislike the most about yourself?" "I'm not as smart as my wife"—he clearly knew it too. But Liddy didn't take a chance that her audience hadn't got the joke. She had more.

"As I joined the campaign full time," she went on, "it's inter-esting that a few people challenged me on that and said, 'You should have stayed in your job and never left.'

"And I said, 'Wait a minute. I think what we women have fought for is the right to make our own career decisions.'

"When Bill Brock left the Cabinet four weeks after I did for *exactly* the same reason—to be full time in Bob's campaign as a volunteer (he's now our national campaign manager), I said, 'What's the difference if Bill Brock leaves to be a volunteer and I leave to be a volunteer?' I'm sure he doesn't feel he's set aside his career. And neither do I."

She argued that it was important to participate in the process that selects the "leader of the free world." That, she said, was more important than anything she could accomplish in another year at the Department of Transportation. She skimmed over the criticism she received about leaving her job, then told the group, "We have to have the confidence in ourselves to know that our self-worth is not pinned on being in a job with a title or a job at all. . . . And I want women to feel that whatever they do—and probably the toughest career, and most challenging, is that of homemaker and mother—is a rewarding career."

You could hardly find a more telling image of America's befuddlement over sex and work and marriage in the eighties—a candidate's wife spending perhaps a third of a precious personal campaign stop arguing that she had a right to be there at all. No one found that strange.

The Doles were the adult role model for the late eighties. A two-career, grown-up yuppie power couple. When Elizabeth Dole agonized long and hard and publicly about quitting her powerful job, *Time* magazine observed: "Her quandary struck a resonant chord in men and women across the nation who increasingly confront the same dilemma: when both spouses enjoy satisfying careers, which one takes precedence?" For once it seemed a story stepping onto the political stage actually mirrored changes in society at large.

But Liddy Dole's public dilemma—the first time wifely campaigning was questioned—was only the most visible example of the dilemma faced by most of the spouses in the '88 race. She was not alone in straddling two worlds: In one she sported a suit and carried a briefcase; in the other she wore a hostess cocktail dress.

In early 1988 superwomen everywhere wondered aloud whether they could have it all: marriage, career, children. The news was full of stories of women attorneys, tired of the corporate fast track, who went home to have babies. A year later, in January 1989, a well-known feminist, Felice Schwartz, published a controversial article in the *Harvard Business Review*, "Management Women and the New Facts of Life." She acknowledged that it cost more to employ women than men and called for businesses to develop two tiers of hiring, what critics called a "Mommy Track."

The word of the moment was "choice," and abortion was merely one sense of the term.

"Isn't this what we women have fought for? To be able to make our own choices? To do what we feel is right for us?" Liddy Dole asked a reporter for *Savvy* magazine, when asked why she left her Cabinet post for the campaign.

Lee Hart tried the same logic. She quoted Liddy Dole's words to CBS correspondent Ed Bradley during a *60 Minutes* interview in which she explained her decision to pitch again at Gary's side. "I very much agree with her," Mrs. Hart said in an attempt to answer those who criticized her own actions. "I've always made my own choices." Coming from Lee, Liddy Dole's words didn't have quite the same effect.

After the Hart debacle author Doris Kearns Goodwin, who worked in the Johnson White House and has written on the Kennedys, said, "There's a tendency, I think, recently, because of Lee Hart, to feel pity for these women who are wives of these political figures." Speaking before an audience at the Chicago YWCA, she added, "But I think in a way that's condescending because one has to know from inside the choices that the women themselves have made."

But for the women lighting upon the 1988 presidential stage, as for many American women in the eighties, the choices were not as easy or as clear-cut as many would have liked to think. "What do you do if you're a 'new woman' and over two hundred years of history says this is what a political spouse does?" asked Ruth Mandel, a scholar of women and politics at the Rutgers Eagleton Institute. "You don't let anyone know you don't fit in. Maybe you let your husband know. Or you go to a wineglass or take a tranquilizer. There's no support in this society for you to question that pattern."

Remarkably, as her remarks in New Hampshire showed that day, even a woman like Elizabeth Dole couldn't quite win in this arena of career, marriage, children and, campaign.

Though Liddy told the audience at her Concord, New Hampshire, stop that "a couple of women's group leaders raised questions about my leaving my job," in fact, criticism had come from other quarters as well and Liddy's aides say she was surprised by the unexpected outcry that greeted her decision to drop a federal appointment and sign on as an unsalaried surrogate.

In 1988 Liddy found she had to defend herself for quitting that high-echelon office and taking on the role of full-time spouse of a candidate. Ironically, once she stepped down from Cabinet member to supporting role, some found her less credible than her counterparts on the spouse circuit, whose put-aside careers were less prominent. Robert Dole's grown daughter from his first marriage was trooped out for show. But without a brood of her own little Doles, Elizabeth had to talk about compassion and caring vis-à-vis her virtual 'family'—the hundreds of employees who made up a faceless federal transportation bureaucracy. It was hard to tell whether she had achieved a political ideal by being all things to all people, or had missed the boat entirely.

"I think she was concerned about what it would mean to women if she did [quit]," said Kathleen Harrington, a willowy, attractive aide who followed Liddy from the DOT, through the campaign, to the Department of Labor, where she became the assistant secretary for the Office of Congressional and Intergovernmental Affairs. "She had asked the question and I was one of the fools who said, 'I think that women in America will understand this.' I think and still think that in the majority I was right. Women in the mainstream have understood it."

What disturbed feminists about Liddy Dole's decision, however, was the obvious implication that she, more than any other spouse on the trail, most vividly demonstrated the eighties ideal for women's roles: If Elizabeth Dole couldn't have it all, who could? Even worse, if she would not have this much, who would?

When she resigned at DOT it was front-page news, as the departure of any Cabinet secretary probably would be. But the photograph accompanying the page-one story on the resignation in *The New York Times* for September 15, 1987, wasn't the usual podium shot. Instead the camera caught Bob Dole's broad back with Liddy's arm reaching around in warm support. Peter Jennings kicked off the *ABC Evening News* that night with the story. His lead: "One of the most important women in government has given up her job for a man." Could it be said any more plainly?

"She of all the current candidates' wives could have shown that women can have other roles than boostering their husband's career at the cost of their own," complained columnist Joan Beck in the *Chicago Tribune*.

Shopping around for female role models in the political sphere, *Washington Post* editorial writer Amy Schwartz moaned a couple of months later: "We looked elsewhere in the public sphere. And there we find Elizabeth Dole, prominent, intelligent, independent, publicly implying that no matter how much you love your job, and no matter how important you feel that job is to the running of the country, no less—let alone some kind of minor gratification, or adding to the world's store of knowledge—you still will eventually face the choice of whether to keep that job or do your full duty to your husband. 'It was my personal choice,' Elizabeth Dole declares, meaning that it is impossible to do both."

A less sympathetic reading of the event came from *The Washington Post*'s Richard Cohen, who accused Dole of selling out. In a column headlined LIDDY DOLE BECOMES "THE WIFE," Cohen wrote: "It is true, as Dole said, that she swapped one cause for another—transportation for her husband's presidential campaign. But as the highest-ranking woman in the administration, and certainly as its most visible, Dole has forsaken yet another cause: that of women achievers.

"The problems of two-career couples are real, sometimes painful and occasionally insoluble. . . . By her resignation from the Cabinet Liddy Dole has said that in her case the ceremonial role of campaign wife takes precedence over the substantive one of administration official—that her smile is worth more to her husband's campaign than anything she could do as transportation secretary."

Veteran Republican women like Mary Louise Smith, the party's former national chairwoman and a Bush supporter, sighed to reporters: "She's going from a visible position to being a helper."

Even Liddy's own staff was initially surprised. Harrington, who saw herself as a feminist, confessed she was "disappointed" when her boss quit Transportation. "It was kind of wishful thinking that we could do it all. We can be if we choose to be great wives and great achievers in our own right," said Harrington, who added that she felt better once she recognized that out on the trail Dole was "still achieving," "still empowering women," as well as "doing everything for her husband."

Harrington and other aides were "shocked" by the criticism their boss received.

"I thought, goddamn it, you're doing what men did to us, years ago," Harrington recalled one morning in her office at the Labor Department. "Putting someone in a box and saying, 'You've gotta be this,' and therefore 'that's a success.' You can't make a choice to do something for your mate. If you've reached a certain level, you've got to stay in that box. . . . Here we have women putting women in a box."

Another aide and close friend, Jenna Dorn, who also has followed Liddy Dole from DOT through the campaign to Labor, where she became the assistant secretary for policy, said she and other campaign aides who urged Liddy to quit "really underestimated" the resentment some women would feel when she joined the race. "The vigor with which some people initially responded, you know, it was a surprise to me," said Dorn, who realized, in hindsight, that not every woman has as many doors open to her as Elizabeth Dole. "It is a testament—partly a sad one—to the fact that we're no further along in terms of more women being out there so that women can make those choices. So that Mrs. Dole doesn't have to take the flak for making a choice that was the right one for her."

Ironically, the cost to Liddy Dole, perhaps personally but certainly professionally, might have been greater had she stayed at the DOT. Indeed, not unlike the other spouses on the 1988 trail, she really had no choice but to leave her high-profile job. In fact she had more professional reasons *to* go out on the stump.

Liddy's decision hardly put her résumé at risk. Set aside the convoluted logic of the campaign and Liddy's decision looked like a pretty astute career move on the part of an extremely ambitious politician. She committed herself to a short spell of basking in the reflected glory of her husband's candidacy; then it was back to a powerful position in her own right. Skeptics wondered if her postelection appointment as George Bush's secretary of labor wasn't largely a matter of placating Bob Dole—a potentially dangerous adversary in the Senate. In the long run, though, that hardly seemed to matter. As one of the few women to rise to the highest political circles, Dole had a symbolic importance that outweighed any policies she implemented at the Department of Transportation. Or Labor. She'd already made it to Gallup's 1988 list of ten most admired women in the world. There were benefits to going on the trail as well. She was seen as a team player by others in the GOP, and as an active Republican surrogate during the general election she gained campaign experience that would prove valuable should she be chosen for a vice-presidential slot in an upcoming election or seek office herself.

Had her husband won the election, Elizabeth would have received a lot of credit. Few blamed her when he lost.

"Mrs. Dole would have a whole lot more power now if her husband were president," said Deborah Steelman, the Bush campaign's domestic-policy adviser. "If you're interested in power, then how can you not help your husband? She and he are both obviously interested in power, and to me it was a perfectly logical career decision, not necessarily a wifely submission decision." Being first lady is a lot better job than being labor secretary, Steelman added. After all, how many job-training centers do you want to visit?

Still, there was something about the Doles that nagged at the collective consciousness, something that couldn't be made to seem right. *The Boston Globe*'s Ellen Goodman came closest to putting her finger on it: "The double standard is of a somewhat different order, an updated order." Goodman pointed out that with a woman like Liddy for a wife, Bob Dole earned points for being half of a modern partnership marriage, "while also winning the benefits of a full-service political wife. Even if he doesn't win the race," Goodman mused, "he has won the secret envy of many a modern man. He has all the perks of having a successful wife with none of the problems, all the assets and none of the debits."

Before September 15, 1987, when she announced her decision to resign, Liddy made it appear her choice was not that clear-cut. Two days before she made her announcement official she insisted to *The New York Times* that "her decision was 'extremely difficult,'" in part "because of intense pressure by the Senator's supporters who have told her that her full-time participation would help the candidacy of her husband. . . ."

At the time, she complained that it was "curious" that as a spouse she was forced to make a decision, while the candidates themselves were free to remain in their jobs. "'It is somehow different for wives,'" she told the *Times*. "'All the candidates can continue doing what they're doing. Wives are one step removed. It does strike me as very unusual.'"

Others asked the same question. "There you have that double

standard," Irene Natividad, then director of the National Women's Political Caucus, commented at the time Liddy decided to leave. "Bush is using *Air Force Two*, [Dole] has to use regular planes, and they're complaining."

But before she quit her post her travels had begun to raise eyebrows. *The Washington Post* published a detailed itinerary of her journeys, thinly disguised under the veneer of the DOT, highlighting her visits to primary states. That caused columnists like Rowland Evans and Robert Novak to complain. About two weeks before she quit her job they crowed: "While back in Washington her department copes with an aviation crisis, she travels almost constantly." Reviewing Mrs. Dole's advance travel schedule, one that put her out on the road for three weeks, they added: "Less than half her itinerary consists of non-political events, few of them transportation related. Instead, she talks about both her husband's campaign and her own job. A Dole-for-President lawyer told us that the campaign pays for travels that are deemed to be strictly in the senator's behalf." They conceded: "Any presidential hopeful would pray for such a wife. Yet the senator's opponents question whether that is really the proper role for the transportation secretary, particularly during as troubled a time for the nation's aviation system and so difficult a time for her department."

Liddy Dole's situation was complicated by the fact that she was part of the Reagan team and therefore politically should appear—like Ronald Reagan himself—to be supporting that team's candidate, although Reagan didn't endorse George Bush until he had the nomination locked up. Moreover, her far-from-flawless record at the DOT undoubtedly would have become a target for her husband's opponents. As it was, cartoonists like Paul Conrad of the *Los Angeles Times* had begun mocking her tenure. Early in the campaign Conrad published a sketch of a skyful of airplanes, all kinds of craft—jets, fighter bombers, air balloons, and Piper Cubs—crisscrossing every which way and barely missing one another. A banner trailing one plane hailed: DOLE FOR PRESIDENT. Underneath, the caption quoted Elizabeth Dole: "I want to do for my husband what I did for the FAA."

Close aides of Liddy Dole agreed that, emotional talk aside, she really had little choice but to leave her Cabinet post because of perceived conflicts of interest. "Anything she did as Cabinet secretary would be somehow an enhancement toward her husband's seeking the presidential nomination," said Dorn. "It would also be the time issue. It would have been the perception issue—even if she would have spent fifty hours a week at DOT and thirty hours a week campaigning they would have said, 'She's not doing her job. She's on the road too much.' That could have hurt the candidate."

Moreover, there was internal pressure from within the campaign for her to resign. "We needed her, there was no question. And the senator wouldn't say anything," said Mari Maseng, communications director for the Dole campaign. "He would not ask her to come and we were looking down the barrel of a gun. Super Tuesday was going to be in March. Iowa was coming along but we had to have it. We needed her out there. Then New Hampshire was a big problem. . . . We needed her yesterday and I talked to her all through the summer about coming. How she had to come. Had to come. So did other people. I can vouch there was pressure from the campaign for her to come."

Maseng eventually pointed to the real issue facing Liddy Dole— timing. The question was not *if* she would leave but *when*. Maseng said, "There was a division among a lot of people, whether or not her continuing to be in the Cabinet was not just a big plus, that that was good, too. A lot of people looked at it both ways. But I wanted her to come. I know a lot of other people did, too."

This wasn't Liddy's first national campaign with Bob Dole. It wasn't even the first time she'd been forced to decide between her husband's needs and her career. Whatever emotions she said she felt, Liddy had felt before, causing some in the Washington press corps to question the sincerity of her "considerable personal turmoil." Her decision to leave her post was a joint career decision the powerful couple had arrived at long before the announced date of her resignation, some believed.

In fact, as far back as the fall of 1986 Elizabeth Dole told a group of Washington political reporters privately over dinner that she'd be out of her job before the campaign got into full swing.

If Liddy Dole ever faced emotional turmoil over possibly taking a backseat to her husband, it was in 1976 when President Gerald Ford invited her new husband, Bob Dole, to join his team as a vice-presidential candidate. Back then Liddy remembered her emotions as "definitely mixed." A professional woman with ten years of government service as a member of the nonpartisan Federal Trade Commission, she discovered what it really meant to be a political wife when her old job hit her new role head on and she resigned. In earnest prose Dole explained herself in a custom-published campaign biography, *The Doles: Unlimited Partners*. Shortly after the GOP Convention she recalled visiting a regional FTC office while her husband was addressing the American Legion Convention. "I stood out like a fifth ace in the pack," she recalled. "According to the FTC's scrupulous code, I was no longer a government professional," she wrote. "As of August 19, I was the wife of the Republican candidate for Vice-President."

In 1976, Liddy started out playing the role of the traditional political wife, standing at her husband's side smiling for the cameras. Then she was "caught between conflicting emotions." She wanted to support her new husband, yet play a substantive role that won votes. Personally, she shared the view of campaign workers who downplayed the importance of candidates' wives and families in gaining media attention. At the same time she was under pressure from women at the Republican National Committee and elsewhere to participate in the campaign. The compromise she reached was campaigning on her own during the day and joining up with her husband in the evening, a pattern Kitty Dukakis and other spouses adopted in 1988.

In her book she remembered that earlier 1976 race, and excused the staff for not planning for her and debating her contribution to the campaign. She'd taken a leave of absence from her job only to find that the campaign had not thought out her role, a frustration aides reported she experienced again during her husband's 1988 run when she found herself appearing before tiny audiences in small towns like Waynesville, South Carolina, wondering just what she was accomplishing. "With so many demands over the previous weeks, with a staff to hire and a schedule to arrange, the last thing in the world anyone had thought about was what the candidate's wife should say. I wasn't presumptuous enough to think the voters were electing me, any more than they were deciding between Betty Ford and Rosalynn Carter. They wanted to know what Ford and Carter would do for America. . . . But as an independent career woman, and an FTC commissioner with ten years of government experience, I wasn't going to spend the whole campaign answering reporters questions with a demure 'I don't do issues.'

"I did do issues. Six days a week. The genie couldn't be put back in the bottle."

In 1980 when her husband made his first presidential bid and she was back at the Federal Trade Commission, her professional status became the subject of intense debate though not to the extent it did in 1988. As in 1976, she debated whether a wife could attract enough attention or be asked to address the issues—so that quitting her job for the campaign actually meant something.

At the time, some of Liddy's own friends thought she was "mistakenly putting my own career on hold for his presidential ambitions." But evidently she didn't see it that way. Beyond the personal question of supporting her husband, Liddy seemed to view her decision as she would in 1988, as a career move for herself. "A career is more than a paycheck: it's a series of learning opportunities," she wrote. "A national political campaign, with all its potential for growth as I discussed issues across the country with the press and the public, would be an unparalleled learning opportunity. I didn't rush to judgment. But I had no trouble making up my mind either." Or in 1988, skeptics might add.

★   ★   ★

More than any other wife in the '88 race, Elizabeth Dole came close to breaking with the conventional wisdom that in political households there is room for only one star. More important though, in the 1988 race she and other spouses who were professional women raised the issue of whether a first lady will ever hold a powerful paying job outside the government while her husband held office, something no first lady since Eleanor Roosevelt—who was remunerated as a magazine columnist—has apparently even sought to do.

More than any other spouse Liddy Dole conjured up the prospect of a working woman residing at 1600 Pennsylvania Avenue. What's more, the Doles were a case of a two-career couple in which both worked for the federal government. "Can you imagine?" pondered Irene Natividad. "A woman walking out of the White House with a briefcase?" Early in the campaign, lawyers Elizabeth Dole, Elise DuPont, Hattie Babbitt, and Jeanne Simon and activist Kitty Dukakis prompted analysts like William Schneider of the American Enterprise Institute to predict: "Sooner or later, we're going to have a president with a career wife or husband, and people will suddenly realize that it is inappropriate to ask the spouse to give up the career."

"What's going to happen when we have a woman who wants to continue working? That to me is the only real question," said attorney Deborah Steelman. "Will the law allow her to work, particularly if she's a lawyer? What about conflicts and ethics problems and all that? Will she be allowed to be an independent person?"

Republican women like Steelman looked to Marilyn Quayle as a test case. But the vice-president's wife did not insist on restarting her legal career, something she said she had planned to do before her husband was tapped as George Bush's running mate. Shortly before the inauguration Mrs. Quayle floated a trial balloon and said she would return to work. Once her husband got into office she found that was politically impossible, even though the demands of second lady were "fewer than you think. There are very few things that I am required to do. State dinners and the reciprocal dinners and arrival ceremonies. Other than that, that's it."

Mrs. Quayle said she initially "pooh-poohed" the idea that she would have a "bully pulpit" to highlight an area of special interest. "I didn't really think it was there," she said. But political expediency took precedence over "making a statement" by returning to work, and Marilyn, a religiously conservative woman, decided to try to "carve a little niche" for herself as someone knowledgeable in the field of disaster relief.

But Marilyn Quayle is also a woman whose professional training and abilities outdistance the demands of a traditional and largely ceremonial role. In an interview at the vice-president's residence she said the question of what she should be doing "never leaves— it's always there. What should I be doing? Initially I thought, 'Oh, now who really cares what Marilyn Quayle says about anything?' But it's not *me* saying it; it's the wife of the vice-president. For the wife of the vice-president to take time is a big difference."

Mrs. Quayle said she also insists on continuing to be an adviser to her husband, just as she was on the campaign trail. "Dan . . . feels that in most instances wives have been an integral part of their husbands' careers, so his luncheons or breakfasts with a head of state will normally include his wife and me, and those will be the only wives. It's a working luncheon, it's all dialogue back and forth," she explained. Mrs. Quayle said she and her husband also hold working lunches with experts in different subject areas and with business leaders. "What's really nice is after almost every single one of these we've done—we've done quite a few—the wife has come up to me afterward and said, 'I'm so glad I was included.' Normally, the wives are left out when you get to this level, and we're the ones that've always been there and understand all of this, and it's nice to be included."

Campaign or career? The trade-off for an ambitious woman like Marilyn Quayle was power and influence. Her husband's success was her success even though publicly the choices she had for achieving success in her own right became limited. How much leeway did she really have to take a job once her husband became vice-president? Marilyn Quayle just smiled. "No one's told me anything . . . [but] Dan isn't president. George Bush is."

Feminists like Irene Natividad argue that some women who married presidential aspirants when they were young, before ambitions were fully formed, or before they were achieved, have few choices. "I don't think it's a question of choice very often," Natividad said. "For a major office like the presidency your wife's choices become very limited to a large extent. She could either stay at home and not have anything to do with it, and cut herself off from a major chunk of her spouse's life at that particular time. Or join in.

"If there is reluctance—as some candidates' wives have expressed—it is overridden by the status of the office," Natividad continued. "Even if one decided to stay home and conduct one's own life during a campaign there is a point when that becomes politically damaging. So that, indeed, the choice disappears. But you know, someone who decides to run for the presidency has already had a significant political life. So that question is moot at that point. It's a question of scale. It's from the beginning of the marriage."

Not always. When Dick Gephardt told his wife that he wanted to run for the presidency, Jane Gephardt initially balked. Sitting over coffee in her new house in suburban Virginia, the week before her husband became House majority leader in June 1989, Jane confessed that at first she hadn't wanted Dick to run out of concern for the inordinate time it would take away from their three children and family life.

"Originally Dick started out by saying, 'Let me go out there and see if I have a chance,'" Jane remembered. "It was his main concern. 'I'm only a congressman. Who knows about me? Do I have a chance?'

"By the time we were out there [in Iowa] for a year and the money was starting to come in and all, you do start to get swept up into this wave. To have stopped it would have been drastic. . . . But I always—in my mind's eye—thought, 'I can stop this.' . . . It would take drastic action to stop it."

Running was bad enough. There was also the unspeakable worry that Dick might win. Had they made it, Jane said, she also felt torn about having her husband as the American president. "I'd love Dick Gephardt to be president, but I don't really want *my husband* to be president. . . . I'd love to see him in there, but I'm not so sure that I want this man that I know and love very intimately to be a president. To go through all the hurts and frustrations and the campaign. Because you know how difficult that would be for them and for you and the people around you."

Once the Gephardts were swept up in the race, Jane said, she discovered she had her place, though she had no hand in designing it. "I found I was scheduled to give speeches, maybe five or six a day, and do press conferences and talk shows all the time. I was sort of forced into that role. It was not something I said to the secretary. 'Now look, I want to give five or six speeches a day and give me all the press conferences you can give me.' It seemed to evolve. But it was not something I sought out. At first it was something I was uncomfortable with. After that I became accustomed to it and it didn't bother me as much. I just stepped in and played it out."

Elizabeth Dole, Marilyn Quayle, and Jane Gephardt were not the only spouses in the 1988 race who grappled with conflicts and choices between campaign, career, and family—or for whom marriage to a presidential aspirant provoked soul searching about their own identities and roles.

Jackie Jackson, a woman who described herself as "progressively old-fashioned," married "her first boyfriend" at nineteen when she was pregnant. She confessed that there was a period in her marriage where she too had to come to terms with the reality of life with a man whose ambitions forced her to live life on her own terms. There was a time, ten years ago or so, when Jackie said she didn't want her husband to run for office. "I was content where I was." Politically the time wasn't right. "We have never stepped out before it was time for us to step out," she explained in Jackson's Chicago campaign office in February 1988.

But there was also a time when she had to come to grips with how she saw herself and handle her husband's long absences. Was she merely Mrs. Jesse Jackson, an appendage of her famous husband, or was she someone secure in her own identity? And where was that identity grounded?

In *Thunder in America,* the book they wrote on Jackson's 1984 run, reporters Bob Faw and Nancy Skelton described a poignant scene not long ago in the fall of 1984 when Jackie planned and cooked a birthday dinner for her husband, only to have him dash in and out of the house and run off to a political event. Didn't that hurt, they asked?

"Jackie shrugged," they wrote. "She didn't speak for a moment, only smiled faintly and looked away, out past her visitor to some bygone place, to some simpler time. Then she caught herself, took another sip from the tall glass of Beck's beer, and answered square into her visitor's eyes. 'You know, a little lady, who happened to be black, sang a song a long time ago. I think it was Dinah Washington. She sang: "I don't hurt any more. All my tear drops are dry."'"

In 1988 Jackie put it this way: "Let me see if I can explain this to you and hopefully you can capture the spirit because it may be helpful to other women. Though my husband was away, he was ever present in my home. I think that presence is due to my own strength. I have never been a whiner. I accept my fate and my challenges. I am pretty good with children. I have a sense of pride in that . . . I've always felt physically and spiritually that I could handle things myself.

"I received many requests for Mrs. Jesse Jackson," she continued. She remembered she would go "in to the mirror and see if I could come up with something [they] might accept.

"It was my husband who helped me," she said. "My husband said to me, 'Remember the name your mother gave you and go in that name.'

"Now I know the name that my mother gave me. [That], and my experience with him, has made me who I am today," she said.

"My mother instilled in me God, love, family, and just good values. My husband has couched those values and helped me to mature into a full woman. I appreciate him for that. . . . My husband encourages me to be self-sufficient. True, like some women I do have some desires to kind of go back and have a man do this, have a man do that. But he has actually encouraged my growth and my participation.

"He's not threatened by me." She let out a deep throaty laugh.

In 1988 Jackie was frequently absent from the campaign trail and her absence was noticed. "A lot of people thought it was strange, the fact that Jackie Jackson did not campaign actively. It had to be explained," Dukakis's issues director, Chris Edley, said after the election. When asked, Jackie said she was at home taking care of her children—an explanation that didn't ring quite right since her grown children were campaigning and her youngest child was off at boarding school. Perhaps more accurate was the explanation she gave to Jackson's press secretary, Delmarie Cobb, shortly before the New York primary. "She said, 'I'm beat. I did that in '84 and that was enough,'" Cobb remembered.

Similar comments had popped up in 1984. Jackie skipped the closing night of the Democratic Convention in San Francisco. Her husband had been treated badly by his colleagues, she felt, and so she would not participate. And, as he would in 1988, her husband tried to get her by his side when she didn't feel like it. "We've disagreed before," she told reporters Faw and Skelton, then explained, "My marriage is about five kids and a sameness of purpose and an understanding. I don't have to prove to anyone that I love my husband, that he loves me. And he doesn't have to prove it. We worked different parts of the cities and states because I could do that, and most women can't. Most women don't know enough about their husband's business . . . or have enough independence to be able to answer, when a reporter asks, 'Are you speaking for your husband?' and you say, 'No, I'm speaking for myself. . . .' I don't pay any attention," she said. "No attention," she emphasized.

In February 1988 Jackie talked again about her marriage, describing it and her work as a partnership. She recalled the time late in 1983 when her husband decided to try to help bring home the navy pilot Lieutenant Robert O. Goodman, who was shot down and held hostage in Lebanon.

"It was near Christmas, I believe, and I hadn't put the Christmas decorations up and I was a little sad because I had made this commitment to be over in Nicaragua during that time. When Goodman was first in the news, [Jesse] looked at the boy . . . and he looked at him and he took the paper down to breakfast. He was reading it. He put the paper to the side. I think a week or two later he picked the paper up and it was upstairs in the bedroom in a chair and he said, 'I am going to try and go get him.'

"Well, my husband says these things while I am in bed; I sit straight up. 'Do you know him? Do you know where he is? How are you going to get him?'" she demanded. "I walked out of the room because he still insisted on doing this."

The two then went their separate ways, Jackie said. "I was preparing to go to Nicaragua. . . . It is always a spiritual moment for me, the parting. It's the nature of our work. . . .

"By the time I arrived [back] from Miami to Chicago, people were calling me at two or three in the morning saying, 'We got him!' I said, 'Who?' And they said, 'Goodman! We got him!'

"Every time he does something, everybody says 'we.' I think that 'we' is the connection in our lives. Both of our lives . . . It's almost like being a runner or something. You run with something. You don't run with the wind. Or the distance. You never do anything alone. You run with. To the end of that distance that you are traveling."

Similarly, Jeanne Simon faced her own dilemma when she married her colleague, fellow state representative Paul Simon. Unlike another politician, Elizabeth Dole, Jeanne, thirteen years her senior, gave up her career as a politician to become a full-time political wife. It wasn't easy. One evening in 1988 when her husband's campaign passed through Chicago, she caught her breath in a hotel suite overlooking the Chicago River and reminisced about her own career before Paul. A tall, slender, gray-haired woman who moves with a liveliness belying her sixty-five years, Jeanne graduated from Northwestern University Law School and was thirty-seven when she married.

"I was independent," she recalled in her soft midwestern voice. "I felt that I owed nothing to anyone, which was a good way to feel. Women lawyers were few and far between. I was on the Judiciary Committee. I felt that I was beginning to reach my stride. I was elected, then reelected. Then there was Paul." It was awfully tough to choose, she admitted some twenty-nine years later.

"But you weigh things carefully," she said. "I felt that I was truly a career woman. I was looking forward to hopefully being a judge—I don't think I would announce that to anyone—but that was the way in which I wanted to direct my career. I did like politics, though, that was for sure. I wanted to stay within the Democratic party—and once you've seen your name on the ballot, it's pretty heady stuff."

Her tone was cheery, almost gee-whiz, but it softened as she went on. "Oh, there were some men, but nothing exciting. I was living with my mother at the time." Then the bow-tied Paul came along. "It changes your outlook entirely. But I thought a long time about it. I was giving up a well-established career. The New Trier Township Democratic party, which helped me to achieve that victory, I think were a little let down—but then they got to know Paul."

★　★　★

In 1988 such personal choices and conflicts got played out on the campaign trail where voters weren't exactly sure what traits they wanted to see in a first lady hopeful. Or just what image it was that a candidate's wife was expected to project.

Out on the stump Jeanne Simon sometimes found herself talking not about her good old days in Springfield statehouse politics, but her good old homemaker days with the PTA and Cub Scouts before her two children, a lawyer and a photographer, grew up.

Other women found the role of independent career woman didn't always play well in certain pockets of the country. A reporter for *Vogue* magazine, trailing Hattie Babbitt on the stump, one day noticed voters found her "too" effective. "Hattie Babbitt's so good, she makes you think maybe she wants to be the candidate," a young man said, without approval.

A Dole campaign staffer noticed that Elizabeth's childlessness registered a mild, but discernible, undercurrent at some campaign events. "I got the sense out there that the other guys were afraid of Elizabeth," the aide recalled. "It was interesting, they would contrast childbearing. We'd be at rallies and some of the Bush sons would talk about their mom, saying 'She . . . bore . . . five children. . . . *Five!* Count 'em! *Five!*' The implication was that 'Elizabeth Dole had none!'"

Nor did Liddy Dole's independence sell well among some Southerners. Another staff member remembered, "There was the feeling, 'It's fine that Mrs. Dole wants her career, but that's not the way we do it here.'"

Once she entered the race, Liddy Dole, more than any other spouse, raised yet another sticky question: Just how much of a political partner could she appear to be? Were voters electing an individual or a team to the White House? Was a vote for Bob Dole a vote for Liddy Dole?

One evening late in February 1988 Liddy hit a Chicago fund-raiser where that issue came to the fore. Liddy functioned as her husband's ambassador, especially in her native South and in crucial primary states like Illinois. At the Palmer House, after a day spent flying around Illinois campaigning for local candidates, Elizabeth joined a gathering of wealthy Republicans from Chicago, downstate Illinois, and suburban DuPage County in the hotel's penthouse suite. The Doles' was an uphill fight there, with four-term Republican governor "Big Jim" Thompson and key Republican state representatives backing Bush. Among the guests that evening was W. Clement Stone, the aging Chicago insurance millionaire who somehow has eluded death, though he looked like it. Guests courted Stone, an eccentric fellow and booster of the philosophy positive mental attitude. But many more people wanted to stand in line and get a memento photo taken with Liddy Dole, wearing a China-red silk suit with a black velvet collar. She tried to accommodate everyone.

"Hi!" she said brightly as a woman moved in close for a snapshot.

"Hi! Come on over," she said again, as a middle-aged man was introduced to her. Turning toward the camera, she brightened. Flashed yet another honeysuckle smile with a stranger. The camera popped again.

"Hi! Nice to meet you!" Bright as ever, smile as wide. She and the next donor, who had paid good money to attend this reception, grinned blankly into a flash so blinding one wondered if too much camera light could damage politicians' eyesight, the way amplified music damages musicians' eardrums.

Off and on like a neon sign, Liddy glowed and dimmed. Then, as if on cue, she spun around and was ushered down the hall to a bedroom suite to rest for twenty minutes before she was scheduled to speak at the fund raising dinner downstairs.

Her assistant, Mark Romig, a short, thirtysomething fellow who faintly resembled the actor Joel Grey, brought her dinner—a tray of hors d'oeuvres. "*My* book will be called 'I carried the purse,'" he quipped, moving rapidly down the hall. Then, emerging from the suite, he and Liddy's speechwriter, Stan Welborn, huddled in the hallway with Lee Daniels, the Illinois house minority leader who pushed Bob Dole's race in the state. "I don't want her tired," Daniels instructed the two, promising to give Elizabeth a bang-up introduction when she addressed the "high donors," who were already seated and served in the hotel's elegant green and gilt Empire Dining Room.

Daniels delivered on his promise for a good lead-in, a lead-in that pointed to the complexity of Elizabeth Dole's campaign role. A short, middle-aged fellow in sporty glasses, he talked in a voice laden with emotion. He told the hushed diners—just in case they couldn't tell—that he spoke "from the heart."

Daniels explained why, in a state where the powerful Republican governor was supporting Bush, he backed Dole. "I thought creating an organization for the man running for the leadership of the free world would mean something not only to Lee Daniels, but something to us as Americans," he explained, promising, "I am going to run the toughest campaign for Bob Dole in the state of Illinois."

Strutting his stuff, Daniels warmed for the introduction.

"I am standing before you with one of the most outstanding women I have had the opportunity to meet," he said. "I first met her personally in Washington through the National Conference of State Legislators. I shared with her a podium. I was immediately impressed with not only her personal charisma but her intellect that just shows so much that Duke University degree, Harvard Law School degree, Harvard School of Business master's [actually, the School of Education], and I said, 'Man, this is some kind of person.'"

Then Daniels got to his point. "We have an opportunity to elect a *team* president of the United States. We have an opportunity to select a *person* that is going to be as much as part of this government, a *strong* part, a strong *participant*, a strong *person* behind the president, who *believes* in her *husband*."

Downshifting, he boasted on her behalf, "and today, she campaigned throughout the state for Illinois Republicans all day long. Elizabeth, forgive me for going on and on and on. . . . Because I know that you have to leave soon. Right after she speaks," he alerted the room, "she has to catch a plane out of here so she can get back to Washington, D.C., before midnight tonight. So she can do the laundry tomorrow. . . ."

At the incongruous suggestion of Liddy Dole doing laundry the audience, finishing up dessert, chuckled.

". . . So that she can leave tomorrow for three state tours." It seemed he wouldn't stop. But thankfully he managed.

"I ask you"—he paused—"to look at this lady," he intoned. "And envision . . . Elizabeth Dole . . . First Lady of the United States."

The Midwesterners looked. They envisioned. They applauded.

Liddy rose from her seat at a table twinkling with candles and came up onstage.

It was time for Southern sugar.

"I am touched," she told Daniels, sounding more sincere than he. "I appreciate that beautiful introduction which I will always remember and cherish . . .

". . . Really," she insisted. Daniels, no doubt, believed her.

Then she launched into her stump speech—the talk of leaving her Cabinet post, of likening her decision to Bill Brock's. She repeated the joke about her husband misreading the Sunday-paper headline, then the wisecrack about both of them being the only two lawyers in Washington to trust each other. She laughed again at her own joke. When she finished speaking she slowly gladhanded her way out of the room, then moved swiftly out the hotel's revolving door to a waiting limousine headed for the airport. True to form, Romig was right behind her, carrying her purse. Welborn followed suit, carrying her coat.

The heart of Lee Daniels's introduction was a point Liddy would just as soon have seen ignored. Though not pre-scripted by anyone in the Dole campaign, Daniels's specter of a team presidency clung to Liddy Dole like pesky lint.

On the trail reporters wondered whether, like Cinderella's stepsister, Elizabeth Dole had feet too big for the first lady's glass slipper. Wouldn't the first-lady role be too confining for a woman with Elizabeth's résumé and ambition? Would she want to give up "her position, influence, prestige and salary knowing if her husband wins she will be pushed permanently into second place?" one reporter asked.

Shuttling from Iowa to New Hampshire after Dole and Robertson trounced Bush, CBS White House correspondent Lesley Stahl commented: "I'm very curious to see, if Dole becomes president, what special role Elizabeth has in his administration. Because it will have to be special. It will have to be substantive. It will have to involve power. I mean overt power, not the kind of power Nancy Reagan has. But power the country will see and the country will have to cope with. Power the country will have to adjust to."

In the world of "what-if," Liddy's former press secretary Kathleen Harrington agreed it would have been interesting to see what First Lady Elizabeth Dole would do. "It wouldn't have been a public-relations effort," Harrington predicted. "She would have had a different perspective on working a project."

The idea of a co-presidency made some people skittish, including Elizabeth herself. "My political aspirations are just simply to do everything I can to help my husband," she said while on the campaign trail. "I think there's no question in a good marriage, obviously, you're going to be communicating on the issues and working together. But one thing, clearly, the American people don't do—they do not elect a co-president."

Months after the Bushes settled into the White House, when Daniels's line about "electing a team" was mentioned to Liddy's former campaign staffers, their antennae went up. "That was *not* the party line," Harrington insisted. "That was a Lee Daniels original. Mrs. Dole didn't feel that way."

Judy Harbaugh, Bob Dole's chief campaign scheduler and a woman who has known and worked for the senator for twenty years, concurred: "Our thoughts were 'Now she's on the campaign trail, she's not Secretary Dole, she's Mrs. Dole.'"

But making that shift from secretary to Mrs. Dole wasn't always so easy. If there was any hallmark to Bob Dole's campaign it was disorganization. That and single-mindedness. "He hires bright and aggressive people and is so demanding of them they call him 'Aya-Dole-Ah' behind his back," *Newsweek* stated. "Yet the aloof and acerbic Dole mistrusts anyone's judgment but his own."

When NBC's Tom Brokaw mediated a Bush-Dole interview in the wake of the New Hampshire primary, and Dole snapped, "Stop lying about my record!," many think the remark terminally blemished his presidential ambitions. Even his wife, an aide recalled later, wished he hadn't said it.

More problematic than organizational difficulties for the senator was his solo style of operating, which at times seemed to cause tensions within his marriage.

On March 21, a reporter for *Time* magazine filed this dispatch: "There was another, unspoken factor in Bob Dole's doubts about continuing his campaign: a growing tension with his wife. According to an aide, Dole felt totally rejected after last week's [Illinois] devastating primary results, and has vented some of his anger on his wife. Says the aide: 'He's been an s.o.b. with her.' Liddy Dole, in turn, has been disillusioned over her husband's inability to control his hostility toward George Bush. 'Bob just won't pay any attention to me,' she lamented to a friend."

Reluctant to delegate authority, Dole was tagged "a political one-man band" by critics, even within his own party. Evidently his was so much a solo act that when things looked decidedly bad in the second half of March, Elizabeth learned of her husband's apparent withdrawal from the race not from him but from a listener on a local call-in show. According to a close aide, Elizabeth was substituting for the senator at a previously scheduled radio-talk-show appearance in Wisconsin when a caller informed her that her husband had just dropped out of the race. Astonished, she replied she would certainly know were that the case. Radio staff checked and discovered a wire story, and though Dole hadn't officially withdrawn, he had made noises very much in that vein. After giving a speech in Washington, D.C., Dole had abruptly told a wire-service reporter that it looked to him as if George Bush would be the nominee. The story went out.

"She was just astonished that [Bob] had wanted her to substitute for him on this program he'd originally been scheduled to do, and he popped off," one of her aides said later. "The timing was incredibly unfortunate from her standpoint. She was very distressed." She was angry that she'd "been hung out to dry," at the same time being isolated on the road when high-level decisions were being made. "It was a low point," her aide said.

CHAPTER FIVE

His Views or Hers?

> It is only a very dull woman who is unaware of
> the speculative curiosity mixed with hostility with
> which her every platform appearance is greeted.
> She is terrified that what she says may in some
> way harm her husband and inhibited because she
> is not speaking for herself but for him.
>
> —ABIGAIL MCCARTHY,
> *Private Faces, Public Faces*

Al Gore spent April 18, the day before the New York primary,
trying to make the most of a belated endorsement by New York
City Mayor Ed Koch. Only shortly before New Yorkers would
vote Koch had handed Gore a double-edged sword. The mayor
praised Gore, telling New Yorkers he saw "a touch of greatness"
in the young senator. But whatever good Koch did Gore was immediately undercut when the mayor needlessly warned his large
Jewish constituency, "You'd have to be crazy, as a Jew, to vote for
Jesse Jackson," thereby allying Gore with Koch's inflammatory remarks.

In the middle of the controversy Koch created, the day before
the primary, Al and Tipper Gore wandered the grimy streets of the
Big Apple looking for votes. Pestered by reporters, Al tried to
convince New Yorkers that by coming out only a month before
against Reagan's Middle East peace plan calling for consideration
of a Palestinian homeland, he wasn't pandering to the city's Jewish
vote. In interview after interview Gore explained that his position
was a long-standing one and tried to reverse the conventional

wisdom, fueled by Koch, that a vote for Gore instead of Dukakis in effect amounted to a vote for Jackson.

When the primary was all over, Gore came in a distant third, winning 10 percent of the vote, compared to Dukakis's 51 percent and Jackson's 37 percent. Koch made what NBC News called "the understatement of the year"—"I guess my endorsement was not helpful." David Nyhan, a columnist for *The Boston Globe*, was more blunt, describing Koch's embrace of Gore as "the political equivalent of the kiss of the spiderwoman."

But before Gore was done for, he greeted commuters early in the morning at subway stops. He visited a city hospital and, wearing a protective sterile hospital gown, posed next to tiny AIDS babies struggling for breath, as similarly clad cameramen and reporters traipsed through an intensive-care ward filled with terribly ill children. He and his wife lunched with Koch at a fish restaurant near the Wall Street waterfront. They taped the Phil Donahue show. Then the senator headed to a fund-raiser at a Greenwich Village art gallery.

After lunch, and before Donahue, Gore wedged in an afternoon jog around downtown Manhattan. Then he joined his wife in their ornate suite at Park Avenue's Regency Hotel. En route to the shower, still sweating in a T-shirt and running shorts, mud splattered up his calves, Gore paused over a room-service tray to wolf down Tipper's lunch leftovers.

Would it be a handicap for him if his wife didn't campaign? "Yeah," he replied. "It would just be like saying, is it possible to run a political campaign for president and give your opponent an extra thirty days of campaigning time?" Answering between mouthfuls, "You can do it. It might not make that much difference—but it could be the critical difference."

Either positively or negatively, it seemed. One school among campaign strategists truly values wives for their ability to humanize male candidates. Another posits the view that wives make no difference—except perhaps by hurting a candidate. The second school sends the candidate and his wife on the trail with opposite goals: He's to seek the positive; she's to elude the negative.

During a campaign and, as First Lady Barbara Bush aptly illustrates, even in the White House, it is the rare spouse who—like any other adviser—lets herself be seen at odds with her husband.

But what happens when a spouse has views that become a liability? From a campaign's point of view, it's hard to know how to strategize if a spouse has views that conflict with the candidate's. Not that it happens much—in public, at least.

"I don't think we know what to do," said Democratic pollster Celinda Lake, who worked on gender issues for Dukakis. "For the presidential [race], it is confusing for voters. They understand these spouses have tremendous influence. Nancy Reagan convinced them of that. Also that she had influence with people around her husband."

Lake theorized, "In general, most [campaigns] err on the side of caution. People don't even want to know the differences between the president and a vice-president. They force the images to merge. To vote for a team. It's the same with the wife."

During the 1988 race Elizabeth Dole sidestepped a potentially troublesome DOT record by shedding her job. Tipper Gore, however, carried a negative that was harder to shake. She trafficked in the war of ideas and policy rather than private profit, as many political spouses had done in the past. Tipper didn't have a career, but she had a controversial cause for her spouse to contend with.

In many ways Mary Elizabeth Gore has been a stereotypical political wife. After graduating from high school in 1966 she enrolled in Boston University in order to follow her Harvard-bound sweetheart, Al. She earned her B.A. in 1970 and the two married that May. When he went to Vietnam six months later she moved to Nashville and worked as a photojournalist at the *Nashville Tennesseean*, where Al had been employed. She earned an M.A. in psychology in 1975, at the age of twenty-six, and toyed with the idea of becoming a child psychologist, but gave up both job and career plans when her husband suddenly launched a successful congressional campaign in 1976.

"I've espoused feminist ideology in certain respects," the mother of four told *Time* magazine during the campaign. "But as I've grown older and had more experience, I can see that the role of self-sacrifice has fallen more heavily on the woman—not just in relation to a man, but because of children. Of course, I suppose because I'm happy with my husband and our marriage, I am willing to look at the brighter side of things."

When the Gores first moved back to Washington where they'd

both grown up, Tipper said the first few months were especially hard, so she looked for her own "productive niche." She found it in an effort to alert consumers to the moral toxins she saw in rock-music lyrics. In 1985 she helped found the Parents' Music Resource Center (PMRC), a nonprofit group that achieved notoriety for asking the Recording Industry Association of America to voluntarily label records and videos in much the same way the movie industry labels its products. For Tipper the effort was more than a mission, it was also a way to be someone other than Mrs. Albert Gore II.

"I think it is very important to have your own identity; otherwise you are simply in the shadow of the man," she explained that afternoon at New York's Regency Hotel.

"I think it would be true with any woman [candidate]. I think it is the nature of the beast. It's the elected official, particularly in Washington, that is the person everybody is interested in talking to. . . . I dealt with that early on. I have always had my own issues. My own identity."

She recalled, "There were a number of congressional wives who felt that same way and we got together and formed the Congressional Wives' Task Force back in 1976. I remember going to Mount Vernon College where they had a seminar for congressional wives and someone stood up and said, 'I have a legal yellow pad here and if anybody else besides me is interested in something other than teas, sign up.' And we signed up. . . . It gave us our own identity where it was very hard to carve it out because in Washington, the senator or congressman—that is it. Even at parties you are sort of given this deprecating attitude."

She continued: "Now I have escaped that, because I have been so strongly involved with issues that I am identified with that I have my own identity. And it's perfectly in concert with my own interests. I have a graduate degree in psychology and I believe that we need to look at the messages in our environment and social change. That is what I am interested in."

Having ties to a U.S. senator has not been without benefits for Tipper Gore. She noted, "You have a tremendous opportunity as the spouse of an officeholder for speaking engagements, for ways to influence people." Ironically, being married to a U.S. senator may have gotten in Tipper's way, first as a PMRC advocate and later as a so-called surrogate in her husband's presidential bid.

As Washington-based reporter Fred Barnes pointed out in a review of *Raising PG Kids in an X-Rated Society*, the book Tipper published in 1987 to alert parents to the "increasingly explicit and brutal lyrical content of certain music," she had a hard time finding an audience. "For one thing, there's her husband," Barnes wrote. "Conservatives, potentially her most enthusiastic constituency, are bound to be leery of rallying around the wife of a moderate-to-liberal politician. . . .

"Don't expect liberals to rush to Tipper's side, either. I've talked to some folks who support her husband's candidacy and they're embarrassed by her. . . . They live in fear of being accused of prudery or censorship or being authoritarian with their kids. Nothing could be worse than the shame of suffering such an accusation. . . ."

Barnes failed to mention that feminists were a constituency likely to find certain rock lyrics objectionable and demeaning to women. But image was a problem there, too. "If Tipper's a feminist, she doesn't boast about it," Barnes wrote.

Out on the campaign trail, Tipper Gore defended herself to journalists who asked if her efforts negatively affected her husband's campaign. She was "very sensitive about her reputation as a 'kooky' housewife advocating censorship," the press reported.

Mrs. Gore did little to clear up blurred boundaries between her interests and her husband's. It was often unclear whether her voice was her own. She created problems both for herself and her husband in 1985 when she and other political wives brought their concerns before a Senate hearing presided over by Al. According to *Variety*, the entertainment industry paper, Al "was one of the most active and vocal members of the controversial panel."

As his wife faced off with rock 'n' rollers like Frank Zappa (who wanted to know why, if it was legal to masturbate, it would be illegal to sing about it), *Variety* reported that Al, who was among the first to arrive and the last to leave, "questioned, often vigorously and at length, every witness or group of witnesses to come before the panel, and that in his opening statement he explicitly 'commended' committee chairman Senator John Danforth for convening the hearing."

The witness Zappa, meanwhile, accused Tipper of "connubial insider trading."

In her book Tipper allowed that the hearing put her and her husband in an "awkward position." She wrote: "Some critics mistakenly assumed that he had asked for the hearing, when in fact, both he and I had had reservations about it. I thought the PMRC would be better off working with artists and the industry on their own terms, instead of dragging everybody before the TV cameras on Capitol Hill. Artists were already screaming about censorship, and this would only give them an excuse to raise the specter of government intervention."

Nevertheless the Gores went ahead. As a result, some wondered whether this was not in reality a husband-and-wife act. Wouldn't her effort to inject a concerned mother's moral tone into her husband's long-planned campaign appeal to the more conservative, Southern wing of the Democratic party? More than a few thought so.

Unfortunately for the Gores, Tipper's comments about the issue coupled with her little-girl name, made the project seem less than serious. Initially Mrs. Gore thought her book and work would be irrelevant to her husband's campaign. "In the book, I am speaking for *my*self, and in his presidential race my husband will speak for *him*self," she told reporters. Although she described her husband as supportive of her cause, her own comments betrayed at best qualified support. One time she said her husband "has been 'cute'" about the book; another time, "He never told me not to do it."

Al didn't help Tipper's credibility. As the 1988 race accelerated and it appeared Tipper's interests were hindering his fund-raising efforts, the senator from Tennessee began to remark on his initial reservations about his wife's lobbying. In February 1988 *U.S. News & World Report* questioned the candidate about his wife's involvement in PMRC and ran an interview beneath a headline reading: HOW TIPPER CONVINCED AL GORE ROCK LYRICS ARE "STRIP MINING" OUR CULTURE. Gore revealed, "My first reaction when she started to get involved in this was, 'Please don't do this.'"

Suddenly Gore had image problems coming and going.

Writers in *The New Republic*, a magazine whose top editor was a personal friend of the Gores and who ultimately endorsed his candidacy, first attacked Tipper and then came to her defense. In a snide piece entitled "Tipper De Do Dah," political writer Hendrik Hertzberg noticed how Tipper was tightening up Gore's already uptight campaign look.

"Gore has been totally unable to capitalize on his youth. The question is why. The answer is his wife, Tipper, and her crusade against dirty rock 'n' roll," Hertzberg observed. ". . . the fact that the PMRC's original manifesto was signed by sixteen wives of U.S. senators and representatives, carried an implicit threat of federal action. The Senate hearing sent a similar message. At the very least, the PMRC's most powerful weapon has been the proximity of its organizers to men of official power."

Hertzberg believed that Tipper's "crusade" presented a "negative," as they're called in the election business.

"In terms of its effect on the electorate, the campaign regards the crusade as a wash: It probably attracts as many Southern and conservative Democrats as it repels coastal and liberal ones. The more important cost, observers seem generally to agree, is in the area of fund-raising, where the entertainment industry wields enormous clout."

Hertzberg had a point. In the fall of 1987, with fund-raising not quite up to snuff, the Gores headed out west to Tinsel Town for a private, closed-door lunch with entertainment-industry moguls, who are traditionally Democratic campaign bankrollers. The meeting was requested by Gore's California supporters to "clear up misperceptions about Mrs. Gore's position," Paige Crossland, Tipper's campaign assistant, said at the time. Put another way, it was intended to undo the damage done by Tipper's PMRC.

Eyeing a *mise-en-scène* of wider scope, *The New Republic* pointed out how important Los Angeles and the entertainment industry have been to Democratic candidates. In his story, Ronald Brownstein described Los Angeles as "the Iowa of money." Brownstein pointed out: "What might be called the Hollywood primary has become a crucial early hurdle, especially for Democrats, in the long presidential race. As with Iowa activists, Hollywood donors expect the candidate to remember their name the second time. And the idiosyncratic concerns of Hollywood get the same kid-glove treatment as the idiosyncratic concerns of Iowa."

Unfortunately for the Gores their off-the-record lunch didn't stay that way. After eating, one luncher told *Variety* that the Gores were backing off their hard-line stance. Mrs. Gore called the congressional hearing "a mistake" that "sent the wrong message" to the entertainment industry. Her husband apparently agreed, saying the hearing "was not a good idea."

The Gore campaign told reporters that the meeting had helped "create a more favorable impression of the candidate's wife."

Danny Goldberg, president of Gold Mountain Records and a Tipper critic, disagreed, telling the press instead: "I think he made a political calculation that a meeting could make a cosmetic change in their perceived position, because the entertainment business is important for both money and attention."

Beyond money, the real problem Tipper created for the Gore campaign "was more elusive and interesting"—image. As *The New Republic*'s Hertzberg wrote: "Al Gore is young, handsome, bright and charming. His background as an anti-war Vietnam vet and ex-investigative reporter is the stuff of glamour. His record on issues such as arms control and the environment is creative and trendy. By all rights, his campaign should be crackling with generational excitement. . . . Gore should be riding the baby boom like a surfer. He isn't. The fuss over porn rock has turned his campaign into a Tipperware party. . . . Having a wife who has made herself the surgeon general of rock 'n' roll makes Gore a faintly ridiculous figure. . . . In some subtle and no doubt deplorable way, it unmans him."

Not surprisingly, the Gore campaign did not take kindly to Hertzberg's musings. The piece was "sophomoric," "juvenile," and "offensive," said campaign manager Fred Martin one afternoon, riding around New York City in the press bus, even though it appeared in a magazine published by "a friend"—one who eventually would give Gore a presidential endorsement.

"I thought it was pretty wild guesswork on Hertzberg's part," Martin added. "I thought he was trying to psychoanalyze the electorate. And I think that is pretty risky business."

Later in the campaign, once Martin Peretz at *The New Republic* decided to back Gore's candidacy, the magazine turned kinder and gentler toward his wife. In a later editorial they pointed out that Tipper's critics, "even when they are men of advanced opinions, are patronizing her because she is a woman. It is why they call her 'Tipper' and her effort a 'crusade.'"

Then, in the best antisexist vein they could muster, they editorialized: "Campaigns launched by women often attract that derisive label. Aren't women and crusades both, after all, emotional?" Fifty years ago, they pointed out, Eleanor Roosevelt agitated for racial equality, "a cause widely thought to be favored also primarily by cranks." At the time, "savvy commentators made it clear that even liberal women should stick to their pastel and mauve responsibilities. The secretary of war, Henry L. Stimson, attacked her 'intrusive and impulsive folly.' As with the slanders against Tipper Gore, the most brazen fear-mongering was believed by otherwise skeptical people. Many were convinced that Mrs. Roosevelt was actually intent on fomenting insurrection among Negro domestics, at least for starters. And her husband's well-wishers worried that, by her independence, she was somehow undermining FDR's aura of command. In this regard, we have not changed that much."

True. But there was a big leap between civil rights and rock 'n' roll, as Lee Atwater would discover when playing his blues guitar fell short of overcoming the Reagan record and beckoning blacks to the party of Lincoln.

★ ★ ★

Many candidates' wives have found it difficult to maintain their individuality while meeting their obligations to their husbands. The dilemma is not new; it wasn't lost on Eleanor Roosevelt. As her biographer Joseph P. Lash pointed out, Eleanor, faced a "life crisis when Franklin's election to the presidency threatened to undermine the life she had so painfully constructed for herself independently of Franklin yet supportive of him. In the White House, she feared, she would be a bird in a gilded cage, a creature of routine, pomp, and ceremony."

In her own memoirs she recorded, "I did not want my husband to be president." When he was first elected, she was happy for her husband; for herself, she was deeply troubled. "As I saw it, this meant the end of any personal life of my own. I knew what traditionally should lie before me . . . I had seen what it meant to be the wife of the president and I cannot say that I was pleased at the prospect . . . the turmoil in my heart and mind was rather great that night."

Granted, Eleanor was a special case—she built a life for herself after discovering her husband's romance with Lucy Mercer. Still, in politics, even more than in marriage, compromise is the name of the game. Tipper Gore, for one, confessed that when she gave up promoting her book for promoting her husband, she felt "a bit of a conflict," but explained to reporters, "So far, I'm campaigning [for Al] and being true to myself."

Other wives toed a stricter line. "You've got to believe in this man" is how Jeanne Simon explained the motivation propelling her to participate in her husband's campaign. "If I disagreed with Paul, we'd talk it over privately. But by this time, after being married twenty-nine years, I knew pretty well where he stood, and we didn't disagree.

"I think that perhaps I could have emphasized some points stronger than he did. I was perhaps more concerned about child care, about parental leave, about pay equity for women. But total commitment to the candidate is absolutely the first requirement."

On the one hand, we expect her to be committed and independent, but on the other, never to do anything that can be construed as "betraying" her man; that was how political analyst William Schneider saw these women's roles. "It creates a difficult dilemma."

Increasingly, observers like Lake predicted such discomfort will become more common. "It will be difficult. [Spouses] dislike it intensely. Especially those who have carved out different roles."

As the era of the doting wife goes the way of the passenger pigeon, sometimes campaigns, and administrations, will emit subtle impressions of divergent stands. "For example," said Lake, "you'll hear in pro-choice circles that George Bush is anti-abortion, but Barbara Bush will never commit on it, leaving the impression that she is pro-choice. You just let it out in selective circles."

★   ★   ★

During the campaign, though, most chose to avoid controversy. For Jeanne Simon, an early PMRC supporter, rock 'n' roll was too hot for a presidential race. She backed off.

During an interview with the Washington, D.C., radio host Diane Rehm months after the election, a caller asked Mrs. Simon about PMRC. She mused vaguely, "Oh, the Parents' Music Resource Center? I had forgotten all about that." She remembered: "Tipper Gore and Susan Baker [wife of Secretary of State Jim

Baker] started that some years ago. I have not been involved in it as much as I was in the beginning. I still think pornographic rock lyrics are not desirable. I don't care for them. But it became a matter of being associated with some fundamentalist groups that I did not care to be associated with. I also didn't want to give the impression in any way, shape, or form that I thought censorship was a good idea. I'm sure Tipper Gore and Susan Baker feel the same way, but there seems to be a great deal of First Amendment objectors out there."

There were in Hollywood. And on the East Coast there were more, at least on the day before the New York primary. As the Gores worked New York City, critics of this stripe popped up at every turn, it seemed.

Handshaking his way through the packed streets of Little Italy, Gore stopped before a pasta eatery near Mulberry Street to project—without amplifiers—to all within earshot, "I want to ask you for your support on Tuesday. . . ." As Gore extolled his candidacy a curly-haired thirty-one-year-old musician (accordion, bass, electric guitar) hovered on the edge of the crowd. Standing in a thicket of official Gore posters, Al Zimmerman held up a handmade sign. CENSOR TIPPER NOT MUSIC, it read and that was what Zimmerman shouted, holding his sign overhead.

He drew the attention of a young campaign worker passing out leaflets nearby.

"She's not for censorship, by any means." The young woman came over and corrected him.

"I think she should mind her own business and not try to intrude herself into the First Amendment of this country," countered Zimmerman, whose T-shirt was emblazoned with the Statue of Liberty.

"She's for labeling and not even mandatory labeling, voluntary labeling," the campaign worker rebutted.

"Well, we see what happens in movies now. We have this rating system in movies so you can't make a movie that's really subversive or anything like that. And all the people who want to hear subversive art . . ."

The Gore gal interrupted him. "She's for voluntary writing of the lyrics on the back of records."

"Yeah, well, she's backed off a little because they don't want the entertainment industry against them. And the media, for some reason, haven't called them on this," Zimmerman answered. "They haven't been talking about this at all. The only thing that's happened is there's more accurate reporting of what she said origi-nally."

"Do you know that the founder of MTV is on her steering com-mittee? As is a very prominent First Amendment lawyer?" the campaigner shot back.

"That's part of the problem; MTV just cooperates in this censorship," Zimmerman complained, his sign going higher into the air.

Batting his sign out of the way with her GORE FOR PRESIDENT sign, she snipped, "Get that sign off my head. You think you own the air rights here?"

Pretty, fair, fourteen-year-old Karenna Gore took all this in without joining in herself. The one who started it all by pricking her mother's ears to Prince's "Darling Nikki," a song about a young girl masturbating in a hotel lobby, Karenna wore all black—black crushed-velvet jacket, black shirt, black high-topped patent-leather boots. The suburban Virginia girl blended in just fine with the urban city scene. Preferring to hang out with the crowds and a few friendly reporters, as opposed to appearing in the usual campaign family tableaux that made her "feel ornamen-tal," Karenna talked about how she saw her mother's viewpoint, once the protester got out of earshot.

"She is the most misunderstood woman in America," she mut-tered. "There's so much degradation of women. It's incredible. If you want to know what you're getting, maybe you don't want to support people who portray women that way. And you've got a right to know.

"I agree with the basic idea that consumer information is not censorship."

Going to her mother's defense, she said, "You know, she's just an easy target, she really is. 'She's a bored housewife,' you know. 'Wife of a senator.' I mean, it's really unfortunate what's hap-pened. I think it's really unfair."

Protesters popped up again later in the day when at four o'clock the Gores settled in to a taping of the Phil Donahue show at a

Rockefeller Center studio. It was a predominantly female poly-ester-pantsuit crowd, except for a lone spike-haired punker who would eventually boo Tipper loudly as the taping drew to a close.

Donahue's crew piped old Elvis tunes into the studio where some of the waiting women applied fresh lipstick and blush. The ceiling was crowded with klieg lights that brightened the green ferns hanging in pots over the studio stage.

One of Donahue's producers came out to face the audience angled in ascending rows of seats. Her job: warm them up. Familiarize them with the show's routine. And above all, make sure they asked questions.

But first she previewed two upcoming shows. Donahue needed recruits. "We're looking for men who have left their wives for an older woman—it's usually the reverse," she explained, as if these "mainstream" middle-American women wouldn't know that. "Sign up with Sharon after the show if you happen to fit into any of these categories. Or your friends," she invited them.

"The other thing we're looking for is people who have slept their way to the top. . . ."

The women tittered. Bottoms shifted from side to side.

Then, like an aerobics teacher pumping a class through warm-ups, she started: "How many of you are following the primaries?"

Not missing a beat, she quickly followed up: "Who do you want to be president?"

Shouts rebounded. "Dukakis!" "Jackson!" "Gore!"

She focused them, got their minds burning on the day's topic.

"Were you surprised that Koch endorsed Gore? Will the endorsement help him or hurt him?"

Puzzlement filled the air.

"How many of you are going to ask questions?" she implored loudly. Next came an order: "Don't stare."

Then, "I don't care what you do. But do something."

"Can you do it?" she boomed.

"Yeah!" they shouted back.

Just when it seemed she was finished, she revved up again. "When Phil comes out here and says, 'Who has the first question?,' who am I gonna see?" she cheered.

Hands flew up.

"Stand up, too," she instructed them. "It helps all the camera people get a good quick shot of you. And then I'll tell him to get the focus real good. And you'll look real thin," she promised.

"But don't lean forward," she warned, "because they're bad at that."

As thoughts of cleavage past and present no doubt crossed the mind's eye, the audience erupted in laughter. They were primed to behold Donahue bound into view from stage left.

"We want you in this!" he boomed in greeting. *"This is America!"* he hollered, even more exuberantly than his pepped-up producer.

"Don't worry about saying something stupid. I hold the record!" he reassured them, crisscrossing the stage, moving up and down the aisles.

Somehow this was not difficult to believe.

"How many of you are New Yorkers?" he bellowed. "How many are going to vote tomorrow?"

More hands went up.

Donahue said he wanted to talk to New Yorkers in particular and announced that the three candidates—Dukakis, Jackson, and Gore—had all been invited to appear on his show.

Dukakis had declined to come. Jackson would come tomorrow. On cue, Al Gore walked on.

Right away Phil let him have it. "We are throwing bombs around in the Persian Gulf. We have knocked out two oil platforms, a patrol oil boat, and damaged two frigates. We are responding to one of our ships hitting a mine that was in the harbor. It is believed the mine was placed there by the Iranians, which damaged our vessel, to be sure, and shook up a whole lot of guys. Thankfully there were no fatalities. How do you feel about this?" Phil grilled the would-be forty-first president.

His words slapped up against the proper Gore who, beside the bouncing Donahue, seemed even stiffer and more wooden than usual. It could have been the perfect opportunity to have a good time. A chance for Gore to let voters see an exciting new face. But when Al opened his mouth he managed to achieve a level of dull and dry that matched Dukakis's delivery.

"Based on the information we have now," Al intoned, "I think that it was justified. I think it was appropriate and I think it was what you call a proportional response. That is . . ."

In the course of Donahue's hour, Phil and the audience took

turns pelting Gore with questions. The candidate explained his views on Phil's hypothetical question, as well as disclosed his views on Iran-Contra ("one of the most serious mistakes"), abortion ("pro-choice"), Jackson ("I think it's wrong to cast a vote on a basis of fear, rather than on a basis of hope"), Israel ("I support the Camp David formula"), and homelessness ("more affordable housing").

Finally someone mentioned Tipper. Donahue obliged, and Gore's wife, dressed in her best telegenic red, stood up from the front row to applause and a solitary back-row boo from the punker, who seemed only a bit older than Tipper's teenage daughter.

"I'm confused," another questioner said, "you sound liberal. But a couple of years back I remember your wife had something to do with censorship with rock lyrics and you went to court with Frank Zappa. How do you feel about that?"

Gore corrected her. "I never was in court with Frank Zappa or anyone else. And she is totally opposed to censorship of any kind, as I am."

He went on to give his-and-her views that today's parents should be more aware of a "new kind of increasingly violent and explicit entertainment aimed at children when they're not really able to deal with it effectively. Younger and younger children . . ."

The more Al talked for Tipper, the older and older he seemed to get.

CHAPTER SIX

~~~

The Conventions: A Family Affair

The politicians have an ideal woman in mind and the symbol they are using for that ideal is "family." The earthly manifestation of the ideal are the wives, no longer merely admiring but passionately adoring. . . . "Such a nice family," "Such a sweet family," "A really cute family," delegates at both conventions cooed. So what? Is this a competition for Father of the Year or a Presidential election?

—JANE O'REILLY, *The New York Times*, "Hers," 9/11/87

For eight days in the midst of one of the hottest summers on record, the giant made-for-television campaign commercials that passed for 1988's national political conventions rather resembled a TV sitcom where viewers saw who loved, cared for, and could show off his family—and spouse—the most and best. By convention time, "family values" were a central feature of both campaigns' rhetoric. Heated controversies—gun control, abortion, child care, drug abuse—somehow became neutralized under broader questions of "values"—to the relief of candidates and strategists who were out to woo swing voters, particularly women and Reagan Democrats. To bring meaning and life to the unspecific and essentially specious talk that resulted, candidates' family members were cast in starring roles.

Polished and processed for prime-time consumption, the portraits of the Bushes, Dukakises, and Jacksons that would emerge from the conventions nourished a nostalgia many Americans harbored for an era when families embarked on united quests for a common goal. The media-made tableaux of presidential politics seemed to offer a modern replica of the pioneering American family working together to bring in the crop. The winner, after all, puts bread on the table.

For the winning wives as for the candidates, the convention was a rite of passage, a point of departure when they gained new stature. No longer just candidates' wives, at the conventions they were elevated to a new position: Wife of the Nominee. In that role their participation seemed to underscore the values theme. Each woman came to represent and symbolize her candidate's version of family life and family values.

Kitty Dukakis underwent her transfiguration the evening of July 21 in Atlanta's Omni Coliseum when she strode across center stage into a prearranged embrace with her husband, who mouthed "I love you" so all late-night, prime-time viewers could read his lips. Barbara Bush's passage began more awkwardly—with a pat on the butt from her husband as she left him on-camera during a preconvention interview with Dan Rather. Watching her go, Bush shook his head somewhat disbelievingly and sighed: "Forty-three years, Dan . . . it's a tough learning experience."

It was a bit like an audition for the White House version of *Family Feud,* in which the Duke's Horatio Alger (in the words of one pundit) was pitted against Bush's Father Knows Best.

The ideal of "family life" as broadcast by both national political parties was little more than a made-for-TV image. Nevertheless, that image sustained itself through the rest of the campaign and into the White House.

★   ★   ★

In Atlanta, the big question was how the Democrats would resolve their own internal family feud. Caravaning to Atlanta via a much-publicized "buscapade," Jackson was still smarting over Dukakis's failure to inform him of his vice-presidential choice—before a reporter eliciting his reaction prematurely brought the news. Speculation blossomed over how Dukakis would mollify Jackson and keep an upper hand in the convention proceedings, if not in the press. Once that tempest dissipated, reporters turned their energies to wondering how good a speech the dispassionate nominee would manage to deliver.

It was pretty much the same story with the Republicans in New Orleans. Reporters wondered at length, aloud, in print, and on the

air, about how good a speech would come out of the man branded
as the most "tele-repellent candidate ever." They filled in vice-
presidential dance cards and speculated futilely about who the Republican's mystery mate would be.

From the press's point of view there was one excellent reason
for riding the non-story: Dukakis had virtually clinched his nomination in the New York primary April 19, a full four months before the Democrats gathered in Atlanta. Bush had locked his up on
March 8 after a Super Tuesday sweep. There was still plenty of
interest in the campaign but not much news; and if the candidates
wanted to advance "themes," the papers were hardly in a position
not to oblige them.

Conventions used to be the moment when party regulars met to
actually select and nominate a candidate. With that task now
shifted from the proverbial smoke-filled back room to primary
voters, national political conventions have lost much of their lever-
age and luster. Conventions are no longer moments of historical
decision making—though the nomination itself is playacted
through a drawn-out state-by-state roll call. Rather, they serve
more as grandiose social events, where delegates, consultants, and
reporters hobnob, just as at any trade show.

"There used to be news in delegates choosing the candidate;
there is no longer a choice to make," Reuven Frank, former president of NBC News, commented after the election. In an essay in
the *Gannett Center Journal*, he wrote: "There used to be news in
delegates competing for credentials; elected delegates are now cer-
tified by secretaries of state. There used to be news in fights over
the party platform; the platform is now decided at another time
and in another place. The civil rights struggle and the Vietnam
War, the great dramas of recent American history, were played out
at the conventions before the cameras. There are no such great
dramas these days. There is, in sum, no more news at conventions."

Despite what Frank said, conventions are not without a *raison
d'être*. They can be, according to political pundit David Broder,
"transforming events for individuals, for parties and sometimes for
the nation." It is, after all, at their conventions that candidates
make the psychological leap to the stature of nominees. They be-

come nationally and internationally known. Shown live simultaneously on all three broadcast networks, nominating conventions present one of the few moments in the long campaign when an interested American, a relatively rare creature to judge by the Nielsen ratings, has the chance to ask, who is this man and what is he like?

Equally important, they are a time for the nominees and their parties to launch the themes of the fall campaign, although they compete for popular attention with back-to-school fashions, fall-season TV premieres, and the debut of new car models.

With at least two hours of free air time per night, both parties turned their convention halls into huge, color-coordinated television studios complete with Hollywood production crews, choreographed glitz, "designer" shades of salmon, ivory, and azure (for the Democrats), "traditional" red, white, and blue (for the GOP), and speechwriting teams to carefully compose manageable sound bites in order to better pound home their messages to prime-time audiences.

Conventions are also personal celebrations, where delegates gather after the long primary season to schmooz in a grand family reunion while looking after the business of ratifying and validating their nominee. They are an opportunity for the candidate and his family, whose schedules have scattered them to different states, to rejoice and focus on the immensity of the task ahead. They are a four-day reprieve in which family and party leaders congratulate the winner of the grueling primary season, plump him up, then send him out like a gladiator for the final battle.

With neither candidate especially well known and with no single issue dominating the race, observers like Jack Germond and Jules Witcover noted at the outset of the convention season that "the personal qualities of the candidates are likely to be especially important and probably determinative."

As several strategists on both sides pointed out, voters don't like to put a stranger in the Oval Office. Conventional wisdom had it that the choice to be made in 1988 was between two personalities rather than between policies or platforms.

And so families were trotted out to reveal the vote-worthy personal dimensions of a couple of otherwise indistinct guys.

"If they see a man who's living his daily life like they would like to live their daily life, then they believe in him because they figure,

'This guy's got similar values to me. I can trust him,'" is how Deborah Steelman described the Bush campaign's thinking at the time.

With little public activity scheduled for either candidate, beyond the big acceptance speech, the convention became for their families a carefully scripted series of events and interviews intended to flesh out the candidates' biographies and bring them to life in as many ways as possible.

For the nominees' wives that meant taking center stage. The convention was the big opportunity, a chance not just to show off Mike, but to provide clear images of the man, his family, and his campaign that could be expanded on later. A picture of Kitty had to be assembled and put across as well. "This is when you tell the world who Kitty Dukakis is and what that means to the candidacy of Mike Dukakis," said Heather Campion, who left her job as public-liaison director at the Kennedy School of Government to coordinate Kitty's campaign schedule.

Once it became clear that Mike Dukakis was going to win the nomination and his wife would face a grueling general election, the Dukakis campaign decided Kitty would need a more experienced staff to help her through. Campion had worked for Joan Mondale in 1984, and she joined the staff of twenty. Before the convention, while Kitty was recuperating from surgery for two herniated disks in her neck, the campaign also brought on board Paul Costello, a Chicago public-relations man who had worked for Rosalynn in the Carter White House. Kitty needed an experienced staff. That, given her reputation for volatility, was the opinion even of the "white boys," as her staff (male and female) disparagingly referred to Michael's staff (male and female).

A vital part of the candidate's biography, political operatives felt Kitty had to be presented at the convention as a personality in her own right.

"This is a person who had her own career but had a traditional life, too," Campion said. "We tried to mesh all those things. We spent a lot of time before the convention fleshing out how her schedule could reflect who she was. Who anyone is, is a very complicated thing. You need to be able to bring it into some kind of focus."

Arriving in Atlanta, Kitty faced four straight nonstop days jammed with appearances designed to show her traditional side, besides signaling that she was going to be a serious campaigner in the fall. She gave in-depth speeches on issues. She schmoozed with delegates from key states. She met and talked to women leaders in the Democratic party and the women's movement. In the words of Eleanor Roosevelt, she was on hand "to work in every way [she could] to help her husband achieve his objectives."

In an unprecedented step, *USA Today* fueled that process by asking both nominees' wives to provide grist for the media mill and chronicle their own campaign activities. Starting at the convention, Kitty Dukakis wrote a daily (later weekly) diary. In Atlanta, the Dukakis campaign tactically used this insider dispatch to downplay expectations about Mike's speech and play up his "passionate" side. Kitty dropped such personal tidbits as admitting to falling asleep while reading her husband's speech, "napping" with him in the afternoon, and their dancing without music one night between flights in an empty airport holding room.

Her torch song drew attention to the romantic style of each candidate—and pointed not so subtly to an "affection gap"—something that Barbara Bush found especially irritating, given her image as "George's mother" and the persistent rumors alleging that her husband had engaged in extramarital affairs.

Eventually, when it was her turn, Bar would strike back, ridiculing the Dukakises' public displays of affection as press ploys. Implying they were fake. Adding another facet of unpleasantness to the already nasty campaign. (After the Republicans met, Dukakis punched back, commenting at a press conference: "It is true Democrats tend to sleep in double beds. Republicans prefer twins—one of the reasons why we have more Democrats than Republicans.")

Meanwhile, with the Democrats' polls showing voters hungry for more information about the man himself, Kitty and her children met continuously with reporters during the four days of the convention. Scores and scores of reporters picked and probed into their psyches, family life, and marriages and then spooned out different versions for public consumption.

July 20, the third day of the convention, was typical. Kitty started at an early-morning breakfast with a group of governors' wives and breezed through a tribute lunch where Hattie Babbitt reminded Kitty just how far she had come. "My tribute lunch consisted of two reporters from Akron who offered me a chili dog and diet orange soda—and who afterward kept calling me Jane," Hattie quipped, describing her own departure from the race. Then, after an Atlanta Symphony concert conducted by her dad, Boston Pops conductor Harry Ellis Dickson, Kitty limoed back to Atlanta's Hyatt Regency at 5:00 P.M. for her real work of the day: ten breakneck, back-to-back interviews with local television reporters from across the country—all in seventy minutes.

Room 452 was outfitted like an impromptu TV studio. There were hot, bright lights. A makeup artist. Furnishings to suggest an intimate ambience. Aides scurried about, coordinating arrival and departure times for the TV reporters and their crews. Each station would be allotted precisely five minutes. That came down to no more than ten questions apiece, depending on the journalists' skill and speed.

A few questions turned up in almost every interview. The reporters wanted to know about Kitty's drug problem. About her husband's upcoming speech. His cool personality. Jackson's impact on the convention. Several asked some variation on "What kind of first lady will you be?" or "How do you feel—*now*?" and "What's going through your head, *right now*?"

During the convention a candidate's spouse had no choice but to coolly master the art of producing a telegenic personality on cue. Answering each reporter, Kitty had to seem fresh. Vital. Interested. As though she had never heard any of these obvious questions before.

Watching Marilyn Quayle partake in this routine during the general election, *Washington Post* reporter Marjorie Williams wrote: "The ability to bat out the message on command—injecting all of its original freshness, hewing to all its original safety—that is what political observers refer to when they talk about whether a candidate has the stamina for a national campaign.

"It is hard to say the same thing over and over, especially when you are tired. In giving as many as twenty interviews a day—back to back—five minutes each, bang, bang, bang—the human impulse is to say something interesting. The core human conviction is that each of us is charming enough to win over our listener. Resisting those missteps is the mark of the professional."

Although all the spouses faced these demands through the primaries, it was at the national convention that Kitty was fully initiated into this ritual of satellite-dished-out intimacy. Like her, the reporters stuck close to the obvious and shot for the "feel" of spontaneity. The reporters came in and out. But for Kitty the pace was grueling, the interviews repetitive. Few viewers watching her across the country would realize what her behind-the-scenes ordeal was like.

5:15 P.M. Gabe Pressman, a reporter with WNBC-New York, came in. Dressed in a smart navy-polka-dot suit, Kitty faced him and his crew. Ever since the New York primary, Kitty had looked different. Her hair, previously worn in a short cut, was now stylishly bouffant, highlighted with henna. Her once-nondescript wardrobe was now stocked with designer clothes. Like a movie star heading to the set, she began her day with a professional hair and makeup session.

Kitty faced Pressman under hot lights while a folding screen behind her shut out the incompatible window light and city vista. Fresh flowers softened the low coffee table before her. Her press secretary, Paul Costello, sat watchfully just out of the camera's frame. Also watching the goings-on was an attentive reporter for *USA Today*, chronicling Kitty's daily events for the by-lined campaign diary. The small room was already warm, and the lights and body heat made it uncomfortably so.

5:20. Rene Ferguson, a pretty reporter from Chicago's NBC affiliate, slipped into Pressman's seat. The second in the long lineup. She focused on the day's events and the candidate's personality. Earlier in the day Dukakis had "surprised" Kitty at a tribute lunch held in her honor at Atlanta's historic Fox Theater. Joining her on stage, he joked about how she was often much better received around the country than he, and mentioned a North

Carolina voter who said he supported the governor because "your wife smokes."

So Ferguson asked about Kitty's repeated attempts to quit smoking, seeking a comment about the stress she was under.

"I tried to stop. I made a public comment once. I stopped for five and a half months and decided when I stop I'm going to stop but nobody's going to know about it," Kitty explained.

Ferguson followed up with: "Are there things that worry you about the stress of being a first lady?"

"No," Kitty replied. "We're so involved with the here and now. We're just ending one phase of a very long campaign and beginning another. I haven't thought that much about the pressures and challenges and opportunities of being a first lady."

"These are very dangerous times. Do you worry about the safety factor?"

"I don't," Kitty replied. "Because [Mike] has Secret Service protection and I'm grateful for that. It started about seven months ago and I feel much more comforted knowing that they're around."

Ferguson turned quickly to Kitty's problem with diet pills. "Do you think there is anything that would make that drug problem come back?" she probed.

Kitty had already had one serious drinking episode that only her family knew about. But she replied matter-of-factly, "No. It's been five years. One is always recovering, not recovered. I don't think about using or wanting to use."

Ferguson moved on to discuss the candidate in a way his wife no doubt found insulting. "America doesn't know very much about Mike Dukakis . . . he is cold, not a warm campaigner."

"I wouldn't have married him if he were that way. He's a warm, caring, compassionate leader. Very competent. He's a leader who is creative. He has begun programs that nobody else in the country has in terms of helping welfare mothers get off of welfare . . ." she went on softly, smiling.

5:30. KPIX, San Francisco. This reporter wanted Kitty's reaction to Jesse Jackson. "Do you feel that Michael has been overshadowed in the first two days?" he asked.

"No, not really," she answered brightly. "Jesse has run a good campaign. He got many votes. He had his night last night. Tonight is Michael's night. Tomorrow night is Michael's night."

Next, The Speech.

"Have you talked about that? . . . Do you have some idea of what we can expect?" he wanted to know. Six different reporters asked her this question within the hour. And six times, she graciously gave a variant on "I haven't had a chance to read it."

"Well, what would you expect some of the points in the speech to be?" the correspondent pursued.

Kitty dipped into safe talk about leadership. Homelessness. Day care. Then added a line she'd repeat five times more. "But I wouldn't want to guess about it because writing is not my forte and I wouldn't presume to get involved."

5:37. KIRO, Seattle. Susan Hutchison. This reporter was wide-awake. She sat down right away and came on strong. "I had lunch today with a couple of people who travel on the plane regularly and they said you are the live spark of an otherwise very staid staff. Do you try to be this way?"

Kitty paused, seeming to ask, What could this question mean? That she's fake? That she's high-strung? Emotionally unbalanced? "No," she laughed, nervously. "But I guess I am that way."

Hutchison was on a roll. "Is that natural for you?"

Kitty explained that after traveling with the same reporters for months on end she liked going to the back of her husband's lumbering plane (affectionately dubbed "Sky Pig" by the press corps) to shoot the breeze with them. "You get to know them," she elaborated.

"However, they say they haven't gotten to know the governor." Hutchison did her best to get Kitty to actually say something newsworthy.

Wary, Kitty laughed nervously again. "I think some people are harder to get to know. Michael is much busier than I am," she replied carefully.

"Some people might say that comes across as arrogance?"

Kitty swung back as her husband's defender. She moved to bridge the public and the private spheres of their marriage for Seattle viewers, but not necessarily in a way that the public might find reassuring. She reinforced the idea that privately her husband was very different from the person he might seem on TV.

"Michael isn't arrogant," she insisted. "He's caring. Very determined. And I think that might come off as . . ." she caught herself. "That's not the Michael I know."

Hutchison backed off, tossing a softball. "What kind of first lady will you be, should you win in November?"

Kitty was always asked this question and had an answer ready, though it became threadbare from overuse. The trick here was to make her answer sound heartfelt, this time and every other time.

"I'd be active," she said, listing her many interests. Homelessness. Arts. Refugee resettlement. Preservation and upkeep of city green spaces.

"And yet you just got over back surgery?" Hutchison prompted. "You're doing all right?"

"I'm doing fine," Kitty replied. "I'm trying to walk every other day. A couple of miles."

"Some people say when you have back trouble, it's because you're carrying a heavy burden. Do you feel sometimes that the burden is heavy?"

Kitty dodged the implication here, avoiding verbal entrapment by dismissing rather than discussing the considerable burdens it turned out she was carrying at the time, as her postelection statements would indicate. "No," she said adamantly, quickly citing her doctor's belief that her background as a teacher of modern dance had brought on her neck problem. It wasn't stress, she tried to assure the reporter. It wasn't a heavy burden.

Like this interview, perhaps.

5:44. WHIO, Dayton. 5:51. San Diego. Kitty asked for iced coffee. "It constricts my vocal cords." 5:55. Cincinnati.

6:05. KCBS, Los Angeles. Ann Curry bounded in. A striking Japanese-American woman, dressed smartly in fiery red, she had the looks networks pay for—and the smarts. Curry wasn't interested in the defender-of-the-hearth-and-flame routine. Or idle speculation about Mike Dukakis's speech. She was preparing a story on the gender gap and wanted to talk with the candidate's wife about women's issues. Kitty brightened immediately. This was her kind of reporter and her kind of story. She talked engagingly about reasons for the gender gap. She discussed pay equity, day care, her husband's stand on abortion, his record of appointing women to important positions. Talking issues, Kitty turned on.

6:12. Fox News. 6:19. Pittsburg. 6:26. Knoxville.

When the dizzying round of interviews ended, Kitty had come up with answers to some sixty questions. She had handled the exhausting round like a pro. Before she could leave, however, Bill Reilley, a producer from KPIX in San Francisco who studied communications at Boston University with Kitty, asked to have his picture taken with her. Happily, she obliged her old classmate.

"You get union scale for this," Reilley joked to an assistant shooting the photograph.

"I do?" Kitty interjected.

The hot room broke up in laughter and Reilley pinned a convention Kewpie doll of the governor and Lloyd Bentsen to Kitty's jacket. The laughter reached a higher, semi-hysterical pitch. Kitty looked down at the two figures pinned to her navy jacket. "I must be losing it, if this makes me laugh," she said, shaking her head as she got up and walked toward the door.

Before Dukakis's speech the next evening, a bit of stagecraft was arranged to underscore the Democrats' major themes. First, delegates in the packed convention hall were treated to the debut of a newly composed "Fanfare for Michael" performed by the Boston Pops, under the direction of Kitty's father. Then the face of the governor's Academy Award–winning cousin, Olympia, flashed on larger-than-life screens as she narrated a video snapshot of her cousin's life, including a tour of Dukakis's high school, his neighborhood and home, his tomato garden, and ending up in the garage with his twenty-five-year-old snowblower. "I say Michael gives the word 'frugal' a new dimension," she told the nation. Finally Dukakis entered the Omni from a ground-level door, shaking hands as he mounted the podium to the thumping sound of Neil Diamond's "Coming to America," a pop anthem brimming with immigrant hope and inspiration.

Mike Dukakis capped his nomination by giving the best speech of his life, what one newspaper called "a celebration of ethnicity, optimism and opportunity." Dukakis painted a warm picture of himself as the prosperous son of Greek immigrants. He became emotional, even teary-eyed, when he mentioned his father, and used his own life as a metaphor for the American dream. In an effort to reclaim a word that Republicans had used for years to siphon off Democratic votes, he spoke of how a stronger, more inclusive economy can strengthen *families*. Looking to the future, he closed his speech by invoking Texas treasurer Ann Richards's granddaughter, Lily, and Jackson's youngest daughter, Jackie—as well as "the baby that's going to be born to our son, John, and his wife, Lisa, in January. As a matter of fact, the baby is due on or about January twentieth."

When the speech ended, as balloons and confetti rained down, the nominee was surrounded on stage by his wife and family. The fallen Democratic contenders and their spouses joined the winners onstage in a show of unity. But the Democratic family feud wasn't done for, yet.

A color photograph filling the front page of next morning's *Atlanta Constitution* hinted at conflict to come. Beneath a banner headline—DUKAKIS TICKET OFF AND RUNNING—Mike and Kitty Dukakis were seen onstage with Lloyd and B.A. Bentsen. Between them, smiling and waving and clearly dominating the shot, were Jesse and Jackie Jackson.

★   ★   ★

Dukakis's emphasis on traditional values, coupled with the Democrats' use of patriotic imagery and a show of unity, caught the Republicans off guard. Traditional values and Main Street Americanism were Ronald Reagan's turf, after all. And 1980 had been the birthplace of neither these values nor political cynicism about their abuse in TV ads. Some Republicans felt George Bush faced a more formidable opponent than they'd predicted. The debate over who loved America's families most revved up.

There were at least three reasons for the new emphasis on family values. Both sides were after key voting blocks—among them, women and Reagan Democrats—for whom family held great appeal. Also, with peace and prosperity at hand, no dramatic issues had captured the public's attention; "family" filled the void. And after delaying having families of their own, baby boomers, the most numerous segment of the populace, were finally reproducing. "As go demographics, so goes the election," quipped Deborah Steelman after the final votes were in.

The Boston Globe's Ellen Goodman called the strategy "Wooing the TICKS"—"Two Income Couple with Kids in School and Parents in Retirement." She didn't think it was anything new.

"Every four years there emerges out of the demographics another American Family," Goodman wrote in her column the day after the Democratic Convention. "Eight years ago, the Reagan brand of Family were people suffering from inflation and afraid of the breakdown of traditional values. In 1984, the Mondale Family was downtrodden and dispossessed by the Reagan rich. This year, the Jackson Family were the people who rode the early bus. All through the years, candidates have tipped their hats to the archetypal immigrant family. But by election day, the Dukakis folk hope to claim the TICKS.

"This updated image is not a fantasy. The two-worker family is most decidedly the new norm. Only 22 percent of the voters live in traditional families with a woman at home, and half of those women have worked and expect to return to work.

"But the image is also a reflection of political necessity. The TICKS are the swing voters, the Independent couple who voted Republican last time out. Theirs is the family the Democrats have to woo 'home' to the Party."

That family was the one Republicans wanted to keep in their camp. Because those voters, as Democratic pollster Peter Hart pointed out to *The Wall Street Journal* at the time, could have meant "the difference between 42 percent and 52 percent." In other words, the difference between a Republican landslide and a Dukakis victory.

The vice-president's reaction to the Democrat's performance was admiring. "I think the Dukakis family at the convention did a wonderful job," Bush told Dan Rather in a pre-GOP Convention interview. "I had great respect when I saw his obvious affection for his mother and the way that son did in an interview. . . ."

Then, sounding more like a contestant returning to the semi-finals of *Family Feud* than a presidential nominee, he mapped out the campaign ahead, promising to show off his own family.

En route to New Orleans for the Republican Convention, Bush began talking to reporters about *his* family and values. And like Dukakis, not just because he "cared." After the Democratic Convention Bush had faced a worrisome dip that a *Wall Street Journal*/NBC News poll said put him as much as 17 points behind Dukakis, who also led four-to-one among crucial Reagan Democrats. Although that lead dissipated by the time the Republicans arrived in the Deep South, Bush was still battling troublingly high "negatives." Polls showed that more than 40 percent of voters had negative attitudes toward him, based principally, it seemed then, on his personal qualities, not his record, résumé, or ideology.

Moreover, Dukakis was leading two-to-one among women, ten million of whom were registered to vote. A Harris poll conducted in the wake of the Democratic convention found women favoring Dukakis 64 percent to men's 49 percent. Men, however, favored Bush 46 percent to women's 32 percent.

Lately, the Republican party has been tough to sell to women. Election results in 1980 and 1984 showed between 6 and 9 percent fewer women than men voting for the Republican candidate, according to the Center for the American Woman and Politics at Rutgers University. In 1988 some early analysts hypothesized that Bush's military achievements and CIA record, the mainstay of his primary campaign, left them cold. More than policy, they thought, women were reacting to personality. One telling joke circulated during the campaign: George Bush, it went, reminds every woman of her first husband.

Pollsters soon refined the "personality" hypothesis. They found the actual reason more women favored Dukakis over Bush was rooted in worry about the future. Women thought the country was off on the wrong track. They felt more economically vulnerable than men. "George Bush doesn't know what it means to live paycheck to paycheck," a woman in a New Jersey focus group told Democratic pollster Celinda Lake.

At the end of July Bush met with the editorial board of *USA Today* and confessed that he had to start "stressing the personal." In what was the beginning of his family show-and-tell, a little like taking out his wallet of family snapshots, he said, "I have to open up a little. At our convention you will see the five Bush children, their five spouses and our ten grandchildren. Michael Dukakis speaks Spanish. I have three grandchildren . . . who are half-Mexican."

Talking on the air with Dan Rather as the convention approached, he confided in his half-bashful gosh-darn-it style: "At this level of politics and in this age, we're gonna have to share what gives us our strength. . . . I never like talking about the loss of a child, for example. It's a tough time when young parents . . . but I saw in Barbara an unparalleled strength. . . ." Looking ahead to his acceptance speech, he said: "I haven't shared family so much with the public because it's very special and private. I have to do that more, so there'll be some family discussion in there, I'm sure."

Indeed there was. Besides calling for, in speechwriter Peggy Noonan's words, a "kinder and gentler nation," Bush made the theme of family values central to his acceptance speech, telling America: "An election that is about ideas and values is also about philosophy. And I have one. At the bright center is the individual. And radiating out from him or her is the family, the essential unit of closeness and of love. For it is the family that communicates to our children—to the twenty-first century—our culture, our religious faith, our traditions and history."

Early in the campaign season Bush sheltered his family from the political fray and kept them, as he put it, an "oasis." Soon enough, though, he trotted them out before cameras for all America to see. During the convention's roll call his daughter, four sons, and Columba Bush, his Mexican-born daughter-in-law, who spoke in Spanish, nominated him from five separate states. Columba's son led the Pledge of Allegiance.

Like Kitty Dukakis, Barbara Bush formally "came out" at the convention. As the mother of the big Bush brood she became emblematic of the Republicans' focus on family values. She was introduced by her own biographical video lauding her achievements as volunteer and touting her role as a wife and mother. She spoke to the delegates, talking openly of the death of their four-year-old daughter, Robin, in 1949. She said their daughter's death was "the hardest thing we ever faced together.

"When she was gone, I fell apart," she told millions of strangers. "But George wouldn't let me retreat into my grief. He made me share it and accept that his sorrow was as great as my own. He simply wouldn't allow my grief to divide us and push us apart."

The headlines obliged, telling the story the Bush team needed to tell, but they sounded a bit more cynical than Republican strategists might really have wanted. THE NEW GEORGE, CASUAL FAMILY MAN, said *The Washington Post*. BUSH TROTS OUT FAMILY IN PUSH FOR NEW LOOK, *The Boston Herald* wrote. "Meet the Bushes. After years of trying to keep his family in the background, Bush is unveiling his 'secret weapon' as an election tool."

There's nothing, as the conventions proved, like public intimacy.

George Bush may have closed his eyes to Iran-Contra, but he
didn't blink when it came to inheriting Ronald Reagan's communications techniques. In her 1988 book, *Eloquence in an Electronic
Age,* communications expert Kathleen Hall Jamieson looked back
at the methods perfected by the Great Communicator himself—
and adopted by his anointed successor. "Reagan understands that
television speaks not to crowds but to individuals; accordingly, it
is suited to self-disclosure," she wrote. "While speaking quietly
and conversationally, he confides in us." Consequently, Jamieson
pointed out, "Self-disclosure can accelerate our sense of intimacy
in a relationship. Reagan's judicious use of personal revelation accounts, in part, I suspect, for the fact that even his opponents
profess to like him as a person. Reagan wears this affection as
political armor, insulating him from the slings of outraged opponents and from the sting of unpopular policies."

Jamieson continued: "Reagan's disclosures about his relationship with his wife both underscore his commitment to family
values and rebut critics who, early in his administration, had char-
acterized her as extravagant and uncaring. The warmth and affection they convey about each other silently underscore Reagan's
claims. His effectiveness as a champion of family values is a tribute
to his skills as a communicator. As the country's first divorced
president, a person reportedly not close to his own children, Reagan exhibits his commitment to family by publicly showing his
devotion to his wife."

During convention week Bush's disclosures about his family
helped him get "close" to the public in other ways.

Bush copied his Democratic rival and "surprised" his wife at a
convention tribute lunch held in her honor, introducing her in a
display designed to gain points in the Bush-Dukakis "affection
gap." Before hundreds of luncheon guests gathered at the New
Orleans Hilton, he joked: "So here we go with the introduction.
With feeling. Demonstrable feeling. Come on up, sweetie-pie," he
instructed his wife.

Bar came forward for a kiss and a hug.

"Thank you very, very much," she replied, pausing for effect
. . . "sweetie."

As her husband returned to his seat she quipped in a saccharine-sweet voice: "I hope you can't take your eyes off me." Then turning to the crowd, she added, "See if he looks at me as adoringly . . . as I looked at him." The Republicans broke up. But afterward some observers felt Bar's implication that the Dukakises' affection was fake only added to the negativism surrounding the 1988 race.

At another time, on nomination night, the Bushes invited television cameras upstairs into their suite at the Marriott so three generations of the family could appear together on prime-time television watching the convention—just like many other families in America that night. (Unfortunately, the Nielsen ratings showed a lot of other families were interested in watching other things.)

While the five Bush children were on the floor with their delegations, network coverage switched back and forth from the floor to the Bush family suite where the nominee, surrounded by his wife, in-laws, and a bevy of grandchildren, waited with a charade of anxiety for the roll call—topped by Texas—to confirm his nomination. The suspense was bearable.

The Bushes did await the nomination in their hotel suite. But their full reaction was not exactly as seen on TV.

It would be a family roll call, Jim Baker's idea, according to Bush's fourth son, Marvin. "This is a different campaign. We've got an idea. So here's what we're going to do," Marvin remembered Baker telling the five Bush siblings. "It was appropriate for us to step up and announce our delegates," Marvin said, "because we've all been involved in our state parties. We've all been involved locally. And we were not going to get out there and be theatrical in the way, say, that the Jackson family was able to do. That's just not my style."

Approximately twenty minutes before George junior was to announce the Texas count, a correspondents' pool of wire-service reporters and photographers and one network TV cameraman headed upstairs in the Marriott and set up in an ad hoc living room abutting the Bush family's suite. The room was arranged like a stage set. Hot klieg lights beamed down from a corner. A muted-blue sofa was drawn out from the wall and angled nicely in front of four color-television sets—two consoles side by side with two smaller sets stacked on top. Sounds and scenes from the convention floor poured forth. When the reporters and photographers were set up, George and Bar, the in-laws and grandchildren, came in. Aides guided them to their seats where they gamely faced the press. The kids, some in shorts carrying toys, some in dresses or ties, were hyper. It was way past their bedtimes.

The Bushes "held"—campaign talk for "waited"—for nearly ten minutes. They sat stiffly, making small talk among themselves, and looked straight ahead at the TV sets. Not a yard away, a group of photographers lolled about at their feet. A microphone boom hung over their heads. No one took any pictures. Everyone just sat or stood, and waited for George junior's face to appear. When it did, Bush said, "Here we go. This is the big moment."

Beaming proudly, from the convention floor and through the TV screen, Bush's eldest son intoned: "The great state of Texas proudly casts one hundred and eleven votes for a man we respect and love. Texas casts all its votes for her favorite son and the best father in America, George Bush!"

At George junior's last word photographers began shooting like crazy. The Bushes grinned, laughed, clapped, hammed it up. Bar, heretofore sitting upright, momentarily leaned her head on George's shoulder and smiled sweetly.

When the nomination finally came, the moment the family had every right to enjoy was stripped of any genuine joy or naturalness.

One reporter ventured: "Mr. Vice-President, what are your thoughts? What does it mean to you?"

"I think it was foregone," Bush allowed. "But it's very special."

A few minutes later Doro's face popped up on a screen. Bush turned his attention to her four-year-old son, Sam. "There's your mom," he said. "Go point her out." Referring to the kid's toy gun, he directed, "Get the pointer. Use the pointer. In your hand. That's it. Use your weapon."

Meanwhile, the press contingent moved toward the door. The reporter ventured again: "All set for the speech tomorrow?"

Bush rambled: "All ready . . . yeah . . . ready to go."

"Is it the best speech of your life?" the eager pooler prompted.

"It's probably the most important one," Bush admitted.

The reporters left. Then a second group of photographers was herded in and immediately started shooting away.

Looking at the screens, which intermittently flashed the faces of his children on the convention floor, Bush said: "Hey, there's Neil! There's Doro!" And then as the network came into the hotel room itself . . . "There's Gampy!" Bush pointed at himself on the TV screen for the benefit of his grandchildren who were alternately hyperactive or practically asleep.

The second shift of photographers exited and a third came in. They, too, shot frantically.

Meanwhile the face of Bush's youngest son, Marvin, flashed up. He was tallying the votes from Virginia. "I'm not going to sugarcoat it for you," he told the convention hall. "I'm proud. I'm proud to be a delegate and . . . especially proud to cast votes for a man who is adored by his wife and his five children and his ten grandchildren. . . ."

Bush called over to Marvin's little girl, "Marshall. Look! There he is!"

Two-year-old Marshall toddled over to a television, the screen overwhelming her. Recognizing her father, she started banging on the screen, wailing, "Da-da."

Suddenly, Marvin finished his spiel and disappeared, sending his little daughter into gales of "Da-da!" She pounded on the TV looking for him after he was gone until Marvin's stylish wife, Margaret, picked her up to take her away. As the last shift of photographers left, the Bushes got up to hit the hay. "Thank you, all," Bush said. "Glad you're here."

To be fair, not all of the Bushes' emotive family displays were quite so contrived. The most spontaneous moment in the otherwise programmed convention week came as a result of the Bushes' farewell to the Reagans, who appeared at the convention on its first day. Scriptless, the vice-president got into trouble. Pointing out his three partly Hispanic grandchildren to the president, he referred to them as "the little brown ones."

Reporters pounced on the remark, raising questions about his ethnic sensitivities. The episode seemed to hit a raw nerve with Bush. His son's marriage to a woman of a different ethnicity had an effect on the family. "You have to adjust" is how the president's sister described it, remembering a period when Columba "was having a hard time in Texas on account of being Mexican. She was getting the cold shoulder from all of Jeb's friends."

That marriage had "definitely affected them," Bush's daughter said in an interview at her home after the election. Initially, Doro said, her parents had been concerned. The Bushes didn't meet Jeb's bride until a week before the wedding. "It had nothing to do with her being Mexican. It had to do with the fact that we had never met her," Mrs. Bush said. "When Jeb told us he was going to get married, we said, 'Give us twenty-four hours, and we will be there.'" Mrs. Bush said she considered Jeb's marriage a "sort of strengthening of our family in many, many ways. All of our family."

Doro added, "It was just kind of weird because we had never met her before and I think my parents were just worried about their kids—and just wanted to make sure that they weren't prejudiced against or anything like that, 'cause that kind of thing isn't easy."

But, Doro added, the marriage "made my parents—not that they wouldn't be—but just made them a lot more sensitive to the problems of being a minority."

And so at a press conference the next day Bush—scriptless and furious—chided reporters who, he said, misunderstood his remarks. "This heart knows nothing but pride and love for those three children," he vowed. He certainly seemed to mean it, and Barbara echoed those sentiments when the press repeatedly asked her for her reaction.

Bush's emotional response won him kudos even in the Dukakis camp. Months after the election Susan Estrich recalled the incident and said, "When I heard this remark, I thought, 'Jesus Christ!' [But then] I thought he was great. He stood there and said, 'How dare you! I love those children.' I think . . . it was not scripted. Maybe it was. But my sense was that if he can fool me, he can fool anybody. It didn't come across as a scripted response. Or a prepared response. It came across very much and very honestly as a grandfather talking about grandchildren he loved. That was why it worked. Because for most people, for many people, that was the first moment they knew that he had grandchildren that were partially of Hispanic origin. And in that moment, his reaction was so much a human reaction that people could identify with. I thought that was a great reaction on Bush's part—and, if I can say, an American reaction."

New York Times television critic Walter Goodman seconded Estrich's opinion. Looking back at both conventions, he called Bush's comments "a rare show of honest emotion in a synthetic stew."

But Goodman ended his praise there. Bush almost sidetracked his convention success by overdoing the schmaltz—and by picking Dan Quayle as his running mate, of course.

Quayle, perhaps more than any other pol in the 1988 race, found his own family testily trying to endure with grace under pressure.

When her husband's selection was only a rumor, Marilyn Quayle stepped off the plane in New Orleans to face a mob of media, "more than we could have gotten together in six months in Indiana," her aide Mary Moses recalled. She remembered Mrs. Quayle as saying: "If it's always like this, I'm carrying Certs. I've never smelled so much bad breath in my life." So began Mrs. Quayle's sorry relationship with the press.

As soon as his selection had been announced and the press started nosing into both Quayles' backgrounds, the young senator expressed concern about the effects of it all on his three kids. "What do you fear the most as you go into this very intense pressure?" Dan Rather asked Quayle during one of his first sky-box interviews. "The thing that I fear the most is the potential harm and instability to the family," Quayle confessed, earnestness coloring his voice. "It's *tremendous* pressure. Not just on me but on my wife, Marilyn, and probably even more on my three wonderful children. . . . They're still uncertain about this whole effort: the escorts, the cars, the Secret Service, bright lights, cameramen, reporters. . . . I just don't want them to be hurt by this."

Indeed, the kids were lukewarm. Quayle's nine-year-old daughter, Corinne, told her father she wished Bush had picked Bob Dole over him. And from the way her brothers wanly waved at the crowds, often only after a nudge from their mother, it would appear they felt much the same way.

Before the ordeal was over Dan and Marilyn would have to explain to Corinne that no, her father was not "friends" with a "Playboy bunny." Their eldest son, Tucker, would go on his first date with a couple of teasing Secret Service agents in tow. He was harassed by schoolmates who ridiculed his father.

The media barrage was difficult for her kids, Marilyn Quayle said later, but there would have been a lot more explaining to do if the Republicans had lost. "We won the election, which helps," she said. "If we'd have lost, the children might have questioned whether or not maybe [what the press reported] was really true.

"It was an ugly time," she recalled later. "No one could have prepared our children for the numbers of media down in New Orleans and how little regard they had for our children. I still look back on that, and their treatment of the children was so frightening. They were knocked down, hit by cameras, pushed around to get at us. And it was just very inexcusable and for them, it was incredibly frightening."

She never said why her children were there in the immediate presence of all those cameras and reporters in the first place.

But TV critic Goodman had a good idea why the Quayles brought their kids into the fray. "Before we ever saw Mr. Quayle's children, we heard about them in a peculiar way," Goodman wrote. "Asked why he had joined the National Guard in 1969 instead of going to Vietnam, suddenly the young senator was telling us about his brother who had entered the Marine Corps, his wife whom he met in law school, and the three beautiful children with whom they were subsequently blessed.

"Mr. Quayle seemed to think that he was not only answering the question but doing so in a way that would floor any sitcom fan. The strategy here: when the reporters begin firing, place your beautiful family in a circle around you and duck."

Goodman did not limit his sarcasm to the Quayles. He turned an acerbic eye and pen to both convention displays, commenting at length: "Is it possible that producers in both the Republican and Democratic camps are ignoring what makes the commercial sitcoms popular? The sitcom fan may not have the classiest tastes, but in his range he is demanding. Scriptwriters work hard at turning all the family members into individuals, giving them quirks and eccentricities. In every episode, one of the children gets into trouble or does something wacky or comes through as the hero of the evening. They are full of little surprises.

"But nothing gets lower marks for the politician's family than individuality, and no convention planner loves a surprise. The fog of conformity churned up by the Bush sons was so thick that you couldn't tell one from another on the week's interview shows.

"If the Bush scriptwriters expect to hold an audience, they had better get to work developing a mildly naughty escapade for one of the Bush boys (nothing to do with Vietnam) that can be allowed to become known in October, giving George and Barbara and everybody a chance to gather rhapsodically round and demonstrate family loyalty in a difficult time. Otherwise, the gathering of the Bush clan, wholesome though it surely is, will soon come to seem as exciting as a postage stamp.

"The campaign has hardly begun, and already the reverence for The Family that has been oozing at us from all sides like some patented cream has become sticky.

"Everybody likes children, but nobody can run for three months, or three days, on his family; it's like taking your stand on a bowl of tapioca."

Nor was it just the candidates' children whose performance was assessed. Taking her turn, *Boston Globe* columnist Ellen Goodman went to town on the mini-series she saw transpire between the on-screen would-be first ladies: Kitty, passionate half of the Dukakis duo, and Barbara, mother of those oh-so-many children. Writing after the Republicans closed shop in New Orleans, Goodman critiqued the public love-fests now expected of national politicians. Fidelity, as Gary Hart found out, was a minimum. "It's love in public, absolutely marital and totally safe, peppered with an occasional touch and feel, that has become the standard," Goodman wrote.

Assessing the convention behavior of both nominees and their wives—the Dukakises' passionate kiss, the afternoon naps—George's pat on Bar's derriere, his revealing talk of "feelings"—Goodman went on about what she called the passion for passion in politics: "For most of our national campaign history, the woman was seen standing behind her man, not in his arms. Marriage and children made the candidate appear trustworthy and staid, not love-blissed and sexy. . . . Now we ask our candidates to reveal themselves emotionally. We expect them to have a rich internal life. We want full disclosure on their histories, even their psycho-histories—although heaven help them if they've seen a psychiatrist. We have upped the ante on the amount they are expected to expose."

They are judged in terms of "home life," "emotional depth," "solid marriage."

Goodman attributed the impetus for such public manifestations of affection to the country's "anxiety about love." Indeed, recent statistics showed the relationships of many Americans to be surviving but not thriving. One set of statistics shows of eight thousand individuals responding to a *USA Today* survey in September of 1988, 39 percent of male respondents and 27 percent of females confessed to having an extramarital affair.

"Ours is an era of marriage until love do us part," Goodman contended. "People once found their security in the institution. Now they seek it in the emotion. They long to witness and believe in lasting love. So, like kids, we seek comfort in the couple of grown-ups in the big house who love each other, demonstrably."

★   ★   ★

In the end, the "family thing" and the "woman thing" rang hollow with other convention watchers. Family values embodied in the image of the nominees' wives didn't mean much to many women. Some women activists watched the sitcom for eight days during the summer of 1988, and were angered to see both sides paying what they saw as lip service to women's issues. Granted, many women were showcased at both conventions. Texas Democrat Ann Richards shoved "a silver foot" into Bush's mouth. Elizabeth Dole co-chaired the GOP's get-together and was a featured speaker as well.

But the candidates sent out mixed signals. As Democratic pollster Harrison Hickman told authors Ronna Romney and Beppie Harrison before the election: "There's a whole other kind of chauvinism that we may see come out in the course of this election, which I think is actually worse—those people talk the talk and don't walk the walk. They say all the right things but when the big decisions get made in their campaigns, for the most part, there won't be women sitting at the table."

Both sides signed up and showed off female staffers. Much was made of the fact that the Dukakis campaign was managed by a woman. Less that she got the job by default after John Sasso's dismissal over leaking to the press a videotape that tied Joe Biden to charges of plagiarism. Women advisers helped raise and spend the governor's money. They shaped his policies. But once Sasso returned to the fold, observers wondered if Estrich wasn't obliged to defer to her preferred predecessor.

On the Republican side, there were no women in Bush's inner circle, although they hovered around the edges. The "chicks" was what they jokingly called themselves during the campaign. When it was all over, this loyal brood was left chirping. Of the several women staffers holding key jobs in the Republican campaign, some got powerful jobs but none an inner-circle White House job.

Even the Republicans' female star, Elizabeth Dole, was referred to by a campaign aide as "an audience pacifier—like a lot of women surrogates were." Liddy Dole's name was bandied about as a possible vice-presidential choice, but she was never a serious contender. Polls showed she didn't help on the ticket, but more to the point, as another campaign operative put it, "Of all the talented women in the country, why would you select your opponent's wife? You wouldn't." Indeed Bush did not, selecting instead a man his eldest son's age.

By touting "family" and the women who headed their own broods, the politicians ignored the real state of American families and the multiple needs of women, many of whom care for those families, often alone. Among women aged eighteen to forty-nine, about 90 percent can be considered part of the labor force. "The typical housewife has become rare indeed," according to *American Demographics*. Instead of acknowledging the reality that family life in America has changed, both candidates regressed into a nostalgia about the way things were. Neither proposed much in the way of substantive family policies beyond a feel-good day-care package. Both updated old-fashioned baby-kissing to a new level. When it was all over there were far too many pictures of candidates and their spouses perched on kiddy chairs at day-care centers, and far too few specifics in the policy recommendations made to take care of these kids.

Not all women bought it.

Writing in *The New York Times* after both conventions were through, author Jane O'Reilly put it this way: "Family issues do not include all women's issues, and 'the family' as presented this year does not include my family. I refuse to take the hint that society would somehow settle down as natural law ordains if everyone would regroup into a 'sweet family.' . . . Politicians continue to idealize the family because they still won't understand women's issues or women's needs. . . . It is odd and irritating to be spoken about by men whose notions of women seem to have been formed before 1920—the year women got the vote."

Responding to O'Reilly, one New Yorker agreed in a letter to the *Times:* "By presenting their version of the 'ideal woman, ever so subtly ensconced in the confines of the 'ideal' family, both political parties managed to recast women backwards, while offering theoretical lip service to a theoretical march forward."

Probably the pols really didn't know what to do because voters, confused themselves, couldn't give them a clear cue. In a Gallup poll conducted before the Democratic Convention voters were asked: "Should women return to their traditional role in society?" Sixty-six percent responded no. Then, when asked if "too many children are being raised in day care centers," 69 percent said yes.

Despite his convention performance, Dukakis finally lost the early edge he had among women, who split their votes evenly between Bush and Dukakis. Men showed a clear and decisive preference for Bush. By aggressively going after the women's vote Bush closed the female side of the gender gap. He changed his tone. Stressed his personal family history. Talked about the environment and child care. He showed off his grandchildren in ads. The "kinder, gentler" approach worked.

And Dukakis? Nikki Heidepriem, a political consultant who advised the Democrats on women's issues, said, "My answer when people asked me why we didn't have a better message to women is, 'When you don't have an [overall] message, you don't get a message to women.'" She added, "In a presidential campaign where paid media [political advertising] is the one show, we consistently had appallingly mediocre media."

Another Dukakis operative said that other than at the convention the Democrats were "unsavvy" about using the candidate's family. Part of it was that "Michael Dukakis had a hard time being a schmaltzy guy." Part of it was that family effectiveness "doesn't get polled for properly." And part of it "was when the polls showed people felt Dukakis wasn't passionate, we didn't pull out the family and hype it—he began talking about Nicaragua."

Perhaps the most creative—and accurate—portrayal of the candidates' use of families, wives, and women at the conventions was made by the cartoonists.

In his *Doonesbury* comic, Garry Trudeau refused to let Bush's blatant attempt to get the women's vote go by unnoticed. Throughout much of the campaign Trudeau portrayed Bush as an invisible man, made to disappear by his handlers. In a September 30 strip, an invisible George Bush explained how it came to pass that he was replaced by his evil invisible twin.

The voice of George filled the air: "For months, my people have been pushing me to take the low road, to play down and dirty. But it never worked. It wasn't me. I kept reverting to the quiet, decent guy I was raised to be," he said.

In the next panel Bush went on: "Finally, when I put that stuff in my speech about wanting a kinder, gentler nation, my staff hit the roof!"

"And that's when they panned you?" *Doonesbury*'s Mr. Duke asked.

"I tried to explain I was just pandering to women," Bush protested, "but no go!"

On July 21, the last day of the Democratic Convention, the *Atlanta Constitution* ran a two-panel sketch by Doug Marlette. In it Mike and Kitty Dukakis stood shoulder to shoulder looking out from behind a podium. Mike's arm was firmly around Kitty's back and he said: ". . . and I especially want to thank the woman without whom none of this would be possible." Kitty grinned expectantly. But her smile vanished when in the next panel Dukakis finished his sentence—"Donna Rice!"

As it turned out there would be more to Kitty's dashed expectations than anyone realized.

CHAPTER SEVEN

~

Running for First Lady

> We were very different types of women but were
> stuck with the same label. "The candidate's
> wife," locked into "little women" politics.
> "What's he like? What does he do?" At the same
> time we were expected to be highly opinionated
> and sharply aware of our husband's positions on
> all the issues.
>
> —ELEANOR MCGOVERN, *Uphill*

For Kitty Dukakis the 1988 campaign was more than a race for the presidency, it was a stuggle for a new sense of identity.

Caught between conflicting expectations of how a political spouse should behave, Kitty struggled to escape the confines of "little women" politics. On the trail she resisted the dreary, debilitating role of the traditional political spouse: a podium prop, smiling silently at her husband's side. Instead she adopted the mantle of political partner and surrogate. She demanded and got her own staff, schedule and chartered twelve-seat plane. At the same time she finessed the minefields of appearance, outwardly demonstrating interest in her husband's campaign, but not too much involvement.

Her public behavior mirrored a long-standing internal struggle. Setting her sights on the White House put Kitty on the path to recognition and power—in her own right—something she'd edged toward in her years as one of the nation's most active political spouses. Attaining the political wife's ultimate prize—first lady—Kitty would be able to have her own position and wield influence herself.

138

For the former Katharine Dickson it was both an exhilarating and a terrifying proposition.

There were the richly appointed Gulfstream jet and the designer clothes. The staff who prepped her for interviews and anticipated her needs. But there was also the pressure that prompted her twice in March (before the New York primary) to drink heavily when left by herself in Boston.

"I was just frightened and terribly alone," she explained in her office at the Massachusetts statehouse, a month after completing her treatment at Edgehill-Newport. "The kids were all off campaigning. Michael was off campaigning and I was alone. You can be alone or be with people and still have that sense of loneliness, and I had some of that," she said. She feared "the enormity of what was expected" of her. "I was frightened of the unknown. I mean, this was an enormous responsibility and it was, I guess, just a normal kind of fear of the unknown. There was a lot at stake. And I think I had some fear of criticism, some fear of not measuring up."

Although they were hidden from the public, some in Kitty's family knew and worried about her drinking episodes, but she didn't let anyone know how afraid she was. "I kept a lot of that to myself. Because I didn't want to be a burden to anybody. It was a very intense period of time."

* * *

Imagine life was going to end on November 8, 1988. Imagine how intensely one would live, were that the case. So it went on the 1988 presidential campaign. Engaged in a struggle for their political lives, the men seeking the presidency—and all those around them—were driven to an intense emotional pitch.

Starting around the time of the twenty-state Super Tuesday match in March, picking up immediately after each party's national convention, sweeping through the sixty-some days after Labor Day that comprise the general election, the campaign pace revved higher and higher until it instantly collapsed on election Tuesday in November. Campaign days, previously geared around a state or even a city or county, became structured around how many media markets and time zones a jet could propel the candidate through. Pols—and spouses—who throve on face-to-face contact with voters were out of luck at this stage. Encounters with voters became a rarity. Instead, "civilians" were reduced to the

status of unpaid extras in stylized media events. Candidates complained they didn't meet real people. They did. But they didn't.
"They 'see' real people," a Dukakis aide said, "but they don't get
to talk to them. When they do, they sit down at a photo op. It's all
fake. You know, they *sit* there. They've been told by advance people 'who these people are.' 'This is what you need to talk about.'
The cameras are on." The situation was no different for their
wives.

Mo Udall, himself once a presidential candidate, described the
experience of running for the White House to a *Wall Street Journal*
reporter: "A presidential candidate is a tired man on a jet plane,
surrounded by madmen. "The madmen are his friends and his
campaign staff." Your schedule is made by a bunch of maniacs.
Some work for you, some work for other candidates, and some
work for causes. You fly all over the country—to San Antonio, to
Detroit, to Seattle—just to make the evening news. You don't call
your own shots."

All airports began to look all alike. Speeches sounded the same.
Faces blurred. There was no time to think. No time to absorb new
information or formulate a philosophy or even provide a
thoughtful answer. Candidates simply reacted. Often simply.

Bruce Babbitt found himself ill-suited for a process so at odds
with his ordinarily pensive demeanor. "The tools of modern com-
munication have reduced the distance between voters and candidates to the point where there is no space for reflection and
consideration," the former presidential candidate told a reporter
for *Vanity Fair,* after dropping out of the 1988 race. "Every response must be instantaneous. If hostages get taken in the Middle
East, politicians find out about it at the same time that voters do—
through television. And as a candidate, you find yourself being
asked by reporters to respond instantly to events that are often as
yet only dimly understood. Often you end up merely upping the
level of noise and chaos in the system."

A *Boston Globe* editor found the artificiality of it all unexpectedly reassuring. Writing two days before the election, Martin
Nolan was reminded of the big shows the Nazis put on in the
thirties. He said: "If these traveling charades were really on the
level, their stage shows would resemble the Nuremberg rallies of
1933." At times the staged pageantry and "spinning" seemed to
bring both campaigns close in technique, though not in message.

At the very least, the artifice of it all made Patricia Schroeder's tearful adieu from the race—she "couldn't bear to turn every human contact into a photo opportunity"—more understandable.

"It's like putting on the Ringling Brothers and Barnum & Bailey Circus," Hattie Babbitt said, and that during the *primary* season.

"Boys Town," Jackson staffer Carol O'Cleireacain commented wryly.

"Theater in the best sense of the word" was Kitty Dukakis's assessment, as she hurtled herself through the days between the convention and the election like a fastball toward home plate.

★ ★ ★

At 10:00 A.M. on a hot August morning in Chicago, about two weeks after the Democratic Convention, Kitty and her three aides (press secretary Paul Costello, speechwriter John Keller, and trip director Bonnie Shershow, small in physique but boundless in energy) were in a motorcade of three, complete with police escort. Their cars screeched to a halt before a secure back entrance of McCormick Place, a sleek black-glass convention center that lies like an airport hangar along Lake Michigan. Today Kitty was covering the Midwest, while her husband hit the West Coast, starting his day in San Diego, moving on to Seattle, and ending up in Denver.

The 10:00 A.M. stop was the second of Kitty's day, one that began with a 7:30 A.M. hair appointment, followed by an 8:00 A.M. radio interview, an 8:15 A.M. newspaper interview, an 8:25 A.M. phone call to Jackie Jackson, and a forty-five-minute drive to a funeral home for a 9:00 A.M. visit to the family of the leader of the Polish American Congress—Aloysius Mazewski, a man with whom Kitty had worked on the Holocaust Memorial Council.

Arriving at McCormick Place at 10:15, Kitty had just a few short minutes to pause in a side room, collect herself, and catch a quick cigarette. On cue she bounded up on stage to greet members of the American Postal Workers Union, which was endorsing her husband for president. Stepping in time to the campaign's adopted theme song, "Coming to America," Kitty waved enthusiastically. The audience applauded wildly as her image loomed on large video screens so everyone in the enormous room could see her. Kitty talked to the charged-up crowd about her husband's positions. Equal pay for equal work. Affordable day care. She mentioned a child-care center that had opened for postal workers in New York. She plugged the idea of basic health insurance for all Americans. She pushed for an increase in the minimum wage. And ethics in the Oval Office.

Kitty finished at 11:00 A.M. After thanking the audience for its endorsement, she was whisked to a side room to feed the rapacious Chicago press. Today rumors were flying that her husband had sought psychiatric help for depression after the death of his only brother. Everyone wanted to know what she thought. It was the question Kitty would answer all day—here and later on in Ohio. Kitty was livid with the Bush camp for circulating this rumor and furious at Ronald Reagan for fueling it by referring to her husband as "an invalid." Restraining her anger, she replied evenly that her husband had not seen a psychiatrist. "It's a false rumor that won't go away," she retorted.

11:15 A.M. Kitty conducted a fifteen-minute one-on-one with a local Chicago anchorwoman who, following the pack, asked if and when she and her husband would release their medical records. Michael will do so soon, Kitty replied firmly. "But I will not release my medical records." A year later Kitty spoke of her history of psychiatric treatment for depression. But in the middle of the intense campaign, she replied, "I have shared the history of my recovery. *I'm* not running for office."

Next followed a quick photo session with postal union VIPs. Then at 11:30 A.M. Kitty and her entourage hustled out the door for a twenty-five-minute ride to Midway Airport, where at 12:15 P.M. her waiting twelve-seater Gulfstream jet was ready to take off for Cleveland. Kitty spent most of the hour-long flight giving another interview, at the same time munching on gourmet-style sandwiches served on glass plates by her handpicked stewardess. "I like it that the crust is cut off," she said, selecting a brown-bread tea sandwich, encouraging her interviewer to do the same.

Shortly before landing, Costello tossed Kitty a pack of M&Ms, which she wolfed down. She playfully tossed back a pack of Saratogas. "Here's a present," she laughed.

Costello sat himself on the carpet at Kitty's feet and briefed her on remarks she was scheduled to make at the next stop. Just before the plane hit the ground, she teased her nattily dressed aide about his new suit.

"What label is that?" she wanted to know.

Costello flipped his jacket inside out to show her. "Perry Ellis," he hooted, asking if that was good enough for her.

At 2:15 P.M. (one time zone later), the party arrived in Cleveland. The caravan of six cars, led and tailed by local police escorts, shot through red lights and arrived ten minutes later at Cleveland State University, where Kitty toured a training facility for welfare mothers. After talking to the program directors, she joined nine participants for a chat, not much more than a photo opportunity actually. Kitty and the women sat around a table set up in front of a mini-mob of penned-in press. In this setting, each woman was supposed to share a heartfelt story of how this particular program helped her pull her life together and get off the dole. The women did their best to talk, and Kitty her best to listen. She likened this effort to a successful program her husband launched in Boston and told the array of TV cameras and microphones thrust in her face that if her husband was elected the public could expect more successful programs like this one.

At 3:00 P.M. she thanked the women, then stepped over to a dais, where Cleveland reporters peppered her for fifteen minutes with practically the same questions as their Chicago counterparts.

"How important are the roles of the wives of the candidates in the campaign?" "How much do you influence your husband's leaning toward Israel?" "How about your influence on Cambodian refugees?" And then, "What are you wearing?"

Kitty looked down at her black-and-white-check ensemble. Then she looked back up at the fair-haired boy who had asked the question to see if he was kidding.

"A suit," she reported matter-of-factly, making the reporter look like a fool.

His colleagues laughed and moved on to more substantive queries.

3:15 P.M. The group hightailed it back to downtown Cleveland to the Bond Court Hotel, where Kitty could rest and make phone calls until 4:45 P.M. Then she popped into a downstairs side lobby for three more one-on-one interviews with local television reporters timed to hit the Cleveland evening news.

5:15 P.M. Kitty and company left the hotel for a half-hour drive to a reception in Mayfield Heights with predominantly Jewish fund-raisers. Kitty shook hands and greeted old acquaintances until 6:30 P.M. On the dot, she and her crew climbed back into the limousine and accompanying vans and headed back to the airport.

7:00 P.M. The Gulfstream took off again. This time for Hartford, Connecticut. After another hour's drive, Kitty and her team would arrive at 9:00 that night at the Park Plaza Hotel in New Haven, where tomorrow another tightly scheduled day like today, a nonstop hopscotch from media market to media market, would start all over.

★ ★ ★

In the ten weeks following their conventions, Kitty Dukakis and Barbara Bush both traveled over 50,000 miles. Kitty visited 88 cities in 25 states; Barbara 92 cities in 29 states with her husband and on her own, according to *The Washington Post*'s count two weeks before election day. Kitty gave what her staff estimated were an astronomical 900 TV and print interviews and appeared at 200 events and fund-raisers and at 25 short sessions called "press availabilities" with groups of photographers and reporters. Comparatively, Barbara Bush moved at a slower pace with the media, giving what her staff at the time estimated to be 184 TV and print interviews, 77 appearances at events and fund-raisers, and 13 press availabilities. Sixty percent of Barbara Bush's campaign appearances were made with George Bush. In contrast, Kitty spent only 25 percent of her time campaigning at her husband's side.

Kitty's press secretary Paul Costello viewed it all as a big success. "They treat her as if she were him. She's 'doing' the prison furlough, the tax increase, the health insurance. And it's great for us; the idea that there is a separate person, as opposed to just a wife, means you've got double the opportunities," he told the *Post*.

But Kitty's solo campaign sparked a debate within the Dukakis camp over whether she should be traveling with the candidate or on her own.

"There was a great deal of talk of wanting me to travel with him. And we had to make a decision about what was best for the campaign," she said after the election. "Whether I was with him, which for me was, on a personal level, fine because I loved being with Michael. But on a . . . campaign level that was just wasted time, because I could be speaking for him and meeting people in a different part of the country and carrying the message to people."

While political, her decision was personal in more ways than one. "I couldn't have handled it otherwise. If I couldn't be myself and be a full partner it wouldn't have been enjoyable and wouldn't have been the positive kind of experience that I look back on," she said of her solo campaigning. "I made myself vulnerable by agreeing to answer questions. Mrs. Bush chose not to do that, and that's a choice you have to make. If I wanted to be taken seriously, then I had to be serious about the work I was doing."

Kitty enjoyed traveling with her own schedule. When she was with her husband her role was limited. During the primaries Kitty frequently made joint appearances with the governor, and sometimes found herself standing wordlessly at his side. Once at a campaign rally before a student group at the University of Illinois in Chicago, she sat alone on a bare stage behind her husband as Dukakis spoke almost passionately about his immigrant past to the heavily ethnic student group. She remembered herself on that podium. "That was just dumb. That was very uncomfortable," she said.

Campaigning on her own, Kitty seemed to thrive. When Mike campaigned with her, he blossomed. Somewhere after the New York primary she actually started looking better than she ever had, despite the grueling pace. She radiated a confidence and warmth that audiences responded to, quelling staffers' fears that she would be a liability on the trail.

In March of 1988 her son, John, commented on how he saw his mother change as his adoptive father got closer to becoming the Democratic nominee. "I think she feels very good at this point," he said. "She is making a contribution and that makes you feel very good. She has grown, I think, with this, and she knows that all of us are very proud of her, for whatever that is worth."

But in addition to feeling needed, Kitty enjoyed and relished the attention.

"For many of these women, there is nothing like the rush they feel from the crowds," said Mary Finch Hoyt, former press secretary to Rosalynn Carter. They get chemically addicted to their own body's adrenaline because of the excitement and the stress. "For the first time," Hoyt pointed out, "the adulation is for *them*."

More than a choice, for Kitty Dukakis campaigning became a compulsion. She liked the constant stimulation, the pressure and the rush, and all of the excitement. Temperamentally, the frenzied pace suited her well. More important, it enabled her to find a long-sought-after niche of her own in the political landscape.

Like many women of the generation coming of age in the 1950s, Kitty Dukakis was caught between the sometimes conflicting roles of wife and mother and career woman. Restless and adventuresome, for a long time Kitty had looked for something she would enjoy doing. Something that was *hers*. Just being Mike Dukakis's wife was not enough, her friends and family believed.

"As a governor's wife, she was an appendage of Michael," Kitty's younger sister, Jinny Peters, said after the election. "As a candidate for president's wife, she was doing things on her own that would affect other people. She could have her own set of issues and do her own thing. She had her own set of issues here, she still does in this state. But with a broader scope it would take up more of her time and give her something to be directed to. . . . She would never be happy just supportive of Michael. I think that is one of her roles. But she needs to be her own person."

The presidential race gave Kitty focus.

The daughter of a reticent, exacting mother and an outgoing father whom she adores, Kitty has an outgoing good nature that masks an inner insecurity. "Kitty is very much like me," Harry Dickson told reporters during the campaign. "We don't have too much confidence in ourselves, but we want to prove ourselves."

After coming out of Edgehill, Kitty described herself this way: "Some of us in this world, and I certainly fit into that category, can have all kinds of kudos and attention and people telling us how wonderful we are, and if we don't believe it ourselves, if we don't look in the mirror and love ourselves and care about ourselves, then none of that makes any difference."

Outgoing and popular, but unsure of herself, Kitty dropped out of Penn State her junior year to marry John Chaffetz, an attractive Big-Man-On-Campus two years older than she. The two headed to Texas where Chaffetz joined the air force. But the journey from the Boston Symphony to the Lone Star State was a leap too far for the former Kitty Dickson to make. "I always maintain that it was his mother that made this marriage go," said Kitty's father, who was distraught when the two broke up. "He was an only son. His mother wanted a daughter and she always felt that Kitty was the daughter she never had. She was mad about Kitty. They were kids and they got married and they shouldn't have. He was quite different."

In 1961 she returned to Boston as a divorcee with a three-year-old son. She enrolled John in nursery school and herself in night school at Lesley College to finish an undergraduate degree in education. Not home a month, she was introduced to Mike by her old high-school friend Sandy Bakalar. She remembered him only as "that brilliant Greek kid" three years ahead of her at Brookline High. For the frazzled young divorcee, the no-nonsense Dukakis offered security. He liked her son. That was a plus. He knew where he was going. That too was a plus. When the two met, Dukakis was already planning a run for the state legislature. Politics was definitely in the picture. "Michael was very determined. He knew where he was going and what he wanted to do," Kitty said.

Early on, Kitty "was never interested in politics per se," her father said. Remembering the early days of her marriage, friends described Kitty then as basically a single mother. "Her life was not so easy," Bakalar said. "She was home alone with the kids. I don't think they went to a movie the way my husband and I did. I think she was lonesome for him because he was really out a lot when the kids were little. And she was, of course, less mobile, and they didn't have much money. . . . I think she had lonely days when she was younger."

More open and sociable than her husband, Kitty yearned to find a life for herself out of the house, her oldest friends said. She studied and taught modern dance. After her three children were older, she dabbled in other careers and interests, working for a time with a Boston travel and convention bureau.

"I think she had some hard times just trying to find herself and find out what she wanted to do," Andrea Dukakis recalled in an interview during the election. Bakalar agreed. "I do think she grappled with her identity. I do think that being the governor's wife wasn't self-satisfying. You just can't sit there and be the governor's wife. What do you do? You march in a parade."

The way Bakalar explained it, Kitty was caught. "As Kitty Dickson, she was Harry Ellis Dickson's daughter and as Kitty Dukakis, she was Michael's wife. So who really was she?" Bakalar asked. "She worked on that. We used to talk about things like this. 'Who am I? What do I really want to do?' And it was with encouragement from Michael. He would say to her, 'Do what you really want to do—as long as it doesn't cost too much money.'"

In 1982 Kitty pursued a master's degree in communications at Boston University, but when her husband decided to run for re-election she found a media career inappropriate. Working in the private sector became uncomfortable when her husband ran for governor again after his 1978 loss to Edward King. When he was reelected Kitty became more active in state government, working out of the statehouse and earning a reputation for herself as out-spoken, impatient, volatile, and demanding. In 1985 Kitty ex-panded her work, running a beautification program—Public Space Partnerships—at Harvard University to rehabilitate urban parks.

Kitty's influence on her husband was often talked about in Boston politics, although it is said the governor would withhold sensitive information from his wife because she couldn't keep se-crets. Some of the couple's acquaintances believe Kitty's political instincts were sometimes better than her husband's, though during the campaign some observers felt the complexities of the political landscape eluded her. When supporters started prodding her hus-band to enter the race, Kitty urged him to go for it. "She was part of the for-him-running group. That is where she was most help-ful," one of the governor's traveling aides-de-camp, Nick Mitropolis, recalled. When she saw Michael getting tremendous support from key people in key states who promised to get an organization in place, her enthusiasm grew. It was seductive, friends said.

Oftentimes, back in Boston, when people found him unap-proachable they'd approach his wife instead. "Whenever I try to push for something and I am not having any success, I will always talk to her about it. There's no question I use her," said Dottie O'Malley, former deputy commissioner of Boston's Metropolitan District Commission. There was no question in O'Malley's mind that the governor listened to his wife.

Dissatisfied with litter on the highways, O'Malley said, Dukakis put his wife in charge of cleaning them up because he knew with her drive the job would get done. Though he finally came out against gays raising foster children, Kitty had a more liberal view and got him to thoughtfully consider the issue rather than dismiss it out of hand.

The two have had their share of disagreements and fights over politics and state policies. Anne Hawley, former executive director of the Massachusetts Council on the Arts and Humanities and a close friend of Kitty's, recalled: "We've had some knock-down, drag-outs over the arts council—Kitty, Michael, and me." Remembering a scene in the couple's Brookline kitchen, Hawley laughed: "She comes at him with a force you *cannot believe*, and he—you know, 'the Iron Man'—it doesn't upset him. He just maintains his cool. He'll stand beside the refrigerator explaining why he *can't* do what she wants him to do, and she'll just be *screaming* at him. There's a real intensity there."

The marriage has not always been easy, friends said. "Michael's had to confront things he never thought he would have to confront," Hawley said, especially in the year since his presidential defeat. The couple has worked through some difficult family issues, according to Hawley. "It's a very resilient and American family. They're real people that work all kinds of difficult things through and stay together."

As the campaign progressed and Kitty became recognized as a political asset, she appeared to thrive. The campaign gave her a platform from which to speak on issues she cared about and learn about the concerns of others. It was a broadening experience, exposing her to all sorts of problems and people beyond Beacon Hill. "She loved every minute of it," her sister, Jinny, said. The question of Kitty's impact—as a partner in her husband's politics—became a standard part of reporters' repertoires. "What kind of first lady will you be?" meant more than "How will you redecorate the White House?" When reporters put that question to Kitty Dukakis, it meant "What role do you play in your husband's decision making?"

Kitty was driven to push herself on the trail so every minute counted, aides said. Part of that was compulsion, part chemistry, it seemed. "You could try and slow her down, but you couldn't do it," Heather Campion recalled. "She wanted to maximize her time and just pack everything in that she could. Her human level, beyond-the-point-of-no-return, is much higher than the average person. Much higher." Campion described Kitty as hard on herself. "Throughout the campaign I continually reassured her that yes, she should be tired. . . . She'd say, 'I feel tired.' We would say, 'It's OK. You are supposed to be. This is ridiculous.' She is just a driven person."

Friends said it was harder for Kitty to set limits for herself than it was to keep pace with the campaign's constant motion. It was difficult to keep herself grounded. Despite the low polls she kept the possibility of loss at bay.

Merna Lipsett, an old Brookline friend, laughed as she remembered a day Kitty invited her to go shopping and pulled up to the Lipsetts' front door in a limo, Secret Service in tow.

Other friends watched warily as the campaign's pace picked up and Kitty lost control over her own life. "They didn't treat her like a person, they treated her like a goddess," another traveling companion, Alice Jelin-Eisenberg, said. An attractive, dark-haired woman who worked for years in the statehouse as Dukakis's scheduler and became a public-relations executive at a Boston bank, Eisenberg frequently traveled with Kitty, going to small towns during the primaries. She said she saw her friend treated royally by an ambitious young staff, sycophants, and other hangers-on out to make names for themselves. "I think campaigns are the most unreal life," she said. "All of a sudden everybody's jumping around. Every whim you have—people stop and do it for you. All the fawning—I was so sick of that. Kitty would say something I didn't think was funny and people would start laughing at the drop of a hat. Conversely, she would cry over something and everyone would start crying. I mean it was *ridiculous!*"

The campaign experience forced Kitty to let go of any semblance of what most voters understand as "normal" life. Once Michael announced his candidacy, Kitty had her own staff. Her own plane. Her own agenda. Her own speechwriter. "She was totally 'packaged' for the next couple of months," another friend and traveling companion, Anne Harney, recalled. She remembered Kitty turning to her once in a midwestern airport and asking, "Where *are* we?"

"You're just simply moving so fast that you can't keep up," said Harney, a mother of six, who typically did not jet through three cities in a day and was happy to get back home to Lincoln, Massachusetts, after a few days to rest. "There's an insulation along the way. When you have your own staff in place, you have people who are just feeding you the top of the news. They're feeding you just what you want to hear to keep you 'up.' To keep you 'on,' and to keep you 'happy.' You're being fed just what they want you to hear. You literally don't have time to turn on the news and digest it. Or read the papers. In the last portion of the campaign she literally was almost put in a time capsule and shot into space. You had to almost see it to believe it."

Alice Jelin-Eisenberg watched warily as her friend got swept up in the unreality of the campaign process. Something big happens between the primaries, when a candidate and his spouse are searching for the spotlight, and the general election, when the spotlight is locked on them and shines nonstop, she said. Once a candidate becomes a nominee, the picture shifts from retail to wholesale politics.

"There are two types of preparation for getting to the White House," Eisenberg mused one afternoon in her office. "They're both important. One is the nitty-gritty grass-roots politics. Unglamorous long days. Small towns. One on one with people. There are no television cameras in this place," she said. "The other is the crowds and the glamour and the staff and the media." And television cameras around you, in force, all day long.

Sandy Bakalar, Mike's high-school sweetheart who introduced him to Kitty, shared Harney's and Eisenberg's view of the campaign. "I'm sure this was true of Barbara Bush too," Bakalar said. "You are not grounded. Even though you see the newspaper every day and you know whether your husband is winning or losing, you are not grounded. I think you build yourself a little fantasy cushion around you because you have to keep going. You are a little bit out of touch with reality. There is no other way for you to handle this experience. You protect yourself. And you stay 'up.' And you stay optimistic, because you know that you are onstage all the time. And if you are going to do this job right, that is campaign properly, you are not going to relax for one minute."

The pace and pressure of the presidential race force people to grow and change in ways they would never have imagined, Bakalar added. It forces individuals to leave behind life as they know it. "Once you get into this campaign, it is a one-hundred-percent experience. It isn't ninety-nine percent. You have to change. Anybody who says, 'Yes, well, they seem their same old selves' . . . it's simply not true. You really have to change. Your heartbeat changes. Your pulse changes. And you are going all the time. You sleep and eat and do your job. You are controlled by this big book that you pick up every morning."

In an arena where personality counts as much as, if not more than, intellect, Kitty earned both kudos and criticism beyond Beacon Hill. On a visit to Pekin, Illinois, a tiny town on the outskirts of Peoria, forty-two-year-old Roger Battin, an automotive repairman with the Caterpillar company, listened to Kitty address a group of retired union workers. He was noncommittal. "Apples don't fall far from the trees. You get the wives and the kids. It helps," Battin said.

After the same speech thirty-eight-year-old Pam Gardner was impressed. "I think she knows her husband's heart and mind as well as anyone in the world. I think she can speak real well for him." But Gardner certainly didn't want Kitty bossing the Duke around. "As a woman, I feel there was a problem with Nancy telling Ron what to do," said Gardner, a former dental hygienist and at the time herself a candidate for the local circuit court. "I think he was elected president and I think he should make important decisions. He and the Congress. Not the wife. I think she could offer opinions at the breakfast table, but as far as the president of the United States—he appears sometimes to be semi-henpecked and I don't like that look."

Back in Boston Kitty's old nemesis, *Boston Herald* columnist Howie Carr, who once christened Kitty the "Dragon Lady," couldn't have agreed more. When Dukakis gave Lloyd Bentsen the nod Carr blamed Kitty for holding up the choice. "Thank God Kitty finally made up her mind," he snorted. At another point he warned, "She'll make Nancy Reagan look like Mamie Eisenhower."

Other Boston reporters sensed that while more active than Barbara Bush (and any spouse except, perhaps, Elizabeth Dole), Kitty had toned down her act for the national media. "Kitty Dukakis dislikes any suggestion that she is trying to alter her public image," *Boston Globe* reporter Joan Vennochi wrote in a profile published during the Democratic Convention. "Asked if she is now trying to play the role of perfect political wife, she made a face. 'Me?' Kitty protested."

Kitty did tread carefully. Once the intense convention coverage began hometown reporters like Vennochi noticed: "The woman who was known in Massachusetts for her independent thinking and outspoken opinions now chooses her words carefully in the glare of national press scrutiny. She is still a long way from emulating the Nancy Reagan gaze of wifely adoration. But, faced constantly with questions about how much influence she exerts over her husband, her message is always the same: Michael is the boss. She may occasionally give advice, but he makes all the decisions."

★ ★ ★

Kitty's independence and boldness were risky for the campaign and for herself, as it turned out. At one point rumors circulated among the press that the Republicans planned to try to trip up Kitty because of her reputation for volatility. Indeed, in August Republican Senator Steve Symms of Idaho suggested, without evidence, that Kitty had burned a flag during an anti-Vietnam demonstration in the sixties. It was a vivid image, one that fit well with the Republican effort to paint Dukakis as an out-of-the-mainstream liberal. Kitty was outraged but stayed calm. She denied any such picture existed. None ever surfaced. But the event helped slow further the Democrats' already slow summertime momentum. "The governor did not respond to the Steve Symms attack on his wife. And I'm not sure why," Estrich said after the campaign.

Kitty also was an easy target for Republicans who played on the public's concern that "another Nancy" might take over the White House. Kitty's activities won her headlines and profiles in all the major newsmagazines. Many addressed just that issue. "Take-Charge Kitty, Would She Stir Up Trouble in the White House?" *Newsweek* asked. "Kitty and the Corridors of Power. As First Lady, She'd Rewrite the Job Description," cautioned *U.S. News*. And beneath the headline KITTY PROVIDES THE PASSION, *Time* informed its readers, "She won't unpack in front of him, but they share everything else." Maintaining her docile no-issues stance, Barbara Bush evaded such coverage, following the traditional first rule for a candidate's wife—worry less about scoring a home run than about committing an error.

Privately, Kitty's boldness and independence were risky, too. She couldn't sustain the pace. She was hospitalized twice during the campaign: once for two herniated disks in her neck. Once for what her aides called a "viral infection" compounded by exhaustion. Once she became the wife of the nominee, Kitty had less and less control over her own actions. Aides made the majority of her decisions. But the way she saw it later, it was after the campaign that she lost control completely. "What I had been controlling just could no longer be controlled," she said.

Other spouses, who only tasted the experience in the primaries, found the process of having decisions made for them disconcerting. After the election Jane Gephardt recalled her own trepidation and frustration with being a presidential contender's wife. "The scheduling part of it was the hardest thing to deal with," she said. "The staff just took his life over. I would call up and I'd say, 'This is something very important, Katie's dance recital or whatever, and it would be terrific if he could be home for this one thing.' It's 'Well, sorry. But there's this, and this, and this. It's all much more important than Katie's recital.' You have no say and no influence whatsoever," she sighed.

Mrs. Gephardt also said the worst thing about the campaign for her was that she no longer controlled her own life. "I was so used to controlling the house, the kids, and everything. Suddenly I was having other people telling me what to do, where to go. I'd say, 'I don't want to do that.' And they'd say, 'Too bad. Sorry.'"

Jane Gephardt found herself fighting her husband's staff particularly over Dick's schedule. "That's where it affected me first. I'd try fighting it. I'd fire off memos every once in a while about this and that, and all my frustrations with the schedule. Things would change for a while but then they'd go right back." Originally staffers promised Mrs. Gephardt that the candidate would be free one weekend a month. That was reduced to Sundays. Then Sundays disappeared. "I finally realized I had to accept what was going on and not fight it so hard. I wasn't getting anywhere. I was just making everyone angry."

Campaigning for almost two years, longer than any other spouse, Kitty Dukakis said the hardest part for her was always being away from her husband. Both Kitty and Mike complained about long separations and staff tried to bring the couple together as often as possible, but schedules frequently pulled the two in different directions. "I wouldn't characterize it as putting strains on our relationship," Kitty said carefully in the middle of the long primary season, but allowed, "It *was* difficult to be away from each other."

Like Jane Gephardt, Kitty freely contacted her husband's staff, chiding them on everything from his schedule to designing a response to Bush's negative ads. Though some staff complained of less access to the candidate when she was around ("You can't get in the suite at six A.M.") and others said she periodically "drove them crazy" with her calls, staff sometimes turned to Kitty as an ally. Frustrated with the governor, they often found her helpful in ironing out differences. She urged her husband to bring John Sasso back.

Campaign manager Estrich recalled wanting to keep the candidate in New York the night of the April 19 primary. "He and I used to fight a lot about time in Massachusetts versus time out of Massachusetts," she said. The night of the New York primary, Dukakis wanted to return to Boston. Estrich felt he should stay in New York. Frustrated, she caved in, figuring she'd get him back to New York at a later date. Before the candidate's schedule was finally fixed, Estrich recalled, "Kitty called me up and said, 'What are you doing? We have *got* to be in New York. We've *got* to be in New York.'

"I said, 'Well, I think it would be better with the media and the press attention and the significance of that primary. I prefer to be in New York. But I thought I would give in to this. . . . So at this point, it is all yours.' That would be my attitude," Estrich remembered. "'Now this is yours. I am happy in New York. But I used up everything I had last week. You deal with New York.' And she did."

Kitty's relationship to her own staff was close. Her immediate staff came to serve as a surrogate family, although they were employees. "When you're together almost twenty-four hours a day I think one of the musts, whether it's the candidate or the spouse of the candidate or anybody else, unless you have the kind of relationship I had with Paul [Costello] or that Michael had with some of his staff people, it doesn't work. It just doesn't work," Kitty said when it was over.

Paul Costello, the first male to take a press secretary's job for a presidential candidate's wife, made Kitty feel "safe," she said. When she was worried or scared, he told her she could do it. When she wanted to tell a reporter off, he'd quiet her down. He helped her formulate answers to uncomfortable questions. "Paul was the one, and I'm not sure I would have thought of this, when Lesley Stahl asked me about Nancy Reagan and her clothing, I said I felt that she should be remembered for her positive things, her drug work."

He "made an incredible difference in my life," she said afterward. "I had great confidence in his understanding of me as a person and how far I could be pushed. He knew when to criticize, and he knew when to compliment. . . . I'm not going to diminish some of the qualities that I have, because I feel good about some of those qualities, but you can be terrific on one level and not have a person who understands how to market [you] and how to pull all those things together and pull the strings that make that happen. He just knew technically what to do. He knew emotionally. And we had fun."

Back in Boston Kitty's operation suffered from some of the same internal rivalries that plagued the rest of the Dukakis campaign, where the "Boston clique," as they were called in-house, cut others out. Predictably, tensions surfaced between her staff and her husband's. Initially, her schedule was not well thought out. But she was more carefully deployed after new staff came on board following the Democratic Convention. Still, her staff found themselves scurrying after the "white boys" to get the latest developments and statements. After the election some staff felt they weren't "taken seriously" by the governor's staff. They felt Kitty was undervalued as an asset to the campaign. His staff didn't really figure out how to effectively use her until the final days of the campaign when she began introducing her husband at emotionally charged rallies. It was at the instigation of her staffers, for example, that Kitty appeared with Lesley Stahl on *Face the Nation* three weeks before the election.

"I think that happens all the time in campaigns, especially among spouses," said Costello, who harbored his own dreams of a top White House job. "It comes down oftentimes to sexism. The campaign doesn't realize how important an asset she is. Most times they pay attention to the spouse [only] when the spouse is raising hell, as they call it. Then the campaign sort of goes, 'Oh, God. We gotta do something. There's the wife problem,' or something like that. But in presidential campaigns, the wife is an integral part," he continued. "She should be viewed as an integral part. And I don't think that, oftentimes, is taken into consideration."

Her friend Anne Harney was more matter-of-fact on the sub-ject: "They built her up, but you know, after all is said and done, she's still only the wife."

At times Kitty seemed to resist the traditional role. Sometimes campaign staff had to urge Kitty to join her husband on the stump. "Kitty herself felt she should travel alone and I had to convince her at one point that she needed to travel with him," Heather Campion recalled. "Part of the reason was that while Kitty was getting good press alone, Barbara Bush was traveling with her husband. I was afraid that the world was going to see George and Barbara Bush and ask, 'Where's Kitty?' The world had come to know the Dukakises as such a close couple that I thought, if we don't arrange for that to happen a little bit more than it was—it was not happening at all in August and the begin-ning of September. . . . I would have liked to see her with him more."

Campion was not alone in that view, for in the end what matters most in an election is what most voters see on TV in their living rooms every night, not what happens out on the stump. The nightly news ranked higher than Kitty's own effectiveness. "I thought she was terrific on her own," Estrich said. "Having said that, I thought that the most important thing was how the gover-nor looked on TV every night and that he looked better, seemed better, seemed happier, his face looked better, warmer, when she was with him. So that it was important to have her with him as much as she was comfortable doing and he was comfortable doing and was happy."

More, one surmised, than Estrich was able to make happen.

* * *

Kitty did play the role of traditional wife one Monday morning in September when she awaited a visit at her home from Barbara Walters, *20/20*'s doyenne of electronic touch-and-feel journalism. Walters arrived early on September 19 via stretch limo, to walk the Brookline streets where she too had grown up and gone to school, and to oversee her staff as they fashioned a TV studio out of the Dukakis family's living room. Wearing an orange couturier suit with bright gold buttons, and the season's required long gold chain necklace, Walters scouted around the small house and took in its ambience before Kitty came downstairs. When one of Walters's assistants carried a huge bouquet of fresh flowers from the prop truck through the front door, she nixed the display, snapping, "Take them out. There are no flowers. The house isn't decorated. Don't bring them in."

She was right. Kitty's abode, a modest Victorian duplex, wasn't decorated. It was trashed by the ABC technical crew. Dropcloths hung over the living room's tall bay windows to allow cameramen to shield and adjust the light. Video consoles were lined up in the dining room, where Costello and a technician reviewed various angles and shots. Costello eventually overruled Walters's decorating technique, placing a more modest floral arrangement within camera range, and set up the backdrop where Kitty would sit, arranging framed family photographs on the mantelpiece.

While aides scurried around, Kitty, wearing a denim jumpsuit and moccasins, came downstairs for a preliminary talk with Walters. The two celebrities sat down across from one another in living-room chairs for some preinterview, get-acquainted chat and a makeup session. As they talked, their respective makeup artists feather-dusted their faces under the television light. Thick brushes swooped this way and that across foreheads and cheeks. Hairspray gagged the air. The two women chatted on as if nothing unusual was happening and they were alone together in the room.

In the 1988 race marital and familial imagery regularly upstaged so-called real issues. Portraits of both candidates' marriages became a subtle part of the political panorama and a staple of the national press. By and large Bush profiles focused on the three generations of their family. Dukakis stories showcased Kitty and Mike as a loving, though unlikely couple, a study in contrasts. She was the fire to his ice. Or so it went in the press.

"The way Michael Dukakis shares his life with Kitty Dukakis illuminates a good deal of how he shares power, deals with challenge, and what makes the man run," psycho-journalist Gail Sheehy wrote in a *Vanity Fair* article titled "Fire and Ice." But what Sheehy failed to consider was that when fire meets ice, something—or someone—must melt or smolder. More often than not, it seemed that someone was Kitty.

Another writer, Susan Buchsbaum, in a post-election analysis of

Kitty for *New England* magazine, wrote of the two: "Kitty and Michael have been caught up in a co-dependent relationship in which each partner has participated in the other's deceit. She asserts a false sense of well-being, and he doesn't challenge it."

Whatever the actual dynamics between the two, Kitty said she loved Mike: a candidate seen by the public as a not very likable guy in a year when likability, Ronald Reagan style, seemed to be a requirement for residing at 1600 Pennsylvania Avenue.

People who had worked with the governor complained that he expected them to live up to the same standards he held up for himself. On television that came across as smugness and superiority. "In character and demeanor, Dukakis is not a person who creates warm, friendly feelings among those seeing him for the first time," *The Washington Post*'s T. R. Reid wrote from the trail in early October. "The Democratic nominee is a serious, dogged worker who maintains high standards of personal discipline for himself." Indeed, the candidate was distant. Remote. In interviews on TV he talked about himself in the third person, as though describing someone other than himself. He could have been describing a different candidate.

One of Kitty's jobs was to try to fix all that. She insisted over and over again to print and broadcast journalists that her husband was not the cold fish he appeared to be. "I wouldn't have married him if he had any of those negative qualities," she repeated. But saying someone is likable at home, in a marriage, is very different from his *being* likable to an electorate. Just as conveying a sense of character is different from depending on character witnesses—like a wife—to win votes.

No matter how much Kitty protested and talked about Mike's warmth, her husband remained the little machine from Boston, as some of the hometown folks termed him.

But Kitty tried her best, especially on that warm September morning with Barbara Walters. After hours of chitchat in Brookline, Walters boiled her network interview down to the requisite ten minutes and *20/20* broadcast the piece on September 23, two days before the first presidential debate. "Do you know this woman?" a voice announced over snapshots of Kitty from the campaign trail. "She could be our next first lady. . . . By learning more about her, we might learn more about the candidate. For many people the first chance to judge Michael Dukakis will be when he debates George Bush this Sunday night. But there are other ways to judge the candidates, like looking at the company they keep, their running mates, or their roommates." The voice explained to viewers, who might have wondered, why they should pay attention to what Kitty Dukakis had to say.

For the next ten minutes, Kitty had *plenty* to say. On screen, she was compelling. Walters did her best, and touched on Kitty's reputation for outspokenness and volatility. The prospect that she might be the first Jewish first lady. Walters asked Kitty about her problem with drugs. Hitting a homer on that topic, asking the question on America's mind. How could it be *possible*, if she and Mike were as close as they said and seemed to be, that her husband didn't know she was popping pills all those years? Walters wanted to know. "And when you finally went to your husband and said, what? For nineteen years you haven't known me, or. . . ?"

"It was very hard to admit that I had to use a substance in order to function. That I couldn't be myself," Kitty replied softly.

"Has he ever wondered if maybe you're on them now?" Walters came back. "Since he didn't know then?"

"No," Kitty said simply.

Walters got Kitty to admit she couldn't get up in the morning without popping a pill. "Did people like you as first lady [of Massachusetts]?" Walters asked.

"I'm not sure. I didn't like myself. I think that was the telling thing. I wasn't happy with myself." And later—"I had a different personality in terms of volatility and I like myself better today."

"Why do you think now you did it? After your husband found out once, why did you continue? Did you feel like you were a burden to him?" Walters kept on.

It was the stuff of human drama, as Kitty's postelection behavior would sadly bear out. Splaying her guts on national TV, Kitty was riveting. Paradoxically, that was *just* the problem with the Walters interview. What voter cared about Mike Dukakis's policy on the deficit when he or she watched this woman, his wife, talk about speeding for twenty-six years in secret? Kitty had so many stories of her own to tell, and tell them she did, that she detracted attention from the story of the private Mike Dukakis. She upstaged him. He was only tangentially involved, yet he was the one running for president and that was why Kitty was on TV in the first place.

The whole episode raised the question: Was this any way to judge a candidate? Well, yes. But then again, no.

What did voters learn in this interview that might have helped carry Mike Dukakis from Beacon Hill to the Oval Office? That Kitty was feisty? Jewish? A former amphetamine addict? That she and her husband liked holding hands? How did learning about a woman's private struggle with diet pills help voters decide whom to vote for?

In a politically manipulated environment where the electorate often struggles to know as much as it can about its candidates but often votes blindly, the voters turned to, and some in the media fostered, this false cult of personality. Most voters favor anything that gives them a clue to what makes a presidential nominee tick. Subtle evidence, like a candidate's relationship to his wife and family, can be an indication on some level of who this fellow actually is. Nancy Reagan's domineering behavior certainly pointed to Ronald Reagan's essential passivity, even though every word that came out of their mouths during their campaigns and in the White House indicated otherwise.

Oddly enough, as the theater of Kitty and Mike took to the airwaves, on one level it did work. Watching the Walters interview, voters saw breaks in this marriage where there shouldn't have been breaks. Kitty raised more questions than she answered. Did the Dukakises have the discipline of the leadership caste? Did voters want to put Mike Dukakis in the Oval Office if his family life was so damaged? Was the public entitled to know about Kitty Dukakis's rocky medical history? Did her volatility account for Mike's coolness and control? Did his knowledge of his wife's problems and inability to handle White House pressure explain what many viewed as his reluctance to jump full force into the campaign?

Again, was this any way to judge a candidate?

The question was as confusing to family members as it was to voters. How were they to behave, knowing that the electorate would judge their candidate by judging them? "I think there is a lot of insecurity that comes with being a candidate's wife," Andrea Dukakis said. "Because you are there and you are accepted, but the candidate is the one that is being voted in. You are on that wave. There is the whole issue of whether that is a valid way of judging the candidate. I don't know. Does it say anything? Even if it does, do we have a right to know? Is there another example in our lives of knowing about someone's character? Like when we go to a businessman, do we want to know about this? Not really. That is allowed to stay separate. So suddenly in politics, why does that make you different?''

The interview didn't say what it could have. As Walters and Hugh Downs, a former game-show host turned TV newsman, engaged in their closing *20/20* banter, Hugh turned to Barbara and mused: "Barbara, watching your interview here makes me realize people appear to be more interested now in the wives of these candidates than they were a while back. Is this because they feel, or they're more alert to, the possible influence of these women on their men?"

Barbara replied, "Oh, I think so. I think even the word *concerned* we might substitute for *interested*. Since Nancy Reagan and Rosalynn Carter, we realize their husbands come home and talk to their wives. They do have some influence. And certainly Michael Dukakis relies a great deal on his wife. Critics say she's more liberal than he is, or she'll want an office right next to him. She says, that's nonsense. But it reflects the fact that we know they do come home . . . although Michael Dukakis and George Bush say, 'We make the final decision.'"

Asking about Kitty's influence on Mike acknowledged that Kitty wasn't just a window through which voters could hope to get a glimpse of the true Mike. Indeed, that she couldn't be. It recognized that she had opinions of her own, and her husband took them into account. The question of a spouse's influence and how accountable she would be for that influence was actually as much an exploration of what the candidate was like as a recognition that the spouse was an independent person in the marriage. The issue was routinely touched upon in the 1988 race, though, as the Barbara Walters interview with Kitty Dukakis showed, it wasn't explored adequately.

CHAPTER EIGHT
Private Life on Public Display

I've heard a lot of this gossip over the years, and
I've asked: "Why aren't you covering this? Why
aren't you publishing this?" As far as I'm concerned, it's a perfectly legitimate topic. The press
didn't invent the practice of candidates using their
families as selling points. Politicians who use their
families to create a public image have no [grounds
for] complaint when the press demonstrates that
image is false.

—BILL GREIDER
Rolling Stone Washington columnist

On Wednesday, October 19, the Dow Jones Industrial Average
dropped 43 points as a rumor shortcircuited Wall Street: *The
Washington Post* was planning to publish a story alleging a George
Bush extramarital affair. The market recovered after the editors at
the *Post* went out of their way to say no such story was pending.
But the damage was done. That evening Dan Rather put the story
on the national map by tying the market drop to a rumor concerning "Bush's personal life," as he worded it.

On the following day, Dukakis's deputy national field director,
twenty-eight-year-old Donna Brazile, told reporters on the press-
bus in New Haven, and again en route to New York City, "I
wasn't on the stock market yesterday but I understood they got a
little concerned that George was going to the White House with
somebody other than Barbara. I think George Bush owes it to the
American people to fess up. . . ." Reporters asked for clarifica-
tion. Were Brazile's remarks on or off the record? On the record,
it seemed. Brazile repeated herself in three separate sets of interviews. Were her remarks a real effort by the Dukakis camp to get a

"George-Bush-has-a-mistress-story" out? Or were they the remarks of a burned-out campaign worker? A brilliant but young black woman whose disillusionment with "white boy" politics, as she called it, was no secret. At the time, it wasn't clear.

For the Bush campaign, the Wall Street drop and Brazile's provocative remarks, which kept the story alive another day, couldn't have come at a worse time. The election was only nineteen days away. Polls showed the race beginning to tighten. Both campaigns—and their ever-present media entourages—were bounding toward New York City for the Al Smith dinner, a fund-raiser for the Catholic archdiocese where candidates traditionally throw barbed humor at one another.

For candidate Bush, the A-question had surfaced yet again. Bush was in the same boat as any other presidential contender in the post-*Monkey Business* atmosphere of the 1988 campaign. While his opponents and their spouses volleyed responses to the adultery question, and Jackie Jackson got the press off her husband's back, the Bush camp dodged the persistent rumors of their candidate's marital infidelity, which peaked the day after the Dow Jones drop. Up until then Bush had successfully avoided answering the question. At the time of the Iowa caucuses he came the closest he ever would to addressing the subject during a debate preparation, when aides thought the question might come up and that he should be ready. Staffers arranged for Illinois Congresswoman Lynn Martin, Bush's national co-chair, to act as a moderator and ask: "Yes or no—have you ever committed adultery?" Bush snapped back: "None of your damn business!" A reply that reportedly made "some aides cringe and others cheer," in the words of *U.S. News & World Report*.

Later in the race, in June 1987, campaign manager Lee Atwater refuted the rumors at an off-the-record lunch with two *Newsweek* staffers. However, when it appeared that *Newsweek* and other news outlets would continue to try to substantiate the rumor, Atwater huddled with George Bush, Jr., who reported that he had asked Bush about the rumors "point-blank" and, "The answer to the Big A question is N.O." *Newsweek* ran the remark in its June 27, 1987, edition in "Periscope," its gossip column. For the next fifteen months, things stayed quiet.

Then, on October 14, the *L.A. Weekly*, an alternative newspaper, came out with an entire issue devoted to what it called "The

Dark Side of George Bush." Among the articles was one titled "The Mistress Question." Thousands of copies of the free paper surfaced and were distributed the day of the second presidential debate on the UCLA campus, where it took place. In England, the Fleet Street tabloids went wild. Although there was a lot of off-the-record gossip, the major American news outlets continued to view the story as unsubstantiated rumor.

On Thursday, October 20, the day after the Dow Jones drop, Barbara Bush joined several women editors and writers in the New York press for a previously scheduled lunch at the tony Four Seasons restaurant. Earlier in the summer, *Woman's Day* magazine brought the same group together to hear Kitty Dukakis, giving the newswomen a chance to meet the two women who wanted to be the next first lady.

"A barracuda-like group," one that "would critique a funeral" is how one participant described her sister lunch mates. It was a well-heeled, well-shoulder-padded group who gathered for a luncheon of chicken with porcini mushrooms, snap peas, and apricot torte. A crowd anxious to check out Barbara Bush and her feelings about the story sweeping Wall Street. In the whole campaign one couldn't have found a better example of how Mrs. Bush could shrewdly keep control over what was for her perhaps the most embarrassing, or painful slur of the entire 1988 campaign. Unlike Kitty Dukakis, who often seemed to deal with uncomfortable questions emotionally, Mrs. Bush expertly staved off the questions in the first place.

Knowing what she might be up against, a group of sophisticated New York City news sharks, Bar had reviewed the advance guest list, and carefully and strategically worked the room when she arrived. Bar came on like gangbusters, whereas Kitty, who had much more in common with these women, had swept in with her aides and hurriedly taken her seat. At the lunch for Kitty one editor had poked fun at Bar for "needlepointing the American flag on her husband's underwear." But today, with the next likely first lady on hand, she and others who had smiled at that joke now fixed polished smiles at Barbara Bush. Like most everyone else, she was dressed chicly, in a chalk-striped navy suit.

After the meal, the program called for Mrs. Bush to give a few remarks and take questions. When her moment came Bar stood and faced the writers and editors, many of whom were not especially enamored of her politics or her life-style. It was a match, a test, of sorts. Mrs. Bush proceeded expertly. First, she stalled for time. Then she disarmed the women with her self-deprecating humor, subtly dissuading them from asking the question foremost in their minds. When she launched into the body of her remarks, she spoke in a voice that reminded every woman in the room of her own mother's—and not when Mom sang lullabyes. "I'm sort of tired today and slightly weepy, so be careful," she instructed one luncheon guest so the whole room could hear. Her meaning was clear. The barracudas became goldfish. Questions and answers lobbed back and forth, like a gentle game of badminton. Feminists and Mom, at truce over tea.

While stalling, "so we won't have too many questions," Bar won the women's ears by immediately telling them that she was sympathetic to the writers in the crowd. She explained how she got roped into writing a weekly campaign diary for *USA Today*. "I'm going to be absolutely frank with you," she said, as if confiding a secret, though it was a story she had told time and again beyond the sophisticated surroundings of the Four Seasons.

"*USA Today* called my office and said, 'Kitty Dukakis has said she would write an article for *USA Today* for the convention. Would you?'" Bar said she would if Kitty did.

"Then they called me, and said, 'Do you believe Mrs. Dukakis says she'll write an article for *USA Today* once a week from the convention on?'

"And I said, 'Well, I think I'm being had now,' but I agreed to write a column as well. Then, about two or three days ago they called me and said, 'We wonder, would you mind going one week past the election? Mrs. Dukakis said she would.'

"I said, 'Well, Mrs. Bush said she won't.'"

The group laughed sympathetically. "And I won't, because if we win, which I think we're going to do, I hope George will take me off for a little vacation. If we lose, I sure as heck am not interested in writing a column for anybody."

Mom: 1. Feminists: 0.

Then, in her best mother-knows-best voice, the one that meant there was *no* room to move, she cut off serious discussion of her husband's position on women's issues before they could begin.

"Let me just say that I have made it a practice for forty-three years to tell my husband when I agree or disagree with him, and I don't tell anyone else when I agree or disagree with him. I think you know how George stands on abortion, ERA, gun control, and if you want to talk about it, that's fine. I'll listen. But I'm not going to change my rule after forty-three years at lunch today, win or lose the election for it."

Mom: 2. Feminists: 0.

When questions finally did begin, no one swatted very hard. With gentle viciousness, someone asked if Mrs. Bush had "heard about fashion" or read fashion magazines. "I read them all," Bar assured them, laughing. She reassured them if she was no Rosalynn Carter, hauling a sewing machine into the White House, neither was she a Nancy Reagan, boosting a bevy of expensive designers. Though "I will confess to you that if I were a size two or a four, I rather suspect the designers would want to give me clothes," she said, delivering a backhanded compliment. She admitted that just that morning she had had clothes fitted, things ordered months ago, and explained, "I just never got around for fittings, which shows how really fashionable I am." Then, "I think Nancy Reagan has done a wonderful job for American designers, honestly, and as I say, if I were a size two, they'd give them to me too.

"But I pay for mine," she snipped, delivering a jab—ever so slight.

Talk turned to her role in the campaign and motherhood. "I'm unhappy when I'm in Washington, when I'm not out working because I get so nervous. I'm better when I'm outside working for George," she confided.

Then she told a story about two of her sons, Marvin and George, "who were supposed to be hardhearted Hannahs during the last debate." Afterward, the vice-president called his eldest son to review his performance, only to discover that boy George and Marvin had gone to the movies. "They couldn't stand the heat and they hadn't heard the debate. Marvin told me George got him up twelve times to run out and call a friend and see how [their father] was doing." The women cracked up. Bar earned herself another point.

Given the news from Wall Street and the group before her, Bar didn't ignore the subject of her marriage, just skirted around it, angling it in its most positive light. Recalling her senior prom, Bar confided, "I don't think I ever shared this, but that was the first time I was ever kissed. My children almost throw up: 'You mean you married the first man who ever kissed you?'" This was the first time many had heard the story of Bar's first kiss, now a staple of American folklore. The room filled with laughter.

Then she went on to share a bit more family history. She was brought up by parents who told her—as George's told him—not to talk about yourself all the time. It was good advice, she confided, for staying married for forty-three years. "If you think about the other fella, and talk about the other fella, and care about the other fella, it all sort of seemed to come back.

"But this fall, I have felt like I've been on the couch," she confessed. The vision of Mom at the therapist's amused this therapy-ridden set and got them howling again. "I've learned more about my mother this year than I thought I knew." The group laughed harder. "I don't like to do *that* talking."

Then her tone shifted from all-business to soft and confidential—"You know, people say to me now, 'What's the secret of a happy marriage?'" This scene unfolded in love-torn Manhattan. Heartbreak hell. In the mind's eye the barracudas returned to their girlhoods, sitting on the edge of the bathtub listening to Mom. They were all ears.

Bar confided: "It's just come to me a little late maybe. But that really is the secret of a happy marriage. Just thinking about George. What makes him happy. What makes him comfortable. He does the same for me. And he wouldn't, if I didn't do that for him."

The women willingly suspended their disbelief. Even though from the outside Bar's marriage seemed to be an institution, much like a bank, something has kept her and Poppy together all these years. Maybe it's their humor, as their friends and family said. Maybe it's all those kids. The money? Power? Maybe it's that they're seldom alone. But who doesn't want a happy ending? No one at lunch that day challenged her. Like Lee Hart standing by Gary's side, Bar got her man over the infidelity hump. With her around, who could ask the A-question? No one did.

When it was over, Bar had won the set hands down, according to the reviews. "Competent. Poised. Charming. And deft at being able to dodge a question," said one luncheon guest.

Why didn't she bring up the sensitive topic? *Ladies' Home Journal* editor Myrna Blyth replied, "I'm an editor of a monthly magazine. I think everyone behaved in a way that's most useful to their journalistic needs," dodging that one almost as smoothly as Bar did.

New York magazine editor Bernice Kanner said she didn't ask the hard question that she wanted to: "to define 'family values.' She would have defined it and the innuendo was cruel. All the press who knew about this didn't talk about the [alleged] affair. I don't want to hurt this woman. She's a battle-scarred veteran," said Kanner, sounding more like a sister than a shark. On Bar's style: "If it's calculated, then it's a calculation that seems so genuine. We weren't eating out of her hands but she won us over."

Sondra Haley, Mrs. Bush's willowy twenty-seven-year-old press secretary, wasn't quite as lucky as her boss. Over lunch she was asked about the Wall Street drop. The question didn't merit an answer, she replied politely but firmly.

Hers was more of a response than George Bush's press secretary Sheila Tate would give later that evening at the Waldorf-Astoria. Before and after the Al Smith dinner she was badgered by reporters who wanted her comment on the Dukakis aide's remarks and "resignation."

At the dinner that night Dukakis personally apologized to Bush for his aide's remarks, and Paul Brountas, Dukakis's campaign chairman, dressed in a tuxedo, stepped before television cameras and said that Dukakis "expressed his regrets." Regrets about what? The rumor created a dilemma for the media. How to explain what happened without repeating Brazile's remark—"The American people have every right to know if Barbara Bush will share that bed with him in the White House."

In the filing center in the Astor Salon that evening, reporters covering both campaigns debated how to cover the day's events. Some, like ABC's Sam Donaldson, groused, "Dukakis has been doing most of the complaining about the tone of this campaign, but Brazile's remarks make it harder for him to claim the high moral ground."

Despite Tate's persistent "No comment," the story made news in the New York papers the next morning. KEY DUKAKIS AIDE QUITS OVER RUMOR—"Called on Bush to 'fess up' to reports he had love affair" (*Newsday*) DUKE AIDE QUITS—"Says she regrets telling Bush to 'fess up' to sex rumors" (New York *Daily News*).

Charles Lewis, Washington bureau chief for the Associated Press, told Eleanor Randolph, *Washington Post* media writer, that he felt that "the Dukakis campaign aide . . . was clearly speaking in her role with the campaign. This was not a casual conversation on the bus. . . ."

The Dukakis campaign denied the story was planted. Susan Estrich said after the campaign that the Dukakis campaign did not want to appear to be trafficking in rumors. "What was working for us best at that time was that we had finally been able to make George Bush begin to pay the price of what we called his negative lies campaign," Estrich said. "The last thing we needed was a backlash of sympathy for George Bush—him being the target of the same kind of rumors—so that everyone would say they couldn't stand the election."

Randolph reported: "When AP was satisfied the rumor was in context and they had the Dukakis staff denying that Brazile spoke for the candidate, the wire service distributed one of the most detailed stories about the rumor Thursday." The AP story for Friday-morning papers included the initials of the Bush aide named by the *L.A. Weekly* and alluded to by Brazile. It also included a comment from Bush press secretary Sheila Tate that the rumor was "warmed over garbage," Randolph wrote.

The *L.A. Times* ran the AP story, too. Editor William Thomas told Randolph, "This is one where nobody's ever pinned anything down. It's one of these when you are forced to take notice of something you would really rather not take notice of at all."

In the post-Hart campaign atmosphere reporters simply weren't sure where to draw the line. Some argued that despite how it may have seemed to the public, new rules were in operation and those rules were tougher, making it harder for reporters to publish sex scandals. *The New Republic*'s Michael Kinsley outlined the new rules as he saw them: "Rule 1. The hanky-panky must be ongoing. If it has ended, even recently, it falls off the edge of 'relevance.' Rule 2. It must relate to some previously raised issues regarding the pol in question. Hart was already alleged to be a womanizer: this was considered a flaw in his character; the Monkey Business illuminated that flaw. . . . Rule 3. The philandering politician must be caught virtually in the act. . . . *The*

Miami Herald saw Hart and friend enter his town house later in the evening and leave it the next day. . . . Rule 4. . . . The victim must invite the fatal scrutiny. Gary Hart told *The New York Times*, 'Follow me around, I don't care. . . .'"

In Kinsley's view, the development was an unfortunate one. He opined: "Despite the risk of excess, more journalistic enterprise in pursuing monkey business would be a healthy development for two reasons. First, because politicians put their 'private lives' legitimately at issue when they bring their families into the campaign, a virtually universal practice that was especially egregious this year. In doing so, they are making a statement about themselves that ought to be exposed if false. George Bush didn't say, 'Follow me around,' but he did say, reacting to a 'Where was Teddy [Kennedy]' banner at a rally, 'I was at home with Barbara.' Michael Dukakis, desperate for warmth, had his wife as much as telling reporters he was good in bed.

"Second, because it's up to the voters, not journalists, to decide what's relevant. Denying voters this information, for fear they will give it more weight than it deserves, is patronizing."

By Kinsley's approximation, the press didn't go far enough on the Bush rumors. Certainly no candidate doled out his family for more public consumption than he. But facing deadlines that evening in New York, few reporters were quite that cerebral, and continued to debate just how far to go in policing a candidate's private life and character.

★ ★ ★

During the time they were plagued by rumors of marital infidelity, the Bush camp maintained their no-comment policy. "The media has a pretty universal rule that holds pretty well," Tate said after the election. "They will not report the substance of a rumor unless it's been confirmed or unless you say something about it. We simply refused to comment. All during that [time] we said, 'No comment.' Kept it at that. But it was right there getting pushed up all the time for about a month."

Early on in the race aides had met with Bush when the rumor first surfaced to figure out how to respond and how to handle Mrs. Bush's sensitive feelings on the subject. Months after the election, Craig Fuller, Bush's chief of staff, replayed a scene for *Washington Post* reporter Donnie Radcliffe. Aides were discussing how to handle the rumors, talking with Bush on the porch of the vice-president's house. Suddenly, Barbara arrived and asked why everyone appeared so worried. When told, she responded, "That's ridiculous, the answer's no. Forget about it," Fuller reported. Bar added, "What are you even talking about it for? Why are you guys even here?"

But the campaign consciously dealt with the rumor, meeting it head on with George junior's denial in *Newsweek*. "It was a conscious decision for this reason," Lee Atwater told the group of reporters and operatives who gathered at Harvard early in December 1988 to discuss the campaign. "Tuesday of the week prior to that I received in one day some phone calls from the press about this thing. It was hysteria. I've never seen anything like it. The second day, the rumor hit the Hill, and from twelve to five o'clock we literally got probably forty or fifty calls from the Hill. The third day, it started melting down into the states, and we were getting calls in from the states. At that point what I figured would happen, after observing the Gary Hart episode, is that a favorite game would be played. It's the old game we saw a hundred times; *Time* calling up and saying, 'Well, *Newsweek* is going with it. We heard *Newsweek* is going with it,' or '*The Washington Post* is going with this. CBS is going with this thing.' Everybody was manipulating the media.

"It became clear to me that no responsible organization was going to go with it. But it was a lead-pipe cinch that some midlevel or off-the-wall paper was going to go with it by the next week.

"Just think about this, fellow campaign managers," Atwater told the group. "You have had over five hundred calls from virtually every important person in the media. You know it's going to get out. So you're dealing with this situation. Does it get out with some mid-level newspaper and then everybody says, 'Oh, well, we hate to do this. We didn't want to touch this story. But now it's out, and so we've got to put it on the front page'? You're dealing then in a totally rearguard defensive posture because what you have got to do is explain. So when you see a Mack truck coming down the road at you, you ought to try to deal with it on your own terms."

Atwater continued: "What crossed my mind was that we needed to get it out on our own terms and in midair to shift the nature of the story from the rumor to who was the dirty trickster putting out the rumor.

"By the way, when the story came out [in *Newsweek*'s "Periscope" section on June 27, 1987], within twenty-four hours it was flat dead. Why? Because the whole story shifted to whoever was putting this out was a dirty trickster and this was vile, et cetera, and no one would put it out."

Initially, Mrs. Bush and some of her children tried to deal with the rumors through humor. "How can George Bush have an affair?" she quipped to one reporter. "He can't stay up past ten o'clock." Bush's son Neil said he thought the Republicans had floated the rumors to add a little muscle to his father's "wimp" image.

But as the stories persisted, Bar became testier, more defensive, her words sharper. "Malicious, vicious, ugly untruths. I don't want to talk about it because it isn't true," she'd say. "It's insulting to me."

When asked months later about this turn of events, Bush's eldest son, back in Texas, nearly shouted into the phone. "Garbage!" he cried loudly, refusing to talk about it further.

Despite the widespread view among friends and family that Mrs. Bush keeps a "stiff upper lip," one aide said Bar was very disturbed by the rumors. The aide recalled Mrs. Bush "getting very quiet," especially when she'd spot signs in crowds alluding to the rumors. "The response I saw from her was that she was very troubled by it, and her staff said she had a few sleepless nights."

"I wouldn't say she's got thick skin in any way," her sister-in-law, Nancy Ellis, added. "I think they just have to live with it. Like a rainy day."

Smart and tough, Bar also capably defended herself and her husband against this and other uncomfortable questions. Her friend Andy Stewart aptly described Bar's style, the essence of which was on display at the New York luncheon. "She could shut things off in a firm way, the things she didn't want to discuss or felt were too unseemly, or felt were the joker's business."

Bar's ability to be blunt in the face of "unseemly" questions became even more apparent five days after the lunch, when ques-

tions continued to pop up during a two-day swing through southern Illinois, a key battleground state. During a visit to the Illinois
School for the Deaf in Decatur, Mrs. Bush held a general roundtable discussion with local media. In the middle of the questioning
one reporter prodded: "Mrs. Bush, do you recall the Dukakis aide
that resigned last week after . . ."

"*No!* I don't recall her," Bar interrupted, with a forceful stare.

He kept going " . . . after allegedly telling rumors about your
husband's personal life . . ."

She interrupted him, cutting him short. "*No! I don't recall her.
I'm not going to dignify that!*" She replied loudly, insistently, her
stare turned to flint. This was the same answer she gave to *CBS
This Morning* host Kathleen Sullivan, who'd phrased her inquiry
more delicately, asking Mrs. Bush if she was worried about the
fact that the stock market "would actually fluctuate on any rumors
concerning your husband."

As she faced the Illinois reporters, in a split second Bar's flinty
stare became a glower beamed not just at the reporter asking the
question but all the others around the table. Swiftly, before her
mood permanently soured and she shut off, another reporter
changed the subject and got in a question about literacy in Illinois.

★   ★   ★

Unlike Kitty Dukakis, who traveled with a speechwriter and press
secretary with White House experience, Barbara Bush hit the road
with two young women: her personal aide, Casey Healey, and
Sondra Haley, her press secretary, who were twenty-six and
twenty-seven years old at the time. During the campaign Lee Atwater told the press, "There was no particular strategy about how
she was used because she is 'good either way'—with or without
her husband and amenable to either situation. She's got her own
following, her own group she can communicate with," Atwater
told *The Washington Post*. "As a campaigner, she's by far the most
sought-after surrogate we've got. Beloved in the South, loved in
Iowa. Every time I went there, they wanted more and more of
her."

Unlike the Dukakis campaign, Bush operatives felt their candidate's wife should not be out front and talk on issues. "It's really a
mistake," Sheila Tate said before the election. "Once you start
that, you've got to deal with every issue and she's not the elected

official. She's not running for office herself. Any first lady who starts moving on the policy side, people don't like her. They really don't. There's a very thin line a first lady or a first lady-candidate walks."

She added: "There's nobody better, though, than the wife of the spouse to talk about what the person who is running is like."

Mrs. Bush highlighted her interest in literacy, visiting schools, Head Start programs, and day-care centers. She attended fund-raisers and greeted GOP workers at Republican headquarters. Any event was OK with her except youth rallies and some parades. "I feel slightly silly sitting on the back of a convertible as the grand marshal of a parade—I'm waving like I think I'm Miss America and I can see people saying, 'What *is* she doing?'" she said.

In the chaos of the campaign, where schedules change on a daily basis, Tate said, "We heard about and got her schedule after the fact because we were so tied up with *his* schedule. We paid attention to whether or not the events that George Bush was doing were enhanced by her being with us. Often she was more valuable somewhere else, instead of standing off in a corner of a stage. And I think she felt that. She kept saying that she wanted to do things . . . she really wanted to work."

On a number of occasions during the campaign Tate said, Mrs. Bush felt underused.

There was also a "tendency by the staff and the press to under-estimate her," Representative Lynn Martin told *The Washington Post*. "Barbara Bush is pretty tough and wanted Bush to be made aware of what he's up against."

There were times on the road when Mrs. Bush's staff felt they really were part of "the other campaign," as some reporters referred to the spouses' efforts. "I think she sometimes feels like she'd like to keep doing more when she's with him. That's the sense I get," Tate said. "Just things she's said to her staff. You know, 'Can I do some interviews? Is there something else I can do [besides just stand there]?' When we go to a city and she needs to be there, if she can do the local interviews, that's wonderful. It really helps a lot. She feels like she's accomplishing things. Instead of just sitting in a hotel room."

As with Kitty Dukakis, there were times when Mrs. Bush's staffers had trouble getting information they needed to keep abreast of the ever-changing campaign, especially when they were campaigning separately from the vice-president. Sondra Haley periodically expressed frustration at George's staff, who weren't attentive to the needs of Mrs. Bush's campaign. Riding in a van through upstate Pennsylvania at the end of September, Haley spoke in exasperated tones of difficulties in getting updates on issue papers or background, "the daily stuff that gets circulated.

"Some people, you tell them once, 'Here we are and we need it,' and we get it every day," she said. "You can't be shy. If you take a backseat you're not going to get it every day." Haley said she'd have to remind people to include her in meetings. "I don't think they're trying to be exclusive. It just doesn't come to their mind. They never had a Mrs. Bush press secretary. You have to just get it into their minds. . . . I'm just a little terrier nipping at everybody's heels," she laughed.

Operatives in both campaigns felt the impact for the nominees' wives lay principally in secondary media markets, rather than major media markets like New York or Los Angeles, where they had to compete for press attention. By the general election, both spouses were carefully targeted.

Because Kitty Dukakis spoke on issues and earned lots of press attention, and because of leaks from aides that Barbara Bush's appearance was not a "plus" to the campaign, at times it appeared that the campaign was deliberately giving Mrs. Bush a low profile. Haley explained that away. "Every day you hear, 'Mrs. Bush should get out and do more. She's so great, why doesn't she do more? I don't know anything about her.' That's just the way it is in her role. She gets the local coverage or attention. We go in and sure you're going to read about our visit in the Pittsburg papers, but you're not going to know in Washington where she was. We don't have the three [press] buses traveling that are going to shoot all across CNN and the national networks."

Back in Washington, Mrs. Bush's chief of staff, Susan Porter Rose, worked with campaign operative Paul Manafort and others to coordinate her schedule, plotting her steps according to daily tracking polls and using her to counter appearances by surrogates in the Dukakis camp.

A former admissions officer at Mount Holyoke College, Rose became Mrs. Bush's White House chief of staff. A native of Cin-

cinnati, Rose grew up in Indiana where she earned an M.A. at
Indiana State. She came to Washington from Mount Holyoke in
1971. Before that she was an assistant dean at the George School, a
Pennsylvania prep academy. In 1980 Barbara hired Rose as her
chief of staff. Prim and proper, she favors tailored dresses and
pearls like her boss. In her late forties, she is married to a Washington lawyer, and has one young son.

Susan Porter Rose set the tone for Barbara Bush's team. In the
East Wing of the White House, as on the campaign trail, Rose
called the shots. She was the standard-bearer. One of that breed of
efficient, super-cautious aides-de-camp who fill the halls of official
Washington. A professional flack, her job was and is to protect
Barbara Bush from pesky reporters who ask troublesome questions
like how much of the taxpayers' money did Mrs. Bush spend on
entertaining while her husband was vice-president.

"The entertaining they have done has been private," Rose told
The Washington Post reporter who wanted to know shortly before
the Bushes took office. Reminded that $285,000 in public funds
were allotted for maintaining the house, $75,000 for entertaining,
Rose dismissed the question: "This is not where our time and attention is. . . . We are not going to go into this."

During the campaign Kitty's staff worked *with* their boss, becoming almost like family. Barbara Bush's staff appeared to have a
different relationship—working *for* her, though Rose said she and
her boss share "a bond." Kitty took advice on what to do from her
handlers; Bar resisted that, setting her own agenda and goals, Rose
and other staff said. Mrs. Dukakis was known informally to all as
"Kitty" during the campaign. But it was always "Mrs. Bush."
During the campaign, access to the vice-president's wife was carefully controlled, just as it was for the Republican candidate, and
ultimately the Democratic nominee.

Unlike Kitty Dukakis, who appeared to use every opportunity
that arose to garner media attention, Barbara Bush rarely gave interviews in cars (or limousines) or on planes, her staff said. As
with her husband, the vice-president, information, even that of
minor importance, was carefully controlled. This caused some of
the press corps to complain, as was evidenced on September 8
during one of Mrs. Bush's visits to a day-care center outside Philadelphia. The event was typical of many Barbara Bush attended
through the fall.

The unspoken goal of the event was for Mrs. Bush to publicize her husband's concern for day care, though her aides tried to de-politicize it, saying Mrs. Bush was there to learn more about education. As soon as she arrived Mrs. Bush posed for pictures with center officials, who politely announced, "We are glad the vice-president decided to embrace day care; we think with a bipartisan effort, we can make progress." Then Mrs. Bush was whooshed inside for a private briefing.

While she was briefed, local reporters, a couple of photographers, and a couple of camera crews were herded into a children's room, baby blue and decorated with cows and sheep, where they, too, were briefed. Sondra Haley instructed them on how this event would be orchestrated and what kind of images they could expect this photo op to yield.

"The children will sing a song for her. They will be on the floor," Haley explained. "Then, after that concludes, we'll put you all back in that corner over there. Mrs. Bush will go to this chair," she said, pointing to one of a group of plastic seats designed for two-year-olds, "and then there will be another little program. That way you can get another close shot of her. OK?"

The camera crews and photographers nodded agreeably.

"Is there going to be any chance to ask her questions?" asked a reporter from the *Philadelphia Inquirer*.

"No, not right now," Haley responded.

"So she'll be unavailable for questions?" he repeated slowly, wanting to make sure he heard her correctly.

"That's what we have right now, but you know that might change," Haley said in a tone indicating it was unlikely things would change.

With no opportunity to interview the vice-president's wife, print reporters began groping for a story. "There's no news here so I'm going to have to invent some," groused Gar Joseph, a *Philadelphia Daily News* reporter. He'd had the same problem the week before, he said, when he was assigned to cover George Bush crab fishing at the shore. "These tend to be strictly TV events. There is nothing of substance that ever happens," he complained. "If you report what they say, it's the same stuff over and over again. This stuff is really for TV. It's not for newspapers. So when you're writing for a newspaper it makes it a challenge."

But the day's event posed problems even for television reporters after they and the kids ran through a practice session with fourteen toddlers between the ages of eighteen months and two years. They sat in a semicircle on the floor, wearing red paper cutout hats with their names on them. "This group," one reporter commented dryly, "has a ways to go before they can vote."

"Who's coming to visit us? Did you forget?" Natalie Pearlman, a middle-aged redheaded day-care worker, urged her brood. But the kids were distracted, looking up at the cameras looking down at them. "What's her name?" Pearlman pushed her charges to perform. After several hints and memory jabs, one toddler came through. "Bush!"

It was part of the policy at this day-care center that parents had to sign release forms allowing their kids to be photographed. So that day only those children whose parents had agreed that they could be photographed were in the room. The center's policy said nothing, however, about the children participating in a political event and it became evident from a television reporter's probing that the parents might not be aware that their kids were being used as political props for the Republican campaign. Asked about this, Pearlman was taken aback. "This [event] doesn't necessarily express anyone's political views," she insisted.

Finally, the wife of the Republican nominee made her way into the pale-blue room and lowered her five-feet eight-inch frame into a two-foot-high chair at a little table filled with tots.

Pearlman sprang back into action. "Do you know who this is?" she asked the toddlers, who blinked distractedly into the blinding camera lights and paid her no mind. Mrs. Bush had been through this scene many times before. She reassured Pearlman that she knew the kids did this every time. It came with the turf. These events tended to follow a kind of script. There was a certain sameness to them all. Mrs. Bush would play her part. The kids would slowly fall into line. Camera crews sprang into action. Photographers got some snaps. The job got done.

Since this event took place at a Jewish day-care center and Rosh Hashanah, the Jewish New Year, was just two days away, the kids shared the tradition of eating apples and honey with Mrs. Bush. All except two-year-old Elyse Roller, that is. Elyse sat right next to Bar and would have none of it. Dwarfed by all the adults standing around her, and upset by the commotion, Elyse looked down at the dancing teddy bears on her T-shirt and pouted.

"I worry Elyse is a Democratic radical in the making," a TV reporter quipped. "And that someone will pull out this video and use it against her twenty years from now."

The photo op unfolded. It couldn't have been more tame, until suddenly Tia O'Brien, a reporter with the NBC affiliate in Philadelphia, got into a tiff with Mrs. Bush's press secretary. Haley was getting her feet wet on this trip, recently having been promoted from a staff scheduler. O'Brien was annoyed because she felt Haley was trying to dictate her cameraman's shots throughout this predictable, no-news, garden-variety photo op.

"She tried to pull the camera person away and stop her in a *very* uncontroversial setting," O'Brien complained afterward. "She kept trying to direct the shots. . . . I felt she had a scripted shot that she wanted us to follow. And I don't think that's her job."

The event didn't win Mrs. Bush kudos among print reporters, either, especially those who, when no discussion of the vice-president's day-care package was forthcoming, were left with little story to write. "I think the press covers these wives in the traditional sexist manner," said Gar Joseph. "Part of that, though, is because of the type of events the wives go to. Part of that is because they have nothing to say. And they're doing what their husband's staff has told them to do."

NBC correspondent Tom Pettit couldn't have agreed more with Gar Joseph after the day he spent tagging along with Mrs. Bush in southern Illinois on October 26. With the polls showing Bush's lead over Dukakis shrinking, both camps went after pivotal states like Illinois, where twenty-four electoral votes were at stake.

It was a typical trip, Haley announced, with events set up like the one in Philadelphia: a stop at a Head Start program. A "meet 'n' greet" with local GOP workers. A tour of the Illinois School for the Deaf. A visit to a Project READ program at a housing project. Lunches at two small restaurants.

With the polls narrowing and the race coming to a close, media interest in Mrs. Bush, scant earlier in the campaign, picked up toward the end. On this day, besides Pettit and his NBC crew, a reporter from Texas, another from Ohio, and a CNN team tagged along, as did a crew from Tokyo. It was a little like the coverage the candidates got back in Iowa before the caucus date drew near, but a far cry from the traveling road show each candidate pulled in the general election. Unlike her husband's multi-bus caravan, Bar's was a mini-motorcade. Local cops, her limousine, Secret Service, followed by a couple of press vans, all whizzed in unison through stoplights in small towns where the roads were lined with onlookers and schoolchildren alerted to her visit, holding blue BUSH/QUAYLE signs. Her motorcade also attracted the attention of the driver of a red pickup truck; he followed the mini-caravan from one stop to another, parking by the road and holding out a big red DUKAKIS/BENTSEN sign for all, including Mrs. Bush, to see.

After attending a Halloween Party at a Head Start program Bar stopped at the Adams County Republican headquarters, a small white clapboard building in the center of Quincy (pop. 39,600), where she cheered on the troops. She then headed into the basement of the building for interviews with local reporters, most of whom are based at the state capital of Springfield, 107 miles away. Today's news had Michael Dukakis accusing Bush of using racial innuendos to steer votes away from the Democrats. Reporters wanted to know what Bar thought about that and the negative tone of the contest in general. Ever her husband's ardent defender, Mrs. Bush insisted that this campaign was no worse than any other she'd seen. She refuted the Dukakis camp's charges that her husband was running a racist campaign. "I noticed that many of the broadcasts last night said there's absolutely *no* evidence of any kind of racism," she said. "So maybe it's sort of desperation."

When another reporter asked her to what extent she thought her husband was responsible for the "dirty campaign" and how much it bothered her, she lashed out angrily at the Democrats. "I don't think we're running a dirty campaign," she insisted. "We're running on our record. He's running away from his record. And if our telling what his record is, is dirty, so be it."

She set the record straight on who started all of this. "Certainly this campaign, starting with the primaries, when they did that unusual dirty trick to Mr. Biden, has been riddled with filth. And that's about all I'm going to say on the subject."

Done, she moved into another room for one-on-one interviews with local press. As she walked by, a radio reporter from Springfield talked loudly into his microphone, giving a pointlessly detailed account of the goings-on, a blow-by-blow description of her every step as though describing a boxing match.

"That was Mrs. George Bush here in Quincy," he started, watching as Bar moved from one room to the next. "Down in the Republican headquarters she is doing some private interviewing now. . . ." When she thankfully disappeared behind a closed door the reporter spotted NBC correspondent Tom Pettit and thrust his mike into Pettit's face for a live interview.

"Were you with Mrs. Bush?" the reporter inquired.

"No, this is just part of a project we're doing on the wives of the candidates," Pettit explained. "We've been traveling around with Mrs. Bush, the wives of the top four candidates. Mrs. Dukakis and the two vice-presidential wives."

"What have you found so far? What is the purpose of the wives traveling?" the reporter asked.

"Damned if I know." Pettit laughed in a puzzled way. "I've never been able to figure that out. I always thought they'd do better if they stayed with their husbands and, you know, just were supportive and helped them out and did what they usually do, which is to offer the closest advice and counsel that you can have in a campaign." He went on, "Modern politicians somehow think that sending the wives out on solo efforts is vote-getting. I'm not sure I believe that."

"Did I get the wrong impression, or is the press intimidated by talking to the wife of the vice-president?" the reporter continued, referring to the media roundtable Mrs. Bush had just completed.

"No. I don't think they're intimidated," Pettit answered. "I just think they're bored."

The reporter then wanted to know what Mrs. Bush's visit meant to Quincy nationally. Pettit, who up until now had looked pretty bored himself, warmed up a bit. This question was a little more up his alley. "Well, it means a lot in terms of Illinois because Illinois has so many electoral votes," he explained. "It's a big battleground. Two candidates are considered to be within range of each other. So while it may not put Quincy on the map, it may help put Illinois on the map election night. So I think it's very important. It tells you how important this state is to the presidential candidates."

The Springfield reporter closed out the interview. "And your coverage will be seen when?" he prompted.

"The coverage of this?" Pettit asked. "It'll be Saturday or Sunday on *NBC Nightly News*."

The man from Springfield continued talking into his mike, blow by blow. "Tom Pettit here with NBC . . ." Then, "Mrs. Bush now is finishing her private interviews with local television reporters. . . ."

Pettit turned away, rolling his eyes.

Out on the street, the impression Mrs. Bush generated was very different from that held by the out-of-town press. What was a sizable crowd for Quincy turned out to greet her. Back upstairs inside the Adams County GOP headquarters, Quincyites had cheered and whistled as Bar inspired the troops to get their neighbors out, and thanked them for their hard work. When she spoke she faced a sea of posters. One stood out: WHITE HAIRED LADIES FOR BUSH! Bar effusively thanked its artist, Pauline Freier, a little woman, white-haired herself, who lived in Quincy. "I just love her attitude about herself," Freier later explained. "I love her self-esteem. She doesn't have to dye her hair and do all these things. She's so real. I thought I'd encourage her."

Outside, as they waited for a glimpse of Bar before she slipped back into her limousine, more kudos came her way from the locals lining the sidewalk. "I've seen her on TV. She is a warm person. I just really appreciate her coming to Quincy. It says a lot about her that she went to the Head Start program. It says a lot about education and education is important to me," said twenty-nine-year-old Carla Churchill Lentz, a teacher married to a hog producer.

"I think she's going to turn things around or she could," added Jane Nolan, another Quincy native standing nearby.

Voters that day responded to what they perceived as Bar's warmth. Her earthiness. The fact that she is a mother. Ironically, in this age of visuals, it was Bar's looks—once thought to be such a liability in her case—that earned her points among this small town crowd.

Looking over the first-lady candidates, thirty-three-year-old Ann Genteman said that of the two, Kitty Dukakis "makes a real good appearance and is very well-spoken. She's attractive. She appeals more cosmetically to a lot of people." But Genteman's respect went to Bar, because "she sticks by her guns and I don't think she's kissing up to anybody. That's the impression I get when she's interviewed. She is herself and to me that really is her strong point."

In mainstream America, Bar also gave people like Genteman, who managed a commercial rabbitry in nearby Rockport, the impression that, unlike Nancy Reagan, she wouldn't be "running the show." People get disturbed, Gentemen thought, if the first lady is overstepping that boundary and taking too much control. "It's difficult to put into words. . . . You don't want to have the sense that the first lady is running the show from behind the scenes. I think that would upset any thinking person. Because then you're going to think the president is a wimp. It's 'What kind of a man is this? We elected him, but yet . . .'"

On the basis of what she'd seen on TV and what she glimpsed that day at the small GOP headquarters on Broadway Street, Gentemen believed whatever input Bar had would be positive.

"I've always had the real strong impression that she's genuine and sincere and I appreciate the fact that she doesn't pander and kowtow—as far as dye her hair, lose weight," explained Genteman, approving of Bar's matronly image. "I have a lot of respect for her that she is herself and she sticks by her rules and her beliefs about what is right for her. I really respect that." To Genteman, Bar came across as very warm and genuine. Down-to-earth. "It's the main quality we look for in someone like that, particularly in being first lady. Because right away, you're going to make the connection, Is a woman like this married to an idiot? No. Her qualities to me are going to mirror a lot of his. I think a woman like that is going to be married to a quality man."

Read those lips, George Bush.

CHAPTER NINE

A Political Wife, Properly Speaking

> The key attitude [for political wives] is public deference to her husband, private loyalty and modest refusal to take any credit for his brilliant success. For the intelligent wife, this requires a daily display of diplomacy that borders on outright fraud. Let's not be coy: a lot of these women are smarter than their husbands. The wife's dilemma is particularly acute today as feminism makes its impertinent demands. She has to be innocuous without being inane, which as all modern examples prove, is impossible.
>
> —SUSAN RILEY, *Political Wives*

Out on the campaign trail Barbara Bush, like Kitty Dukakis, was frequently asked how much she influenced her husband's decision making. She disliked the question. She also wished reporters wouldn't ask her what kind of first lady she'd be. "I know about as much about politics as the ant that just walked by. . . . I don't fool around with his office and he doesn't fool around with my household," was her standard reply. The line made Barbara Bush appear to be out of the fray, unconnected with the fine points of her husband's campaign and career.

When pressed, Mrs. Bush would concede: "You ask any woman who has been married to a man for forty-two years if she would be interested in what he was doing and the answer is 'Yes, of course.'" She'd also say she would not hesitate to tell George Bush what she thought if she saw something or somebody hurting him. "I'm a very normal human being. I would certainly say to him, 'George, I think Jane Smith is doing you a disservice.' But I wouldn't say fire her or fire him. That's not really the way we work. . . ."

185

Her response was that of a classic political wife, and sounded very much like her compatriots on the trail and the reply her predecessor in the White House gave when she campaigned. "What you see is what you get," Nancy Reagan would say. Mrs. Bush and many other spouses in 1988 regularly repeated the line. History almost guarantees it to be a false front.

Barbara Bush's "daily display of diplomacy" and her behavior as a proper political wife who dismissed politics as too unseemly to get involved in was a public stance that at times appeared to be at odds with her private self. Her self-portrait and claims of political ignorance were not echoed by either her children or the people who worked to get George Bush elected. Politically and substantively there was more to Barbara Bush than she allowed. In 1988 Barbara Bush was very much a force to be reckoned with.

During the 1988 campaign, George junior said, his mother was known as a "terror with the staff."

"She definitely has her opinions on things and there is no doubt that my dad hears from her," her daughter, Doro, claimed.

"She won't have an office in the White House next to my father's, she won't have a seat in the Cabinet Room, [but] I think she will be just as influential as Rosalynn Carter" was the opinion of her third son, Neil.

And her talkative eldest son, George junior, painted an ever-more-vivid picture of his mother as a player on her husband's team, especially when it came to dealing with staff and domestic-policy issues. "There were times that people did some things that I think upset my mother. . . . Leaks, and staff siphoning credit for ideas originating with the candidate, especially infuriated her." When that happened, her son said, he would mediate between his mother and the staff. "I would then go talk to that person and inform them that they had made a mistake and that they needed to amend their ways—and explain to them that if they weren't careful, the wrath of the Silver Fox would fall upon them."

Bar's anger apparently was not without consequences, according to her son. "Who knows what would happen?" he asked. "It may not happen immediately, it may happen as time would go on. When you have a family [member] start talking to 'the man' about how terrible someone is, the tendency is for the confidence of 'the man' to be eroded in that person. So if the chorus of negatives arose unanimously against anybody in particular or any policy or any way things were happening, that generally had an impact on the campaign."

In the opinion of the president's eldest son, both the staff and the press during the campaign—and afterward it would appear—failed to take into account George Bush's rapport with his wife and family. "A lot of people underestimated George Bush's love for his family. He respects and loves his sons and daughter and his wife and he listens to us." Because Bar's opinions carried weight with George Bush, her son said, "a lot of those people lived in fear of my mother . . . although they didn't show it. My mother was viewed as a very smart, intelligent, savvy person. People needed to be aware of her presence. No one wanted to irritate her. . . ."

When asked if her son's assessment was correct, Mrs. Bush didn't deny it. "I think people are slightly afraid of me," she conceded.

Oatmeal Lace cookies aside, Barbara Bush can be a regular Ma Barker.

★   ★   ★

Though her attitude is one of public deference, for years Barbara Bush has been an integral part of her husband's team, helping lay the groundwork for his rise to the presidency. It was in 1977 that Nancy Ellis first learned of her brother's intention to seek the presidency. She and Barbara were on a return trip to China. "He was getting his Fund for America's Future going," Ellis explained. "Bar said to me, 'You know your brother is going to be president of the United States, don't you?'

"I said, 'Oh my God!'

"And she said, 'Well, he is, and I just hope I am going to be up to it for him. I just hope I am going to be able to do all that he needs and expects of me to do.'" Realizing what it might mean for her should he succeed, Bar began thinking about "a cause" in 1978. "I really worried, I ought to have an issue," she has said.

She has taken small, steady steps. For years Bar has been an avid notewriter, mailing out her own batch of handwritten letters, ever widening the circle of friends who made up the constituency that helped elect her husband in 1988. Her Christmas-card list numbers in the thousands. In Texas and later out on the trail with her husband, she developed her talent as a campaigner and political helpmate. She can glad-hand a room of potential voters like a pro. At times, it seemed she and her husband had a routine down. "When we go to a reception," she explained one day in the summer of 1987, "I don't stand by George. First of all, I'd be stampeded. That's foolish of me. I mean, I'm not that dumb. Secondly, you cover more people. So I go in and watch him go to the right and I'll go to the left. Or vice versa." They'd meet in the middle, splitting the work in two.

She's a quick study. "It takes twenty minutes for me to get to know somebody," she has said.

"Her instincts and judgment of people are superb. She has a strong political common sense," Janet Steiger explained. She has a razor-sharp memory: whether it's for a conversation she had with a staffer she hasn't seen for six months, or the name of a child she read a book to at a Head Start program. "She is remarkable about the kind of things that she remembers," Elizabeth Kuhl agreed. A neighbor who lived near the Bushes on Palisades Lane in Washington, Kuhl recalled that when Bush became vice-president, the couple's many relatives stayed with neighbors during the inaugural festivities. "I was delighted she remembered that her sister-in-law, Margie Pierce, was a classmate of mine from college," Kuhl said. "There was no earthly reason why she should have remembered that. I think she remembers names very well. Now whether that comes naturally or she works hard at it, I don't know. But I think that's something she's very good about . . . remembering names and faces . . . and not just politically important people."

Friends and family describe Barbara Bush as "smart," "strong," and "extremely well organized." She is also a woman who has developed her own circle of women friends, without whom she says she "couldn't live." According to Commissioner Steiger, "She has awesome managerial skills. I've often said she could run General Motors and I swear to God it's true. Awesome. Much of it, yes, she had to do by herself. [While in Congress] George traveled a great deal back and forth. Traveled a great deal. You do it by yourself. But it was just assumed Bar could handle anything anyway." Her worst failing, Steiger says, is that "no one can possibly do anything for her."

Bar has never shied away from giving her husband advice on his career path—though he has not always heeded it. She told George

Bush not to take up Richard Nixon's offer of heading the Republican National Committee as the tides of Watergate edged near. "The chairman of the GOP National Committee was the job I told him not to take," Mrs. Bush said. "'Accept that job over my dead body.' He came home and said, 'Guess what the president asked me to do?' I said, 'Do anything but that. You're a *statesman*, stay out of that. . . .' Well, he came home that night with that job. It looked like a can of worms and was I ever right!"

Barbara Bush has repeatedly said that sharing her husband's work has been extremely important to her. When asked during a campaign trip what needs of hers were being fulfilled by her husband's run for the presidency, she was momentarily baffled. "That's a hard question," she said reflectively. "I don't have those enormous needs. I mean, I've always felt a need to be part of his life. You certainly are in this case. . . . From campaigning, I feel the children and I are on a much bigger—equal—level. That we all have this in common. We all have funny stories. We're all doing this together . . . sharing more."

She has also explained that the secret to the success of her marriage, beyond humoring her husband, was in not letting him drift. "I think togetherness is a very important ingredient to family life. It's a cliché and we use it too much but I think for a husband and wife, the way to stay close is to do things together and to share. If he just comes home as mine is apt to do, saying, 'Nothing,' when you ask what happened that day, then you've got to probe a little and listen to telephone calls a lot," she told the *Chicago Tribune* in 1986. The toughest times in her marriage, as she's said, were when her husband headed the CIA and they couldn't "share."

"A very hard time for her was the Watergate time," noted Nancy Ellis.

"The CIA was a very lonely job, she did tell me that," Ellis added. "Nothing is shared. 'How was your day?' 'Fine.' Then the man comes in and locks up the briefcase in a safe in the bedroom at night and clicks it shut and the first thing in the morning when he is up, he is taking it back out. The driver comes to take him to work."

Despite his wife's profound unhappiness with his CIA job, Bush wanted to stay on. He asked President Jimmy Carter to keep him there, even promising to stay out of the national political arena, the CIA's former second in command, retired Admiral Bobby Inman, told David Nyhan of *The Boston Globe*.

"As a late bloomer," it took time for Barbara Bush to learn to assert herself and get more involved in politics and her husband's career. Through the disappointments, the many moves, and the insecurity endemic to political life, Barbara Bush has displayed a toughness and independence developed through the death of her first daughter, Robin, and nights "eating on a tray by herself," as Doro put it.

China was a turning point. Mrs. Bush put it this way to the *Los Angeles Times:* "I don't mean to say I didn't do a lot of things before, but I was always a nice little follower." China, still closed at the time to Americans, was an adventure. "I think it just taught me that I could be good. I don't think that I was not confident before, but I would say that I was you know, C+ in confidence. I was perfectly happy living in my own little family spot."

Close friends describe the couple's relationship only in the most glowing terms: "I think they thoroughly enjoy each other," says Barbara's longtime friend Andy Stewart. "But they're not the way some people are, where they only just want each other. Their world is a great big world and the center of hers certainly is George, and I guess always has been. . . . He's the kind who wants people around him all the time."

How does Bar feel about her husband's active socializing? "She jokes about it," Mrs. Stewart said. "But the very quality of reaching out to people, they both have, and I think she'd go bonkers if she couldn't do that."

Mrs. Bush communicates with her husband, she says, "by osmosis." "You should recall the day your husband proposed or the day he told you he's going to run for president. I don't have it down as a red-letter day," she has said.

The Bush children claim never to have seen their parents quarrel, certainly a record worthy of an Academy Award—for over forty years of good behavior. Nancy Ellis says the two never quarrel because "they are always so busy that they never stick around to quarrel. They are really working all the time. She is a worker. The scrapbooks that she had done and her diary that she is doing. They are busy, busy people. I think quarrelsome people are people who spend long evenings going into the relationship. 'Some months ago, you said this. Or you said that. Or you didn't do this.' But they are always on to the next thing."

"They are like a team but they are pretty independent," Doro said of her parents. "It is like they are going on the same track right next to each other . . . my mom right next to my dad."

★   ★   ★

In the 1988 campaign, Bar kept a discreet distance from staff and press but kept a close eye on goings-on. One key avenue for her to tap into the campaign was through her children, especially her sons. When the campaign first kicked off the Bushes' youngest son said his mother was worried about the political operatives around her husband, the so-called "handlers." "I sensed that she was concerned a little bit about that whole aspect of having a bunch of handlers treat her husband like a puppet," Marvin said after the election. "You know, as though he couldn't make decisions on his own. I think she feels that my dad's political instincts are better than [those of] any person involved in the campaign. From that point of view, I think she felt that it was almost an awkward process to have a consultant for seemingly every particular aspect of the campaign."

Marvin continued, "I think that's a natural thing for people who come from a background of being involved in congressional campaigns and Senate campaigns and even the 1980 campaign that brought us on the presidential primary. It was a smaller, more cohesive unit. What we've seen is all of a sudden, it's like a big corporation running for office. I think that made her a little uncomfortable, seeing her husband, whose greatest strength in her eyes is his warmth and his personality, being packaged. There was a concern during that period. I do remember her feeling—I think she was hoping—that the real person that we know in her house would somehow come across."

To make sure that happened, George Bush's eldest son left Texas and signed on with the campaign in Washington, D.C. Before the election, Mrs. Bush said she often turned to him. "George junior, he's an enormous watchdog," she said. "He is wonderful. . . . George calls a spade a spade."

In 1988 much was made of the candidates' "joint" family decisions to run for office. Mike Dukakis reportedly asked his wife and each of his children at a Christmas roundtable to consider the effects on their lives if he were to run. He wouldn't do it, he said, if anyone disagreed.

"We had a long discussion about it, where at the beginning my father said, 'Let's play What-If,'" John Dukakis recalled. "Believe me, What-If at that point was a rather slim possibility. He encouraged us to talk about mostly what it would mean personally for us. Sacrifices. Problems. But to be obvious, before that discussion, my mother and I were well known to think that this was a good idea.

"In that discussion, ultimately, we came to a consensus that this was something we were behind him on," he said. "We encouraged him to make a decision one way or another. And told him that we would be involved to varying degrees in it, if he wanted us to. We were all very supportive of him. Nobody said 'No.' Some of us said we were a little apprehensive."

On the other side of the ballot, the decision was fundamentally George's. Mrs. Bush at times told reporters she had "no choice"; her husband had decided to run. But Bush did gather his family around and asked for their support, claiming he couldn't run without the team effort of his whole clan. In the spring of 1986, the Bush extended family gathered at Camp David to hear campaign operatives outline strategy.

"We were all taken down to Camp David," the president's sister, Nancy Ellis, recalled one day in her historic home in Lincoln, Massachusetts. "President and Mrs. Reagan, George and Barbara, their five children, my three other brothers, myself, and our spouses. We flew in, and then that Saturday in that Camp David conference room, we all sat down and we met the demographics guy and Lee Atwater and they told us how this campaign would be packaged and the strategy, and we had charts and maps. Then my brother said, 'Now, I am not going to do this, if we don't have one hundred percent behind me. I cannot do this without your support and feeling that you are all with me, because it is going to be a hard thing to do.'

"So then they threw it open to suggestions and questions, and Marvin suggested, 'I think we ought to use Mom more. . . . She is this tremendous force. We have to get her out there, and on her own and everything in the primary, to make use of her.'"

Atwater's reaction?

"None. Inscrutable." The president's energetic sister laughed out loud. In Ellis's opinion, Atwater originally was not much on family. "I think he felt this was an unnecessary weekend, really. . . . I don't think he realized in the beginning how important it was to my brother. It was enormously important to him."

Marvin Bush said he encouraged greater family participation because he thought one of his father's biggest failings as a politician up to that point was not blowing his own horn. The game plan this time around called for Dad to trumpet a parental tune. "I think one thing that my dad, and maybe our entire family, has learned over that period of time," Marvin said, "is that—albeit unnatural at times—you know, why not show off the fact that one of George Bush's greatest qualities is that he has been able to keep a family very close, while at the same time encouraging each and every member of that family to take risks and to accomplish whatever their potential might allow them to accomplish."

It was at that family meeting that George junior decided to join the campaign, mostly out of family members' mistrust of Lee Atwater. Recalling the Camp David gathering, George junior said: "The way this came about, I challenged Lee Atwater at the meeting because he was Charles Black's partner and Charles Black was Jack Kemp's campaign manager. So I had real trouble understanding how loyalties would work. Who would he be loyal to? Charles Black, hence Jack Kemp, or George Bush? And I wanted him to explain that to us all. And so he did, you know, in fairly good fashion.

"And Jeb chimed in with his famous quote: 'If there's a hand grenade rolling around George Bush, we want you diving on it first.'

"So then we finished our discussion, and Lee Atwater walked up and said, 'Are you guys really worried about my loyalty?'

"And we said, 'Absolutely.'

"And he said, 'Well, if you're so worried about loyalties, then why doesn't one of you come here in the office and watch me, and the first time I'm disloyal, see to it that I get run off.'

"I happened to be the one who was able to come up here, and I did it," George said.

George junior ran unsuccessfully for a Texas congressional seat in 1978 when he was thirty-one. Early in 1989 he became an owner of the Texas Rangers baseball team after deciding—partly on the basis of his mother's advice—not to run for governor. "She will give you her opinion. She speaks her mind. She was on the front page of the Texas newspapers saying I should not run for governor of Texas," George junior said. "Front page. Banner headlines. In bold print: MRS. BUSH TELLS GEORGE NOT TO RUN FOR GOVERNOR."

Expounding on his role in his father's campaign, he explained in his mile-a-minute hot-dog Texas twang: "Access is power in Washington. OK? And I had more access than anybody to George Bush. And whether or not the gunslingers and inner-circle whatever you want to call them, whoever they thought they were—I might be sitting there talking about how well the dog retrieved the ball—they don't know that. They think we are talking about how bad they are. How good somebody else is. So I ultimately became a conduit. Many people tried to take ideas to George Bush through me. Complaints or suggestions. Generally in a campaign, complaints. Very few times do you get kudos. Generally campaign people are taking kudos for themselves, giving complaints to the candidate. So I became a filter for a lot of news—most of which I never passed along to the man, because having run for office myself, I had some kind of an inkling of what he was going through."

Pausing to gulp a breath of air, he continued, "I helped referee power struggles. I shielded people from Mother. If she were upset about something I would help vent it. She could vent to me and not therefore adversely affect some of the players. You know, I was the enforcer when I thought things were going wrong. Because of the access I had to George Bush, I had the ability—and I think I used it judiciously—I had the ability to go and lay down some behavioral modification. So as a result I had the confidence of . . . most of the top people in the campaign."

Not everyone on the Bush campaign corroborated this version of George junior's role. One aide said the younger Bush was "used" a lot by staff and hangers-on anxious to get the candidate's ear.

Mrs. Bush's eldest son reinforced the view of his mother's watchful relationship with her husband's team. "Staff just knew that she was outspoken enough and honest enough with her opinions that if something were going on—particularly disloyalty to George Bush—then they would hear from her," he added.

Leaking inside information to the press made her especially angry. "I'd put that down at the top of my list of least favorite things," she told reporters in a group interview shortly before the inauguration.

"They had a fit over the staff. When a member of the staff said this or that," Nancy Ellis said.

Indeed, *Newsweek* magazine quoted a senior staffer describing Bar as "challenging a campaign staffer who she thought had ill served her husband. It was the only time I've seen her bordering on unpleasant," the aide said.

How did Bar view Lee Atwater? "He's the same age as her sons, so I think she treated him accordingly," Sheila Tate said elusively.

"I think she sees him as a son whose hands need to be slapped once in a while," echoed another White House aide.

The occasionally reckless Atwater sagely paid attention to Barbara Bush. At the GOP Convention he described Mrs. Bush as a cheerleader, revving up the troops "during this so-called Iran-mess" and after the Iowa defeat. "There's never been a tougher period in any campaign in the country than the day after the VP lost that Iowa caucus. I felt terrible. Here I am, the campaign manager, and I did feel at fault," Atwater said. "Frankly, I couldn't have done my job if it weren't for the attitude she had because I felt terrible about that thing."

He added: "I've managed I think thirty-two campaigns. If you're in my job and the candidate's wife don't like you, you're in a heap of trouble. No matter how smart and no matter how good you are, she gets the last word."

Rich Bond, a former top aide, said that Mrs. Bush feels strongly about "the type of people her husband has around her"—and, he might have added, the image they project. On the campaign trail and afterward, Mrs. Bush demonstrated a deep sense of propriety. Speaking about herself she said, "You have to be careful you don't put yourself in a position where you commercialize the White House, or cheapen the White House. That's very important." While that feeling held true for her, it also held true for her husband's staff whom she watched for signs of self-aggrandizement.

After the Bushes were ensconced in the White House and Lee Atwater was promoted to chairman of the Republican National Committee, the thirty-eight-year-old posed for *Esquire* magazine's June 1988 issue saluting a flag in red running shorts with his sweatpants dropped to his ankles. *The New York Times* reported, "Mrs. Bush saw a little red herself." Rumors had been circulating that Bar was unhappy with Atwater's moonlighting as a rock 'n' roller, playing his guitar in nightclubs after hours. The *Times* reported that Mrs. Bush felt Atwater's "Bad Boy behavior was 'trivializing' the image of the party her husband heads."

Always a diplomat, Mrs. Bush called the *Times* piece "mischievous." She said she hadn't even seen the story when it appeared, and she denied harboring any bad feelings toward Atwater. But she had kept a close eye on a flap surrounding an RNC memo that appeared early in June which implied that House Speaker Thomas Foley was a homosexual and she had definite thoughts on that. "It was the most outrageous, unattractive, not nice memo, and I was ashamed of it, as was my husband."

Elaborating, she said: "I think [Atwater] is one of the best politicians I know and someone on his team made a terrible mistake. But they won't make another one, will they?"

In Washington it is also believed that it was in part Mrs. Bush's displeasure with her husband's former top aide Craig Fuller that cost him the coveted job of White House chief of staff. During the campaign Fuller was rumored to be leaking stories to *The Washington Post* and was dressed down by George junior. Mrs. Bush reportedly felt Fuller had isolated her husband from other aides in an effort to get the top job. According to news reports, Mrs. Bush made her displeasure known. As Maureen Dowd reported in *The New York Times:* "The story is legend in the Bush inner circle that once in the campaign, when the Bushes and Mr. Fuller were in the cabin of Air Force Two, Mr. Fuller was going through a stack of phone messages that he had let pile up for several days.

"Pitching her voice so that her husband could overhear, Mrs. Bush said innocently to Mr. Fuller: 'Are you just going through your messages now?'

"When he replied that he was, she went on silkily: 'Keep looking. When you get to the bottom of the pile, you'll find a couple from me.'"

"Mrs. Bush did get on Craig Fuller about not returning her phone calls," confirmed her chief of staff, Susan Porter Rose. After the campaign Fuller went to work for a Washington public-relations firm. Now he quickly calls her back, another aide said.

Despite what Mrs. Bush said publicly about not knowing diddly about politics or the inner workings of the campaign, she knew the detailed developments, aides said. The staff realized that Mrs. Bush was indeed very plugged in. "Mrs. Bush is not demonstrable in that confidante role, but I know she knows everything because in casual conversations [during the primary season] . . . it was clear she knew what was the turnout, what was the problem, what screwed up," said Mary Matalin, a field organizer during the campaign and later Lee Atwater's deputy at the Republican National Committee.

Matalin elaborated: "After the Ames event [an Iowa straw poll hijacked by supporters of Pat Robertson, who trounced Bob Dole and George Bush], she knew exactly what happened and she understands the tactics and she understands the strategy, although she never interferes. She never got on the phone and said, 'How many people are you turning out in Polk County for the straw ballot?' or anything. But she clearly knew after the fact what had happened and what were the causes of our failure in that thing. So she does know everything and I presume she discusses that with her husband."

Once the dismal Ames results rolled in, Bar may have skipped directing Matalin, but top aide Rich Bond didn't get away so easily. According to political analysts Jack Germond and Jules Witcover, the evening after Bush's poor showing in the Ames straw poll, Mrs. Bush summoned Rich Bond up front in *Air Force Two* as the vice-presidential couple returned to Washington. "She wanted to know point-blank why her husband had lost in a state where he had beaten Ronald Reagan seven years earlier. She told Bond that she expected him to get back to Iowa and park there from then until the caucuses were over. For the next five months he did just that, with only occasional trips home. . . ." they reported in their book on the 1988 race *Whose Broad Stripes and Bright Stars?*

Early in the 1988 race Mrs. Bush explained her participation in her husband's campaign this way: "I listen" and give input "only if somebody asks, 'What do you think about that?' Or, if I really think something's . . . you know, I might reinforce what someone else says."

Bush himself pointed to his wife's influence. At times he advocated an itinerary recommended by his wife, aides recalled, because the president said, "Bar tells me I've got to do this."

Bush's campaign adviser on domestic issues, Deborah Steelman, remembered Mrs. Bush's participation in strategy meetings in the spring of 1987 when the Bush camp hammered out policy and issues at the couple's Kennebunkport estate. Steelman described Mrs. Bush's style. "She sits through the briefings, and she weighs in at the precise moment that she knows she has to," Steelman recalled. "She doesn't waste a lot of discussion. She doesn't ask the staff a lot of questions, but if she can see Bush getting certain information, then she'll weigh in. When we had the two days in Kennebunkport, she sat through all the briefings and asked some good questions and gave her opinion at a couple of key times. . . . You could tell she was very interested and wanted him to know how she felt about certain things. . . . She's not at all intrusive, but she clearly knows the issues she cares about."

Mrs. Bush accounted for her participation in staff meetings this way: "I've been sitting in on all the briefings, but I don't go to national defense briefings. I'm not an economist. I did sit in on some of the economy meetings in May. I sat in on all of them, actually. [But] I really don't have the background to talk about the economy. Other than the very simple facts of what the interest rates were and what they are now. What unemployment was. What it is now."

Beyond that, Barbara Bush closely monitored the negative tone of the campaign—a subject she frequently talked about to local reporters who badgered her on this as the Democrats' complaints got louder. She "read everything," said one aide.

When the handlers in Washington sent out speeches that were filled with what Bush termed "red meat," Bush would take out a lot of it. He recognized the need to define Dukakis, but would insist on being factual, an aide said. "He would discuss any weakness in Dukakis's record as long as it was factual. That was his bottom line." His wife "did not like attack politics," Sheila Tate said. "When she'd be with us for a few days you'd see her softening effect on him. The campaign, of course, would urge the attack. She would moderate that."

When certain passages of her husband's lengthy convention speech had to be cut for time, Bar insisted George keep one passage in: "I am a quiet man but I hear the quiet people others don't."

However, like her husband, she was not against using negative ads when she deemed them necessary. In New Hampshire, aides credited her with persuading Bush to run the "Straddler" ad attacking Dole's position on tax increases, *Newsweek* reported.

Infuriated by the tone the Democrats took at their convention, she remembered the slights well. "It's sort of funny to me, after seeing the Democratic National Convention where a former president of the United States called George Bush silly and effeminate. . . . It sort of set an interesting tone," she told reporters on the trail. She felt the Democrats started it all. Ann Richards—whom she referred to as "that woman"—"didn't set such a great tone, I didn't think."

She was angered by Jimmy Carter's description of Bush, she said, and noted with satisfaction that the former president later dropped Bush a private note of apology.

Yet as the campaign drew to a close, she urged her husband to tone down attacks on Dukakis. She was concerned about the dirtier aspects of the campaign. When unsanctioned campaign literature popped up around the country, she got on the phone to Jim Baker to find out what was going on. "Yesterday, I talked to Jim Baker and said, 'Jim, what was that awful thing Governor Dukakis was holding up on the news?'" she told the newswomen who heard her at the Four Seasons luncheon in October.

"And he said, 'I'll be darned if I know. It did not come out of national Bush headquarters.'

"Now whether it came out of some enthusiastic person who's for you, there's not an awful lot you can do about that," she said. "I don't know where it came from, but I asked Jim.

"He said, 'I'm gonna look into that 'cause I don't like George's name on anything like that.'" The Bush camp later disowned this salacious material.

"I'd like all positive ads," Mrs. Bush told the group, then rationalized. "But that evidently doesn't work all the time. It's no worse, incidentally, than other campaigns I've been in. . . . We've been through such smear campaigns that you can't believe."

But those were down and dirty regional races in Texas.

Though critical when negative ads were used against her husband, Mrs. Bush had no objection when George Bush's campaign used them later on. In an interview in the White House after the election, Mrs. Bush was asked her opinion of the Willie Horton ad. "It was a very good ad," she said. "It had nothing to do with race at all. I think most Americans still feel that way. When you see a man who has killed several people brutally, who has been let out on leave, it doesn't matter what color he was—and nobody thinks that it was a racist ad. That's just another, if you'll excuse the word, liberal way of getting back at the president. It was never meant to be a racial thing at all. Willie Horton could have been white, green, anything. It was an outrage."

More significant, beyond campaign squabbles, were signs of bedroom policy making. Mrs. Bush helped shape her husband's views on certain domestic issues, especially education. "I'm much more interested, frankly, in child care. There are issues that have been there always but are now coming to the fore," she said in an interview prior to the Republican Convention. "I'm sure someone had AIDS before 1980. I never heard of it. I'm sure we had homeless, but they were exceptions. They still are exceptions, actually, 'cause we're talking about a small number. But we don't want them to grow and we want to help them. I guess we've always had problems with affordable housing. But I wasn't as conscious of it. There are a lot of new things that have come into focus that I'm interested in because they all have to do with people."

She had a quick grasp of her husband's economic position. One day during a campaign bus trip around Chicago, she quickly briefed reporters on what took the "voodoo" out of Reagan's economic policy. "If you think back, what [George] called 'voodoo economics' was strong taxes, strong defense, and no cutting of government programs. He said you can cut taxes but you also have to cut government spending. That was voodoo economics," she explained. "When it changed to cutting taxes and cutting spending, it stopped being voodoo economics."

But it was on education, her expressed area of concern, that she has been most articulate. "We both feel Head Start is the *real* answer for getting kids into the system where they really know how to read, write, and comprehend," she told reporters one day on the trail. In an interview she confessed, "Did I bring to his attention facts and figures about education? Yes, I think I did. . . . But I think I brought a lot of focus. I didn't urge him to be the Education President, but I was delighted when he was. I think if you go to bed and wake up every morning with a woman who's talking about it, maybe it makes a difference."

Indeed it does. Doro recalled her mother's reaction to the president's emphasis on education during his first budget address to Congress in January 1989. She remembered, "My mom turned to me and said, 'See how your father talks about education? I told him. A year ago, he wouldn't have been this strong on education.'"

★ ★ ★

As her husband has taken on increasingly important jobs, Barbara Bush has shown that she is tougher than her public image. Publicly, Mrs. Bush's language is peppered with hyperbole. "Wonderful," "Enormous," "Sweet," and "Precious" are among her favorite descriptors. In private the story can be different. During the campaign, writer Gail Sheehy once asked a close aide if Bush and his wife "talk tough in private." Sheehy reported, "The aide chuckled and replied, 'Hell, yeah.'"

Chris Matthews, the *San Francisco Examiner*'s bureau chief, noticed Mrs. Bush's penchant for winging underhanded verbal zingers, remarks that sometimes come out sounding needlessly defensive. "Forget those cuddly grandmother stories," Matthews wrote in a profile after lunching with the first lady at the White House. "The wife remembers. Ask her whether husbands should spend more time at home with their children and Mrs. Bush's synapses are brutal. 'Well, if you are a very lucky couple and maybe you are like Jane Pauley and Doonesbury. I mean, he does a lot with the children, as I understand it. Well, I mean, that is lucky, because his job is such that he can work ahead and he could stay home with the children.' Bam!"

Indeed, after a visit to a program that served poor women in Pittsburgh, Mrs. Bush's language became graphic. Afterward she described one participant as "smelling like a billy goat." On a plane ride back to Washington she chastised her aide Casey Healey, who was gnawing an apple down to the core. "Casey, stop eating that damn apple, it's disgusting!" Casey just smiled. At other times she'd insist to her staff, "We are having *fun*. Your feet are *not* tired!"

"When displeased, she has a freeze like nothing you've ever seen," reported Susan Morrison, who was Bush's spokesperson in his 1980 campaign. "She sets a standard of behavior, and she expects everyone—family and staff—to live up to it. She bitches at you about smoking, manners, dress, and staying out too late—things your mother did when you were fourteen and fifteen years old," Morrison told Washington writer Sandy McElwaine in *Lear's* magazine.

Several of Bush's advisers have acknowledged that the president is capable of holding a grudge, but credit the first lady with being the couple's institutional memory. "She'll go to bat for me, sometimes more than I'm inclined to myself," the president has said. "She'll take 'em on head to head, dog eat dog. And that's fine. I'm glad to have her defending me. I'd rather have her on my side than not. She's been there for forty years."

When asked if his mother is the memory bank in the marriage, George junior said she was, and elaborated: "Institutional memory doesn't mean she's the type of person who spends time plotting to ruin somebody's career. She's not that way. She is a kindhearted woman as opposed to a meanspirited woman. But she doesn't like it when people betray or are disloyal. There are times when people are so worried about themselves that they forget 'the mission.' She doesn't like that and so there she is quick to point it out; may point it out directly. I think it's good she is that way. It keeps people on their toes. . . . She is a quick burn. She expresses her displeasure and goes on to the next subject. So institutional memory is one thing. Grudge-holder she is not."

Barbara Bush does indeed remember slights and registers her disapproval in her words and, more directly, in the tone of her voice. One day midway through October, the Bushes conducted a daylong bus tour through central California. The vice-president headed the caravan in Asphalt II, a custom-outfitted recreational vehicle. Joining the Bushes that day were California Governor Deukmejian and his wife, and the celebrities of the day: martial arts king Chuck Norris and two aging Beach Boys, Mike Love and Bruce Johnston, whose new single, "Ko Ko Mo," had just topped the charts. (A fact they never failed to mention as they kicked off rally after crowded rally throughout the long day.)

During a twenty-minute ride between Ripon and Modesto, a "pool" of three reporters boarded Asphalt II to catch any newsworthy utterances Bush might make. En route to Modesto Bush sat with Beach Boy Love and Norris. The three men munched on hickory nuts, bragged amiably about their ocean powerboats, and swapped exercise regimens. Occasionally Bush got up to pour himself out the window and wave to crowds lining the roadways.

White House correspondent Terry Hunt was on board as part of the reporting pool. Also aboard was *Time* magazine correspondent Alessandra Stanley, who supplied her colleagues with a "pool report" that wryly described the scene from inside Asphalt II: "Mrs. Bush sat next to Mrs. Deukmejian, scribbling notes for her *USA Today* diary. Bar asked the pool how big the crowd [at the last stop] was. When someone answered vaguely, 'Several hundred,' she said of his mediocre crowd estimate, 'That stinks.' But, she added, 'I'm sympathetic to you writers now that I'm one, you have to keep taking notes all the time!' She playfully blamed Kitty Dukakis for her new assignment, saying that once Mrs. Dukakis started doing diary entries at the Democratic Convention, she had no choice. 'I didn't sign up for this, it was thrust upon me.' (Deukmejian, seated behind Bush, was silent and mainly looked out the window.)

"When Bush teasingly reminded 'Bar' that AP pool reporter Terry Hunt had been the one to report her '84 gaffe about Ferraro ('rhymes with witch'), she demurred, saying it wasn't Hunt, but someone else. 'Not this precious one,' she said patting Hunt's hand, as if defending a wrongly accused four-year-old. Adorably, but wrongly, Terry Hunt assured her that he would *never* have reported such a thing, and she replied tartly: 'I would have. If I remembered it.'"

When Hunt, forty-two years old at the time, returned to the press bus, Bar's patronizing comment stuck. "Precious one," Stanley ribbed him.

★   ★   ★

Public posture aside, beneath Barbara Bush's calm exterior, and the Secret Service moniker "Tranquility," hides an intense woman. She was a smoker for twenty years. She grinds her teeth at night. "It really is terrible," she said in one interview, pointing to a ridge across her front teeth. "I wake up in pain."

An old acquaintance, Phyllis Draper, whose husband is administrator of the U.N. Development Programme, once described Mrs. Bush's hostessing style: "Like that old saying—she's very calm on the top and paddling like hell underneath."

Out on the trail, as when hostessing a dinner, she wouldn't let anyone see her sweat. In a final Sunday morning interview with Lesley Stahl, she was asked if she was worried. "I don't feel confident. I don't feel tired. I feel great. Just as you should feel right about now," she said noncommittally.

Where she *was* committed was in protecting George. During the 1988 race she kept tabs on his schedule, trying to get him back to D.C. at least on Sundays for a "down" day. "She knows him, how far you can stretch him and when he has to rest. Because he is the type that goes, goes, goes," an aide said.

Barbara's sister-in-law credited her with getting the vice-president out of town the week of the Democratic National Convention. "I think it was her idea to call Jimmy Baker and say, 'Why don't you two go fishing in Wyoming?'" Nancy Ellis recalled. "She said, 'He just cannot [stay in Washington] because it is going to be the most unbelievable abuse. It is just going to be a nightmare sitting and watching it.' And they got way out in the wilderness and found this wonderful place where they could be miles from a TV. I think she masterminded that. I know she had something to do with that. She was on the phone with Jimmy."

During the final few days of the race Bar admitted she was having a hard time falling asleep. "You wake up thinking of those things you've left undone probably. At least, I do," she told the press during a bus tour in Illinois. "You think it's either way too long, the campaign. Or you think not enough time. There are a lot of places to go. Another reason we're not sleeping too well . . . is if you know you have to be up at five-thirty, we look at the clock half the night." The press, keeping similar hours, laughed sympathetically.

Last-minute jitters aside, Barbara Bush was not immune to the stress other wives displayed on their sleeves. Once in the White House Mrs. Bush said, "I don't ever feel panicked about anything anymore. I really don't feel it. I used to think, 'I'm not prepared. I'm just not going to be able to even face it, can't sleep at night until I come up with something. I don't feel that anymore." Looking back on the campaign, Doro LeBlond remembered her mother's periodically frayed nerves. "The campaign was horrendous. It was horrible," Doro said bluntly after the election. "Everybody's nervous around you. You have these people around you who are just like . . . one false move and we are dead, you know. But Mom and Dad have such great senses of humor, it helps you through.

"I traveled with my dad the last five days of the campaign," she continued. "It had nothing to do with me. I just think it had something to do with someone from his family being with him. Someone told me, Roger Ailes or whoever it was, 'You cannot believe how much more relaxed your dad is when you are around.' And I think he just meant having someone who is around him who is not going, 'Your hair is wrong.' 'You can't say that.' Whatever it is. Dad never listens."

Doro recalled an earlier time in the campaign when her father's chances looked bad. Prior to a primary debate at Dartmouth, she joined him and staff members in a New Hampshire hotel room for a debate briefing. She watched as staff drilled her father on subject after subject.

"Mom was there in the next room," Doro recalled. "She couldn't listen. She was doing her needlepoint at about one hundred miles an hour."

When staff had finished their briefings, Doro said she watched her father put the papers aside, lie down, and within five minutes start to snore.

Amazed at his reaction to the pressured situation, she turned to her mother and asked, "How can he do that?"

Needle jetting back and forth, Bar replied, "I don't know," and waved Doro in for a chat. "Come in here and talk to me," she invited.

Her daughter's conclusion: "Mom was probably more nervous than dad was during the campaign, sometimes."

CHAPTER TEN

❦

Hurtling Toward a Loss

A political star mobbed a few years before, every
utterance worth a thousand Xeroxed copies and
front-page stories, is dropped by the press and
other politicians when he loses power. Though
the politician may voice the same views, post-
defeat, the value has gone from his words. What
was puffing him up was not so much the bril-
liance of his thoughts or rhetoric but the importance of his position. This is, of course, the most
fundamental lesson a politician learns, but it is
still bitter fruit—especially when one has been a
national hero.

—MYRA MACPHERSON, *The Power Lovers*

There are only a few key moments in a presidential campaign,
once the field has narrowed and the final contenders are streaking
across the country at breakneck speeds. A stellar convention
speech, a gaffe, or an ill-timed answer to a debate question can
make or break a candidate's chances. In 1988 it was CNN anchor-
man Bernard Shaw's opening query to Mike Dukakis during the
second presidential debate on October 13 that many felt sank the
governor's candidacy.

Despite Dukakis's winning performance in the first debate at
Winston-Salem on September 25, under the constant pummeling
of the Bush camp the Democrats had never really built much momentum coming out of their summertime convention. When the
two contenders met for their final duel at UCLA's Pauley Pavilion,
facing several hundred members of the media and several thousand guests, Dukakis desperately needed to score points.

Just minutes after the debate began, Shaw, who moderated the
debate, delivered the opening question. He asked: "Governor, if
Kitty Dukakis were raped and murdered, would you favor an ir-
revocable death penalty for the killer?"

Ignoring the visceral logic of the question, Dukakis gave this reply: "No, I don't, Bernard. . . . And I think you know that I've opposed the death penalty during all of my life. I don't see any evidence that it's a deterrent, and I think there are better and more effective ways to deal with violent crime. We've done so in my own state. And that's one of the reasons why we have had the biggest drop in crime of any industrial state in America; why we have the lowest murder rate of any industrial state in America."

Dukakis continued. No mention of Kitty. No display of emotion. It was a vague, rambling answer. Public opinion rests in part upon a candidate's ability to demonstrate expected emotional responses, and Dukakis's answer to Shaw's "Kitty question" only served to solidify the perception of the governor as an aloof man, unable to share his feelings and connect with average voters.

Behind the stage at the Pauley Pavilion, back in Boston headquarters, and in between the two coasts, there was collective disbelief. Democrats' hearts sank. "I remember sitting in one of our offices with about eight people watching the television," said Chris Edley, Jr., Dukakis's issues director. "As he gave that answer, several of us kind of pressed our lips and shook our heads gently. . . . Then Bush gave an answer and he was terrific. And the same thing happened. The same exchange of looks. I think there was a sense, 'That was it.' That the election was over at that point."

Edley, who had helped with debate preparation, said Dukakis was nervous and overprepared. The candidate had not been feeling well that day. A final morning review had been canceled. He'd slept in the afternoon. "When that question came across, it seemed clear to me that what he did was he said, 'Ah-ha! Crime! Here is the answer. Here is what I want to get across,'" Edley said. "Rather than being more spontaneous and taking the question on its effective terms. I think it is understandable." Edley conceded his interpretation wasn't widely held. "Most people think of him as Ice-Man Dukakis. I thought of it as Mike Dukakis being very nervous, knowing how much is at stake in this [second] debate and looking for an opportunity to make certain kinds of points after having been beaten for three months over Willie Horton and not being tough on crime."

Actually, melting Dukakis's Ice-Man patina was just what CNN's Bernard Shaw had in mind when he asked the question. In an interview with *Washington Post* TV critic Tom Shales about a

month after the debate, Shaw explained, "I realized that in asking
that kind of question it would arouse emotions, but I meant the
question to Dukakis to be a stethoscope to find out what he was
feeling on this issue. Bush had been beating Dukakis severely
about the head and shoulders, charging he was soft on crime.
Many voters perceived seeing and hearing Dukakis, but not feeling
him. I asked that question to see if there was feeling."

Shaw's question and Dukakis's response infuriated Kitty.

Publicly she expressed anger at the question, calling it "inappropriate and outrageous." But aides and close friends later said
Kitty's immediate anger was directed at her husband, who
shocked her by a response which she felt sabotaged the election. If
body language talks, the couple's behavior after the debate spoke
volumes. While Bush and his family hovered onstage talking with
panelists and soaking up a few extra minutes of TV attention,
Kitty perfunctorily embraced her husband, who turned on his heel
and stalked offstage. She followed, paces behind.

Was she angry? "I think you can assume that," one of her aides
said later. "Then she felt bad she was mad at him."

In an interview months after the election Kitty held to her initial
public stance, still describing Shaw's question as "outrageous" and
"inappropriate." She insisted she hadn't been angry at her husband, but did concede, "Michael had a golden opportunity and he
missed it. He realized afterward what he had done. . . . I felt sorry
for him, because I know how painful it was," she said.

After the debate another aide remembered Kitty looking for advice on how to handle inevitable inquiries from reporters who
would want a response to the rape question. He suggested:
"'Look, I think Michael gave the right answer. The fact that I'm
filing for divorce has nothing to do with it.'" The two shared a
laugh.

After the debate, Dukakis dropped further in the polls and he
scrambled to recoup his losses. He allowed Shaw to put the question to him again, weeks later, on November 1. In a second interview, a limp would-be replay of what might have been, Dukakis
recast his answer. "Kitty is the most precious thing that I have in
the world and obviously . . . I would have that kind of emotion,"
he told Shaw.

"Would you kill him?" Shaw queried.

"I think I would have that kind of emotion," the governor replied, this time trying to give the much-desired expected response. "On the other hand, this is not a country where we glorify vengeance. We're a country that believes in the law and I believe very strongly in the law."

The answer was improved, but most voters had already reached their verdict. "The rape thing was a killer, particularly with women," said Democratic pollster Celinda Lake. During the second debate the Bush camp had monitored voters' responses with hand dials. "Women in particular were blown away," Lake reported. "Even more than men. They never came back."

Not surprisingly, Dukakis's answer thrilled Bush's media guru, Roger Ailes, who felt it showed the governor's true colors. He told an interviewer: "He is truly a bureaucrat. He does not understand vision at all. It's just off the radarscope," Ailes said two days afterward. "Dukakis became a defense attorney for the murderer, as opposed to the outraged husband of the victim. He literally took on the position of the defense attorney. And that said it all. That said it all. . . . Actually it was an outrageous and even unfair question and showed anger on the part of Bernie."

Dukakis never closed the gap. In the final, waning days of the campaign Kitty and Mike's fatigue was palpable. But their fatigue was mixed with an infectious, anxious optimism. Approaching the last days, Dukakis appeared to one of the traveling press corps as "a man who wants to feel he ran his hardest in the stretch." Dukakis finally hit his stride as a campaigner, delivering some of his strongest speeches before his largest, most enthusiastic audiences. What had been an awkward, jerky back-and-forth tango between candidate and crowd became a lively twirl. Polls showed undecided voters breaking the governor's way—the gap between Dukakis and his opponent narrowed as they sashayed back and forth across the country like two guys playing tag. Although the crowds swelled, there was a bittersweet feeling among Dukakis supporters, who cheered but who seemed also collectively to sigh, "Why couldn't he have done this sooner?"

After lurching across the country, campaign organizers decided to bring the candidate and his wife together for the final sprint. Previously when the candidate's spirits ebbed or he had appeared rudderless, staffers had put Kitty or one of his daughters on the plane "to boost his spirits and restore a sense of grounding to his life," as *Newsweek* reported it. In the final days Sasso too got on board to deal with the candidate, while back in Boston Estrich handled the demoralized staff. "John, I know, made certain decisions about not giving him polling information, and about how much he told him and how much he didn't, and what he told him and what he didn't," Estrich explained. "He very much managed Dukakis throughout the general election, but especially during those last couple of weeks."

For months reporters had noted how much better the candidate performed when his wife was around, prompting a spate of bedroom jokes. Even the Bush camp eyed Kitty watchfully. Focus groups held by the Bush camp prior to the Democratic Convention showed Dukakis's "negatives" went down when he appeared with Kitty.

Sensing a surge among undecided voters, Kitty pitched back and forth from euphoria to bitterness. Early in the last week as Dukakis celebrated his fifty-fifth birthday and even larger crowds responded strongly to Dukakis's populist cry of "I'm on Your Side," Kitty appeared to be in high spirits. She told reporters, "It's just intuition. It's something in the crowds." Her enthusiasm was also sparked in part by a new role the campaign found for her to play while she was with her husband. She began introducing him at rallies, attempting to display the passion so many said he lacked. "It was a cheap way of getting schmaltz," a Dukakis aide commented later. "We were totally unabashed about it." Unfortunately, it came too late.

★   ★   ★

Early on the morning of October 27 Mike, Kitty, and company arrived for a meeting with supporters at the Martinique, a gaudy dinner club in a suburb near Chicago's Southwest Side, one of the city's largest bastions of Reagan Democrats.

It was a "deese, dem, and dose" crowd that greeted the couple in a Las Vegas-style vermilion ballroom, lit by Plexiglas-crystal chandeliers at 8:30 A.M. that day. The kind of crowd that howled when a local Cook County pol recited the legendary deathbed wish of LBJ—to be buried in Chicago so he would never lose his right to vote.

Many in the group were manifestly doubtful of Dukakis's chances of winning. Bush had been tailgating Dukakis throughout the Midwest, especially in Illinois. Though polls overall looked bad, polls in the state showed the race was very tight. So tight, in fact, that on election night CBS's Dan Rather made a false call, erroneously putting Illinois into Dukakis's camp.

With only twelve days until the election, the precinct workers needed an injection of adrenaline. They needed to see the candidate to believe themselves that they could win. They needed backbone.

Neil Hartigan, the Illinois attorney general, tried to give it to them. A fading redhead whose hair often clashes with his worn-for-TV scarlet ties, Hartigan spoke with classic Chicago-style hyperbole. "The attempt by George Bush to portray Mike Dukakis as something he is not—to smear him—is one of the most offensive things I have ever seen in American politics. And those of us in Cook County thought we had seen everything," Hartigan shouted, trying to warm up the crowd a few degrees before Kitty and Mike arrived. The crowd roared its approval, maybe fondly remembering the tales of stolen ballot boxes afloat in the Chicago River, turning the tide for JFK by 8,800 votes.

Hartigan continued, "We have an obligation to ourselves if to no one else to get the message of the Dukakis candidacy to the people of our community." He droned on.

A few minutes later Kitty and Mike burst into the room. Dressed in a fiery red suit, Kitty led Mike to center stage. The Bio-Mechanics, a band outfitted in evening wear for this early-morning gig, opened up too loudly with "One" (Singular Sensation). The couple moved toward the stage, grabbing hands with the eager pols. Kitty appeared upbeat, electric, a cheerleader, as she energetically waved to the crowd and flashed a brilliant smile. Three days later she would collapse in Minneapolis with what her aides maintained was a raging fever and viral infection—a condition much more serious than anyone let on at the time.

As the crowd roared "WE WANT MIKE!" Kitty stepped up to the podium and the governor stood back—in a reversal of the routine they'd perfected over three hundred days ago in Iowa.

"It's good to finally be back with my husband," she began, to the crowd's appreciative laughter.

"I'm really pleased to be here this morning, to introduce the next president of the United States," she went on. "This is the man who stood by my side and comforted and helped me when we lost our first child," she told the quieting room.

"And this is the same man, when I made a decision to confront my dependency and said to him, 'This may not be the best time, you're in the middle of a tough reelection campaign.' And his answer to me was 'You're more important than my reelection.'

"Is that compassion? Is that caring? Is that sensitivity?" she asked persistently. The questionable exploitation of expired offspring for political advantage may have been tasteless, but the crowd came alive.

She proceeded. "And when my husband is elected president of the United States, I'm going to have the same husband I had when this campaign began nineteen months ago. Not a facsimile. Not somebody manufactured. Not somebody molded in the vision of someone else. With the same integrity and dignity. I'm so proud of the way he has campaigned for this great office. The next president of the United States, Michael Dukakis."

The crowd went wild. Reporters nodded approvingly.

"He should take her with him wherever he goes," columnist Jules Witcover volunteered, as he scribbled down the Dukakisisms of the day. "I'm sure she does good elsewhere but it helps him and she always looks so upbeat. He is so much better when she is with him. I've said that from the beginning."

Dukakis came forward and put his arm around Kitty's waist. The two soaked up the cheers before he proceeded with his speech.

Outside, the couple didn't hang together quite as tightly. After the rally a different scene unfolded. Heading toward the motorcade's lead limousine, Kitty tripped herself. Three Secret Service agents caught her before she could hit the ground. Photographers caught her as well, on film. It was a fleeting moment, but one that also caught the attention of ABC's Sam Donaldson, who thought enough of it to record it in a campaign diary he published after the election. "As Mike and Kitty Dukakis left the morning rally in Chicago and were about to get into their limousine, Kitty stumbled and fell to the sidewalk. The Secret Service agents immediately helped her up, but Dukakis had been turning to his side of the car and was not close enough to grab for her when he saw it happen. His reaction was to pause slightly and to make sure that she was all right, but he made no effort to go over and help. He simply resumed his passage around the limousine. To me, this was just another example of how dispassionately Dukakis acts in situations where other people would react emotionally. His partisans say this would be one of his strengths as President, but it is one of his biggest weaknesses as a candidate."

An hour later the entourage arrived at the Harlem High School gym in downstate Rockford, Illinois. A twenty-minute hop via "Sky Pig," Dukakis's slow-moving press plane, followed by a forty-minute road trip: A dozen or so buses with scores of reporters caravaned through late-October cornfields. As in other schools in other parts of the country, handpainted signs yelling DUKE CARES ABOUT KIDS and WE LOVE KITTY were taped up on the school's gym walls, heralding the candidate's arrival. The school's emblem, an oversized, monstrous orange wolf, rose up along another wall. The press had been to hundreds of events like this, but here they found what must be one of the biggest trophy cases in all of high-school America. The rotundalike glass case dominated the school's main hall, crammed with golden youths frozen forever in various basketball poses.

In the gym a dozen girls, look-alike friends, scattered themselves like pick-up sticks, every which way on the floor. Their hair, styled in the wispy blond look actress Farrah Fawcett made popular years ago, made them seem dated, as did their pastel sweatshirts, tight-bottomed jeans, and white canvas tennis shoes.

Looking around the packed gym, Jim Sullivan, a retired machinist, said, "I didn't know there were this many Democrats in Rockford." Sullivan said he'd just finished reading a book about the Reagan administration and the Iran-Contra affair and volunteered: "I came to hear Dukakis because of the Republicans' utter contempt for the voters."

As in Chicago, Kitty came before the thumping crowd to introduce the candidate. This time she pitched passion as she told a story about her husband's sensitivity toward her son by another marriage. "When I first went out with Michael, I was concerned about the fact that I had a young son, a three-year-old, and wondered whether or not he would accept John," she told the crowd. "I needn't have worried. Because his love and caring and sensitivity have been there from the beginning and it has been a joy to watch that love grow and flourish through the years.

"It was Michael Dukakis who has been by my side—when we

lost our first child, when I made the decision to confront my dependency," she repeated. "And I wondered aloud to him whether my timing was right since he was in the middle of a tough election. And his answer to me then was 'You're more important to me than anything else.'" She insisted to the crowd that Dukakis cared deeply about his family and could care about their families as well.

The crowd roared its approval.

"Am I not married to a great woman?" Dukakis beamed as he once again settled into his place at Kitty's side—while Neil Diamond's "Coming to America" blasted out of loudspeakers and the balloons hung over the podium began to dribble down like bubbles.

Kitty's new campaign role earned her favorable reviews from the press. Four days before the election, *Washington Post* columnist Mary McGrory took note that Dukakis's managers had "finally tumbled to the obvious fact that Dukakis does much better when his wife is beside him. They booked them for several joint appearances last week. John Sasso had the further inspiration to have the fiery Kitty introduce the candidate at several stops, to great effect.

"She brought genuine passion to the proceedings," McGrory wrote. "At Independence, Missouri, she spoke forcefully of her husband's sensitivity, citing his support when their newborn child died. It may not have been a presidential topic, but the Bushes brought up the subject with accounts of the death of their 3-year-old daughter. Mrs. Dukakis has none of her husband's reluctance to carry the fight to the enemy."

Indeed, as she introduced her husband during those final days, Kitty's fury at what she called "the vitriol of the Bush campaign" was apparent. "It's so much uglier than I think any of us anticipated. You've got to hope that whatever it is you're doing counteracts that kind of thing and that truth reigns," she said to one member of the media. Inadvertently, to the surprise of his inner circle, at a speech during a whistle-stop train tour through the Central Valley of California, Dukakis had begun calling himself a liberal. The word had simply slipped off his tongue, aides said later. Not surprisingly, the Bush camp duly ridiculed the governor. But once the word was out there, Kitty pumped it, putting her own spin on the "L-word." *The Wall Street Journal* reported:

"Introducing her husband, she refers to Republicans harping on the 'L-word' or liberal, but turns the attack back at Mr. Bush. 'There has been one "L" word my husband's opponent has used in this campaign,' she says. 'Lies.' The pressure of the final campaign push provokes a roller coaster of emotions, and the governor's wife, Kitty, isn't given to disguising her feelings: her face betrays a fatigue and some bitterness. The combined effort of her passionate introductions of the candidate and her anger at the Bush camp had Dukakis joking . . . 'If she were running, we'd be twenty points ahead.'"

It was, as the reporter pointed out, "a thick disguise of his own downbeat feelings." And for Kitty the effort of the last week of the campaign was only the beginning of an emotional roller coaster that would continue for months. First there was election day to get through. Then the aftermath of the defeat. A year after the election, the turbulence the loss seemed to have triggered inside her still hadn't begun to subside.

★   ★   ★

A long line stood outside the polling place at the Boston Public Library on Cambridge Street, a red-brick building near Massachusetts General Hospital. It was only 10:55 A.M. on November 8 as a chartered bus brought the sleepless press pack to the Four Seasons Hotel in downtown Boston. Reality began to sink in. Many had been on the road intermittently with Dukakis for twenty months. In the last seventy-two hours, they'd blitzed 8,500 miles in eleven states.

T-shirts distributed to the press said it all: I SLEPT WITH MIKE DUKAKIS. NOV. 5, NOV. 6, NOV. 7.

After the three-day, four-time-zone blur, this is what it all came to: voters standing in line, their participation in the election process measured only by the length of time it took them to get in and out of a polling place. From the look of it early in the day, some in the press thought the predictions might be off. Maybe after all the mudslinging and negativity, people would be inspired to turn out and either give George Bush the "mainstream mandate" he said he so desperately wanted, or enable Mike Dukakis to beat the odds in an upset that hadn't been seen since Truman beat Dewey.

The stony candidate and his entourage had arrived at around 10:00 A.M. at Logan Airport via a red-eye express that began on

the West Coast, stopping for a 3:30 A.M. rally in Des Moines and a
7:00 A.M. rally in Detroit. In his cross-country foray over the last
ten days of the campaign, Dukakis spent $18 million of his entire
$42.5 million war chest. In the final couple of weeks' push, he
outspent George Bush by $2 million.

Flying home with the candidate, Kitty had veered off in a last-
minute attempt to swing Pennsylvania voters her husband's way,
and greeted commuters at 7:00 A.M. in Philadelphia's 30th Street
Station. "This schedule was planned by a twenty-four-year-old
male," said a dead-tired Bonnie Shershow—joining other dazed
staff and press in an early-morning luggage hunt, after the candidate and his wife had greeted Boston well-wishers and headed off
to vote.

While the press corps journeyed from Logan Airport to downtown Boston, the candidate and his family motored to the Theresa
Morse apartments for the elderly, a polling place about two blocks
from Dukakis's home. The governor, Kitty, their three children,
and his mother, Euterpe, checked in at the polling room and
voted. As Dukakis exited his booth, the omnipresent Sam Donaldson, on hand for the ritual of Watching the Candidate Vote, asked:
"Who did you vote for?"

"You, Sam, you," Kitty joked, before Dukakis supplied the
network correspondent with an appropriate sound bite: "I voted
for Mike Dukakis and Lloyd Bentsen and I'm proud of it." A
small crowd nearby cheered dutifully. Outside more onlookers
roundly cheered him. He shook some hands and then got into the
limousine for a two-block ride back to 85 Perry Street. As the
family headed toward the house, a reporter cornered Dukakis's
eighty-five-year-old mother, asking her what she expected the out-
come of the election to be. She raised two fingers in a "V" sign
and said, "Victory."

The governor's daughter Andrea said simply, "It's good to be
home."

Ordinarily on election day there is not much for a candidate to
do but vote and then go home and wait for the returns to come in.
But Dukakis broke with that custom, darting out in the afternoon
to do some last-minute satellite feeds, beamed up from Boston's
WGBH to local stations in distant cities. On paper, the campaign

was pulling for eighteen targeted states. That afternoon, exit polls momentarily showed Dukakis within two or three percentage points of winning in some key parts of the country. It looked as if there might be just enough electoral votes to pull through. So the candidate was dispatched to scramble for fourteen last-ditch interviews in an hour and a half.

Viewers in Chicago saw Dukakis live on the evening news on WBBM-TV, the CBS affiliate. Makeup barely masking his fatigue, Dukakis made a last-minute plea to voters. Only an hour and forty-five minutes remained before the polls closed in Illinois. As the Duke's ashen face flashed on the screen, he implored people to get out and vote. "It's a cliffhanger. A lot like 1960. People in Chicago remember just how important Illinois was to JFK," Dukakis pleaded. "A last-minute drive could make an enormous difference."

WBBM's Walter Jacobsen, known for his scrappy style, pestered him. "Governor, where do you get those figures?" Dukakis ignored him. He didn't seem interested in putting up with another reporter's question, he only wanted to talk to Chicagoans watching the news who might still go out and vote.

Just after 6:00 P.M. East Coast time, Dukakis's son was doing his own version of get-out-the-vote in Boston. At the World Trade Center, the campaign's election-night headquarters, John spent a few minutes of his own talking live on the radio in a staccato keep-the-faith voice. His father's TV interviews were not planned, John related to Radio 1030 in Boston. "But in the afternoon we had every indication that this is going to be a very tight race throughout the country and especially in some key states. One state could make the difference. One vote in every precinct like in 1960 could make the difference. And that's why he went to the studio and is beaming himself across the country to different stations. To get out the vote."

Looking back at this marathon run, what could have been done differently? the radio host asked. John, who had hit forty-three states on his own, ignored the question. Until final numbers are in, he pleaded with listeners, go out and vote.

"Well, when we win," he insisted, "I think we'll be very satisfied with the way things have run. We're feeling very good about things. . . . We've been working hard. . . . Mike Dukakis and Lloyd Bentsen's message of being on the side of working families has made a real difference. Many people out there have felt that they're being controlled by the pundits and the pollsters. They feel they're being told how to vote and I think also people have felt they've been taken for granted by the Bush campaign for the last several weeks."

Was Dukakis ever discouraged? the reporter asked.

John skipped over this one. "I don't think so. If he was, he never let on to it. I think he's always believed in his candidacy and this was a year for Democrats."

"Some of the key states that people are saying Duke must win: California, New York, maybe even Texas," the interviewer prompted.

"I'm not sure," John said. Now was not the time to talk losing. "I think looking back we'll try to add up two hundred seventy and how we got to that. That's really the crucial thing at this point. There are many key states out there and real possibilities," he insisted urgently.

Wrapping up, the reporter then said what John wouldn't: "The Dukakis family [is] still believing that America can come about tonight."

Early in the day the airwaves were flooded with news reports predicting big voter turnouts. Massachusetts Secretary of State Michael Connolly expected a turnout as high as 86 percent. In St. Louis election officials expected between 73 and 75 percent. In California, where there was talk of voter gridlock over a confusing ballot, the secretary of state said turnout could be as high as 75 percent. At Harry's New York Bar in Paris, patrons participated in a straw poll—most going for Bush. When it was over, voter turnout overall was the lowest since 1924.

The election was over almost by the time aides started to arrive at Perry Street to watch the initial returns. In a year when the networks had promised cautious reporting of voting results and promised to take the long view, when ABC anchor Peter Jennings claimed, "We might have a real, old-fashioned election night on our hands," no such thing occurred. Not on the air more than a minute after opening CBS's election-night coverage at 6:00 P.M. East Coast time, Dan Rather called Indiana and Kentucky for Bush. Rather reported that Bush had gotten off to an expected early good start, with 53 to 47 percent of the vote going his way. "But there's so few votes counted, that it doesn't mean much just now," Rather allowed. As if to excuse himself for what he was doing. Rather underscored that the polls were still open in many states and then directed viewers: "Let me emphasize that the polls are still open and voting continues in many parts of the country at this hour. So if you haven't voted, just do it. Please go out and vote. Then come back and see your vote count," he invited viewers.

Polls closed in Florida, New Hampshire, Vermont, Virginia, and South Carolina at 7:00 P.M. eastern standard time. By 7:10 P.M., long before the polls closed out west, all three networks called Alabama, Georgia, Florida, and New Hampshire for Bush. At 8:00 P.M. polls closed in sixteen states. On CBS Dan Rather put nine of these in Bush's column. Shortly afterward Rather said Ohio went to Bush. It was a state that has picked the winner of every presidential race for fifty years and one Dukakis needed badly. Ohio gave Bush a total of 227 electoral votes, out of the 270 needed to win. Around 9:15 Bush won Missouri, giving him 277 electoral votes, seven more than needed. Rather announced, "Our CBS news estimate is that George Bush will be the next president of the United States." It was 6:15 in San Francisco. The polls were still open, but it was all over for a Dukakis presidency.

★　★　★

Kitty's aide, Bonnie Shershow, arrived at the Dukakis home on Perry Street at around 8:30 P.M. "The only people in the house were the family and a couple of staff people from the statehouse helping with dinner." Exit polls came in regularly from headquarters on Chauncy Street. Despite the tension, "It was very low key," Shershow said.

Another top aide described the scene more grimly: "It was like a wake."

"People were drifting around televisions in the living room," Shershow added. When the moment of defeat occurred Shershow remembered, "Kitty and I were standing in the kitchen and Michael came in wearing a maroon sweater. 'We just lost Missouri,' he said.

"And she said, 'Does that mean it's over?'

"And he said, 'Yeah.'

"And she said, 'How're you doing?'

"He said, 'I'm sad.'

"Then we just did a little small talk," Bonnie said. "But you know, it was sad. . . . It is. He worked hard. Everybody worked hard. But sad was the way it was. . . ."

Later that evening a limo took Kitty and Mike from Perry Street to the World Trade Center, where the candidate would publicly concede defeat, face the press, and console disappointed campaign workers. When they arrived, the couple took a back elevator to a private meeting room in the marble-walled skyscraper to talk with supporters and staff before meeting the press. Dozens of key players spilled out of the room, consoling one another. Campaign confidant Paul Brountas. Press secretary Dayton Duncan. Some over drinks, some with slaps on the back. Dukakis's younger daughter, Kara, walked into the room, signaling the arrival of the candidate. Dressed in black, she looked as if she'd been crying and was greeted by several of her girlfriends who flocked toward her, hovering protectively. "He can't believe it," she whispered of her father, disbelievingly. "He's in a rage."

After briefing the staff, Mike and Kitty then headed down to face the press from a podium embellished with a painting of the Statue of Liberty and shooting stars across a pale-blue backdrop. "D-U-K-E" was spelled out in balloons. Rows of bleachers were set up just across from the stage—a multitiered media stand was packed with photographers and blazing camera lights. A campaign sign, THE BEST AMERICA IS YET TO COME: DUKAKIS/BENTSEN '88, hung to one side.

Before getting their cue to start down a runway leading to the elaborate stage, Mike and Kitty stood by a side entrance staring blankly into space. Kitty, dressed regally in rich purple, looked down at the floor. To reporters watching them, the two appeared utterly dejected.

Then with supporters shouting "DUKE! DUKE! DUKE!" the governor, surrounded by his family, ceremoniously conceded defeat. After congratulating the vice-president for a "decisive victory," Dukakis faced his troops. Many young people packed themselves up against the stage. Dukakis tried to be positive. "I don't want you to be discouraged," he told them. "I want you to be encouraged by what you've learned. . . . There is nothing you can do in this world that is more fulfilling and satisfying than giving of yourself to others and making a contribution to your community, your state, your nation, and your fellow citizens." He was proudest, he told them, that thousands of young people had become involved in his campaign.

The crowd responded with somewhat obligatory-sounding shouts of "'92! '92! '92!" Grim-faced, Kitty came forward to stand at her husband's side. It was a tough moment, reflected in Kitty's and her family's frozen faces. The crowd continued to applaud and cheer. Kitty smiled back gamely for the cameras one last time. Dukakis's daughters fought back tears. Finally, stagehands, performing the equivalent of lowering the curtain, unloaded silver campaign confetti that fell like raindrops.

Later, in yet another crowded ballroom, a more select group of campaign workers milled around tables laden with trays of hotel cheese and dip, and waited anxiously for their candidate and his wife to arrive. Out of the view of the press, this would be the final dance, the last symbiotic embrace between the candidate and his staff. The last twirl of "he's good—we're good—Democrats are good—I'm good."

John Dukakis got up to say a few words.

"I think one of the most moving parts of this whole experience for our family was the convention. It wasn't just the acceptance speech . . . a lot of it was the staff party afterwards. Because all of you were so together. And while my dad has said there were ups and downs as part of this campaign . . . we certainly have the best staff of any presidential campaign."

John was drowned out as applause suddenly erupted and his parents walk into the room.

The crowd sent its love. This was family. No hostile press were around the room. Although they had worked for him for more than a year, many in the room had never spoken to Dukakis at length. And so they pressed closer and closer to the podium, behaving like any crowd of supporters.

Standing before them, basking in the glow, Kitty and the Duke seemed momentarily reenergized by the applause.

A staffer replaced John at the podium to usher in the final adieu. "All the staff collected a lot of our extra salary," she began, to hoots of laughter. "And came up with a present. It was nicely wrapped, but the Secret Service ripped it open," she said as she handed Dukakis a box. The candidate pulled out a spiffy new suede jacket. It replaced the look-alike version he'd borrowed from his advance man Jack Weeks. Ironically, in the pit of defeat the staff's gift seemed to be a last futile attempt to make Mike Dukakis into a man he was not. Dukakis tried again.

"Do you all know the story of this jacket?" he asked the crowd. Most of them did and laughed in anticipation of the retelling.

"I had one of those Seabee sports jackets, which I've always thought was perfectly fine," Dukakis began. The crowd laughed again.

"And," he continued slowly, relishing their every reaction, "I haven't kept it for twenty-five years, but it's been around for a while. And," he insisted, "it's perfectly fine.

"I brought it with me when we did the tour of Yellowstone. But everyone insisted that I wear Jack Weeks's suede jacket." More laughter.

"And . . . I thought that, you know, certainly Jack . . . was . . . kind of . . . yuppieish." At that apt description the group went into gales of laughter—for the handsome advance man Jack's penchant for dressing had provoked bemused comments from fellow staffers and ribald commentary from disheveled members of the press for months.

"He thinks of himself as a solid outdoorsman," Dukakis grinned, "but on the way back in these crazy last few days when we covered eighty-five hundred miles in eleven states in about two and a half days"—he sounded again as if he were facing the press—"I had to conclude that Jack Weeks's suede jacket was a pretty good way to address crowds at airports. . . . Now, obviously Jack Weeks's suede jacket belongs to Jack Weeks. Thanks to you I now have a suede jacket."

The crowd cheered. The staff woman bounced back up to recapture her place at the podium. It was Kitty's turn for a gift.

After more than two years on the campaign trail Kitty Dukakis had traveled a long, long way. She'd invited recognition that she was more than just Mike's wife. In two years, she'd evolved from a stiff, anxious speaker who worried aloud about how well she was received while delivering her husband's pat phrases—"Good jobs at good wages" and "the Massachusetts Miracle"—into an issues-oriented, Republican-bashing professional surrogate.

Kitty had tested the conventions of the past that bound political wives. She wasn't deferential. She didn't pretend to dislike politics, and she didn't try to stay out of the fray. She contradicted her husband in public—sometimes in front of reporters. She got involved in political decisions. She was a player at the kitchen table and wasn't shy about saying so. Her causes were controversial. She spoke out on foreign policy. As a Jew, she had taken flak for marrying a Christian but she took the campaign to Jewish communities in New York, Florida, and other states. She overcame her own doubts about Jesse Jackson and defended him. She helped quiet fears among Jews that Dukakis had cut a deal with Jackson on Middle East policy matters. She spoke of "people making mistakes," "retribution," "change and all the rest of it," despite her personal feelings that Jesse was "very difficult," "not very helpful," and "a negative force at many times."

Kitty's views on Cambodian refugees and strong feelings about reuniting families torn apart by war caused some to wonder what she would stir up with the Immigration and Naturalization Service, should her husband get elected. It was she, not the candidate, who announced the details of the campaign's position on AIDS to a crowd of more than a thousand in San Francisco.

She had very much wanted to carry that dynamism into the White House.

"I think she realized she could make a difference in the White House," her friend Anne Harney said. Harney recalled a time flying with Kitty from Cape Cod to Washington when she was scheduled to testify before a Senate subcommittee hearing on refugees. Anne remembered, "The pilot said, 'Hey, Kitty, you want to fly over your house?'

"And Kitty said, 'Why not?'

"So this little Learjet went n-n-n-n-r-r-r and went right down over the White House," Harney said, "and I looked down and I said, 'Kitty, can you believe that you might be living there?'

"She said, 'I just don't even let myself think about it.'"

The two talked about the possibility of Kitty's being first lady. "I said to her, 'You know, as the governor's wife, you can get things done that I can't,'" Harney recalled. "'You can pick up the phone and tap in to the number-one person on a project, and you have real clout. As first lady that clout will be even greater. You can really focus on the things that you care about and make a difference, whereas the average woman can't do that. Even the most powerful average woman can't do that. Whereas the White House has that availability. Has that potential."

Matter-of-factly, Kitty said, "That's right."

After tagging along the Dukakis campaign trail for more than a year, *Boston Globe* correspondent Tom Oliphant, a veteran of six presidential campaigns, had noticed Kitty's performance. He wrote: "Mrs. Dukakis makes clear a hundred times a day that she is not running for president herself, but her campaigning is almost never 'wifey'—it is overtly, unabashedly political. It is also essentially without precedent in modern presidential politics. For all the attention paid recently to Nancy Reagan's White House machinations and deep if occasionally intrusive involvement in her husband's presidency, Mrs. Reagan in public is still accurately summed up by her adoring, never-wavering stare at President Reagan while he speaks. And in 1980 and 1984, she never came close to addressing issues or offering opinions. But this has also been the rule on the Democratic side. Such wives of liberal and liberated Democratic nominees as Eleanor McGovern and Joan Mondale avoided partisan activity throughout their husbands' abortive quests, and Rosalynn Carter, while an activist president's wife, played a traditional role on the campaign trail.

"Without much notice, Kitty Dukakis is shattering these conventions daily as she tours the country. It is for her a natural role, given her high visibility in Massachusetts over the years, and it is taken for granted by most people in the press."

What was not clear, Oliphant and others pointed out, was how or whether voters were influenced by Kitty's campaigning and if what was good for Kitty was good for the campaign.

Urged on by an ambitious professional staff anxious to achieve success for themselves as well as for their candidate's wife, Kitty spent most of her time on the stump alone. Inside the Dukakis campaign her performance earned good reviews. "She sparkled," said Dukakis issues director Chris Edley, recalling the governor's wife one day on the stump in California. "She was really impressive. It made Michael's speech that followed seem kind of flat and listless. He was good, but she just sparkled."

When it was all over, Kitty said she was never sure how effective she really had been on the trail. Sometimes she wasn't even sure where she was going or why. Other women, relegated to the same campaign role in the past, had similar doubts.

"Whether the efforts of a political wife are truly effective, whether she actually influences a voter's vote, whether she can accurately portray her husband as a human to the public, is open to question, and I believe . . . other campaigning wives would agree," Eleanor McGovern wrote in 1974, after her husband's unsuccessful race. Kitty wondered the same thing.

"I don't know how you measure how many votes I got for Michael," she said after the election. "I don't know if that's measurable. It probably isn't."

The Dukakis campaign never commissioned a poll to find out. And none of her achievements were reflected at all in the gift the Dukakis staff had hurriedly prepared for Kitty that evening of her husband's defeat as she stood by Michael's side. There was no recognition of her professionalism. No recognition of her contribution to the campaign. Instead, the squealing staffer offered, "A romantic dinner with her husband at Jasper's restaurant!" "Woooooooo . . ." the young crowd responded. Kitty grinned gamely and thanked them all as warmly as she could.

★   ★   ★

For Kitty Dukakis the painful process of dealing with defeat escalated day by day. George Bush would have a couple of months before the inauguration to start his new job, but Mike Dukakis had to deal with the Commonwealth of Massachusetts the very next morning and promptly took the "T" back to work. He had budget problems to face—no one knew just how big at the time.

At 2:00 P.M. the afternoon following the election, Kitty joined her husband and son at the candidate's wrap-up news conference on the race. Dressed in a burnt-orange dress and jacket she sat beside John and watched her husband face a last barrage. Dukakis reiterated his congratulations to Bush "for a decisive victory." He thanked the press. "I know it wasn't easy the last few days. I apologize for that. You all look a little better than you did yesterday." In fact, they didn't.

Casually dressed staffers sat beside reporters in the packed room of the Four Seasons Hotel. Almost everyone still looked beat. Dukakis himself was only a slightly better shade of gray.

The first question to the governor came from Sam Donaldson, who in his customary way was perched in a front-row-center seat so as to be inescapable. "Some were arguing that peace and prosperity were so strong that no Democrat could have won," Donaldson said. "Where do you think you went wrong?" he asked bluntly.

"There's plenty of time for analysis," Dukakis started. "If you look at the results, maybe with a different combination of factors it was winnable. I think I lost states representing about one hundred thirty-three votes by four percentage points or less. If we won those states, we'd have had two hundred and fifty electoral votes and been very close to a winnable majority. . . ."

If. If. If.

The questions continued and covered the expected bases: What were the effects of negative campaigning? "The distortion of my record." Should he have responded to the negative attacks sooner? "One of the lessons of this campaign is you have to respond and you have to respond quickly." Did he spend too much time in the Massachusetts statehouse? "I think it would be a tragedy if one either had to be unemployed or hold an office—and I don't mean this in any way to belittle the vice-president—but to hold an office which doesn't have any statutory responsibility." The reply earned him a chuckle.

In his very last press conference Dukakis's answers were short. To the point. He had nothing to lose by clipping his answers. What will be Bush's biggest problem? "The federal budget deficit." How would he describe Bush's mandate? "I don't see a mandate." What contributed most to your defeat? "I don't think there's any question that the negativism that we had . . . is something that had an impact on me. . . ." Did he feel any sense of personal bitterness? "I'm not a bitter person. . . . Am I disappointed? Sure I am. It was a distorted campaign. It was a campaign that distorted my record and I think did not set high standards for the kind of campaign we want for the presidency and may well set a standard that we live to regret."

The best line of the hour came when Joe Day, a political reporter for Channel 7 in Boston, reminded Dukakis that the man he'd called "the sleaziest," Jim Baker, was already the secretary of state. "I believe in the redemption of souls, Joe," Dukakis quipped. Reporters, many of whom had been with the man for over a year, laughed out loud and applauded Michael Dukakis's rare display of unscripted humor.

Two days would go by before Kitty would face the press by herself. There were seventeen hours of sleep to get and a lunch with staff to attend. By Friday many reporters had left Boston but there was still a short lineup for interviews.

Mike, his last interview behind him, had let his Secret Service detail go on the afternoon of November 10. That evening he went out grocery shopping with his stepson.

For the first time in months no one screened visitors who arrived at 85 Perry Street on the afternoon of November 11. Inside, the house was abnormally quiet. A couple of aides in casual attire moved about—slowly, answering the phone and the door as an occasional delivery man dropped off yet another bouquet in a house beginning to mount with bouquets. The living room, clean and empty, functioned as intended, no longer an improvised television studio. A bank of plants tucked between the peach-colored sofa and the front bay windows of the house looked well watered in the afternoon sunlight. A silver-framed photo of Kitty, dressed in flaming red and surrounded by her family onstage at the Omni Coliseum, sat prominently on a side table. Family doodads rested on the fireplace and tables: a collection of Japanese dolls, a Steuben glass apple, a small Greek bust, two old-fashioned square brass clocks.

Only a lone television plunked on the floor next to the marble mantelpiece hinted at the activity of a few days before. That and a florist's note tucked into a two-foot-wide bouquet of pink day lilies and wildflowers in the hallway. If the flowers set off a metal detector, the note said, it was because they were wired together.

John Dukakis walked through the house greeting reporters gathered to talk to his mother for what might be the last time. Sporting chinos, running shoes, and a bright red Bradley University sweatshirt he picked up in Peoria, Illinois, he wolfed down a sandwich as he walked. His sister Andrea, fresh from a shower, came downstairs to pick up a bouquet sent as a gift for her twenty-third birthday. John's wife, Lisa, in the final stage of her first pregnancy, opened mail at the kitchen table.

It felt surprisingly like any household where the kids were gathered for a holiday or special family occasion. Mike was at the office. The house seemed almost back to normal until a camera crew bounded boisterously through the front door and one by one reporters lined up for their interviews. The list wasn't nearly as long as it had been earlier in the campaign. Three local reporters, television and print, wanted to know what had come up only once in Mike's Wednesday press conference: How did the candidate feel? And how would the Dukakises adjust to the defeat and return to normal life?

Unlike her children, when the lady of the household descended the stairs she was elegantly dressed in a smart, form-fitting red-and-black tartan jacket, fashionably short skirt, and gold-tipped Chanel pumps. But fancy clothes couldn't mask Kitty's fatigue. She looked exhausted. Drawn. A reporter surprised her, telling her how sad she'd looked on election night: "Very much in control, but sad." Her face was angular and stiff from tension. As she talked, her deep husky voice took on different tones, depending on the reporter's question. Sometimes she spoke authoritatively. Then her voice grew thin, almost reedy—as it caught with emotion.

Fatigue aside, Kitty had a job to do that day. One more time she acted as the window to her husband's emotions. Donned the mantle of her husband's defender. Reporters again turned to her to ask, "When did you know it was all over?" "How did the candidate react?" And worse, "How does defeat *feel*?"

Above all else Kitty was there to reassure the local press—and more important, the taxpayers of Massachusetts—that they still had a governor who cared about *them,* who, after an absence of almost a year, could face the resentment that would come after he had failed to grace the state with a favorite son in the White House. He was ready to deal with problems left behind while he sought higher office. She was there to reassure everyone that the governor was okay and would quickly and happily get acclimated to living again in his home state as its highest elected public servant. It wasn't until months later that it became clear that nothing could have been farther from the truth.

Despite her exhaustion Kitty seemed to know instinctively that was the only message that she had to get across. She had to reassure her audience that Mike Dukakis was not too big to run the state. That he hadn't outgrown his britches. That dreams of meeting Gorbachev aside, he hadn't forgotten who he was. Where he was from. What his job was all about.

"So you didn't wait at all, I see, with the Secret Service protection?" asked Adam Nagourney, a short chatterbox from the New York *Daily News,* who for once had taken off his signature Yankees baseball cap. "And I guess, in a way, that must drive home the fact that it's over?" The first of five half-hour interviews got going.

"Oh, yes," Kitty replied. "That's reality. I think it's important for him to begin—and everyone handles this differently—it's certainly going to take some time. You don't go through what he's gone through and the family's gone through for twenty months and decompress suddenly. There's a whole physical and psychological part that's going to take some time." She spoke slowly, thoughtfully.

How can you prepare for a defeat of this magnitude? Nagourney wanted to know. Did she ever sit down with her husband and talk about the possibility of defeat?

"You know, we all deal with the possibility in our own way. I think each one of us having gone through '78 . . . I had a sense that things weren't going the way they should, certainly six or seven weeks ago," she explained. Yes, they had a sense of what could happen. No, they didn't spend a great deal of time talking to each other about losing.

"I think we knew we had a job to do and needed the energy to do the job that had to be done. There were so many people depending on it," Kitty said, adding, "You couldn't help but be fortified by the hundreds of thousands of people who came out at these rallies by the end. . . . [And] on the other hand, there's always—until it's over—there's always the sense of hope. I think we had several hours of hope on Tuesday afternoon. . . . So close. They really were. So many of those important states we were two and four points apart and so there was a sense of excitement and possibility. And there really was a surge. That surge wasn't manufactured at all. It was really there those last couple of weeks."

When Nagourney asked Kitty how her husband reacted when he realized that the race was lost, her voice constricted. "Fine," she said shortly. "You know, I think all of us were ready for the campaign to be over, come what may. And certainly disappointed and sad about it. But very philosophical and I think healthy in our attitudes."

"It must have been tough," Nagourney offered. She agreed but swiftly moved on to emphasize the input of support from family and friends. Also important, she said, was the sense that they "had done everything that could be done," especially in the last month.

She conceded Bush did a better job of pushing negative buttons. "I don't think there's any question that—I think Mr. Atwater was the one who said that they had a job to do—and George Bush was willing to do anything to reach that goal." Overall, she found such campaign tactics disappointing. "I've said over and over again, you can make judgments about the values and character of a candidate by how that candidate performs. Mr. Bush was willing to make all kinds of statements and charges and advertising that were just . . . calculated and, in many cases, totally untrue.

"I mean the flag burning was just a part of that," she went on. "They had no picture 'cause there wasn't any picture. And yet when you say something—regardless of its truth or not—it begins to take on a life of its own and there are so many of those untruths, as it turns out, that are thrown out there. . . . I think there are many people in this country who believe that if it's in print it must be true."

She agreed that Lee Atwater understood that concept a lot better than most.

After Kitty quenched the reporters' curiosity about the candidate and his ability to adjust to normal life, talk turned to her. Kitty told reporter after reporter that afternoon that she was happy to be home. Someone asked, "How will you deal with a transition like this emotionally? You've been on top of this wave."

Her voice softened, while her body and face stiffened uncomfortably. Her liquid eyes gave her feelings away. They were piercingly, hauntingly sad. "Yeah. I think it's going to take some time," she said. "We're disappointed. I feel sad about it."

Almost every reporter at Perry Street that afternoon asked Kitty that painful question. Each time she reshaped her answer slightly. The fourth time she was asked if it would be hard for her and the governor to adjust, she said simply, "No, not at all."

Kitty admitted that the campaign had changed her. "I do know that none of us will ever be the same again." Although subsequent events would prove otherwise, that day she said she felt stronger. More confident. More capable. Even though she "got tired very often," her energy level grew. She was inspired by people along the trail, she said. And her horizons were broadened in ways she didn't think possible.

By late afternoon, past four o'clock, two television crews had come and gone. A quiet chill of early winter settled over the house. The last interview of the day would be with the big hometown paper. *The Boston Globe*'s Joan Vennochi, five months pregnant, disarmed Kitty by making baby talk for a few minutes. "How did you get pregnant on the campaign?" Kitty asked. Vennochi laughed, explaining that she left the trail months ago to rejoin her husband in Boston.

Joan, a dark-haired young woman in her mid-thirties, apologized for what she said would inevitably be repetitive questions, then teased gently: "But maybe you'll give a real answer."

"Well, I think I've given real answers," Kitty started. Vennochi's chatty technique helped some. Kitty got as honest as she was going to get.

How did she handle the flag-burning rumor that Senator Symms began? Vennochi asked, as had her predecessors that afternoon. Kitty responded that it was then that the full breadth of the Republican strategy hit her. "I think I knew at that point that this was going to be a campaign that was full of distortions. . . . We discussed it and I talked about it being outrageous and untrue."

Why didn't Dukakis fight back sooner? Along the way, did she say to her husband, 'Mike, do something'? Vennochi queried. Kitty said sometimes she did because "people were talking to me along the campaign trail." But never having been involved in a national campaign, her husband had to listen to his own instincts as well as the people around him. "I'm not convinced . . . that it was Michael's lack of response to the negative campaigning that lost this election," she mused.

"Were there times when there were charges, or even things the press wrote, that made you angry?"

"I think I got angry when Senator Symms made that outrageous charge. I certainly was disturbed at the kind of manufacturing of untruth that began with psychiatrists and medical records and Michael's patriotism . . . the impugning of Michael's patriotism. But you can't stay angry in the context of a campaign because you're not very effective if you are."

Why was this different from '78?

"There were gnawing feelings that were there. And a certain reality quotient that we didn't expect in '78. All of us, in our own way, were making those preparations. This is a very mercurial kind of atmosphere to be in. It's a roller coaster."

John Dukakis ducked his head into the room. Kitty reminded him to run an errand before the stores closed. Andrea popped in, excusing herself politely, and said that she wasn't sure whether her girlfriend would make it to her birthday dinner celebration that evening.

The conversation wrapped up and Kitty readied herself to meet the governor at the statehouse. After sitting through all the interviews, Kitty's press secretary, Paul Costello, beelined it to the phone. Within minutes he was joking, seemingly relieved to have come to the end of his day of holding the hand of the bereaved. In a few days he headed off to California for a vacation.

Heading out to the driveway, Vennochi paused and started to laugh. Standing by the front door, she pointed down at the floor and giggled, spotting a large pile of the candidate's telegenic red neckties in a corner of the hallway—ready for the dry cleaner's.

CHAPTER ELEVEN

Coping with Defeat

Given the widespread view of presidential campaigning as an exhausting, demeaning, soul-
destroying horror, it's remarkable how many
people, having done it once, want nothing else in
life but to do it again. The experience is intoxicating, in both senses: it exhilarates even as it poi-
sons.

—HENDRIK HERTZBERG, *The New Republic*

June 16, 1989. Seven months after the election. Three months
since her treatment at Edgehill. Kitty Dukakis breezed with a
smile through the halls of the Massachusetts statehouse, bounded
through the foyer of her husband's office, and turned toward her
own. Wearing designer garb, a flashy aqua and black polka-dotted
jacket dress, Kitty settled behind her desk for a chat with a
reporter. Her spunk was back. She looked as good as she ever
had on the campaign. At the time it seemed everything was once
again OK.

Her office, located just down the hall from her husband's, reflected facets of her personality with mementos from her life. A
whimsical pink paper butterfly kite flew from the ceiling. One of
her husband's pressed suits hung on a hanger behind the door.
His official portrait filled one small wall. There were snapshots of
her kids, a poster of wildflowers from Martha's Vineyard, a
Jerusalem candle and trinkets from other travels. A standard-issue
air conditioner worked away noisily in the tiny room.

On this warm summer day, halfway into the first year of the

Bush administration, Kitty talked at length about the campaign, about Edgehill, and about her life. "In the final analysis," Kitty said, "I was grateful things [the election] worked out the way they did because I know I wouldn't be able to handle it. . . . I very much wanted Michael to win, but in hindsight it would have been difficult," she said. "It's a hard thing. I wanted it very much, and who knows what would have happened [had we won]? Except the progression of this disease is such that I would have eventually gotten into trouble. . . . And being in the White House and getting into trouble is really hard. It would have been very hard to get help in that kind of situation."

★ ★ ★

When Kitty Dukakis checked herself into Edgehill-Newport, questions immediately arose over whether or not she was indeed an alcoholic. "Until shortly after election day on November 8, Kitty never had a problem with alcohol," her husband told the press. And none of her staff—and none of the people who traveled with her, including Paul Costello and her close aide Bonnie Shershow—ever saw her abuse alcohol. At most, they said they saw her take a drink or two at the end of a long day. But after the campaign she admitted she had been drinking on the trail, binging heavily at least twice before the New York primary. Kitty later said, as she had said of her amphetamine problem before, that she was good at hiding her drinking. "Like all alcoholics, I was very clever. I didn't drink in front of anybody. And so nobody saw me drinking," she told a group of Villanova University students only a week after coming out of treatment. Still, given the rigors and demands of her schedule on the trail, many wondered how she could have functioned effectively had she been drinking heavily. At the time even some of her close friends were skeptical. Her problems turned out to be more complicated than that.

"I personally don't believe she's an alcoholic. I just think she was very depressed and she used that as a crutch. She was very sad after the campaign," one friend said right after Kitty came out of Edgehill. "She'll get over it."

Whatever she or her doctors chose to call it, what was clear, and became clearer with time, was that Kitty was extremely down and drinking dangerously, to the point where she frightened herself and her husband.

Friends said the letdown from being the toast of the town to being a wife at home with too much time on her hands was more than Kitty could bear. "She wasn't doing a whole lot," Shershow said. "She went from having every minute scripted to having no structure at all."

Dukakis himself initially tied Kitty's problem to politics, telling reporters "a combination of physical exhaustion, the stress of the campaign, and the postelection letdown" caused it. His comments produced headlines: "Kitty Dukakis in Alcohol Treatment Program: Governor Blames Campaign Stress for Wife's Problem" (*The Washington Post*); "Kitty Dukakis Seeks Treatment: Problems with Alcohol Blamed on Election Loss" (*Rocky Mountain News*); "Thrown by Loss, Kitty Enters Alcohol Clinic: Duke Cites Exhaustion, Stress, Letdown" (New York *Daily News*).

When Kitty had her chance to explain what had happened, she insisted to reporters that she was an alcoholic and had been before her husband was defeated. Subsequent events would make it seem far more likely that Kitty had been battling serious depression. In an election year—and an era—when candidates for president cannot admit to suffering from depression, let alone seek treatment for it the same appeared to hold true for their wives. Barbara Bush decided not to seek help even when, as she said, her husband felt she needed it for her self-described yearlong bout with depression. Kitty got help, but if she was suffering from depression—as many of her friends thought and as she later acknowledged—at the time she wouldn't, or couldn't, say so. When specifically asked by a reporter if she had sought treatment for depression at Edgehill, Kitty vehemently said, "No!"

Kitty also denied that her problems were caused by the presidential race. "It was not the campaign that caused it," she explained. "It could have been any crisis. The campaign was a very positive experience, and the only thing that happened wrong was that we lost." Given the engrossing life-style of national politics, Kitty's deep involvement in her husband's campaign, and the way she seemed to thrive on the celebrity status it gave her, many wondered how Kitty could separate the stresses of the campaign—and the stresses generated by the loss—from the heavy drinking she said she engaged in periodically on the trail and afterward.

★   ★   ★

The psychological aftereffects of political defeat are only beginning to be documented and understood. Defeat is not something most politicians dwell on or like to discuss publicly. Kitty Dukakis's experience pointed to the complexities of one woman's fragile psyche and personal trial with substance dependency accompanied by depression. But Kitty's experience also raised questions: Could she have handled the pressures and demands in the White House? Given the scurrilous nature of the 1988 race, it's not difficult to imagine what might have been made of tidbits from Kitty's medical history. Innuendo tactics aside, was that information that voters had a right to know? On the trail and afterward, Kitty said no. She wasn't the one running for office, after all. On a more personal level Kitty's experience also raised questions about the demands she put upon herself, and the demands of a political system in which a female spouse is primarily limited to sending the message: "Your candidate, my husband, is an honest, caring family man whom you can trust."

"In a campaign you are so focused that when it's over it's like there is nothing left. The support groups, your staff, the campaign committees disband. When the goal is not achieved, you're suddenly left with: 'Where do we go from here?,'" said Carolyn Mutz, an educational psychologist and wife of Indiana's former lieutenant governor. In 1977 she helped start a support group for political families called Partners in Politics. "It is a very difficult transition. I can see that would involve a grieving process. It's a loss like a divorce is a loss. A death. A job. It's a loss of a direction, a goal, a focus, and it has to be considered that way and there has to be time to heal." But, Mutz continued, "Our culture doesn't allow political people to grieve. Doesn't allow them to be human. That's a very important part of the process. They really block that. You're supposed to really act like you didn't really care. The trick is not to get caught up in other people's expectations."

"Generally members of a political family have an investment in the candidate's career," said Mwalimlu Imara, a professor at the Morehouse College of Medicine in Atlanta and a member of the board of directors of the Elisabeth Kübler-Ross Center in Virginia. Also an Episcopal priest, Imara has counseled political families who have found it more acceptable to seek help from a priest than a psychiatrist. "[That investment] influences how they deal with one another, how they interact with the public and most other life decisions. The degree to which each family is involved in the political career differs. But even in families where a political spouse is out working on a separate career, a lot of decisions hinge on what the politician does.

"Losing kicks that basic foundation out from under them. Suddenly the dynamics of how the family interacts are abruptly changed. Just as a family has to learn to grieve and get over a death, so too does the losing political family have to reacquaint itself with a life outside of politics or outside of a particular elected position."

William S. Appleton is a psychiatrist at the Massachusetts Health Center and an assistant clinical professor of psychiatry at the Harvard Medical School. He has counseled political families and studied the effects of an election defeat. Though each individual copes differently, reactions to a loss can be "curious," he has written. Defeat can be especially difficult for the candidate's spouse.

In a paper titled "Psychiatric Danger of Running for Office," published in the journal *Perspectives in Biology and Medicine*, Appleton wrote: "The pressure on a politician's wife to serve her husband selflessly comes from him, from his political family [or staff], and from the public. She is supposed to participate in a certain way, to accompany him smilingly in parades, at public functions, dinners, and coffees, to convey an image of the happy American family with which the voters can identify. . . . She is expected to participate in the campaign even if she has no interest in it at all or finds it painful to appear in public. One wife took her role so seriously that she believed she was responsible for her husband's defeat in a close election.

"Thus a political wife is expected to conduct herself as a Victorian woman, to submerge her own personality and devote herself to the career of her man. The modern spouse may not want to do so—with resulting marital discord—or may try to cooperate against her real wishes while feeling depressed and angry."

Appleton also noticed that in the aftermath of a defeat some political couples he had observed were "so used to being apart that they had to continue the pattern once the election was over. Like couples whose children grow and depart, leaving them alone with one another for the first time in perhaps thirty years to find they no longer know or enjoy each other, many political couples seem to dread one another's company in an almost phobic way. They arrange never to be alone together, much the way a person arranges never to be in an airplane or an elevator."

Perhaps most difficult of all in the families he studied was getting back to life as it was before the election. Appleton wrote: "Return to private life is accompanied by disorientation and feelings of unreality. Just as a man must undergo a marked transformation at the beginning of his campaign, so he must, like a returning veteran, undergo a reconversion to ordinary living at the end. After nine months of viewing life almost twenty-four hours a day in terms of winning office and getting votes, and having talked almost entirely to members of a small political-family group, the candidate and his wife no longer know whether matters which once seemed vitally important are in fact significant at all."

For months after his defeat, his popularity plummeting, his political problems rising, Mike Dukakis shunned the press. Weeks passed before he and Kitty took a vacation. Though in January 1989 he announced that he would not seek another term as governor, it was not until his 1990 State of the State address that he publicly discussed the presidential defeat. His manner was viewed by some as arrogance that only fueled resentment among Massachusetts voters who'd cheered their favorite son but were furious about the state's fiscal problems. Periodically, a few concerned aides and reporters got a glimpse of how the governor was doing. One aide visited Dukakis a few weeks after the election and described him as a "depressed" man. The aide was at a loss as to what he, or anyone else, should expect. "In psychotherapeutic terms, what is a healthy response to this situation?" he asked. "I don't know. What's the model? I don't know. These are complicated people. You have to figure out the context for judging them."

Robin Toner covered the Dukakis campaign for *The New York Times*. Late in February 1989 she elicited just a few words from the governor and wrote: "Dukakis looks like a changed man. His eyes are dark with sadness, a look not unlike that of Walter Mondale in 1985 or Jimmy Carter in 1981."

Sandy Bakalar, who has known Mike Dukakis since high school, said when she saw her friend Michael turn into candidate Michael she didn't like what she saw. "I saw my friend Michael all alone in a bubble and I wouldn't want to see that again," she said. "This is the leader of the democratic free world. That is him alone. He has to stand alone. No amount of manipulation can detract from that. . . . And while I think my candidate was a wonderful candidate, I think what he did was he stood alone but he was really lonely alone."

The way Bakalar saw it, Dukakis could not get angry. "He couldn't defend himself in any kind of personal way. He could depersonalize. That has always been fine for Michael," she explained. "But he has never been big ego—'I this,' and 'I that.' He has always been a 'we' person. He has always been pulling people together. I think when it came to stand up and defend 'me,' 'I,' 'Michael S. Dukakis,' he just couldn't do it. I don't know why he couldn't do it. Was that a function of his feeling lonely?" she asked. "I don't know. I don't know if it separated him from the people he was really close to who were working for him. . . . He got so involved in the process that he lost his identity. He got so involved with being in Iowa here, and that place there, and that place there, that the big picture gets lost. George Bush didn't lose it, but Michael's style is very different than George Bush's."

In the spring of 1989 the wounds were still wide open among family members. Asked how the governor was doing, John Dukakis deflected the question with one of his own. "What did Walter Mondale say when someone asked him recently how long it took him to get over the 1984 loss?" John smiled wryly, then supplied the answer. "'I'll tell you when it stops hurting.'"

"The loss affected everybody in this campaign, including Kitty," her brother-in-law, Al Peters, said. "There was a letdown for everybody who was involved in the campaign. It was a grieving process. I could say, in my own case, certainly the grieving process lasted a good three months. That was common for most of us—it took two to three months, including Michael, I believe. I think that Kitty, since she probably was at a higher place during the last month of the campaign, came down off that combat high, so to speak. She probably had a further distance to come down than some of us who weren't quite so high."

After she seemed to have gotten some perspective on the campaign, Kitty said in June 1989 that the election had left her and her husband in different orbits. Unlike the past, when she nursed her husband back from his gubernatorial defeat, this time she said she felt the loss as much for herself. "This time, unlike 1978, although I was concerned about Michael, I was really wallowing in my own pain so much I really wasn't very helpful." Feeling alone and unsure of what she was going to do, she didn't know "what life had in store for me." There was a book contract and a speaking tour. Both would keep her locked in the past, unable to move on. "None of that seemed terribly relevant," she said. "I just was feeling very sorry for myself. I didn't know quite what I was going to be doing."

And Kitty was alone. Within days of the defeat her campaign staff had left town. Her two closest aides in Boston, Chris Noel and Bonnie Shershow, declined Kitty's offers to stay on staff at the statehouse and help her shape her postelection life. Some of her closest friends said they were unsure whether she wanted company or not and held back. No one was fully aware, it turned out, of the depths of Kitty's despair. Weeks went by and several dangerous drinking bouts occurred before Kitty's first "cry for help," as one of her intimates called it, began to be heard.

For spouses, defeat can be especially hard since they often get more emotionally involved in the campaign than the candidates and have difficulty believing the public doesn't see their husbands the way they do. For months afterward, Kitty continued to urge her husband to consider running again in 1992, believing that he could make a political comeback.

In 1975 Abigail McCarthy commented on the aftershock of her former husband, Gene McCarthy's, 1968 loss, telling *The Washington Post*'s Myra MacPherson: "No one understands what it is to nurse a man through defeat. There is a depression of cataclysmic proportions—a loss like a death in the family. He questions how 'wanted' he was . . . when it's over there is such a sense of defeat."

Betty Ford described herself as "bitter and depressed" at her husband's election loss to Jimmy Carter after "twenty-eight years of faithful service" to the country. "I thought the American people had made a big mistake."

When, in turn, the Carters were defeated in November 1980, Rosalynn Carter was similarly devastated. Not only did the Carters face defeat, but the couple discovered they were almost broke since their personal finances had been mismanaged while held in a blind trust. Mrs. Carter remembered her husband asking her one day long before then, when they were still in the Georgia state- house: "When my term as governor is up and we come home to Plains to live, what are we going to do the second day?" At the time the two had laughed. "Now it was no laughing matter," she said in the book she and her husband wrote together about their adjustment to life after the White House.

Although Carolyn Mutz knew of Kitty Dukakis's problems only through television and newspaper stories, she offered the term "postelective depression" as a working diagnosis for someone who had spent two years in pursuit of the presidency and failed. Mutz told reporters that problems like Kitty's could come partly from a feeling of helplessness, losing control of her destiny, and a lack of meaning in her life. She said the life of a candidate's wife is one constantly filled with activity, "but there is little time for reflection on the meaning of the activity. And there is the conflict between the unrealistic expectations by the public and the reality of being human in a normal family.

"Politics does take over your entire life," she said. "It takes over your social life. Your family life. It is your husband's working life. It's a two-person career—where there are certain expectations for the partner and no paycheck. There is no time to pursue your own career and build up your own self-esteem."

For someone like Kitty, who has described herself as low on self-esteem, public life on one level may have only exacerbated a feeling shared by many performers and candidates: that you are only as good as your audience tells you you are.

"It's important . . . to always make certain that one hundred percent of [one's] identity doesn't become a function of how many people decide to vote for you," Hattie Babbitt said at the time Kitty entered Edgehill.

Kitty insisted to the press and to friends that her personal inse- curity was at the root of her reaction to the defeat. "Who knows?" Sandy Bakalar asked. "She thinks that insecurity has been there for a very long time and that bandages were slapped on. The cam- paign was maybe a big bandage . . . and also a kind of placebo. When that was removed, you stand there naked."

Al Peters, a retired dentist and himself a recovering alcoholic, who helped Kitty make her decision to enter the Hazelden clinic in

Minnesota in 1982, tied his sister-in-law's postelection condition to her addictive personality.

"After the campaign was over, a lot of the restraints were removed, as far as behavior was concerned," Peters said. "You don't have to have your hair done every day, your fingernails done every day, be wearing designer clothes every day. If you wanted to have three drinks instead of two, that's all right. So the natural restraints on her drinking were removed and she progressed into the early stages of alcoholism quite rapidly, which is not unusual. Alcoholism takes many different courses in many different people. In women, for example, it can progress far more rapidly and acutely than in males, because of biological factors."

In Peters's view, the presidential campaign did not cause Kitty's postelection problems. "It's like saying if she had diabetes, she could say that diabetes was caused by the campaign, or she came down with cancer," he argued. "A chemical dependency is a disease. Stress does not cause chemical dependency . . . but the stresses of a campaign can accelerate an already existing, underlying chemical dependency.

"Society has difficulty in understanding and conceptualizing Kitty's alcoholism because it was in its early stages. But there's no question that Kitty is an alcoholic, and that we were able to achieve intervention of alcoholism in the early stages.

"Alcoholism is a disease of feelings, essentially," Peters went on, talking one spring afternoon in his airy, plant-filled home on Cape Cod. "The tendency is to cover up your feelings as a consequence of your alcoholism and not display them publicly. . . . Everyone who uses any drug, including alcohol, uses it in order to feel better, or comfortable at a social gathering, more congenial, happier perhaps, no doubt; courageous perhaps if you're facing an anxiety situation; you know, to reduce anxiety. Chemically dependent people end up using in order to feel better or to change one's feelings in a positive way. But they end up feeling worse after they've used, and they end up using just to feel normal, and then no matter how much they use, they don't feel normal.

"But I think that in order to learn to live drug free, you have to learn to cope with feelings."

★   ★   ★

By the time a politician wins a presidential nomination and has brought his family to the top of the political heap, they all must be inured to the vicissitudes of political life. Maybe they must even thrive on them. Although would-be presidents and first ladies go to inordinate lengths to seem like "just folks" and to "care" about people, the higher they rise in politics, the further removed they are from the public they would serve. This irony is an occupational hazard of public life.

Kitty appeared to yearn to make the leap into that realm where presidents and first ladies live. Though the downshifting and readjustment afterward proved traumatic, during the campaign she seemed to understand the necessity of transcending the everyday, and was all too ready to do so. Her husband, to his political peril, couldn't shift gears, some said. He insisted on keeping one hand in the Massachusetts statehouse and the other on his twenty-five-year-old snowblower.

Watching the governor cling to the familiar drove some campaign aides crazy. Patricia O'Brien, Dukakis's first press secretary, watched in frustration as the governor resisted becoming "the larger-than-life leader" Democrats yearned for. "As the front-runner, Dukakis lost the normalcy of life that he most treasured," O'Brien wrote in an essay published by Columbia University's Gannett Center for Journalism, where she turned up after leaving the campaign. "When we would pull into his driveway after a campaign trip at three in the morning, he would gripe about not being able to trim back the rose bushes. He regretted not regularly riding the streetcar from his home in Brookline to the Statehouse. Reporters liked to refer to it as his 'beloved' trolley, but only ordinary people do that, not people running for President."

In O'Brien's view, Dukakis was "clinging to normalcy." She wrote: "Two things about Michael Dukakis's run for the Presidency seem true. First, content with the Governorship of Massachusetts, he didn't really expect to win the nomination when he announced his candidacy. Second, once nominated, he didn't hunger enough. 'Enough' is to plunge into isolation and live wholly for the race. Above all, 'enough' is the ability to see oneself as more than an ordinary person. Becoming a symbol of values and direction for millions of people is not an easy job qualification to fill, but great leaders do just that. Maybe Dukakis's ego wasn't large enough. Although large egos make most people odd and unlikable, they have produced Presidents without awe, who look on the White House as their rightful, natural place. Michael Dukakis, to his credit and his detriment, is too much a man of common sense to envision himself easily as President."

During the campaign, it appeared easier for Kitty to throw the safety net away.

After the election, it seemed to some of the Dukakises' close friends that the loss spun Mike and Kitty into separate spheres of grief—each was unable to reach out and comfort the other. One close associate likened their response to that of a couple who has just lost a child, an experience the Dukakises had already shared, and even made into a set piece of their campaign speeches.

This loss was different. More individual. For Kitty it was exacerbated by a volatile, depression-prone personality.

Anne Hawley, former head of the Massachusetts Arts Council, has known Kitty for thirteen years. The two shared a long-standing interest in the arts. "If you're someone who's subject to great highs and great lows—if that's the kind of person you are, and that's the kind of person Kitty is—you feel life so intensely at both levels and there is not a lot in between," Hawley said knowingly one afternoon in her office overlooking Boston Common. "The combination of highs and lows. The attacks. The 'being loved' is just awfully complicated stuff for any human being to go through."

Hawley viewed Kitty's experience as "a modern tragedy." She elaborated: "I think if you look at anybody who is living on the edges, with the kinds of risks they take and the kinds of exposure they give themselves, you're going to find intense vulnerability at the other end. . . . It's hard for me to think of anyone who is very exceptional at what they do who isn't subjected to this"—she paused to find the right word—"internal despair. If you don't feel it, you're partly kidding yourself and you're not fully human. I think that's what's going on with Kitty."

The demands of a presidential campaign have kept and continue to keep qualified individuals from the Oval Office. When asked why he didn't want to run for president, Speaker of the House Tom Foley, for one, said: "In order to run for president, you have to have the fire in the belly. You have to really desire that office. The kind of demands that are made on the family, the individuals, for months, even for years, the kind of casting everything—life, fortune, sacred honor, finances, debt—into the question of being the nominee, much less the president, you have to really desperately want the prize. I don't have the passion to be president."

Eleanor Roosevelt, perhaps the most admired of modern first ladies, might well have endorsed Foley's view. Looking back over her many years in public service, she measured the toll of politics on her family life. "I doubt if the public realizes the price that the whole family pays in curtailment of opportunity to live a closer family life," she wrote in her memoirs. "Much has to be sacrificed by all to the public interest and there is little or no personal compensation for the members of the family.

"There are, of course, pride in a man's achievement and gratitude if he is able to help his countrymen and the world. . . . When sufficiently disciplined, a family may be glad that a man has the opportunity to fulfill his heart's desire and they will work with him in every way they can to help him to achieve his objectives. But something of the personal relationship must be lost. It is the price paid for a life spent almost entirely in public service."

The magic of the handlers and spin doctors aside, the reality is that all family stories don't reflect as much sweetness in life as they do under television lights. Betty Ford has written honestly of the personal troubles she and her family endured while in the White House and after, when she and her husband settled in a new house in Palm Springs, California. "For anyone who thinks otherwise, let me tell you being an occupant of the White House is no breeze. You have no private life, the demands on your time are constant, you are under terrible pressure," Mrs. Ford wrote in her 1987 book, *Betty: A Glad Awakening.*

Perception, not reality, is what counts. Dukakis campaign manager Susan Estrich singled out the 1984 Reagan/Mondale race as an example where Democrats lost on "family issues" to a man whose ties to his own family appeared tenuous at best. "The reality was that Ronald Reagan never saw his grandchildren and Fritz Mondale was a devoted family man," Estrich said. "But the perception has Reagan associated with family values and Mondale somehow puffing a cigar in a room with the union leaders."

When the facade breaks down, especially in the midst of battle, it can doom a campaign. One need only think back to the pain Gary Hart's family must have experienced in the 1988 race. Before he reentered the race his wife spoke movingly about what her family had suffered. Lee told reporters: "No single individual, no group of individuals can ever hurt or cause such pain to this family again."

But in 1988 Gary Hart certainly, and other politicians as well, brought that pain on themselves and their families by inviting the press in as uncomfortable witnesses. Lee Hart, for example, agreed to an interview with CBS correspondent Ed Bradley for a *60 Minutes* show broadcast on December 20, 1987—the day after her husband jumped back into the race. Speaking awkwardly and nervously, she called her husband's escapade with a Miami model "very, very stupid," but insisted, "I never felt humiliated." Mystifyingly, she then added: "One of the things I appreciate about Gary is he doesn't use his family for political purposes. Not one time, Ed."

In a gentle response that earned him his year's paycheck, Bradley replied: "Some would say you were being used now."

It wasn't just the Lee Harts or Kitty Dukakises from whom the 1988 race exacted a toll, however. While John Dukakis was working overtime on the campaign, Lisa took to her bed with complications late in her pregnancy. Her husband was often needed in two places at once. After the election the Dukakises' younger daughter, Kara, dispirited by the election defeat, opted to continue her studies in Spain for a while. And it was a much more worldly-wise Andrea Dukakis who arrived at a Manhattan eatery for lunch on a rainy afternoon in April 1989.

Dashing out for an hour's lunch from her job on ABC's *20/20* (she has since left and become a recruiter for the New York University School of Drama) the Dukakises' pretty daughter waltzed in wearing a stylish overcoat, her dark hair pulled up under a black fedora. This sophisticated young woman was very different from the thin girl in an ill-fitting dress who the year before tentatively addressed Des Moines supporters sporting bright red WE'RE GONNA CAUCUS FOR DUKAKIS buttons. "I have very mixed feelings about the election process," she said over lunch. Looking back, the hardest part was watching her parents have to handle the defeat. But she called the campaign a positive experience in that it brought a close family even closer. Unknowingly echoing the Bush kids, she said, "You have the feeling that no one but you knows what you're going through."

Andrea confessed to having mixed feelings about the prospect of a President Dukakis. "I very much wanted my dad to be president," she said earnestly. "But those feelings were very separate from me being the president's daughter. I worried I would lose him. I worried seeing him so preoccupied and never having time for anything else."

A month later John Dukakis passed on similar sentiments. For the thirty-year-old the election loss was sobering. Hurt stained his voice as he spoke about the past months. When he began his career John's movie-star looks had taken him to Hollywood where he got bit parts in a handful of feature films. Returning east, he adopted politics, working for Massachusetts Senator John Kerry before joining his stepfather's campaign. After Dukakis's defeat, he was hired by sports agent Bob Woolf to make deals for athletes and rock bands.

For a time, John was heralded as the next generation of Dukakis politician. Speeding in a campaign car from downtown Chicago to O'Hare Airport in the heat of the Illinois primary season, he ebulliently looked ahead to his stepfather's victory and a political career of his own.

Was he interested still? John looked out at the Charles River from his new office in a Boston skyscraper, and it was clear things were a lot less heady and seemed very different now. "I still think about running, getting involved in politics, but I think that's going to be a long way off," he said. "I need to get involved and learn something completely separate from that. And I'm a little wary. I'm probably more reticent than I was about subjecting my family, my emerging family, to that kind of life. Because even though I think we grew up in as normal a political family as humanly possible, it still is a strain. It's still tough to explain to a young child why you or somebody you love is being trashed in the press. Or why you're popular at one moment and the next you're worthless."

Looking across his desk at framed photographs of his infant daughter, Alexandra, he mused: "I'm enjoying a relatively normal workday and going home and spending time with my family on the weekends. I'm not ready to trade that in yet."

When the possibility of his parents moving into the White House loomed, John said he worried about raising his first child in the shadow of the White House. He was also concerned about the effects it might have on his sisters' lives, since they were young and unmarried. "I can see how it can be very damaging for people, especially if they're younger—who get involved in this and leave their own life—lose their childhood in something like this. It's very seductive," he said. Even for an adult who at times found himself putting on a face he later didn't recognize. "Did I smile sometimes when I didn't want to? Yeah, of course. Sure," he said. "You have a persona that sometimes comes on which you have to have because you can't sustain yourself for six events a day. Six speeches. Six photo ops. Six mini–press conferences. I've seen some of the pictures of me from the convention during interviews, and I don't quite recognize the person that was involved." He paused to form his thoughts. "It's a slightly different persona that goes on up there. And I think that it's easy to lose yourself. Especially if you win."

★   ★   ★

When Kitty returned from Edgehill on March 8, she and the governor posed for reporters on their front lawn before enjoying a home-cooked meal of lasagna sent over by a friend. Dukakis smiled, his arm swung around his wife's shoulders. "Doesn't she look great?" the governor asked rhetorically, throwing his question out toward the cameras. After months of practice on the trail, Kitty always managed to look great. That wasn't the issue. How *was* she, *really*?

Fresh from Edgehill, there was something disquieting about Kitty's homecoming when she smiled and posed for pictures standing before her Brookline home, as though it were just another campaign photo opportunity. There had been something cold in the official way the governor had announced his wife's need for treatment. And something chilling in the press conference that would occur the day after she returned. It was as if the governor and his spouse were announcing another highway program, not her road to recovery.

But the callousness surrounding Kitty's homecoming paled by comparison to what Betty Ford faced in 1978 when she finished her traumatic month of treatment for alcohol and drug dependency. In her book Mrs. Ford put the best "spin" possible on her homecoming. "In the beginning, you are more fragile than you—or other people—realize," she wrote. But her own account of her homecoming shows just how erosive public life can be for a vulnerable individual. "I came home from Long Beach—they had cameras there to televise my leaving—and discovered I was on instant display. I had been twenty-eight days in treatment, I was still going through drug withdrawal, which takes one to two years, and I found I was expected to greet a lot of Republicans who were having a reception at my house. Not only that, but NBC was coming in to do an interview," she wrote.

"I broke down and cried, I begged not to have it happen. But the TV crew had already arrived from New York. Nobody had consulted with me, nobody had consulted my doctors; it was typical leftover White House programming. There's going to be a television interview, we expect you to be ready. Finally, I agreed to sit in the study on the couch next to my husband, and the TV people asked me how I was, and I said I was just fine, gritting my teeth behind my smile.

"To me, it was a cruel intrusion; it was as if they had bought a piece of my life that I had no intention of selling them."

Given the relentless pressure to perform, whether self-imposed or imposed by a political staff, the pressure from the media, the lack of control she exerted over her own life, the insensitivity to her needs—which were considerable at that point—Betty Ford's words seem surprisingly mild. Though no longer in the White House, Mrs. Ford was a public person and her story still newsworthy.

After the election some of Kitty's friends believed she had to come to grips not only with the political defeat but her own feelings of rage: rage at her husband over losing the election, at a staff who failed them, then moved on, at a public who sided with an opponent she had so little respect for. She had to regain control over her own life again, after being controlled by others for more than two years. She had to accept what was beyond her control.

The experts at Edgehill tried to guide Kitty back on track and sort through an apparent emotional maelstrom. "Edgehill is directed toward self-awareness, including awareness of what your feelings are, and dealing with them appropriately or in a way that makes living comfortable," her brother-in-law explained. "It relies quite heavily on group therapy, in addition to individual therapy."

Kitty put it this way: "I'm human and I have a disease and I recognize that, and so does my husband. If there was anything that I could do about it . . . there really wasn't. It's not a question of control. It's a question of willingness."

When Kitty came out of Edgehill some family members balked at the idea of her holding a press conference. After discussion among the governor, John Sasso, Paul Costello, and other key advisers, Kitty faced the press on March 9, 1989, at Boston's Park Plaza Hotel. There she spoke of how much she liked the theme song "All I Ask of You" from her favorite Broadway musical, *The Phantom of the Opera*. The lyrics sang of freedom. Freedom to grow and to change. "That's what I was talking about to the press," she said later. "I needed that freedom to do what I had to do." She talked about masks and read the poem "Behind the Facade," given to her by a fellow patient at Edgehill. "So many of us who are alcoholics play games, put on masks, and want to be different people than we are. What we do with this disease is fool ourselves. We're not very often satisfied with what we are and who we are," she said afterward.

At the press conference she told reporters this would be the last time she would face them. "I need privacy for my recuperation," she said. There was little to worry about there. Not many reporters were that anxious to pounce and pursue the inner workings of her postelection trauma. In fact, some reporters and top campaign aides who knew her well were amazed she was "doing any press" at all when clearly she was going through a very rough time. Leaving the press conference, some members of the media felt uneasy. "I felt like I just looked into someone's bedroom and I'm not sure I like it," Adam Nagourney of the New York *Daily News* said immediately afterward.

Mark Starr, *Newsweek*'s Boston bureau chief, agreed that the press conference made him uncomfortable. "But I didn't feel blemished or prurient," he said. "I also didn't ask any questions. This privacy stuff is all a little uncomfortable. But much of the media interest stems from genuine affection and Kitty knows that. It's the media attention that resulted in her getting five thousand letters at Edgehill. So there's an up side and a down side."

Indeed, despite what she said about not wanting to talk to the press, within a week Kitty was back at it, talking to Philadelphia reporters before a speech scheduled at Villanova University. "I am not going to talk personally about my recovery, because I have been told by professionals in the field that it is not healthy for me to do that. But I am going to speak about the disease of alcoholism and drug addiction." Kitty sounded almost as if she were talking about a distant other self. Despite her intent she did speak personally, confessing to students that she drank in hiding during the campaign. A short time later at another speech in California, she told members of the American Psychological Association that she had sought psychiatric help for years. By bringing attention to her problems, aides said, she felt she could draw attention to the problems of others. Still, her public appearances did not sit quite right.

"Why did you choose to go on a public speaking tour so soon after your recent treatment, rather than shunning the spotlight for a period of recovery?" a student bluntly asked her after her Villanova speech, titled "Women and Politics."

"That is a fair question," Kitty replied, but she made light of it, answering, "I signed a contract the third week of December." She and the students shared a laugh. "I'm glad I did that."

Given that a presidential campaign is an intoxicating experience, a drug of sorts all its own, some observers wondered whether Kitty simply wasn't looking for another fix. Admittedly low on self-esteem, Kitty got from the campaign reassurance she badly needed. When it was over she seemed to continue to yearn for the reinforcement she had found, and earned, from the political world. Was she, as her father told *New England Monthly* writer Susan Buchsbaum, "making a career out of a catastrophe"?

In the last days of the campaign, and immediately afterward, Kitty told reporters that she had tried to prepare for the loss. Her husband thought she had. He told *The New York Times:* "She knew we only had an outside chance of winning toward the end. And for the last couple of weeks, for the first time she was saying, 'I'm ready to take a walk by myself someplace.' So she wasn't under any illusion about the difficulty we faced. That's why what happened later was so startling."

Once she had gained some perspective, Kitty realized what her friends had seen much earlier: Given the pressures of the campaign, there really was no way for her to prepare for defeat. "It's very hard to adequately prepare yourself. You can think you're preparing, but you're really not," she admitted. "Part of losing is growing up enough to accept what has happened. To go on in life after . . . I didn't do that."

Sandy Bakalar said the defeat was "the biggest loss that she has suffered," and, as Kitty had in 1978, likened it to "a death." Sandy described Kitty's initial resistance to go out right after the election. "I remember talking to her about Thanksgiving dinner and I said, 'You are not going to cook dinner, you are exhausted. There is a little food shop near here that makes wonderful food.'" Kitty plaintively asked Bakalar to help her shop because she didn't want to go out alone.

"She really felt abandoned and alone. Maybe she thought people loved her because her husband was running for president. I think he probably felt the same thing. 'Who am I?' And 'Who are my real friends?' All of us were her real friends. All of us. But then there is the point that I think she had to face this thing alone."

Kitty's sister, Jinny, also recalled her resistance to being seen. Jinny remembered: "Afterward she said, 'Every time you are going places, it's like going to a funeral. It's like there's been a death in the family because everybody empathizes. Sympathizes.' So it is painful every time you go out in public."

Kitty said Edgehill helped her deal with the defeat. One of the hardest aspects of losing, she said, was feeling she had failed and that she, like lots of others on the Dukakis campaign, no doubt, could have done things differently. What was even harder to let go of, though, was "giving up the feeling that you could make a difference. That's the other part of this thing, this grandiosity, that you can save the world and make a real difference," she said.

Kitty said one of the most important things she learned in Edgehill was that she didn't have to do things alone, that she didn't have to depend on herself all the time, that she could "reach out to other people." She also credited the campaign with helping her to appreciate that. During the campaign, she said, she learned how to depend on others in a way she had "never depended on anybody before."

Sounding very much like her husband, she said, "I had to rely on other people. I'm a very strong person. I'm very definite in my ideas about things. And when you have that kind of personality, ego gets in the way. You think you can do things better than anyone else. That's just not true. . . . I know that today. That's very humbling and very important for me."

Once spiked with campaign jargon, Kitty's speech, in the year after the election, now became colored with talk of "my personal disease." She swapped long-term hopes and a dashed dream for the "one day at a time" philosophy extolled by Alcoholics Anonymous. For the void left by the lost camaraderie and excitement of the campaign, she substituted the fellowship of AA. She became a regular at AA meetings. "One of the things you learn in treatment, if you learn anything," she said, "is you've got to accept the things you can't change. . . ."

For a while it seemed Kitty was doing just that. "Now she is really getting to know herself," her old chum Sandy said in the spring after Kitty finished treatment at Edgehill. "She can look in the mirror and not just see a candidate's wife or a beautiful woman, or a person with a master's in communications, or an authority on travel or the Holocaust. She is looking at this person in the mirror and saying, 'Who am I?' and 'What am I going to do?' I think the speaking is really helping her discover herself. She's got a new self."

Her close friends and relatives said that in a strange way they had gained from the election loss. Jinny Peters said she "hated to see Kitty suffer" and felt "terrible" to say it, but "part of me enjoyed it, because finally she reached out to me and I was the only one that she reached out to." For a change, Jinny said, she could help. "Most of the time she is such a rock that she never needed me. That was kind of a nice feeling. I'm a nurturing person to begin with and I like to be able to nurture her."

The effusive Sandy Bakalar shared that sentiment. Finishing a cup of coffee in the living room of her expansive Chestnut Hill home one afternoon in March, she looked out toward a rolling back lawn filled with her husband's sculpture collection. She laughed, remembering how Kitty had come over just the other day to get Sandy to grind her coffee beans because Kitty's own grinder was broken.

After hours of talk about the campaign, of reflecting on the highs and lows, her good friends' marriage, their early days together in Brookline, their children and divorce, Sandy said if Mike and Kitty had reached the White House, "it never would have been the same. I never would have ground her coffee beans. She would never have bounced in here yesterday showing us pictures of [her granddaughter] Alexandra. I would have really lost a friend, and you know it." Cigarette smoke wreathing her blond hair, Sandy went on, "It is very selfish of me but when she left here yesterday with her dear coffee beans, I thought, 'I can't believe she's back. I'm glad she's back.'"

But Kitty wasn't back. As John Dukakis said, his mother is a woman who "can't sit still." In the year after the election, she tried to stay very busy. Watching her in the spring, her friend Anne Hawley assessed Kitty's postelection activity this way: "I think Kitty finds herself in motion. I think having these things to do gives her satisfaction that she's back at it again and that's comforting. I don't think she wants to go back . . . it just seems pretty clear just from what she's doing, she doesn't want to go back to being the spouse of the governor of Massachusetts. I think she's kind of left that. And if she doesn't do those other things, what is she going to do?"

Ironically, Kitty's career as a public speaker and author took off just when her husband's popularity was at its lowest, ever. After years of fast economic growth the Massachusetts Miracle lay in tatters, a joke. The governor was forced to raise taxes 15 percent to meet a projected $800 million budget deficit. The state's financial ranking dropped to the lowest in the nation. Dukakis's approval rating plummeted to 26 percent. "He couldn't get elected to dogcatcher," one Massachusetts politician groused. The cuts eliminated many of the programs Kitty had worked for and was interested in.

Friends said the governor's decision in January 1989 not to seek reelection in Massachusetts freed Kitty to move into a niche of her own. "I think there's a bond that's in a political marriage that's hard for us to understand," Hawley said. "Every couple has their trade-offs. I think she's accepted that. On the other hand, I think that right now she's at some level decided to move on and he hasn't, so she's just going to do it. We'll see."

In June Kitty conceded she and her husband were "at different places." He was still the governor. She still had certain responsibilities as the first lady of Massachusetts. But she had new opportunities. Doors opened for her. For the first time Kitty began to earn sizable sums on her own from the book contract and speaking tour, payments as high as $12,000 per speech. Her friends thought she had gained confidence. She bought herself a new car, a white convertible with red interior complete with car phone. "A movie-star car," as one friend called it—one that Mike, ever mindful of his image, wouldn't let her park in the driveway.

After Edgehill Kitty kept up a brisk pace. She opened a second office outside the statehouse. She faced pressures to complete the book, a project aides helped her set up in an effort to fill the void of the campaign loss, but a project that by some reports filled her husband with trepidation. Kitty worried about the appropriateness of disclosing certain insider details. Costello disputed that. "She wasn't worried and Michael was proud of her. He loved the book." In September she took an Outward Bound trip in Utah. In October she gave thirteen lectures in twenty-two days. Afterward, Kitty spoke to *Boston Globe* reporter Carol Stocker, who spotted signs of trouble: "Kitty Dukakis does not have the veneer of a politician, or even a good businesswoman. There is no mask, just the simple need to control herself and her situation. It's the main protection she has for a fragility that is palpable. She has given hundreds of interviews during her public life, but in this one she is shaky and self-conscious like a marathoner learning to run again after a bad accident."

Kitty's hectic travel schedule and comments by the governor fueled rumors that the couple's marriage was troubled. At the end of October, as she always had, Kitty insisted to Stocker, "This has not been an easy year for him in many ways. [But] I think these last eight and a half months have brought us even closer together. We were very close before, and when we went to treatment together, we both benefited. . . . We just feel much better about each other and us as a couple."

The governor participated in his wife's treatment program at Edgehill and has attended AA meetings with her, according to close aides.

Fighting his own political battles, her husband watched as his headstrong wife went her own way.

"Kitty can't stand being out of the limelight. I don't know what to do," *Time* reported he told a close aide. "There was little he could do," another confidant agreed. "Michael's been through hell. He's a saint," said yet another. Ultimately, Costello reported the governor as saying of his wife, "We can never let this happen again. You can't let this schedule go overboard."

Watching Kitty on the run, some friends feared for her as she continued to put up what they saw as a front, never quite believing she was the successful career woman she seemed to be. "Kitty is of a generation of women not fully prepared for independence," Shershow said. In her opinion, Kitty was trying to turn her personal experience into something redeeming. "During the campaign she had found it hard, frankly, to talk about her drug dependency to high-school students. But she felt it was helpful for others to hear that. She does value her position in the limelight to do something of value. She needs to have a sense of mission."

Others saw in Kitty the classic symptoms of euphoria exhibited by alcoholics in the early stages of recovery. "She was simply riding for a fall," said an old acquaintance familiar with the problem.

And fall she did. On November 6, 1989, Kitty was again alone in bed at her home in Brookline when she drank the only alcohol she could find at home, rubbing alcohol. At around ten o'clock a friend called and Mike went upstairs to tell Kitty to expect a visitor. She was semiconscious. The governor called the family physician and Kitty was rushed to Boston's Brigham and Women's Hospital where her stomach was pumped and she underwent tests.

As they had in the past, the Dukakis camp tried to conceal the real story. There was talk of a suicide attempt. Her aides denied it and talked of "exhaustion and symptoms of the flu," just as they had when Kitty had collapsed in Minnesota during the campaign. After a chaotic press conference, the Dukakis family doctor released a statement saying Kitty had a long-standing battle with depression. Kitty had suffered from severe depressive mood swings for years. She was taking antidepressants prescribed by her psychiatrist, potentially lethal when mixed with alcohol. Some of Kitty's closest aides knew of her history with depression during the campaign, but "there was never a time when it was a problem." This time, Paul Costello said, "Kitty reached 'a *low* low.'"

Kitty's friends and former aides said many factors contributed to Kitty's postelection condition. "People don't understand what losing the presidency does to people," Costello said.

"If you struggle with depression it's so terrifying you don't think it's ever going to go away," Anne Hawley said. "A high level of structure keeps it away, can help keep it at bay. When you have it recurring and have this just devastating loss on [top of] that, you have a context that is emotionally lethal. One thing you need when you have this problem is structure and business. That's what was removed along with being excoriated by the press."

In Bonnie Shershow's view, it was hard to separate what was the political system and what was the depression. She said, "Maybe the system is the medium for the depression. It has to be factored into the equation. I don't think you can dismiss the problem with the role political spouses find themselves in. This situation is not one that lends itself to feeling strong and capable and all the things that make up an individual carrying their own weight. In some ways it downplays you as an individual and treats you as a subordinate."

When Kitty Dukakis drank rubbing alcohol on the eve of the anniversary of her husband's defeat, it was not just his loss that was on her mind. In the wake of the end of the campaign and her treatment at Edgehill, Kitty had gone on to invent a new identity for herself. No longer the "Nominee's Wife," or even the "Wife of the Losing Presidential Contender," she presented herself as an upcoming author and spokesperson for alcohol abuse and addiction therapy. On November 6, the book that had kept her locked in the past was almost complete. She had canceled her last wrap-up session with her ghostwriter, almost as if to keep it all from really ending, a friend said. Her speaking tour was coming to an end. She'd asked an aide, "Are you sure there are no more speeches?" She didn't have any plans for the foreseeable future. As she had in November the year before, Kitty Dukakis faced a frightening, daunting chasm. She'd come full circle. Once again, Kitty would have to reinvent—or face—herself. This time to really recover from the campaign and all that had happened in between.

CHAPTER TWELVE

❧

First Lady Victorious

> It was our first day in the White House, and
> though we should have been exhausted by the in-
> auguration, the parade, and the thought of attend-
> ing all seven balls still to come that night, the
> excitement of the day and exploring our new
> home made us tireless. . . . We were all thrilled
> and awed, to be in this beautiful place.
>
> —ROSALYNN CARTER,
> *First Lady from Plains*

"I think election night I saw them as tense as I'd ever seen them. But everybody was tense, you know. Gosh almighty," said Barbara Bush's old friend Andy Stewart. "It had been such a long campaign and the press was predicting a landslide here or Dukakis surging forth suddenly. We were all at this family get-together in Texas, down in Houston. Just those good friends, you know, that they've always had every election night. Just for a few minutes I probably saw as tense a time as I'd ever seen. But everyone was feeling that way, because it just didn't seem possible that it really was going to culminate."

Reality hit Andy Stewart on January 20, 1989, standing on the Capitol steps at George Bush's swearing-in ceremony. "My husband had sworn him in twice before [as vice-president]. Then I just realized. It was very teary. I looked around and I saw these great big, grown-up men friends with tears going down their cheeks. Men they'd known forever. It was so moving. But it didn't seem strange. That was the thing that was so interesting to me. It didn't seem strange. It was just terribly crowded. I don't know how much doubt

258

they may have had, but I know their friends didn't have any doubts that once they got in, they'd be able to handle it all."

While the Dukakis camp grappled with the agony of defeat, for the Bushes the story was different. It was time to party and savor the GOP's victory over the Democrats. Limousines logjammed the capital for days. In 1989 the Republicans spent some $30 million to put on a week-long extravaganza welcoming George and Bar into 1600 Pennsylvania Avenue. Shortly before the inauguration, in her last interview at the vice-president's residence, Mrs. Bush was asked about the expense. If that kind of money was raised privately for the inaugural, could it also be raised for the homeless?

"No, it couldn't," she replied nonplussed. "You wouldn't raise the money for that purpose. These people are raising it because they worked for years and years to elect a president. It just couldn't be done. If it could be done, we would do it." Mrs. Bush wasn't worried about the expense of it all. "It's putting a lot of people to work, giving a lot of people jobs. So no, I don't feel badly about it. If it were federal money I'd feel absolutely outraged, but it's not."

Besides, she said, many events were planned for the public. "We wanted very much for it to be a people's inaugural," she said that day, sitting at her dining-room table in the Naval Observatory. Looking ahead, she spoke of plans to open the White House to the public. "I think we'll be at the door" shaking hands—"not with thirty thousand people. I think just to get it started probably." Then she outlined what she expected would happen next: a series of celebratory events.

After her husband's speech, she said, "We're having a luncheon at twelve o'clock with two hundred and fifty relatives. After the parade we've set up a buffet for those twenty-eight people [staying at the White House] to wander in and eat well. I envision, I'm probably nutty, but I envision the girls coming in and taking naps maybe." (Her daughter and four daughters-in-law, she meant.) "The children sort of exhausted and taking naps. People going in and getting a bite to eat when they're ready. So I've asked them to put out a hot buffet that will sit out with little burners. Because then they have to all get dressed. I think Mrs. Bush [George's mother] who is *very* frail . . . she'll be in bed. And I envision the daughters-in-law coming in with the ball gowns to show her. And

George and I going in to show her . . ." Then off they'd go to five inaugural balls.

Events transpired more or less along the lines Mrs. Bush envisioned. Friday evening after the inauguration, after lunch at the Capitol, the seemingly endless parade, a quick bite to eat, and the donning of elaborate gowns, the Bushes made fourteen stops on their grand tour of balls. They rode around the capital in a huge motorcade more than twenty vehicles long. The couple started the evening with vigor, but noticeably faded as the night wore on. President and Mrs. Bush danced at five of the evening's events, but only a twirl or two.

The couple's last stop of that night was at the Washington Hilton ball, attended by what one aide called the "mega donors." As elsewhere, people had waited for hours to catch a glimpse of the new president and first lady. But the two didn't show up until 12:30 P.M. When they did, Mike Love of the Beach Boys got them both to join him in singing "Ba, Ba, Ba, Bar-bara Ann." Mrs. Bush said no more but, according to a reporter writing from the scene, "was the hit of the evening in her royal blue dress with the velvet top and satin skirt. All the ladies loved it. They gasped with pleasure when they saw her and pronounced her beautiful and said the wait had been worth it."

With many streets blocked off for the inaugural, traffic that evening was a nightmare. Unlike the usual Reagan practice, the Bushes' motorcade did not use sirens, but they didn't need to because all the streets were blocked off and empty. At one point along the way, Bush's new chief of staff, John Sununu, hopped into one of the press vans for a jaunt from the Capital Hilton to the D.C. Armory. He told traveling reporters that he "wanted to see what it was like." According to those on the scene, the tuxedoed Sununu had to crouch in the press van because there were no extra seats, and apparently he wasn't offered one.

For the most part, reporters said, the new president changed his material at every stop. But by the sixth event he started repeating stories. "The one about how nice the accommodations at the White House are," one journalist reported.

In the rush of events it was hard to absorb it all.

Later, Mrs. Bush said of the inauguration, "Well, I didn't feel any different than any other equally happy time. But it was awesome. . . . It was very nice [to be] surrounded by so many people we loved. Walking up Pennsylvania Avenue—we did it Columbus Day. It wasn't that much different truthfully. Except there was enormous goodwill."

Bar's friend Janet Steiger said that the "reality of having all those kids and grandkids in the White House on the night of the inaugural, she has mentioned that as being a reality striker."

On Saturday night, January 21, the partying continued at the "Celebration for Young Americans Ball," where Bush campaign manager Lee Atwater made his national debut as a Republican rock 'n' roller jamming on stage with music legends Ron Wood, Percy Sledge, Joe Cocker, and others. The *Chicago Tribune*'s Tim McNulty, assigned to "pool" reporting duty that evening, provided his colleagues with an insider's idiosyncratic memo of the scene—a memo that, like most other "pool reports," never made it into print. McNulty, a bearish bearded man, spent the evening running after the Bushes and—though tuxedoed—maintained a war reporter's pace as he followed the first couple's mad dash from one spot to the next. McNulty wrote:

> George Bush, 41st president and rhythm and blues rocker, joined his children and grandchildren at the Convention Center where he jammed with Lee "Put on Your Red Shoes, Momma" Atwater. Wearing his tuxedo and black leather boots with the state colors and the outline of Texas, he [Bush] rocked and riffed and strummed with a white electric guitar presented by rhythm and blues artist Sam Moore. It said "The Prez" in front. Bush called it "the most active event of the inauguration." By other accounts, it was fifty times livelier than anything else this week.
>
> Lee Atwater set the tone with his Chuck Berry moves. Marvin Bush put sunglasses on the new chairman of the Republican National Committee and he took off—doing a split on stage, kneeling and then writhing on his back, all the time singing and working his guitar. President Bush had been escorted to a table to watch the entertainment and he rocked with the music, though not exactly in the right time. Mrs. Bush had much better rhythm. With hundreds of people in the stands of the Convention Center and scores of family members and new White House employees closer to the stage at tables, it was a knock-down fun affair. The Bushes beamed as they joined the musicians on stage.

("It was the blonde leading the blonde," a black newswoman cracked afterward, describing the same scene.)

Earlier that Saturday night, the Bushes had appeared at another party, the Texas State Society Ball. In McNulty's words: "It was more sedate, with only the expected whoopin' and hollerin' at the 'Black Tie 'n' Boots' ball at the Washington Hilton. Bush first appeared in a low-ceilinged overflow room with Barbara Bush in a red dress with a black lace overblouse. That is, something black and lacy covering the bodice of her red dress," wrote McNulty who doesn't know beans about fashion but as the reporter on the scene tried his best to provide some detail.

He pulled slyly on his right trouser leg to show off his boots for the first time of the evening. He said, "We've had a great, wonderful day." He was introduced by Charles Stenholm (D-Texas), who joked that Bush was a "card-carrying member of the Texas State Society." He showed off a check that he said was from Bush for his 1989 dues. Bush spoke of "how important it is to be the custodian of the peoples' house. . . . Bar and I are happy. We're very, very pleased." He joked with Texans he recognized from the 1950s. One woman yelled out, "We love you, Barbara."

When Mrs. Bush got to the microphone, she raised her eyebrows at her husband, who was now freely raising his pant legs to show off the boots, and she said: "What I ought to do is make George stand on his head and really show you those boots!"

Moments later they joined a much larger, louder and raucous group in the ballroom where he did the boot thing again.

Stenholm said there were 5,600 in attendance and an equal number who couldn't get tickets to get in. . . . [Inaugural organizers] Penny Korth and Bobby Holt and their spouses accompanied the First Couple, along with George W. Bush Jr. and his wife, Laura.

Bush looked over the crowd, giving thumbs up signs and other friendly finger gestures, some Texas steer or Longhorn thing. He added: "I don't want Ann Richards to think I'm not a Texan!" as he again showed off his boots. The man who made the boots (Rocky Carroll, but that's only phonetic spelling) was in the crowd.

The crowd sang, "Texas Our Texas," or a song like that. Stenholm presented Mrs. Bush with a check (amount unknown) for a Texas literacy program. She opened the envelope, looked at the check and raised her eyebrows and gave a thumbs up sign. Stenholm then gave Bush [cowboy] boots for all ten grandchildren with the word "Gampy" on them.

Bush said he has been getting a bad "rap" about the cost of the inaugural celebration. "More Americans have been able to participate in free events than in any other inauguration in history."

Mrs. Bush said people have been coming up to her all day asking, "Does the president like this?" Or, "Does the president like that?" She said she was about to say, "How should I know?" Then she thought, "My God, it's George!"

"He is the president. He's going to make a darn good president," she said. Later she added: "I worked awfully hard this week to make you very, very proud of me. Next week, I'm going to be Barbara Bush again."

Barbara did work hard. Beyond the partying some serious business was going on during inaugural week. For the new first lady inaugural week meant setting out to define a style and tone for the administration. It was another hoop to hop through for the new president's wife.

"The wife of the nominee, whoever she is, can hurt a campaign, but the first lady is the key to the whole tone of the administration," said Sheila Tate, who after four years as Nancy Reagan's press secretary had sound opinions about such things. "All you have to do is look at the style, the tone of Nancy Reagan's first year," Tate remembered one fall day after the campaign. "It all came together the day the story about her ordering the china came out the same day that ketchup was deemed a vegetable for school lunches. I'll never forget that moment, recognizing the significance style and tone has in the fortunes of an administration. I mean, that became fodder for all the opponents of Ronald Reagan."

During her eight years up on Observatory Hill Barbara Bush had walked her dog and seen her husband emasculated by a job, of which she once said, "I think a good vice-president goes through what a good wife goes through." She had also observed Nancy. And one thing Bar learned from observing Nancy was that if the former first lady was good at anything, it was making a gaffe. From the costly White House redecoration during her first hundred days, to possessing a "little" gun, to perfecting "The Gaze" at husband Ronnie, to consulting an astrologer and orchestrating the ouster of Chief of Staff Don Regan, Nancy Reagan was a study in what *not* to do as first lady. Then, as if that weren't enough, there was the multimillion-dollar Hollywood-style, glitz-and-tell story of *her* White House years. The book provided fodder for the gossip mills inside and beyond the Beltway. Lips that were sealed while the Reagans were in power opened up in their wake.

Publicly Barbara Bush pooh-poohed the press stories that surfaced about what many described as her distant relationship with Mrs. Reagan—a woman whose private coldness but skilled public display of warmth (especially before whirring or snapping cameras) amazed even former first lady Betty Ford, who is no novice to the political stage. But friends and family indicate the relationship between Nancy and Bar was far from intimate.

"A wicked little grin comes on her face whenever Nancy Reagan comes up," a White House aide said.

The two got off to a difficult start. Their husbands, after all, had been rivals. In 1980 when Mrs. Bush had to make the switch and work *for* her husband's rival, rather than *against* him, she frankly admitted, "I'll work, but not my heart out." Theirs were different politics: Reagan's conservative ideology versus Bush's compromising moderation. Then there was Nancy's bad-mouthing of George during Iran-Contra, expecting him to be the fall guy for Ronnie. There were the infrequent invitations to the White House. The Bushes and Reagans never dined alone together after Reagan's first year in office, Nancy said. Equally irksome to the Bushes, who have made the thank-you note into an art form, was Reagan's ambivalence toward a George Bush presidency, the reward for eight years of loyalty and good behavior. Though their well-bred Yankee manners stopped the new president and his first lady from grousing, the president's sister, Nancy Ellis, felt no compunction in expressing her sentiments in her hometown newspaper, *The Boston Globe*. The minute the mantle of nominee was handed over to her brother and the incumbent departed New Orleans on the first day of the Republican Convention, Mrs. Ellis wrote this dispatch as a guest columnist: "The president addressed the convention, and we honor the Reagans. What a night for them: It's a love-in. But I am nervous. First comes Mrs. Reagan. She looks beautiful and is touching but does not mention Barbara. I want her to do so; I want her to say how valuable BB [Barbara Bush] has been as a compatriot in politics these last eight years, how BB has stood beside her, or slightly behind her, and what a great first lady BB will make. But no mention of this, and the blue sky changes to a white sky."

Such was Mrs. Ellis's polite way of describing a dampered day.

And so there was a national sigh of relief when the president's helicopter lifted off from the Capitol's backyard on January 20 and took Ron and Nancy off to fashionable Bel Air, blowing a copter storm into the faces of the new tenants of the White House who bade them adieu. Upon arriving in California Ron and Nancy bemoaned the constitutional technicality that cheated Americans of Reagan's leadership for a third term. The Reagans couldn't have been more wrong. Although he was leaving office with high approval ratings, if Reagan had been eligible to run for a third term, 54 percent of the public said they wouldn't have voted for him, according to *Time*.

On the campaign trail reporters had annoyed Mrs. Bush by constantly asking "What kind of first lady will you be?"

Though she hinted at it throughout the campaign, Barbara's answer first got out on the morning of January 19 in inaugural week when some six thousand people filled up the Kennedy Center's three auditoriums—the Concert Hall, the Eisenhower Theater and the Opera House—for a special event honoring Mrs. Bush. Well-dressed party faithful from across the country filed in at fifty dollars apiece to welcome the new first lady and to enjoy the National Symphony Orchestra, the Preservation Hall Jazz Band, the Mora Ariaga Mariachis (starring Bush granddaughter Noelle), the Houston Symphony Orchestra, and other entertainers.

Barbara Bush made the rounds, visiting each hall, taking in a few tunes. She was presented at all three stops by the soon-to-be second lady, Marilyn Quayle, who after a few words of introduction wept with unbelievable emotion each time.

Mrs. Quayle began by telling each of her audiences that she had a tough act to follow up on Observatory Hill, the vice-president's official residence. "When George Bush was elected vice-president of the United States, Barbara Bush became president of the Senate Ladies. We are a very unique group. We're totally nonpartisan," Mrs. Quayle explained. (A spinoff of the Red Cross, the group meets monthly to roll bandages and the like for local hospitals.)

"When Barbara came into our presence as our leader, she didn't just act like a figurehead. She came to our meetings. She took each one of us to her heart. We all became her friends and she helped all of us who came to Washington without friends, without family, and treated us as her family.

"That's Barbara Bush. She goes beyond herself," Mrs. Quayle continued, her voice choking with emotion.

"To everyone she meets . . . she spurs them on to be better people, and to do better things with their lives . . . and I get weepy when I talk about it." She gulped for breath. (Mrs. Quayle later said that Bar had turned over her own Red Cross apron to her, a kind of passing on of the sacred beanie, "because she knew I wouldn't buy one.") "How wonderful Barbara Bush has been to all of us in the Senate. To our families. To making our lives a little more special. Barbara Bush has done this for people around the country and around the world. Each life she touches she makes a little bit better because she came into their lives."

There was more. Mrs. Quayle went on, her voice trembling. "Barbara's a woman of great character, indomitable spirit. High energy. And a very, very keen wit that she uses to great effect with her friends to bring us all great joy. She's beloved of all the Senate Ladies. In a very short time she will become a most beloved first lady of our nation . . ." As she spoke, tears glistened in Mrs. Quayle's eyes.

The first time Mrs. Quayle gave this introduction—and wept—it was with apparent conviction. The Quayles, after all, had been run through the ringer. Bar had been a big support, it seemed. Marilyn's gratitude would be plausible.

The second time she went through a very similar but slightly reworked version of the same introduction—and wept—the depth of her emotions seemed, well, suspect. It was Bar she was introducing, after all. And Bar had just *heard* her effusive commentary moments before.

By her last performance—all three witnessed only by Mrs. Bush and her entourage, and the small reporting pool herded from auditorium to auditorium—wry jokes about crocodile tears seeped out among the press.

"I think in the next administration we're going to be known as the weeping sisters," Mrs. Bush told one audience, which laughed gently at her reference to Mrs. Quayle's comportment.

It was also at this first-lady event that Mrs. Bush took her first steps toward projecting her own image and making a statement about who *she* was. After Marilyn's words, Bar stepped out from behind the center-stage podium. Three times she implored her audiences, "I want you all to look at me very closely." The crowds laughed and cheered.

"Please notice the hair," she invited each audience. More laughter and whistles.

"The makeup." The laughter grew louder still.

Then, unbuttoning and opening the jacket to her deep-blue Scaasi suit, she flashed the green and purple rose print lining, matching the print in her bowed silk blouse. "The designer clothes." Three times, one audience of Republicans after another howled in glee.

"I want you to watch me all week," she said, pausing for effect . . . "And remember! You're not going to see it again!"

Of course they would, but on that day she brought the houses down. Videotape rolled. Still photographers shot frame after humorous frame of a winking, grinning, self-deprecating Barbara Bush showing herself off.

It was that simple. The tone was set. The message clear, if unstated. "The subtext of all that is 'I am not Nancy Reagan,'" said Lewis Gould, a historian who specializes in the history of first ladies at the University of Texas at Austin.

Our new First Lady: "Mrs. Not Nancy" is how the fellows over at *The New Republic* cleverly put it.

★   ★   ★

In her first one hundred days, the artificial timetable invented by the press to gauge the tone of the new administration, Bar built on that image. She scooted around the country to some forty solo publicity events, visiting the poor, the ill, and the homeless in an effort to capitalize on media attention that inevitably would fade. She had her picture taken reading to minority children. She was pictured holding a baby sick with AIDS. The events were similar in design and staging to her campaign appearances. She oversaw the establishment of the Barbara Bush Foundation for Family Literacy, an organization designed to bring private funds and focus to those family reading programs around the country that succeed.

Mrs. Bush made her first public outing on January 31 to Martha's Table, a day-care center and soup kitchen for homeless adults and children in a poor part of Washington, D.C. There were plenty of well-to-do faces that day as more than two dozen reporters, photographers, and television technicians were jammed into a press pen set up inside the modest building to witness Mrs. Bush taking her first steps as first lady of the United States. Donning a red apron, Bar joined a shy-looking volunteer at a table set up in the center of a big room in perfect view of the press pen and for ten minutes or so folded a couple of meat and cheese sandwiches while the photographers maniacally documented the moment. Then she moved on to a gathering of kids and read them a story while the journalists watched her and the kids watched the journalists.

Unlike Eleanor Roosevelt, or Rosalynn Carter, or Betty Ford, who took hands-on roles in their husband's administrations, Mrs. Bush prefers not to see the first lady role in substantive terms. "Thank heavens there's no job description," she told a reporter for *USA Today*. "You write it yourself and nobody else, and that's what I'm up to. I love my life. I don't consider it a job."

What Mrs. Bush does do is designed to complement her husband's presidency and generate good publicity for him by creating the image of a person who "cares." "The East Wing [where the first lady's staff works] sets the tone and if the West Wing [the president's side of the White House] doesn't pay enough attention to what that tone is and what's happening, they'll run into problems," Sheila Tate said. Looking back on her own experience, Tate recalled: "They really will, 'cause it'll politicize things so quickly. All of a sudden it looked like the Reagans were very acquisitive and only interested in their own comforts. She was spending money like a drunken sailor. It was very damaging. It took a long time to beat our way out of that hole."

Mrs. Bush's chief of staff, Susan Porter Rose, explained her views of the first lady's role in her spacious office in the East Wing of the White House. She said that Mrs. Bush wants to highlight administration initiatives. "I think she has the general goal of wanting in all ways that she can to help this administration. . . . Her approach is one that she has first of all thought through in a very conscious way, and it's tied to this very profound belief that he's the elected official and what he thinks about is what matters. It's a principled consideration on her part."

As on the campaign trail, Rose calls the shots for Mrs. Bush. Asked about Barbara Bush's management style, Rose described her as trusting. The two work well together, Rose said. "She's trusting of me. Now, that's not to say that she doesn't convey how she wants things done, or that she doesn't have definite views about things and a lot of input into things. But she trusts it's going to get done. She trusts she's going to like it. And I think she trusts that it's going to be comfortable for the people we're working with, whether they be the other people on the present staff or whether they be the people that we're working with to set up a trip or an event."

Rose detailed her definition of first lady. "I think as first lady one of the things she does is reflect the human side of this man who has been elected president and reflect their family and their values. Now, what she did on the campaign trail was to reflect the human side of the candidate, and as people meet her, she brings him to them in a lot of ways."

Did the first lady have to have a project? Rose, who previously worked in the White House on Pat Nixon's and Betty Ford's staffs, elaborated: "How the first lady handles her life and what she chooses to do is really her own decision and if someone chooses not to have a project, I think that's entirely up to them. Now in this day and age especially, when I think there's been a greater focus since the sixties on women and their accomplishments, I think that would be harder. But I still think if you had a young woman who had little children or something like that and was shy in personality, I think that person would have to make her own decision about that. But I think most people would see it as such an opportunity to make a difference in something. I think it would be very hard not to have that feeling about it. But I'm not somebody who thinks that expectations ought to be imposed on a first lady."

In Rose's view, "One of the things that's a given in almost every case is that people really do expect and hope that the first lady's going to be a good wife to the president. They like that. People like that. I think they feel more comfortable that the first lady and the president are working together and helping each other and being important parts of each other's lives. And also when they are a family, as they certainly are with the Bushes, a big family, you know, you gotta look out after the family, too."

Are there expectations that the first lady will have an impact on women's issues? Rose didn't think so.

Nor did Mrs. Bush. Though she is not a feminist, Barbara Bush is admittedly a "woman's woman." She has said, "I really like women . . . and I couldn't *live* without my women friends . . ." Only one of her twenty-two-member staff is a male. She wanted a woman press secretary, "not because I am a chauvinist, but because I think a woman understands a woman better, that's all. For me," she said, and hired a black woman, thirty-seven-year-old Anna Perez. Mrs. Bush is interested in the needs of poor women and women who have been left by their husbands and need job training. She is concerned about the problems facing teenage mothers. But, she said, "I am not going to be one who's speaking out on women's issues, so-called." She makes no connection between these women's needs and what Americans have traditionally come to perceive as women's issues: pay equity, abortion rights, and an equal-rights amendment. Nor has she lent her voice toward shaping a national family policy: a guaranteed work-leave for employed parents after the birth or adoption of a child, for instance, or financial aid for the working poor to obtain quality child care.

After several months in the White House, in an interview in early April Mrs. Bush described her own sense of her role and how it differed from the second lady's. "I think we are doing less foreign countries and will do less than as vice-president. We spent over half our time traveling. A relatively short amount of time, but we went to seventy-eight foreign countries. So I think that life was much more representing your country abroad. Although certainly, I had the president of Costa Rica's wife for lunch yesterday. I had Mrs. Mubarik for tea and Mrs. Shamir tonight. I do see that as a part of it, a very important part of it all on home ground." Because of her previous experience, she said, "I have been thinking globally for a number of years."

On the domestic front as a hostess, she said: "I am not a hands-on first lady as such. I trust [White House social secretary] Laurie Firestone and Gary Walters, who is the head usher. They are wonderful, once we make the decision. Our biggest problems are guest lists [and] trying to merge in people you want to have, and those are *major* problems."

Mrs. Bush also described her role as that of a publicist. "That's much more important for me now," she said in a White House interview. "I would be a hands-on volunteer if I thought it would do the most good. The truth is, it wouldn't. The most good done by me now is getting out and saying to the people who work for MADD [Mothers Against Drunk Driving] or child help, or drug abuse, or crime prevention, or visiting nurses, or whatever it is, you're doing a wonderful job and we need more of you."

Overall she said she saw the job as "really dealing with people. I ran out and watched the former head of my Secret Service when I was [wife of the] vice-president play horseshoes today. I am a people person. I have a tea at three today; Casey Healey's [her personal aide] mother and grandmother are coming up. I had all these doctors this morning and gave them a tour. Yesterday we had a recording-for-the-blind reception. In the morning I did a press conference for abused children about which we got no press at all. Not one living bit. And I could have told you that, but you have to make the effort. It is too bad because it is really a wonderful program."

Mrs. Bush said she was disappointed by the lack of publicity. "I don't care for me but for them. I cared because they were hopeful. But I see that over and over again. It is just not newsworthy. It is too bad. We had a lot of people who came a long way for that press conference."

As her remarks about her press conference indicate, like a lot of public figures Mrs. Bush wants press attention, but only on her terms—as publicity, not as scrutiny of her actions as a public person. She is aware of the distinction. She once said, "I read an article where Helen Thomas [senior White House correspondent] said, 'We want publicity when we do good works. But we don't want it when we try to go off privately. We can't have it both ways.' Well, maybe that's true. I don't know."

As much as she regretted lack of press coverage that day in April, Mrs. Bush has displayed both amusement and a marked dislike of being in the limelight. Rose said, "I think she's someone who's content with a lower profile. She wants the attention brought to what she's doing rather than to her. Now you can say, well, it's not going to separate and the fact of the matter is that's partly true, but that's still how she feels about it."

After her first visit to Martha's Table, aides later said she was "stunned" and put off by the press attention.

"She's ambivalent about the spotlight on her," her press secretary, Anna Perez, said during the first couple's trip to Canada.

"I don't think she's crazy about it. She doesn't seek it. It's there," her friend Andy Stewart agreed.

Despite her initial efforts to woo select reporters with invitations and lunches up in the family residence, at times Mrs. Bush barely seemed to tolerate the press. Once her first one hundred days were through, Mrs. Bush admitted the rush of events had worn her out and she was going to slow down. "I'm lucky if I get through the day. I don't mean I'm overextended," she told a group of reporters during a roundtable discussion, "but I'm sixty-three years old and I need to be babied a bit. Nobody asks me to do all these things—I do them because I want to. But I have overscheduled myself. I'm not going to go into retirement, I'm just not going to try to do twelve events in one day. That's silly."

Besides, she had already done her most important job: Her image was firmly in place and she could now carefully pick and choose her public events.

"On the foreign trips she really does not want to go off and have a big splashing separate schedule. She wants to do things that, first, countries want her to do and the embassies feel are a good idea. And rather than be out there making a big splash in some way, she wants to complement what [the president's] there to do," Rose explained.

However, it wasn't her desire to complement George that caused a problem. On the contrary, her low-key approach to publicity has created some embarrassing and much-publicized moments. In February 1989, for instance, when Mrs. Bush traveled with her husband to China she didn't want to turn every meeting into a press event, so she brought only her press secretary and no other staff. As Mrs. Bush visited the Forbidden City, ancient home to Chinese emperors, and toured an exhibit about Pu Yi, the last emperor and the subject of Bernardo Bertolucci's film, Chinese security guards pushed and shoved Mrs. Bush's entourage into a door so hard that a White House photographer's jaw was dislocated. "This girl's job is to take my picture, and she got hit," Mrs. Bush scolded the guards at the time. "She works for my husband. Ask them to calm down," press on the scene reported.

Asked about the quality of the advance work (referring to staff groundwork and preparation for the moment-by-moment itinerary of a visiting dignitary), Anna Perez, said, "What advance?"

Reporter Craig Hines of the *Houston Chronicle* suggested to Mrs. Bush that in light of the shoving incident, "the trip seems just a little lightly advanced. Are you happy with that?"

The first lady disagreed. "You're just saying that to be rude because you know I don't want to be advanced."

To some Mrs. Bush seemed almost to be resisting the visibility of her role. "She does have this idea that she can do things the way she did them before, and it just can't be," a senior White House official told a *Washington Post* reporter.

Later Susan Porter Rose said: "I think that's going to have to be just something that kind of evolves in her thinking. You know, she doesn't want the focus on her and she thinks it can happen without anything like that. . . . I think her mind kind of has to adjust to thinking about it in the sense that she just wants to be sure that she is not front and center."

When the Bushes traveled again to London for the NATO summit, reporters sensed that Bar was still resisting media attention. Lois Romano of *The Washington Post* wrote from London:

Media interest in the first lady has been moderate at best—which is the way she seems to prefer it. Choosing low-key cultural and educational activities close to her heart, she gave a pretty good indication here of how she'll handle foreign travel during her White House years.

Even American press interest in her on this trip has been inconsistent, with some events attracting only one or two print reporters. That's a far cry from the Reagan years, when five or six news organizations would send reporters just to cover Nancy.

There has also been a sense here that, mediawise, the first lady does just what she has to do—and no more.

She startled Italian and American reporters in Rome, for instance, when she abruptly cut press queries about her husband's "cautious" attitude on arms control.

To the dismay of her staff, the incident was recorded by a network pool and widely reported at home.

A few days later, during her morning tea with Hannelore Kohl in Bonn, she again showed some impatience with press demands. As the West German chancellor's wife bent over backwards to help photographers, Mrs. Bush asked: "Don't they have enough yet?"

But her staff seemed to realize this week that even for someone who doesn't enjoy coverage, there is room for compromise. After hearing complaints that it was impossible to get near the First Lady in Rome and Brussels, her office began inviting a pool writer to accompany her. And today at Brixton, the First Lady appeared much more willing to pose and talk.

Earlier, in Kennebunkport, Mrs. Bush had a different reaction to her newfound celebrity. She laughed as she described a scene during a walk with her daughter when she and her husband came back for their first visit since the inauguration. "Three women almost drove off the road. They were funny. And Dorothy LeBlond did not help me at all," she began. "A woman came around the back road. Pulled up in the car and said, 'My God. Oh God! MY GOD!! It is you. It IS YOU!!' And Dorothy fell over laughing.

"I thought, 'The poor woman.' She got very embarrassed and Dorothy was screaming with laughter. We were afraid she was going to turn the car around."

Laughing, Mrs. Bush continued. "Then another lady, Japanese, I think, stopped me. Screamed with excitement. Carrying on. Touched me and then we heard her for quite a while.

"Unfortunately, we passed her again later and the Secret Service said, 'You're lucky she's not driving.'"

* * *

Since she moved into the White House, Mrs. Bush's friends said, she has enjoyed sharing her new life. "These, after all, are extraordinary adventures, and she shares them. Half the fun is sharing, from her point of view," Janet Steiger said. "She's very generous about it. She's just always acted in that same fashion."

Shortly after moving into the White House and tapping into the budget provided for the president's family's personal use, Mrs. Bush often invited her friends over for lunch and gave them a tour of her new surroundings. "She frequently has friends over to the White House privately," Steiger said. "As you know, they only publish a guest list for official functions."

Commissioner Steiger described a birthday party Bar threw for women friends of Mrs. Stewart, who just "roams in and out" of the White House. Mrs. Steiger recalled: "Bar took such glee in this. You really would've thought she made [the cake], she was so enchanted with it. The cake was quite a large cake. And it was a tennis court. It had a sugar-candied racquet, absolutely perfect racquet on the top. It was simply marvellous. The most magnificent time was had by all. Especially Andy."

Not long after the inauguration Susan Porter Rose said: "One of the things I find amusing, and I don't know why it strikes me as amusing but it does, is that she just loves having lunch [with friends] in different nooks and crannies around the White House. I think that is just terrific. I laugh and laugh about that," Bar's chief of staff said. "There's a kind of freedom that goes with it, in the sense that you're there. You know, the obstacles have been removed. You're there. Not that they have spent eight years panting to be there, I don't mean that at all. But here they are; it's theirs to make of it what they can and will. And I think there's a liberation to that."

Mrs. Bush seemed to agree. "I have friends over for lunch almost every day," she said in February 1989. "I want to sit down and show it off. . . . One day Mrs. Stewart and I picked a sunny spot nearly a mile down the end of the hall to lunch just for fun. You can have it anyplace. You can have the solarium. You can have it anyplace your heart desires. We had people, friends, come and spend the first weekend we were here. . . . Then we had friends last weekend at Camp David who came back to the White House with us for the night from Houston just for fun. The social life is all right. 'Cause George Bush keeps us on our toes."

Indeed. During the initial days at the White House the Bushes engaged in a compulsive round of socializing, wooing members of Congress unhappy with the negative tone of the campaign, and journalists as well. The night she was invited to join the Bushes for dinner, Jessica Lee, a White House reporter for *USA Today*, said, "I couldn't get over it, a Washington reporter parking in front of the White House." Ms. Lee is the owner of a rusty blue Datsun sports car, according to *The New York Times* reporter who elicited her quote. Dinner and a tour of the White House, complete with a viewing of a signed draft of the Gettysburg address and the awesome Lincoln bed, became a regular story in the newspaper society pages. (The Bushes finally gave a video tour to ABC's Sam Donaldson and Diane Sawyer, so the public could see it, too.)

★ ★ ★

Though Mrs. Bush balances politics with her friends and family, and keeps a close eye on White House goings-on, in conversation she marvels at life in the White House and prefers to emphasize the softer side of her life. The ease and glamour. The chance to meet the world's most accomplished people. "An enormous perk of the job," Mrs. Bush said. She described a visit by dance impresario Martha Graham, now in her nineties. "There were moments when she talked where [this greatness] all came back. I could see her dancing and she looked like . . . a young girl," Mrs. Bush marveled.

She was also impressed by a rarely seen, softer side of Margaret Thatcher. "It's interesting when you get to know people a little bit more on a personal level. I think you think of Margaret Thatcher one way. When you meet her you're sort of overcome by another side of her. For instance, you know, I have enormous respect for her as a woman who is the head of a world power and very influential in the European Community, which is really a power. But when we went to visit her, I was really overwhelmed by her enormous courtesy and hospitality and the female side came out. . . . She took me upstairs to show me the room herself and said, 'I thought maybe you'd enjoy these books and I thought of you when I saw this.' I thought that was very sensitive and it was a side of Margaret that I don't think others will see and I enjoyed that."

She continued: "You also have a feeling in common with people like that, which is a surprise in a way. Because they have children. They have grandchildren. They can't see them as often as they'd like—you sort of put a wall around your children so that they'll be protected. Anyway, I think you have something in common with them."

Another thing Bar found fascinating was swapping notes with other foreign leaders' wives. After visiting with Mila Mulroney in Canada, Mrs. Bush reported: "We talked about other world leaders and their wives, and we had very different impressions. We had *very* different impressions and I told George, too. He was interested. But it was just fascinating to me. The women that both of us have met with and done things with. Now maybe it makes a difference, too, if you're the wife of the prime minister or the vice-president's wife. Maybe there's a difference in there, who knows? Or maybe it makes a difference if you're from an African country or French-speaking. Or if you're in the Commonwealth. There are a lot of things that could have made a difference. But I was fascinated with the people that I adored [and] she didn't. And people she did, I wasn't too sold on."

The couple also appeared to enjoy state dinners, not necessarily cozy occasions. Mrs. Bush said she had an especially good time at the dinner in June for Australian Prime Minister Bob Hawke. "He's what you call a relaxed guest. You know, Australians are very much like Texans, anyway. I don't know why. There's a sort of feeling of continuity there."

That evening Mrs. Bush had especially enjoyed the entertainment. "Leontyne Price just happens to be a favorite of mine and an old friend. During dinner, out of the blue, she broke into song. I can't remember the song that she sang, but the violinists were playing. They didn't play Vienna waltzes for some reason, they played singable songs. And she started to sing—I think I wrote it in my diary—but whatever she sang was—I mean it was so special to have that voice in the middle of dinner singing out. . . . There was a magic about that evening. I don't think the food was any better, but I think just the choice of people. I mean every table looked like they couldn't bear to stand up after dinner; they just wanted to stay where they were."

Since joining the world's power elite, Mrs. Bush has undergone a personal transformation of sorts. Like Kitty Dukakis, who underwent a visual makeover on the campaign trail, Bar *looks* different. She has shed her matronly looks. Despite the off-hand way in which she and her designers dismiss her clothes, she cares a lot about her looks. No different from most American women, she *loves* looking good. When she bumped into her daughter and two of her girlfriends while walking around the grounds of the Kennebunkport house, the group caught up on inaugural gossip. Today everyone was dressed in jeans. Doro's friends teased Mrs. Bush on how beautiful she looked during inaugural week. "We loved the inauguration," she said to the young women. "I heard you were all there and I saw none of you. It was a wonderful vacation. It was so much fun. You wouldn't have recognized me if you saw me. . . . I had lipstick on and makeup."

"Oh, you looked so glamorous," one of Doro's friends replied. "Sca-asi . . ." she drooled teasingly.

Mrs. Bush giggled like a teenager. Then did a little dance. A bit like the twist. "Scaasi! Scaasi! Scaasi!" she laughed delightedly, jittering back and forth. "All Scaasi clothes!" Doro and her friends roared with laughter then clambered back into their car and took off.

In an interview in Kennebunkport, it became apparent she was extremely sensitive to how Americans were receiving their new first lady. "I look at my mail and try to get the gist of it. To see if it's really not saying, 'Listen, you are a pig and we hate you,'" she said bluntly. "None of them have said that so far."

Contrary to popular belief, Mrs. Bush has been having couturier fittings ever since she was in the vice-president's house. "She has people that she's used through the vice-presidential years, and she still uses them," Susan Porter Rose said. "And she goes up to New York, and they do designs, show her swatches of fabric, and she makes choices." Shopping off the rack went out a long time ago, although she did purchase a "cheap" pair of shoes for the inaugural balls. "I bought twenty-nine-dollar [ones]—I think it was," she said. "Had them dyed to match the dress because I knew I had to give them away. Every inch of my feet told me *never* buy twenty-nine-dollar shoes. Ever! I wore them again for the diplomatic reception. And barely . . . I mean, they are the *worst* shoes you ever knew. But everything I wore had to be given away. The fake pearls. The dress. The stole. The ravishing pocketbook. All go to the Smithsonian."

Mrs. Bush has her own checkbook and always has had. "I never have to ask [George] for money. I have another source I go to," she explained. "Don Rhodes. He handles all our financial things. George said to him, years and years ago, this is what the children get for allowance every month, and whenever Barbara Bush asks you for money, give it to her. Not bad, huh?

"I heard George say one day—which really shocked me, he might not say that anymore—Bar is really good. She never spends too much money. I have a guilty conscience every day of my life. But I don't buy things unless I really feel I need them. I am getting more spoiled now," she confessed. "I think I shocked Casey [Healey] because I sent her out to buy tennis shoes the other day. I saw some Reeboks, all-white. I like all-white and she brought back two pairs. And I said, 'I will take both.' And she said, 'What?'

"Now we go to Camp David. Now we are here. Then we go to Maine. And I think I am old enough to have tennis shoes at each place. That's four of them. So I don't have to worry. I bought three bathing suits the other day—they are not lovely. I hate them on skinny, lovely things—there is a lot of fabric."

One of the designers from whom she buys, Arnold Scaasi, has said, "Fashion isn't her main concern at all. She wants to look good and then forget about it." But Bar loves good clothes. Mingling with other guests in the front hall of the White House after a state dinner honoring Australian Prime Minister Bob Hawke, William Draper, administrator of the U.N. Development Programme, joked about a little shopping trip to Scaasi's Bar took his wife, Phyllis, on. Draper laughed as he told the story of how later on Bar asked him if he was still mad at her because of the expense. "It's heavy on the checkbook," Draper said laughing, looking over at his Scaasi-gowned wife.

In contrast to the brittle Nancy, Mrs. Bush has used wit to elude criticism for wearing expensive designer clothing. On the president's first trip to Europe for the NATO summit, Mrs. Bush wore different clothes for every occasion. When a reporter mentioned it, she quipped, "I hoped you'd notice. I killed myself."

Nor has she been criticized for redecorating several rooms at the White House and Camp David with the help of society interior designer Mark Hampton. "You walk into the residence and she says every day, 'Thank God for Nancy Reagan.' She did nothing but compliment Nancy Reagan while she made a lot of changes. Very smart," a former campaign aide said, recalling how the Carters lived with severe structural problems, shunning the federal funds appropriated for White House redecoration rather than deal with the expected political fallout of refurbishing the White House. "Barbara Bush changed three or four major rooms up there without any problem at all because she just kept saying she didn't need to change a thing. That is a masterful political way to handle that situation."

Hampton, who helped Bar decorate the vice-president's residence, said she had done "a general sprucing up" at Camp David. "Anything that Mrs. Bush puts her hand to becomes fun because she's so involved in it," Hampton told *The Washington Post*. Mrs. Bush agreed. "It is fun. And the people are spectacular. I have never known people so dying to take care of your every want. It is a wonderful house. A very happy house. Filled with sunshine and the most beautiful food you ever saw in your life."

CHAPTER THIRTEEN

❧

Life at the White House

I'm way behind in the work I've got to do, and there are so many new people in my life, I've been neglecting old friends. When I retire, I'm going to lobby for a salary for First Ladies, because it's much more of a 24-hour job than anyone would guess.

—BETTY FORD, *The New York Times*, 12/8/74

Before moving into the White House, Mrs. Bush had frequently expressed misgivings about life at 1600 Pennsylvania Avenue. "I think how awful it must be for Nancy Reagan not being able to walk around the lawn, having strangers wandering through the downstairs rooms all morning," she told a *New York Times* reporter in 1982. "There are enormous downsides [to being first lady]," she repeated to a group of reporters gathered for a pre-inaugural interview at the vice-president's house. "I think Nancy felt besieged at times. And I think she was criticized for things that she shouldn't have been. I mean, I honestly think that if someone gives you the money, raises the money privately to buy china for the White House, the American public ought to say thank you instead of being critical."

Her son Marvin said, "I think after being in what I would consider the nicest house in Washington, the Observatory—it was a home. It was a big Victorian house—I think she was worried about moving into the White House and feeling like she was in a museum."

Once there, she talked openly about maintaining an open-door policy and stressed the importance of not becoming too isolated. After years in Washington Mrs. Bush has a heightened consciousness of hangers-on and the fawning that come with being in power. "Some of us have been around long enough to know what it means," she said. "I don't know if people tell you the truth."

Nancy Ellis remembered Bar telling her, "'You've got to come and stay, otherwise it will be like being a prisoner here.' I think she keeps herself from being trapped and will continue to do that. . . . I think they will open it up a lot more so they are not sitting up there, just the two of them, on the second floor," Mrs. Ellis said. Mrs. Bush expressed those sentiments herself to a group of reporters who interviewed her over lunch one day in the spring. "I am not going to let him be a prisoner in this house, and we are going to go out and we are going to do things—we're just going to go out. Both of us," she insisted.

Andy Stewart added, "They're such outdoor people. They're such active, do-it-yourself types. I mean she plants the trees, and the bushes, and the gardens, and does all the stuff around. And walks, five or six miles a day, and all that. So that's curtailed. [The other day] we were kidding [that] it will be years before she will drive a car. Isn't that extraordinary for someone who has done everything all her life for herself? I mean, some people are perfectly happy to sit back, and they say the one thing they want when they get older is to have someone drive them around because they can't stand the traffic or something. But not the Bushes."

When she had thought about the prospect of her friend Kitty Dukakis moving on to the White House, Sandy Bakalar had said the one thing she feared most was that she'd lose her old friend. "Do you think that Barbara Bush is going to be able to sustain the relationships that she had?" Bakalar asked. "She is really going to have to give them up—that is a real loss."

Barbara Bush has struggled against that. "The place is different. The role is different. The responsibility, God knows, is different," said Andy Stewart.

"The pressures are not only global, but intergalactic, truthfully," Janet Steiger said. "And there is always this awesome sense that, after all, every word from the mouth of the president of the

United States can go through the entire world. You sort of feel they belong to the world now. It's amazing she can find time to see friends at all," added Steiger, a regular White House guest.

Steiger said there had been times when she felt Bar might have been able to use her friends more. "In general, some of these roles have a real quality of isolation. They are so incredibly demanding. You are so incredibly busy all the time that just taking the time for chitchat with an old friend who knows your kids by name can become a luxury. This is true of an awful lot of people who are close to Bar . . . the same really unbelievable demands. I don't think people understand the scope of those demands. . . . She's had to reach down to friends for all the years I've known her."

Steiger insisted that "one of the more amazing things" about the Bushes is that they never allowed their friendships to drift. "They stay in touch." Still, "There is a difficult role for friends of these incredible people. Everyone is reluctant to impose on them in any way. I think there are times when Bar could've used more of us and more contact and yet you certainly don't want to intrude because you know the incredible demands on her time. So it really is, has been, on their shoulders to stay in touch with everybody. More so than on yours or mine."

Doro said she has talked with her mother's friends about staying in touch. "People are afraid to call," her daughter said. "She can't always see everybody and do everything" but is insistent that her friends stay in contact. Doro recalled a phone call from her god-mother, Betsy Heminway, who asked: "'Should I call your Mom?' And I said, 'Yes, absolutely. Because first of all, she will feel left out if you don't talk to her about it. And secondly, she would want you to call her.'"

Speaking for herself, Doro said, "Sometimes I think I'm going to tell Mom some stupid trivial thing or something. But she wants to hear all that. She wants that. She doesn't want to be treated any differently. Of course, she is going to be a lot busier always."

Barbara Bush's friends and family say she has tried to keep things the same. "We haven't changed," Mrs. Bush insisted in an interview. "George still takes a shower with the dog."

But circumstances got beyond her control at times. During one of her first days in the White House, Mrs. Bush ventured beyond its gates to walk her dog. She tried to show friends Blair House, where visiting dignitaries stay across from the White House, only to find it locked, and she was unexpectedly mobbed by reporters who caught her while they were waiting to interview Henry Kissinger. Mrs. Bush said she hoped if she continued with such impromptu stops she could "wear the press out." Millie, her much-maligned spaniel, has helped Mrs. Bush retain a sense of normalcy. "That dog is her security blanket," Mrs. Stewart said. A dog running around the White House chomping on a tennis ball also functions well as an icebreaker and helps cut through protocol pretty quickly. Walking her dog—to whom she talks constantly— enables her to have time to herself and helps provide a balance in a life filled with strangers and shifting political loyalties. "Family, friends, and faith are the three things she holds on to for dear life," one of her White House aides said.

Marvin Bush, who lives ten minutes away in Alexandria, Virginia, also said, "things haven't changed" between him and his parents since they got into the White House. "I don't feel that I've lost them at all because they're the ones who drive the way we feel in this situation. They've made it easy for us. They've created an environment where it's no big deal. I've always been respectful of my parents' time, you know. Maybe it comes from being one of five children. But I make it count."

His mother makes her time count, too. Her friends say one of Barbara Bush's strengths is her ability to focus on, and enjoy, whatever she is doing at the present moment. "She really reaches out. You feel like you just *met* Barbara Bush," said longtime aide and family friend Alixe Glen, now a deputy White House press secretary.

★   ★   ★

Lunch and puppies aside, the transition into the White House was harder than the Bushes let on, especially after the grueling campaign. Some of Mrs. Bush's closest friends said they felt she needed more time than she had to adjust and for her role to emerge. "I would have thought that it didn't start off with quite such a bang, that you had several months to sort of ease into it," Mrs. Steiger said. "She told me two weeks before the inaugural, they would hit the ground running with great speed. There wasn't any easing in. The mail was already stacked in huge piles. I don't know if she feels that way. I feel that way."

In fact, Mrs. Bush said she *did* feel that way.

"You know, we were so busy. Even the transition isn't long enough—and yet it is plenty long because it's hard for the former president. . . . You are plotting and planning at getting things ready—plotting is not a nice word but I mean it in the nicest way. We moved in with twenty-eight people [who] stayed for two or three days. I think we were very lucky that way too, because I think other people haven't had that opportunity to hit the ground running."

"She works all the time at her desk. Just the paperwork was unbelievable," Doro said.

"I'm sure she sometimes feels like her life is not her own," Marvin added. He also said he believed his mother, like himself, was not enthralled with the idea of President George Bush. "First, it doesn't take a rocket scientist to see what it does to these people physically. I remember Jimmy Carter. I remember seeing a before and after picture of him, and it just seems like it wears these folks down. . . . She knows that I know that she and I share this quality. So when we're talking, it's like we're *hermano y hermana*, talking about this thing. We're on the same wavelength. I think, deep down, she would've been just as happy if he didn't run, too."

Life in the White House took some adjusting. "She's the type of person who used to do a lot of piddling around the house, and she's organized. She's incredibly organized," Marvin said. "I think that she misses time alone, just being able to run across the city and do whatever she wants to do. You know, you don't have the privacy you did before."

Marvin continued: "I think it is lonely albeit surrounded by humanity every minute of every day. I think it's a very lonely position. . . . You know, if you have an experience and you want to share it with somebody who's been through the same thing, it's a tough position to be in. Because only three or four people are there to share your thoughts and none of them are your best friends."

Mrs. Bush lost a considerable amount of weight those first few months. The change was noticeable though she denied it, even when reporters asked her about it. Explaining it, Bar faced the reality of the White House fishbowl. In early February she admitted she had lost weight but insisted it was excess weight gained on the campaign trail. "I gained thirteen pounds and lost them, but I lost them in the White House running up and down the marble stairs. You spend hours running up and down those stairs," she said. A month later she invited a small group of reporters to lunch at the White House for a wide-ranging discussion. When a reporter again asked her politely if she had lost weight, Mrs. Bush replied, "Yes. Now do you want to know why?" She then went on to explain that her weight loss, twenty-one pounds, was due to Graves' disease, a thyroid disorder, which she has described as the "biggest challenge" she has faced since her husband took office.

"It was an interesting approach to break this in the residence," said one reporter who was there. "They bring you into their territory. The level of politeness is very high. They're in control."

Frank Murray, a White House correspondent for *The Washington Times*, also viewed the lunch as a "very well-managed way to inform the world that she was sick," rather than releasing the information to the White House press corps at a daily briefing session. "They decided if she talked about enough things and combined it with the puppies, it would blunt the isolation of the medical situation, which on a quiet news day could have been played up."

In an interview at the White House in April, Mrs. Bush said her first few months were pressured. "I thought I lost weight because I was being overworked. Seriously, it wasn't a joke. I honestly thought so. Because we were up at six, going until not too late at night, ten or eleven, but with absolutely *no* time to sit down and read a book. Three hours of mail a night. A lot of reading that I really should do. And it just seemed to me that I was being overworked. Plus, of course, six puppies. It seemed to me that I just didn't have any time alone. But now I have scheduled two tennis games in a week. In the early morning I have been swimming a mile a day."

Mrs. Bush also changed her schedule, in part, she said, "because the doctors told me to, just a little bit." At the time, she added, "We are still getting things under control." She also tried to take it easy, she said, because her new medicine made her lethargic. Or, as she put it: "I was feeling the effects of this new medicine which makes you collapse."

★ ★ ★

Beyond adapting to the hectic White House pace and life-style, Mrs. Bush began to see, soon after moving into the White House, the effects the presidency would have on her family. The most visible were changes made for security: the bulletproof glass that replaced the old leaded windows at the Kennebunkport house. The Secret Service detail that began following the kids after death threats arrived. There were other family considerations, as well. From the start Bar has worried about "the terrible thing politics does to your family," as she put it in 1980 when her husband first sought the presidency. It can either tear you apart or pull you together, George junior once said.

Like the Dukakis siblings, members of the Bush clan said they felt the campaign experience brought them closer than they otherwise might have been. Marvin Bush explained: "Certainly it's made our family more cohesive. I know just among my siblings and myself—having shared the same experience is a valuable part of our relationship. Otherwise, it would have been quite natural for us not to stay in touch with each other."

He elaborated: "My brothers and sister and I, we live in five different states. My Dad's two runs for president really brought us closer together by being able to share the experience. It's like you've been in a war together, and you've shared the good moments and the bad moments."

Disagreements on issues are kept quiet. "George Bush told me abortion is the one issue that no one in his family agrees with him on," a senior campaign aide said after the election. Though he is less apt to say so now, Marvin opened up enough in 1980 to tell a reporter, "Look, I don't always agree with the guy. I don't like his stand on abortion. But he's worked his tail off. He deserves to be president."

George Bush's career has affected his children's lives in other ways, affording them opportunities they might not otherwise have had, and denying them others. "I have enormous worries about that," Mrs. Bush said shortly before the inauguration. "Only because we chose." And their choice has driven what their children can and cannot do.

All of the Bush children had put their lives on hold to join the presidential campaign. Both Bushes have expressed ambivalence about the effect the presidency might have on the lives of their five children and twelve grandchildren. "He was reluctant for me to join the campaign at first," young George said of his dad. "When I told him I was moving from Midland to Washington, I don't think he was real comfortable with the idea. He did not want his desire to be president of the United States to affect my life and what I was doing in any adverse way. He thought that pulling up stakes and moving my family to Washington was too big a sacrifice to make on his behalf. After I convinced him that this is what I wanted to do and it fit into my life nicely, simply because I had merged my business out of existence basically, then he finally came to terms with it. And then he was helpful in helping me forge a role that enabled me to be very useful to him. But at first he was reluctant."

The Bushes' second son, Jeb, eventually resigned his position as secretary of commerce of Florida in order to campaign. Neil, a Denver oil entrepreneur, took time off. Marvin, a Virginia real-estate developer, took a leave of absence.

After the election the kids scattered again. George junior returned to Texas where he first thought of entering the governor's race, then, dissuaded in part by his mother, bought a baseball team instead. Jeb and Neil returned to Miami and Denver. Months after the election Marvin confessed he was still "paying back" his two partners in Alexandria, Virginia, for the time he was away from work. The Bushes' youngest child, Doro, was the one whose life seemed most permanently altered.

During the campaign Doro frequently left her husband and two children at home in Maine to stump for her father. After the election, she took a job as a special-events coordinator with the Maine Department of Tourism. In August 1989, during the family's annual summer holiday in Maine, the Bushes announced that she had separated from her husband of seven years, Bill LeBlond. "She grew up and he didn't," a White House aide explained.

A shy woman, Doro blossomed on the campaign trail, by all accounts, as she crisscrossed the country for her father. During the campaign Doro, like her mother, referred to herself as "a late bloomer." After the election she confessed to a reporter, "I'm twenty-nine and I still don't know who I want to be."

On a cold February evening in her comfortable home in a cul-de-sac in the tiny town of Cape Elizabeth, Maine, Doro assessed the impact of the campaign and her father's election on her own life. She talked about her family, her father, her husband, and shed some light on Bush family dynamics.

Still trying to come to grips with it all, Doro talked of a recent visit to the White House. "I was down last week and walking through the White House, seeing people react to [my parents]. Or call him Mr. President, because we don't really—it's like the same deal. You look at these other people who are practically falling back out of their way and stuff and it is like—whoa! Just the importance of it kind of hit me there. Then, seeing my dad in these incredible meetings that go on for hours. Just the magnitude of the job kind of sinking in and seeing what my mom was doing.

"It's not a place I would like to hang out too much, I've decided," she said of the White House. "I will go visit a lot but it is just—I don't know—it's just very serious . . . it is hard to be totally relaxed. . . . I think it will be better to be with them other places to be able to relax and have fun."

Talking in her living room, as her two children were being fed by a nanny and her cat wandered over and around the chintz-covered furniture, Doro described a sheltered girlhood. Her father, whom she spoke of lovingly, was lenient with her, she said. She held a soft spot in her father's heart. She recalled as a little girl asking her father to "tell me about Robin" as he tucked her into bed. "I don't know why—just curious or something—and we would go through this every night. My dad would cry and I would cry and go to bed."

Doro talked about the campaign, her mother, her father's political losses, her parents' relationship, and their relationship with her. She also talked about her husband. "Growing up," the Bushes' daughter said, she "never had any boyfriends." Then at college in Boston she met Billy LeBlond, a quiet young man who now manages his own building company.

"I think my mom was finally glad," Doro said. "She was like, 'Good.' But I didn't really know how to tell my father that I had a boyfriend."

She remembered: "Billy sort of moved into my parents' house one summer. He liked to go to the tennis courts really early in the morning and was living a little further away. So I said, 'Mom, can Billy spend the night?' Because we had like this boys' dormitory upstairs.

"And Mom goes, 'Sure.' And she sort of got to know him. He was really quiet. But he sort of met everybody. And she said to him, 'Now, Bill, anytime you want to stay the night . . .'

"Well, he took her literally. And practically spent every night.

"And my mother said, 'I like that Bill. We both wake up at the same time, which is five A.M. He walks by, and gives me a little sign language. And he is a nice guy,' she'd always say."

Moving upstairs to her bedroom to curl her hair with electric rollers before heading out to dinner, Doro continued chatting. She showed off a picture of her father on her bedroom wall, signed on the back. She picked up a picture of her brothers with the family's housekeeper, Paula Rendon. Then she spoke softly, thoughtfully. "But my family is a hard family to marry into, because nobody is quiet," she confessed. "I'm sure it can be highly intimidating, especially my brothers—as much as I love them. But it is not easy. They're all power kind of guys. . . . It is really hard."

Before taking office George Bush told his offspring that he was concerned they not appear to benefit from his position. Prior to the Republican Convention Bush wrote notes to each of his children advising them to avoid even the appearance of conflict of interest, no matter what opportunities they might sacrifice. Since then, according to Mrs. Bush, they have. "Several of our boys have called their father or talked with White House ethics counselor C. Gordon Gray and have turned down things they've been offered in a business sense," Mrs. Bush said. Early in 1990, the Bushes' third son, Neil, was tied to the savings and loan scandal.

But since George Bush entered office some of his children and extended clan have taken on another role—serving as conduits to the White House from the world beyond the Rose Garden. The president and his wife are people who seek information from a wide range of sources before making decisions, and that includes family members. "That's one thing we are really working very hard on," Mrs. Bush said, "to be sure that we don't see less and less people and get less and less correspondence. That's something both of us feel very strongly about. I know it's hard to be sure you keep open and he feels very strongly about it. He fools everybody by getting on the phone. He stays in touch with about seventy-five people."

Since the election, Bush's eldest son has advised his father on Cabinet choices. According to *U.S. News & World Report*, he warned his father that Texas developers were alarmed at the idea that James Schlesinger might become energy secretary. Young George conceded that he talked to no more than five oilmen about the appointment. "The message wasn't, 'Well, take him or don't take him,' it was: 'There's a rebellion down here. Be careful,'" he told the magazine. Schlesinger was never offered the job.

Similarly, Jeb Bush, Florida's former secretary of commerce, whom some in the family expect to run for governor someday, talks with his father on various issues, including Central America. Shortly after the inauguration Jeb spoke with his father about "the Nicaraguan thing," *U.S. News* has reported. "He spoke of the influx of Nicaraguans to South Florida as a serious problem straining state social services, since some refugees were forced to live in Miami's baseball stadium." Arriving in the Florida Keys for a fishing trip a few days later, Bush said he intended to take another look at immigration law, calling Florida's "increasingly burdensome problem with Nicaraguan refugees a top priority." The magazine also described Jeb's role as more "conveyor than convincer."

Other family members also function as pipelines to the president. Trying to describe a typical family get-together, Nancy Ellis recalled participating in a forum for candidates' relatives during the 1988 race. "I remember being on the program with Mrs. Gore, other relatives . . . and Simon's daughter was saying, 'When Dad and I have dinner, I give him input into Illinois farming, things I see around the country.' It came to me and I thought, 'Jesus, what am I going to say?' And I said, 'When we get together we just shoot the breeze and get caught up on all our friends.' We are so dovetailed in with different people. We talk about them and the funny things that happen. George is liable to say, 'Have you met Roger Porter at the Kennedy School? He is wonderful. Why don't you get him out for Sunday lunch and tell me about him?' He is now the domestic policy adviser at the White House," she said offhandedly.

Like her husband, Mrs. Bush relies on family members for information and understanding of issues and social problems. The family's personalizing of issues—like one son's adoption of a child, or another's drug-pusher neighbor, or finding the right child care for Doro's children—all affect the president's and first lady's thinking. Mrs. Bush mentioned that it was Jeb who changed her views about English being declared the national language. "Because Jeb [whose wife, Columba, is Mexican-born] tells me that to the Hispanic-American, they consider that a racist thing." Jeb also heightened her awareness of the link between expanding local business opportunities and the quality of schools in surrounding areas.

It is not quite clear how in tune the well-off and socially connected Bush offspring are with worlds beyond their own, however. One afternoon during a campaign stop in Chicago, the Bushes' affable third son, Neil, chatted about his mother's life and recalled the period when she was questioning what she had done. He then mused aloud about women and families and said, "You know, I think women in general have a much more difficult time with issues that relate to family and profession. I can't imagine wanting to be a professional woman and also wanting to be responsible for kids. You know what I mean?" he asked ingenuously.

*   *   *

Though Mrs. Bush says she "tries very hard to stick to the system" and resists being used as a conduit to her husband, she does talk to him when the issue and time seem right. Staff have described the Bushes' as an "easy working relationship." She will often drop by the Oval Office to meet the president's guests. He will spring in on her White House events. For example, when Mrs. Bush announced her Foundation for Family Literacy at a White House lunch in March 1989, the president popped in to make remarks and lend his support to her effort demonstrating the concept of a "thousand points of light," as he put it.

The way Mrs. Bush describes her relationship with her husband, the two operate on a very high level of *politesse*. "George does not make decisions for his family. He has never once said to me, 'I would like you to . . .' Has he called me regularly with plans for me? Yes. But he does love to go, 'If you are not busy this afternoon, I think it would be great if you did . . .' And usually it is so much fun I am glad to do it. Sometimes I think, 'Oh, I hope George is not calling me yet again. He's got a finger in every pot.'"

Mrs. Bush passed that along the day after she received a spur-of-the-moment phone call from her husband asking her to entertain Mrs. Arias, the wife of Costa Rica's president. Bar was just on her way out to a museum with Andy Stewart and another pal when the phone rang.

"George called and he said, 'What are you doing this afternoon? It would be helpful if you had Mrs. Arias for tea.'

"And I said, 'George, I really can't. I'm going to do this [go to the museum] and then I have to do something else. Then I've got to rest before this dinner tonight'—because I was feeling the effects of this new medicine which makes you collapse.

"And he said, 'Lunch. How about having her for lunch?'

"And I said, 'If you have the nerve to call her an hour before and then to call our staff and tell them I'm having the president's wife, I'd be delighted.'

"And she came. The four of us had lunch and everybody smiled at me, so he handled it well." Mrs. Bush described Mrs. Arias as "very interesting. She had an agenda which she gave through the whole lunch. And I wanted to say, 'We love this and keep on talking, but you are wasting it on me because I don't fool around in the government.' But it was really fascinating. She knew exactly what she wanted to say and she took that opportunity to tell us. . . . She's got her own little plan there which I suspect is his. . . . So George exposes me to all sorts of interesting—sort of like the icing on the cake—things. I enjoy that a lot."

As she felt her way around the White House, like Rosalynn Carter, Mrs. Bush continued to operate the way she always has: to go directly to her husband. From her accounts and those of staff, family, and friends, her way is to weigh in at just the right moment. "I know when he is really uptight and I don't bug him when he is really uptight," she said.

Marvin Bush said, "I think privately she knows how to get his attention. I *guarantee* you that she knows which areas she might have more influence in than others. One area she will not influence is foreign policy. It's just not her thing, but when it comes to other issues where she has had more contact than my dad, then I'm sure he'd probably be interested in her thoughts."

He added: "I think my mom has learned a lot. Maybe one of the things is that if you want to be effective as a first lady or as a spouse of a candidate, to maybe internalize some of the things that you think are not going too well and save it for when it matters. If you have something to say to somebody on the campaign, make sure that you don't express your opinion fifty times in a two-hour period, so that when you *do* say something, people pay attention. Make it count."

By the president's own admission, he seeks his wife's advice. Shortly after the election, on a vacation in the Florida Keys, when asked if he had solicited any advice during the transition, Bush grinned at reporters and pointed to his wife. *The Washington Post* reported: "Barbara raised her eyebrows pointedly as she stood by his side. She then leaned into a microphone to say: 'Just kidding.' Bush, still laughing, responded: 'No, she's not.'"

In the spring of 1988 Bush told David Hoffman of *The Washington Post* that after he had talked about aiding the homeless in a Republican candidates' debate, "Some guy that's all involved in one of these homeless programs wrote Barbara saying, 'I know you care about the homeless, but I listen to your husband [and] he doesn't.' So we got into a big argument. She had been telling me I had to do more, and I think she's right."

When the president met the governors for an education summit in Charlottesville, Virginia, in the fall of 1989 Bar asked her husband to include the spouses in the working sessions.

In Washington, Mrs. Bush is widely viewed as a key behind-the-scenes operator. Some argue her way of advancing her views was in backing certain Cabinet choices. She is credited with urging her husband to promote Louis Sullivan from the presidency of Morehouse College, where she is on the board, to his Cabinet post as secretary of health and human services. When asked why Mrs. Bush didn't speak on issues or explain *her* stands, former campaign adviser Deborah Steelman pointed to Sullivan as an example of Barbara Bush's *modus operandi:* "She can make a Louis Sullivan happen, so why get involved?"

Members of the White House press corps view her as Bush's prime unofficial adviser. "She's a key part of his kitchen cabinet," said the *Tribune*'s Tim McNulty. "And his kitchen cabinet is all over the house. He's got kitchen cabinet advisers down in the basement and up in the attic. In Texas and at the Old Executive Office Building. For all that, he keeps everything close-knit."

In the White House Bar got the chance to settle scores from the campaign. One of the areas where she quickly became most active was in expressing opinions on her husband's staff. Bar's friendship with Joanne Kemp reportedly helped ease the way for her husband's onetime rival's appointment to HUD. And although initially turned off by Budget Director Richard Darman's arrogant and condescending style, Bar had a change of mind and helped ease Darman's way into the Bush camp.

Rich Bond, a former top aide, cited "ethics" as an area Mrs.

Bush feels strongly about. That and "the type of people her husband has around him." As on the campaign trail, now in the
White House, Mrs. Bush is concerned that her husband's staff
keep him well informed. "You want to protect your husband a
little bit. But so far, I haven't had to intervene or anything in his
life and I hope I won't," Mrs. Bush said in July 1989. "Because I
go right to George when I have a problem. And I know people are
scared to death of me, and I'm sorry about that. And George says,
'Leave it, let it lie. It's better that way.'"

One White House aide described the attitude of West Wing staff
toward Mrs. Bush as one of "healthy respect." There's a fine line
of "she won't mess with them if they don't mess with her," the
aide said. "She's no fool."

During an interview at the White House she described a scene
one morning when she walked by the Oval Office on her way for
her early swim. "I saw Dan [Quayle] and George—maybe Sununu
and Brent Scowcroft—sitting there talking very seriously. And
then I swam, thinking about Oliver North, and I hope that—I
know that—Dan Quayle is in on everything, and I hope nobody
thinks that they should spare their president or their vice-president
things, which I think people did during the Reagan administration. It's such a mistake," she said. "If we've learned nothing else
from that horrible time, we've learned that you don't do your president a favor, or your vice-president, by sparing them these
things."

Since she's been in the White House Mrs. Bush has also done
some Capitol Hill shmoozing of her own. She courted Heather
Foley, wife of House Speaker Thomas Foley, inviting her for
lunch when her husband was leading a fight against Bush's plan to
cut the capital gains tax rate. Mrs. Foley is her husband's unpaid
administrative assistant and considered by some to be an extremely
influential woman on Capitol Hill. Mrs. Bush has also persuaded
the president to support legislation forbidding discrimination
against AIDS patients. According to *U.S. News:* "After speaking
with Dr. Burton Lee, a family friend and member of the federal
AIDS commission, Mrs. Bush convinced her husband that people
with AIDS, especially children who have contracted the disease
through blood transfusions, must be protected from prejudice—
and that concern should take precedence."

Mrs. Bush also sees her role as actively protecting her husband.

After the two returned from a Fourth of July holiday in Kennebunkport, where they were deluged by guests, she said: "I have to really protect George a little bit. You know, you have to give him more peace and quiet. George is very much at home and very much at peace with all his family. But he has to be allowed to go fishing alone or with one adult or two." Talking in a maternal voice, as though she were describing one of her sons, she said: "He took boatloads out because he's so precious and sweet. . . . I've learned I have to protect him—no accepting dinners up there at all . . . because he doesn't want to come in from fishing. Everybody just needs time alone. I know I do. . . . I just learned that George needs—I know I need quiet, but George *really* needs quiet."

★   ★   ★

Even though most Americans saw more style than substance in the early days of the Bush administration, when the first polls came out Bar got rave reviews and eclipsed her husband in popularity. Nine months into the new administration 37 percent of people polled by *USA Today* gave her high marks, while just 13 percent gave the president the same grade. In October 1989 *The Wall Street Journal* found the trend continuing. The *Journal* reported: "A number of groups have a more favorable opinion of her personally than they have of her husband's job performance. Among liberals 60 percent have positive views of her, while 50 percent approve of the president's job performance. Among professionals 76 percent have a favorable opinion of her, compared to 62 percent who approve of her husband's performance. While a quarter of black voters disapprove of Mr. Bush's handling of his job, only 15 percent have a negative view of his spouse." And, perhaps most telling, the *Journal* found voters by three to one preferred Mrs. Bush as first lady to Mrs. Reagan.

As those numbers may suggest, one way Mrs. Bush has been especially helpful to the administration has been by creating the impression that—through her—those with more liberal views may have an ear in the White House: especially regarding abortion and gun control. By never saying she actually agreed with her husband's position on abortion, only that she wouldn't talk about how she felt, she kept the possibility open that she was more liberal than her husband. A year after the election, in an NBC interview with John Cochran, she even resurrected the hated "L-word," calling herself a "liberal" on certain social issues. "The assumptions about her position on abortion are true," one close White House staffer contends.

When asked to identify Barbara Bush's greatest potential assets and liabilities back on the campaign trail, George Bush's campaign press secretary, Sheila Tate, offered: "Her humor and her candor. Her humor was the asset. Her candor was always—I mean, on a campaign would always be—a potential liability. I mean, she's sort of irrepressible."

But as became increasingly evident once she'd moved into the White House, Barbara Bush was more repressible than Tate would have predicted. The CIA chief's wife, the woman who clammed up on the Bush family's opinion of Dan Quayle, turned out to be a remarkably secretive lady. In that, she totally followed her husband's chameleon style.

Barbara Bush admits to what she has dubbed "muzzling" herself ever since her husband was first elected to political office long ago in Texas. In formal interviews she hedges what she says as best she can, often negating in the last part of a sentence what came at the start. When it was pointed out to her, for example, that most other first ladies were frustrated by not being able to speak their minds in the White House, Mrs. Bush replied: "Maybe I lost [that right] years ago and just don't know it, but I don't think that's true."

Since moving into the White House Barbara Bush's public stance on issues has become an integral part of the Bushes' noncommittal style, what some perceive as a facility to walk "both sides of an issue," depending on where their political strength lies at the moment. Mrs. Bush, for one, believes strength lies in numbers. Talking one July morning in the White House, Mrs. Bush criticized a *Boston Globe* editorial that took issue with her husband's position on the flag. "They said, 'Now, there goes old President Pander; just because three fourths of the people feel the courts were wrong on the flag, he went along with them,'" she said, repeating their comments. "Well, if three fourths of the people are against it, something is wrong with *The Boston Globe*, in my opinion. I mean, that's what we rule by. The majority rules in our country. And I suspect that seven eighths of the people are against burning the flag. In fact, probably many more than that."

Mrs. Bush went on. "I think when the people speak, there we are. I mean, that's what our country is all based on."

Perhaps the most telling example of that philosophy has been Mrs. Bush's responses on abortion. Shortly after her husband took office, Mrs. Bush made news in a session with reporters at the White House, telling them she was "grateful" that the U.S. Supreme Court had enabled a New York man, Martin Klein, to obtain an abortion for his comatose wife. Following the advice of his wife's doctors, Klein hoped the procedure would speed her recovery. It was delayed, however, when an anti-abortion supporter challenged Klein's guardianship of his wife. The case dominated the news early in February 1989.

She also told reporters that guns scared her and she was in favor of banning automatic rifles at a point when her husband wasn't. She said that military assault rifles like the one used in a California rampage that left five children dead in the summer of 1988 should "absolutely" be outlawed and that unlike Nancy Reagan, she doesn't own a handgun because "I'm too afraid I'd shoot the wrong person."

Relaxing over an early February weekend in Kennebunkport, Mrs. Bush made even stronger comments on the Klein case in a private interview. Indeed, she *volunteered* them, speaking openly on the issue. "This week it has certainly been very moving with that man," Mrs. Bush said. "I've seen him on television twice—the husband—and it has touched me. He has moved me. . . . He wants to get on with his life and he wants his wife to get well."

Not only had Klein's story captured *her* attention, Mrs. Bush said, but it had captured the *president's* attention as well. "He thought it was outrageous that a husband with a wife in a coma had to go through all that," Mrs. Bush said.

The Klein case was a "perfect example" why her husband supported abortions in the exceptions of rape and incest and when a woman's life was in danger, she said. "That is why he has the exception. A perfect example this very week."

After her comments generated enormous attention, Mrs. Bush spent days backpedaling. On a trip to the Far East later that month, she made it official: Barbara Bush would not speak on issues.

"She's not the one who makes policy. She's not the one who lobbies Congress. She's not the president of the United States. To that extent, her opinions are not the ones that should be the focus," Anna Perez told reporters shortly after the Bushes arrived in Japan for the funeral of Emperor Hirohito.

Asked whether Mrs. Bush was being muzzled, Perez said, "Not that I know of," *The Washington Post* reported.

"What if we think her opinions are important?" veteran UPI correspondent Helen Thomas asked.

"Shame on you," Perez said.

"Shame on me for saying the first lady has a right to an opinion?" Thomas asked.

"It doesn't mean she doesn't have a right to an opinion," countered Perez. "She has a right to express one or not."

Later, in a White House interview, Bar explained: "I've made up my mind. Gun control, abortion, all those sorts of issues that would cause controversy. I'm trying to be a positive force on subjects. I want to be very effective with the homeless and with AIDS, and the way not to do it is to get yourself into controversial issues that will divert you from the things you are really interested in. Half the world is for and half the world is against those particular issues and I am not going to get in them or on them."

Mrs. Bush said she is comfortable not speaking her mind in public. She insisted she doesn't feel muzzled or as if she has lost her freedom of speech. "I think anyone who is controlled or disciplined—anyone—as you get older you think out your answers. You realize you have a responsibility. Sometimes I forget."

She has not had any trouble shying away from a public stance. "Because I have perfect freedom of choice to say what I think at home to my husband, which is really where it counts in my case," she says. "I have no qualms about telling George what I feel and he politely listens."

That, she said, is what makes a good partnership. "I think a good mother and father make a decision about a child behind a closed door and then come out united. You don't want your father coming out and saying you can go to the movies and your mother saying, 'No.' And then having the big thing in front of the children."

Not that the electorate is in search of moviegoing guidance.

"I use the analogy because that's the way I think a very healthy marriage is. Why come out and air it publicly? Or publicly argue with your husband, if you are going to argue with him? That's why I've chosen a number of issues not to speak on. Because if I say, 'I am not going to speak on one,' everybody says, 'Well, we know how she feels.' But you don't speak on them; you can do it privately. It just makes news.

"If George wanted to make news, all he had to do was say, 'I just don't agree with President Reagan.' We are just not that kind of people. Someone else has to do that. We are not going to."

By the summer of 1989, when the Supreme Court decision on the Webster case reignited the abortion question, Bar no longer took a stand at all distanced from her husband's. During a July Fourth vacation at the Bushes' summer home in Maine, for instance, a reporter asked her if she would comment on the Webster decision. She shook her head no, and after a pause said, "I go with my president."

Despite that answer, her earlier remarks and her husband's change of mind on assault weapons kept the impression of a more liberal Barbara Bush fixed in the minds of some.

Mrs. Bush's reluctance to speak out on issues, especially abortion, is viewed as pragmatic by some Washington insiders but cynically by others. Disappointed feminists criticized Mrs. Bush for failing to endorse their stand at a pro-choice rally held in the spring of 1989 in Washington, D.C. Barbara Bush's name was cited more than once. Comedian Whoopi Goldberg said she hoped the first lady would "look at men and women here and talk to your husband tonight." Writer Gloria Steinem cited Barbara Bush's reticence as an example of the price to be paid by marrying into power, and led protesters in numerous refrains of the chant: "Free Barbara Bush!"

The evening of that march Mrs. Bush told the network news, "That's what America is all about and it's great." Lest her remarks be misinterpreted as taking a pro-choice stance, the White House officially qualified it, explaining that Mrs. Bush did not mean to say she was pro-choice but that it was a "great" exercise of freedom of speech by more than 300,000 women and men. The same could have been said for the other side.

Sheila Tate agrees that a certain caution and self-effacement is common when women reach the White House. "It's an accommodation you make to political life," Tate said. "Look at every first lady; they've all had to do it. They get too far out on a limb on an issue and all they do is get grief. You know, 'How dare she? She's not an elected official.' 'What's she doing, going to Cabinet meetings?' 'She's got no business in politics.' 'It's embarrassing that she's been sent to represent the country at a funeral.' 'She's overstepping her bounds.' 'She's in big trouble.' 'She's got the right wing of the party screaming.'" Who needs that? Tate wondered.

"Over time you recognize that's just part of the system," Tate mused. "And it's funny how you and your husband, no matter who you are, over time your views come closer together anyway. In politics it becomes very hard to see in black and white. You always see the shades of gray. And you understand the forces that work on both sides of an issue, and suddenly nothing is simple, I think. You seldom end up being a one- or two-issue person, because you're exposed to all of them, and you agree with what your husband is doing on ten different things and that's what you want. So whatever helps solidify his position is in your interest. You identify so strongly with that. You have to."

Biding time outside the White House gates, some Democrats have watched Mrs. Bush's actions with interest—from both a political and cultural vantage. Wendy Sherman, who managed Mike Dukakis's Washington office during the election, is one. "It depends on whether you believe in Machiavellian conspiracy theories or not," she laughed. "There is one school of thought in Washington that her saying what she did on both the Klein case and the AKA assault weapons allowed the Bush administration to have it both ways. They had Bush being tough and Barbara being soft. And that it was calculated.

"The other theory is that nothing was orchestrated. She spoke out in advance of orchestrating and it did create a problem and so she's going to try and be quiet."

In the view of politically active women like Sherman, who managed Barbara Mikulski's successful bid for the U.S. Senate, Mrs. Bush's actions and response manifest this culture's ambivalence about women in or near power. "In the case of a married woman whose husband is the elected official, Americans seem to both want someone who is loyal to their spouse and at the same time they want someone who is their own person," she said. "Sometimes the two don't go together."

★ ★ ★

Before leaving for the NATO summit in July 1989, Barbara Bush chatted again about her role as first lady. Rested from a July Fourth Kennebunkport vacation, she looked well, despite problems with her eyes caused by her thyroid condition. She wore a jaunty-looking Scaasi day dress—bright blue with bouncing red, yellow, and pink squares all over a three-tiered flounced skirt. This Barbara Bush looked totally different from the matron of yore in Connecticut Yankee shirtwaists. Her hair was stylishly done and swept up off her face. She'd been transformed and looked more vibrant than she had in years.

Mrs. Bush nestled into a plush armchair on the second-floor residence of the White House, sitting beneath a Cézanne painting of Mont Sainte-Victoire. She faced another magnificent Impressionist painting of lilac and green water lilies by Monet, which was given to the White House by Jacqueline Kennedy in her husband's memory. "I have a new dress the color of that painting," Mrs. Bush beamed.

The second-floor family residence is serene: incredibly quiet, and filled with light and soft colors. It is a comfortable, careful arrangement of furniture that fosters an intimate atmosphere, despite the fact that the first family lives in what amounts to an extremely long railroad apartment atop a public museum. Off the path of the visitors, the hardship of making the White House a home is exemplified in a little-known architectural feature: All the second-floor rooms jut off a hallway that runs the length of the White House itself. As Doro said: "The house is actually pretty cozy considering how big it is."

Mrs. Bush and some of her friends believe in the concept of life passages. Andy Stewart, for one, believes her old friend is facing the challenge of her life. "I think things sort of come along when you're ready. Maybe a few years ago she wouldn't have seen as many people or traveled as much. Been in positions of such authority or such responsibility. All the way along, as we all know from Gail Sheehy, there are passages, and they come along . . . when you're ready. But she's ready. She's ready."

But like her son Neil's opinion on working women, some of Mrs. Bush's pronouncements make her seem hopelessly out of touch with the reality of most American women's lives. In an interview with National Public Radio correspondent Susan Stamberg in October 1989, Mrs. Bush said those mothers who "opt to work" have to make an added effort to cope.

"And it's hard on you, but you have to put your children first. And I think your boss has to accommodate a little bit. I mean, if you need to go to school to see your child in a school situation, they should make accommodations for it. You'll have to make it up, but that's just a fact of life."

The first lady told Stamberg—married, mother of one son, and a woman who is credited with helping make National Public Radio what it is today—that a woman can't be a bank president and a mother at the same time. "You can't—oh, you can do it—but are you going to give the children the time they need? Now, I'm assuming a bank president has to work like a president of the United States and work fourteen hours a day. If a bank president just works the regular hours, you can do both. But if you're going to work fourteen hours a day, it just isn't fair when you've had children."

Stamberg protested, "But it's such an old-fashioned idea. . . ."

Mrs. Bush *is* old-fashioned, perhaps terribly so, in another area as well. Chatting that day, seven months after her husband took office, she confessed that all her own six pregnancies "were planned." But when it came to talking to her own children about "the birds and the bees," Mrs. Bush paused. "I think children know, now. I mean, truthfully. I'm pretty sure they know.

"I never did things like the pill," Mrs. Bush explained. "I never talked to Doro about taking the pill. I'm a little bit old-fashioned about that. First of all, I'm not sure the pill is good for you. I am not convinced yet that—I know that's really old-fashioned—I'm not really sure that it's safe. I don't know that, but I remember when friends of mine took it, they lost pigmentation in their face and I'm not too sure about it yet. But I also think people abuse it badly—or used to. Maybe they don't now, but they used to badly."

Mrs. Bush continued, "We just talked when it came up, and questions did come up. . . . And I also gave her a little book to read. A friend of mine gave me—her daughter a book and said it seemed to solve some of those small problems."

Despite her popularity, Barbara Bush raises the issue of just how relevant a traditional first lady can be to American women. "Today's young women don't have to look up to the first lady," Michel McQueen wrote in a profile of Mrs. Bush in *The Wall Street Journal* in October 1989. "They can look up to Pat Schroeder, they can look up to Nancy Kassebaum. The world has changed in that there are a lot more women exercising their own political power."

In July 1989, Barbara Bush seemed to be grappling with that very issue.

Not long before, Nancy Ellis had mailed Mrs. Bush an excerpt from *The Autumn Garden,* a play by Lillian Hellman first produced in New York in March 1951. There, one character said to another: "So at any given moment you're only the sum of your life up to then. There are no big moments you can reach unless you've a pile of smaller moments to stand on. That big hour of decision, the turning point in your life, the someday you've counted on when you'd suddenly wipe out your past mistakes, do the work you'd never done, think the way you'd never thought, have what you'd never had—it just doesn't come suddenly. You've trained yourself for it while you waited—or you've let it all run past you and frittered yourself away."

When asked about Hellman's script, the first lady's review was "I loved it. I loved it."

Did the excerpt describe her? "Oh, I don't think she [Nancy Ellis] sent it describing me. . . . It's just sort of something we all believe. It's a sort of moral philosophy of 'You don't just luck into things, as much as you'd like to think you do. You build step by step, whether it's friendships or whether it's opportunities.' The thing, I think, that Lillian Hellman was saying was 'You may miss opportunities if you haven't built those. . . .' I think that's what it was saying. 'You make your own opportunities really, but don't let it pass you by. Be ready when the moment comes.'"

How did that philosophy apply to her own life?

Mrs. Bush was momentarily baffled. "Well, my opportunity came when I was nineteen and I took it," she laughed. "No, that's not true. You're making me a little ashamed because there's a message I'd like to get across. I'm sort of saying, 'Do what I say, not what I do.'"

Then with uncharacteristic uncertainty Barbara Bush added, "I'm not sure I've built my bricks as well as I should have. I'm not sure of that. . . . But I do believe, 'If you don't use it, you lose it.' So I believe in continuing to build. I think that's important. At my age, maybe I should be thinking more than I [should] about building."

CHAPTER FOURTEEN

✦

First Lady or First Partner?

> Why do we want public wives to appear but not
> to act, to be seen but not heard? In today's cli-
> mate of sexual equality, many women may feel
> "oppressed" at the thought of wives who must al-
> ways appear to be in agreement with their hus-
> bands, and are required to do so charmingly and
> convincingly. . . . But we can't have it both ways.
> We can't continue to demand the reassurance that
> public wives provide, and then insist on keeping
> them out of the "hard news" arena.
>
> —JOANNA BOWEN GILLESPIE,
> "The Public Wife as Visual Aid"

The 1988 presidential race reflected the changing realities of
American families and changing realities of women's roles. With
up to thirteen candidates, voters had the opportunity to see the
changes in their own lives and marriages reflected in the country's
political leadership. Thirteen different marriages were subjected to
the kind of attention that at times matched the intensity and insensitivity devoted to show-business romances. They ran the whole
range, the whole gamut. Traditional marriages between a supportive wife and an overachieving husband. Marriages between equally
educated partners who shared the same profession. Marriages in
which wives adopted issues and causes of their own. Second marriages. And an adulterous marriage—which eliminated one contender from the race.

Faced with this revealing spectrum and with Nancy Reagan very
much still in the news, at the start of the race, voters and the
press alike began to ask new questions. Could the spouse of a presidential contender be free to pursue her own career, hold her
own opinions, and advocate her own causes without fear of

damaging her political partner's prospects? Could she be her own person? What was the appropriate role for a candidate's wife? How did these women really fit in with how Americans elect their president? Beyond providing emotional support to their mates, for all their campaigning, did they get him any more votes?

"The bottom line is, would anyone ever vote for or against your husband because of you? That's a question every candidate's wife asks," said Mary Finch Hoyt, Rosalynn Carter's former press secretary. "They all think they do. Because they all get back that rush. That adrenaline. But would you pick your doctor because you like his wife?"

And yet clearly there was more to the question than that. Republican pollster Linda DiVall argued that the doctor analogy didn't hold. "The problem with the presidency is that there's this innate curiosity that everybody has about the candidate, and by extension the family, and they feel it's their right to get to know everything they possibly can, and part of it is getting to know the spouse," she said.

That interest, of course, has been there for years. What 1988 brought was a new focus on influence.

Several women whose careers and causes could have posed problems for their husbands sprang onto the political stage. Careers weren't the only issues. On the campaign trail these women were repeatedly asked how much influence they had. More important, as the unelected half of the presidential pair, how accountable would they be for that influence?

As *The Washington Post*'s David Broder wrote in April 1987:

When marriages are partnerships of independent, able and co-equal people and one of them seeks the presidency, new issues are created for voters, for reporters, and for both spouses. It would be fatuous to suppose that women with years of experience in government and/or clear views on public policy will be of no importance in governments their husbands head. It would be sexist to suggest that they might not be qualified to play some formal or informal role in the administration. But the Constitution did not envisage the presidency as a dual office, and it is not clear what standards or methods are appropriate for ensuring accountability in the unelected half of these modern marriages.

Difficult questions. The array of would-be first ladies this year didn't make them any easier to answer. During this election year there was one woman whose deeply held religious beliefs raised a question about whether she should be watched more closely. There was a woman whose emotional problems, in hindsight, raised questions about whether her husband was a suitable man to be president—and just how much the public had the right to know about a spouse's medical history. Even the traditional woman who ended up in the White House posed her own puzzles. When does old-fashioned reticence shade into concealment? Just how relevant could a traditional woman be to American women? Especially in an era when many more are exercising their own political power, and receiving recognition for accomplishments gained on their own merit.

The 1988 campaign showed that simply being the wife of a presidential contender continued to be a career in itself. Even the wives who had professional careers accommodated their husbands' political needs. Resigning or taking leave from work, they took to the campaign trail full time, and as surrogates virtually doubled the candidates' availability.

In this emotion-driven, issue-lean race, the spinners who looked to tap in to voters emotions most often viewed wives in very traditional, limited roles: as useful pulls on those emotional strings. Some political operatives, reporters, and voters looked at a would-be first lady to uncover her policies and points of view, but the vast majority still expected to hear what she thought about her husband, as if what she said could hold any surprises.

When a wife of a candidate broke out of that mold and started to talk differently, some found her a threat. Consider this letter from a *Chicago Sun-Times* reader named Robert Kuffel who addressed the editor about Kitty Dukakis, "her husband's closest friend and his closest adviser." He wrote: "[That] sent chills down my spine, as it sounds like déjà vu of what we've gone through these past eight years. If 'Iron Mike' is elected president it should be for his ability to govern and not for his spouse. Maybe the official ballot should read Mr. and Mrs. So and So. Remember, voters, we're to elect a president—not his wife, nor his children, nor his parents, not his cat or dog, but him alone."

The fact that so many professional women were involved in the 1988 presidential race raised still other questions that will no doubt return. Should Elizabeth Dole be applauded or condemned for trading on the perception of conflicted career woman for what was in reality only a slippery power play? Was it fair that Tipper Gore was patronized for her cause, discounted as a crusade? Should Jackie Jackson have received more credit for escaping the confines of a "wifely" niche? Was it disingenuous for Kitty Dukakis to rail against the system?

"The rituals are still so powerful and serve some function," said Ruth Mandel of Rutgers' Eagleton Institute. "When we're not following them, we're hard-pressed to know what to substitute. We still want some of the old things."

But the changes played out in the political arena weren't always as smooth as participants might have liked.

★ ★ ★

Most of the less prominent wives shared Elizabeth Dole's view of campaigning as a tremendous opportunity for personal growth and a way to gain influence and power. Even so, some of them joined the chorus that criticized Mrs. Dole for her decision to quit her job.

Hattie Babbitt, in what she affectionately called "her real life," was a Phoenix trial attorney. Through 1987 and 1988 she geared down her law practice as her participation in her husband's campaign geared up. "I practiced law full time through two statewide campaigns and two babies," she said in Iowa before the election. "So I've done that. But frankly, you couldn't do it in a presidential campaign. This is more exciting than practicing law—I've done that for thirteen years."

Hattie said her career echelon could not be compared to Liddy's. "I was disappointed because—though I essentially made the same decision, which was to put my career on hold to participate in the presidential campaign—I wasn't the secretary of transportation. There are lots of lawyers. And more than a few of them can take a deposition as well as I can."

On the trail Hattie said she saw herself functioning much as she did in the courtroom. "I'm a trial lawyer, so what I'm trained to do is argue a case on behalf of a client. I think in many ways what I do for the campaign is to argue the case on behalf of a candidate. I've just got a better client than I usually do. Sometimes my clients are harder to get enthusiastic about."

Perhaps that self-consciously professional view of her role explains why Hattie was one of the few spouses in the race who said she would not function for voters as a "window on to the candidate." She challenged the credibility of a wife's traditional testimony.

"What consultants want both of us to do is talk more about Bruce as a person," Hattie said one day in the dowdy lobby of the low-budget Kirkwood Hotel, where her husband's Iowa campaign was headquartered. "I really don't want to talk about it in public. I mean, either it feels like it's nobody's business or else it's boring. If you give six speeches a day six days a week, how many times do you want to repeat that? Whereas if one day you're talking about our commitment to providing child care, and the next about unacceptably high levels of lead in drinking water, and what causes mental retardation, those are just more fun to talk about. The consultants may be right, but that's my resistance—it's not really interesting."

Tipper Gore shared that view. "Maybe they want me to be up there giving them softball fluff on him," she said, "but I figure that I'm suspect there. Of course I am going to like the guy. I'm his wife!"

Professionally challenging or not, campaigning is hard work and Hattie Babbitt was one of the most forthcoming of the wives about its rigors. After yet another debate among the Democrats, this one at St. Anselm's College in Goffstown, New Hampshire, Hattie waited as her husband, pinned in by minicams, completed yet another round of interviews. With resignation in her voice, she cracked, "This is about as interesting as a bad cocktail party— with no booze!"

After the campaign was all over she told columnist Joyce Maynard: "I've heard one of the candidates' wives say she loves every minute of the race, and all I can say is, either she's lying or she's wacko. It's just no fun sitting in airports. Having every minute of every day scheduled. Hardly ever getting outdoors except maybe for a photo opportunity: a single run down a ski slope for the press and then back in the high heels again.

"The truth," she said, "is it's more fun ending the day in the same hotel room with my husband, but I'd really rather campaign alone. If I'm not going to be home hugging my children, I'd rather be making speeches myself than standing around getting varicose veins."

★   ★   ★

Liddy Dole and Hattie Babbitt, perhaps because they knew what was in it for them, held up well under the stresses of the campaign. Other spouses found the experience much more stressful. Like many women in the late 1980s, these "new" wives found that hands-on juggling of home, career, and family was exaggerated by the demands of the presidential race. Even on the campaign trail it seemed the division of labor between the sexes was expected to operate. Being a candidate's wife meant being a "wife" to the nth degree. The campaign demanded a superwife, an icon. An Everywife.

The wife who seemed to have the hardest time was Kitty Dukakis. Even before her emotional problems kicked in, the campaign clearly gave her more conflicts than anyone else.

Dukakis staffers in Iowa remembered days when they'd request Kitty to appear at an event only to find she couldn't get away from her job as director of a Harvard University design project called the Public Space Partnerships Program. "We'd bitch and scream. But she's the wife of a feminist and it would be silly if she didn't [work]," said Barbara Moses, an attorney who quit her job at a San Francisco firm to schedule Dukakis surrogates in Iowa.

Feminist idealism, however, quickly gave way to campaign exigency. As the demands of the race increased, she "commuted" between Boston and Iowa and other primary states. Kitty's time at Harvard decreased. By January 1988 she was down to working just two days a week. Then, by the first week in February, Harvard was out altogether.

To those few reporters who inquired about *her* career, Kitty replied how difficult it was to campaign on a national scale and keep a job. It's hard not to see in her answer a foreshadowing of her later problems. "It's a question psychologically if I can do both," she once said. "Michael manages to shift gears from the campaign trail to the governor's office. I'm not finding that easy to do."

For a while she had tried. After schlepping back and forth across twenty states for the March 8 Super Tuesday sweep, Kitty talked one evening in the basement of a North Side Chicago nightclub as she listened excitedly to final returns pour in. Earlier in the evening a packed crowd had gone wild as she and her husband stood on a stage backed by a wall of video screens stacked six wide and six tall, beaming an array of early returns and projections. Near midnight, as the network crews rolled up their cables and Mike wrapped up the last interview of the night, she unwound in her stocking feet and smoked a Saratoga.

She cheered out loud when she heard the numbers from Texas, where she had just spent hours in Bush's one-time hometown of Midland, though earning only scant press attention. She shrugged. "You never know if your efforts pay off."

Looking back, Kitty realized the far-ranging itinerary combined with the gamut of issues was unlike anything she'd done before. Looking ahead, she saw a two-week break in April free from primary contests. When asked what she planned to do then, she laughed, thinking perhaps of the staff pinch-hitting for her back at Harvard. "I will be able to spend more time at my job."

Kitty Dukakis was also aware of what she called a "double standard" applied to the female spouses of presidential contenders.

A couple of weeks after Super Tuesday, riding from Chicago to Rockford, Illinois, where she would walk alone and wave to crowds in a St. Patrick's Day parade, Kitty talked about the expectations she felt she faced. The drinking had already started, and her account showed her riding highs and lows, lows that proved hard to pull out of. She said she didn't think any husband of a woman candidate would be expected to do what she and other wives were doing in 1988. "I don't think society ought to force spouses in the political arena to be involved if they don't want to be. We have situations where we have governors' spouses who are working at their own careers and choose not to be that much involved in sensitive areas. As more and more women run for public office their husbands work professionally. . . . You know, clearly we've got a double standard in this country, still. I think if there was a woman running for president, we wouldn't expect her husband to be out there. But that's part of reality. Someday it's going to change."

It's easy to argue that any spouse would do what Kitty and the other female spouses felt they should do. But their only approved public functions, as author Riley said, continued to be largely ceremonial, nonpolitical, secondary. In short, duties traditionally filled by women. Which is why what they did seemed so sexist.

The one male spouse in the 1988 race saw his role rather differently. Only Pat Schroeder's husband, Jim, stood as a counterpoint—and not for long. When his wife decided to make her short-lived exploratory bid for the presidency in 1987, Schroeder, a partner in the Washington law firm of Kaplan, Russin and Vecchi, said he took "sort of an unstructured leave of absence" from his job to help her in her effort. Like his female counterparts, Schroeder got involved in his wife's campaign. Initially, he functioned as the chairman of his wife's exploratory committee, providing far more than emotional support. "We actually moved people into these offices and used some of our space here," he said. "I mean, we had telephones and Xerox machines and some extra space and so we sort of used this as a committee headquarters and, accordingly, I took a lot more time in the effort." Had his wife decided to launch "a real campaign," her husband said, "then you have a different structure, and my role might have been less, or different."

Nevertheless, it appeared unlikely that Schroeder would have taken on a campaign role similar to that of the other candidates' spouses. "I saw my role as schmoozing, meeting people, shaking hands, taking the pulse, asking 'What do you think?,' seeing what was out there," he said. He has avoided playing the surrogate role. In his view, "As a surrogate, the husband is usually not very good. I don't think people care much about husbands. . . . I guess it's just a tradition that we have over the years. We've seen mostly men candidates and therefore people understand that you can't be all over all the time. If the wife shows up, it seems to be acceptable and people accept that, but my feeling was that people wanted to see Pat. Wanted to talk to Pat. And they don't particularly care about me."

Pat Schroeder has said she's never expected her husband to perform like a wife. "What I have done with [my] job that's really quite different from what most politicians do is I have viewed it as my job and not [my family's] job," she told authors Ronna Romney and Beppie Harrison for their book *Momentum: Women in American Politics Now.* "My husband doesn't do thank-you notes, and he doesn't go to Ladies Teas, and he does not go back and campaign and set up housekeeping and smile and do all that, nor do the children. I post the schedule and anything [the family] want[s] to do fine. It's my job and not theirs."

Jim Schroeder described his role similarly. "We have the stereo-type that the wife is supposed to campaign for the husband," he explained. "For men, first of all, there are very few. And then a lot of the men have their own careers and perhaps don't even enjoy politics so they don't get involved at all. Other husbands, like myself, we have some political background." He ran unsuccessfully for the Colorado state senate in 1970. "We enjoy politics. We're happy to pitch in and do whatever seems appropriate."

Even though his wife's bid was only exploratory, Schroeder, like Elizabeth Dole, was asked about the spouse's role. Should there be a Pat Schroeder administration, whose shoes would he fill?

"Well, I don't know, maybe I'll play golf with Denis Thatcher," he said. "I never really thought about it, although my initial reaction would be that probably the first time we get a woman as president or vice-president, that the husband is proba-bly going to have to bend over backward and avoid—there might be a tendency to see the husband as more of an influence or a player. I think probably Denis Thatcher, who [gave] his wife money and support, is the role model. From everything I know Margaret Thatcher is her own woman and, you know, Denis is supportive, and he plays golf, and he goes to his clubs, and he basically lets his wife do her job. I think that is probably where I could come down."

If Pat Schroeder did make a presidential bid, her husband's pro-fessional life would change, he said, as did the professional lives of his female counterparts. Schroeder, like other spouses, especially attorneys, said he would not be immune from conflicts of interest and disruptions of "family time" and separation. As it was, he remembered being in Thailand on business when "someone came in with the *Herald Tribune* and said, 'Look, your wife is running for President!' That's how I found out."

How did that make him feel at the time?

Schroeder paused and grinned. He said something all the spouses of 1988 presidential contenders said in one form or an-other. "I thought that maybe I shouldn't be traveling so much."

★ ★ ★

In 1988 the question of double standards was fleshed out in yet another way, as shown in the case of the vice-president's wife,

Marilyn Quayle. Perhaps more than any other spouse who came to the forefront in 1988, Mrs. Quayle raised questions not just about career conflicts but about a wife's political influence and accountability for that influence.

An attorney, Mrs. Quayle said she would consider going back to work, or even filling out her husband's vacated Indiana senate seat after he was elected to the vice-presidency. But in keeping with the political reality she faced and potential conflicts of interest, Marilyn Quayle nestled into the low-profile role of second lady to the second man. A job that by her own reckoning is far from full time.

Had she gone back to work, she said, she "would be making a statement." But she found she couldn't pursue the areas that she was "best equipped to work in because in this city that's hard. When given the choice of probably taking a job that may not be as exciting or interesting—I mean I can do trust law—you're sitting behind a desk. If I have a full-time job, I'm not going to be able to travel with Dan around the world, and I have found that very rewarding.

"It is hard," she continued. "I am pulled in many directions emotionally. Should I do this? Or that? What really does fulfill personal ambitions and goals and what utilizes your skills as best they can be used? Where is the line between a traditional role and what I had seen many years ago as what I would be doing with my life? Which is totally different than where I am."

Rutgers scholar Ruth Mandel saw Marilyn Quayle as an interesting case study in women's changing roles. "That marriage symbolizes a kind of 'double image' of some sort," Mandel said. "The woman is highly educated, ambitious, and enjoys fulfilling that part of her energies and her identity. The decision to support her husband's career is perfectly consistent with her values. She can sound like both kinds of people." During the campaign, in her speeches Mrs. Quayle at times sounded as if she were a partner in a law firm. At other times she sounded like the traditional supportive wife. "She's a quick-change artist," Mandel said. "She shows enormous flexibility in shifting from role to role with ease. The image of her shifting from identity to identity and the very ease with which she seems to accomplish it is daunting to others. It discloses what women are up against in this period of transition and change. She's probably the best example."

During the campaign, Mrs. Quayle declared herself an influential member of her husband's inner circle—to the point that staff on the campaign and afterward complained about her interference. Mrs. Quayle was furious during the campaign with Bush "handlers" (Stu Spencer and Joe Canzeri, in particular) who, she felt, muzzled her husband during the race while he endured "Candidate's School," as Rich Bond later described it. "'We knew we were going to have to script him,'" Canzeri told journalists Witcover and Germond when the race was over. "'We were continually putting out fires. There was a sense we couldn't turn him loose on your group [the press].' In internal discussions," Witcover and Germond reported in their book on the 1988 campaign, "Quayle had a short attention span. He didn't want anything on paper. His eyes would glaze over. . . . There was an immaturity, but also a cockiness that he could deal with anything."

Mrs. Quayle had urged her husband to break loose from those handlers. When the election was long over she singled out Spencer and Canzeri for criticism. "Those one and a half months that those guys were in charge was an aberration in Dan's career," she said defensively. She categorized their published remarks to Witcover and Germond as "sour grapes. They knew we didn't appreciate or didn't feel they were doing the best job. That's why . . . we kept bringing in more and more of our own people on board to diminish their influence. . . . Those guys are supposedly professionals. Obviously they weren't," she said. Then she added, "Politics doesn't need these sleazy characters."

During the campaign, Mrs. Quayle was questioned about her influence over her husband the candidate, a man widely viewed as not up to the vice-presidency. She was also questioned about her own views, especially her religious beliefs.

Mrs. Quayle and her parents have followed the teachings of Colonel Robert Thieme, a Houston-based evangelist who ministers over the airwaves and through mail-order tape cassettes. Thieme appears to maintain an extreme level of control over his cultlike following, according to journalist Garry Wills, who talked with Thieme in the fall of 1989.

In an interview at the vice-president's residence in August 1989, Mrs. Quayle took issue with published reports that showed, as she saw it, "I was an unbending person who would force religion on others. It was absolutely wrong, totally against my upbringing and what I see as one's faith." Mrs. Quayle believes in such biblical precepts as Noah's Ark and creationism. She has said she believes creationism should be taught along with evolution in public schools.

When pressed about these beliefs Mrs. Quayle recoiled and refused to elaborate. She maintained that her views are her own and said, "They're personal. Everyone's faith is personal. I would never force my faith on anyone. Never have." In a postelection interview she declined to say whether or not her husband shares those particular beliefs of hers, though she did say that it was "their shared religious views" that in part brought the two together. The Quayles met and married within ten weeks.

She has held to that stance while working to help her husband seek the nation's second-highest office and continuing to advise him there.

According to Wills, Marilyn Quayle's behavior is in keeping with Thieme's teachings. "It is fashionable on the political right to attack some Supreme Court decisions as importing a 'right to privacy' into the Constitution," he wrote in "The Private Ministry of Colonel Thieme," an October 1989 article published in the magazine *Wigwag*. "But Thieme puts protecting privacy among the first tasks of the state, and respecting privacy among the first duties of a Christian. For him, the government does not exist to guarantee life, liberty, and the pursuit of happiness but to protect 'liberty, privacy, and property.' The sin he inveighs against most often and ardently is curiosity about other Christians' behavior. He warns his followers against asking or answering personal questions. He attacks counselors, psychiatric or religious, and refuses to counsel his own people. Right doctrine is the only helpful advice, and anyone wanting guidance should go straight to the one true source: 'The Bible is the only accurate discerner of what you think.'"

Mrs. Quayle's religious views were most prominently brought to national attention prior to the vice-presidential debate on October 5, 1988.

The Bush camp felt Mrs. Quayle was "pummeled" in the television interviews that aired then, especially on the morning TV shows—programs not ordinarily known for pummeling their guests. Sheila Tate recalled, "I thought it really crossed the line. I called the executive producer of the *Today* show and complained, and I never do that. I thought they were badgering her on religious questions. About people related to her who aren't even running for anything. I really thought it was terribly unfair."

But when a wife contributes to her husband's policy making—whether it is open as in the case of Marilyn Quayle, or less detectable as in the case of Barbara Bush—where is that line drawn?

Marilyn Quayle says she is no different from any other Quayle adviser. "I don't talk about what I tell him. I don't talk about what he discusses with me. I acknowledge that we do discuss things, but then no member of his staff had better talk about how they advise him and what they're telling him. It's no different than that."

But of course it is. Marilyn Quayle cannot be fired. Only divorced.

★ ★ ★

Political spouses certainly have First Amendment rights and a right to their own lives, but, fairly or not, their actions still affect the public's view of the elected official, their mate. In 1988 political operatives argued that it was helpful to see the spouses because they could flesh out the candidates' biographies. In the ongoing theater of politics in America, the wife provided background information, they said. "Our unconscious assumptions regarding leadership seem to require symbols that 'certify' a leader's respectability, his high moral standards, his appropriateness for public trust—in other words, his 'normalness,'" women's studies scholar Joanna Gillespie has written. "The visible presence of a public figure's wife and family demonstrate a basic civilizing process and that he is committed to civilization's continuity. We read that he is 'domesticated'—channeled sexually and thus not a threat to society." Following that logic, Barbara Bush's effectiveness as a mother and grandmother gives the public assurance that because her husband cares about his own family, he will care about theirs.

There are some grounds for that argument. During the election voters studying Kitty and Bar did learn something. Barbara Bush certainly did not tell voters everything they wanted to know about George Bush. Nevertheless, when compared to Kitty, she showed, so it seemed, that her family was better equipped to endure the rigors of the presidency.

After the election Kitty Dukakis's behavior and psychiatric history with depression opened up disquieting questions that have yet to be answered. Most disturbing: If Kitty Dukakis's bouts with depression occurred regularly every fall, as her family physician has said, how did the campaign plan to handle it? They hired a professional SWAT team of media handlers. The head of it, Paul Costello, maintains he didn't know about the problem. Another close aide did, but said depression never interfered with Kitty's campaigning.

Mrs. Dukakis's condition raised further questions about where the line of privacy falls for family members of public officials. In June 1989 she shared her thoughts on that issue. "We're electing the highest officeholder of our country. For the most part I feel the public has the right to know everything there is to know about that person. Whether stability is a part of that person's life. All of those things are fair game." However, she didn't feel that reasoning applied to spouses. During the campaign a reporter had once asked Kitty if she had been to a psychiatrist. She said she refused to answer. "That was nobody's goddamned business. I've chosen to speak about it since then. What relevance does that have? What of my medical records? What relevance did that have? So there is a line I think," she said.

In light of Mrs. Dukakis's subsequent behavior, some White House observers argue that her medical history *was* relevant, insofar as her history of substance abuse and depression—which dates back at least to 1974—could affect *her* performance in the White House and, in turn, affect her husband. After the election Kitty admitted that she felt she could not have withstood the strains of the White House.

If her husband knew of her emotional fragility, some asked later, why did he put her under such pressure by seeking the presidency, even if she had urged him to do so?

When Kitty was hospitalized on November 6 for drinking rubbing alcohol, such questions were discussed publicly. Journalists asked psychologists about the possible causes of Mrs. Dukakis's emotional state. Shortly after her hospitalization, four practitioners, none of whom had treated Mrs. Dukakis, talked with *The Boston Globe*. "Her troubles may be tied to her husband's, psychologists say," the headlines in the *Globe* read. One expert was quoted as saying: "When someone is going through all that Michael Dukakis has gone through—with losing the [presidential] election and the state fiscal crisis and now having to inflict all this pain on people with budget cuts—there has to be some emotional pain." Another suggested the governor resign to get out of the public eye so he and his wife could work out their problems privately. "I would say to her to get out of the public eye as soon as possible—because being in the public eye puts her under very special stress," psychologist David Kantor, head of the Kantor Family Institute in Cambridge, told the *Globe*. "I would say to her, 'Get Michael out of politics and get someplace where you have some privacy to work on this problem together.'"

The article made the governor appear to be a "culprit in her illness," as *Newsweek* later put it—and prompted the Massachusetts Board of Registration of Psychologists, a body appointed by the governor, to begin an investigation into the remarks, which could have led to revocation of the four practitioners' licenses.

Politically, the intervention of a Dukakis-appointed board looked awkward. The action also had First Amendment ramifications. The questioning of doctors and psychologists to explain medical, or in this case, psychological conditions, is a standard, if sometimes undesirable, journalistic practice.

*   *   *

Underneath the phenomenon of the first ladies race lies a bigger question, one that reflects on women's status in America. Journalist Susan Riley of the *Ottawa Citizen* put it well. "The first question we have to ask ourselves is why, now, are there political wives? . . . Why do we need political wives? Why do we put up with them? Why does society insist on an archetypal wife, an Everywife, a figurehead with no political power but potent symbolic importance? What is the political wife saying about women, about marriage, about the way power is distributed in our society? It sounds as if she is saying that women are status symbols, possessions, mirrors for the men they live with. But aren't those days gone?"

Evidently not. The public behavior of political wives—and of the first lady—and the public acceptance and expectations of their largely ceremonial, symbolic role say a lot.

Despite herself, Nancy Reagan's lasting contribution to the advancement of American women was in blowing the lid off the covert way in which political wives, especially first ladies, operate. The silent helpmate pose, perfected by Mrs. Reagan in her first four years in the White House, and still the ideal, is no longer plausible.

Initially, Nancy tried to keep up the facade. "I watched it very closely these last eight years," her former press secretary, Sheila Tate, recalled. "Nancy Reagan erred on the side of caution on that. She didn't want anyone to think she had influence for the first four years. I mean, I sat through hundreds of interviews with her, and I watched the frustration on the part of reporters because she wouldn't say anything."

In her first year at the White House Barbara Bush continued to do the same thing. Happy to foster her husband's ambition, Mrs. Bush publicly appears to be less savvy, less involved, and less ambitious than her friends, family, and staff say she is.

Once her husband left office Mrs. Reagan made up for lost time on that score by publishing her memoirs, *My Turn*. Much of the negative press that followed was a consequence of what many see as Nancy Reagan's unpleasant personality. But a lot came from what others saw as Mrs. Reagan's meddlesome role. As Tate points out, "If any first lady starts moving to the policy side, people don't like her. They really don't. There's a very thin line a first lady walks."

In some reviews, serious questions about the first lady's role were raised. As R. W. Apple of *The New York Times* asked in his review: "Does the country derive any real benefit from putting an essentially domestic relationship onto such a grand stage? Why do we have a first lady at all?"

There are a couple of answers to that question.

The first lady is, in part, a product of a quirk in the presidential system and peculiarly American attitudes about leaders, according to historian Betty Boyd Caroli. In her book *First Ladies* she points out: The assignment of the president "includes two jobs that are performed by separate individuals in other types of representative governments: a head of state who presides over ceremonial functions, and a head of government who makes major appointments and takes a decisive role in legislation. The American president, charged with both tasks, frequently resorted to sending substitutes on ceremonial and other occasions when a mere physical presence was required. Members of the president's household made excellent surrogates—they signaled the president's approval and also his continued control of government. Martha Washington began what became a tradition when she attended a New York church service while George was ill, and her example inspired her successors. Nearly two hundred years later, Nancy Reagan left her husband's hospital room to return to the White House and announce to guests assembled for a large reception that she was 'the president's stand-in.' Political wives substituted in other ways for their spouses, sometimes maintaining a facade of civility while their husbands feuded. John Quincy Adams observed in 1824 that Andrew Jackson and William Crawford, contenders for the presidency, were avoiding each other socially but 'the ladies have exchanged visits.'"

Caroli points out that the president's living arrangements also increased his wife's role. With both official residence and private quarters combined, it was hard for the wife not to know what her husband was up to. And although it was considered inappropriate for wives to campaign until well into the twentieth century, once they began, they inevitably moved closer to the power circle.

Beyond history, *The Washington Post*'s critic Richard Cohen had another answer to that question. In a December 1989 essay he argued that the first lady was largely a media creation. Just another celebrity to fill the needs of celebrity journalism. "Constitutionally hollow positions—First Lady, vice president—are covered as if they were important. The press has made them America's constitutional monarchs: extremely limited powers, almost unlimited coverage. In other countries, these would be 'balcony' positions, and their occupants would wave to the populace on certain holidays. But for the First Lady, and even the vice president, every day is a holiday."

Cohen is right. On the international front no such status is afforded the wife of the German chancellor or husband of the British prime minister. Wives of Russian leaders were widely unknown until Raisa Gorbachev, who may be better known in the United States than in the USSR.

Even when a wife does have status, women in the equivalent position are breaking out of a traditional mold. In France, Danielle Mitterrand, who at sixty-four is the same age as Barbara Bush, speaks openly of her pursuits apart from her husband. "I am the wife of François Mitterrand, and he happens to be president of the republic," she said in an interview with *The Washington Post*. "So I have a broader tribune." Even though she is the president's wife, she said, she has not "lost my right to express myself."

In Spain, Carmen Romero, the forty-two-year-old wife of Prime Minister Felipe Gonzalez, the Socialist Workers Party leader elected in 1982, ran and won her own seat in the Spanish Parliament. A former schoolteacher and union organizer, Romero told the Spanish woman's magazine, *Dunia*, before her election on October 29, 1989: "I have struggled to maintain my independence. First with teaching. Then with my professional work. My candidacy is nothing more than a new stage in consonance with the previous one. I know this will cause a lot of friction with those who think I have the obligation to accompany my husband on all his trips. I believe this obligation does not exist."

Romero didn't join her husband on his trip here in the fall of 1989.

The *Post*'s Cohen also pointed out another reason why America's first lady continues to have a high profile, especially since 1960—"the approximate year when the first lady became the First Lady . . . would coincide with the election of John F. Kennedy and the emergence of television as the nation's dominant news medium. . . . Among other things, television networks expanded their nightly news shows from 15 minutes to a half-hour. On a slow day, how were they to fill all that time? To the national media, every twitch of the president, vice president and First Lady became news. . . ."

True. The distaff side of the presidency also fits like a glove into White House image making, joining professional public relations to presidential symbols. "Most activities of the First Lady bring her to public events where she reflects the prestige of her husband's high office. The complaint by her staff has been that the West Wing political offices, including the Press Office, have not been sensitive enough to the potential publicity benefits the President can derive from her activities," authors Michael Baruch Grossman and Martha Joynt Kumar wrote in their book *Portraying the President: The White House and the News Media*. Sheila Rabb Weidenfeld, Betty Ford's press secretary, likewise complained in a book she wrote about her White House years that the West Wing failed to appreciate Mrs. Ford's public-relations, ergo political, value.

Not so for Barbara Bush, whose husband campaigned largely on emotions: railing against furloughs and rallying around the flag. Fear of crime and love of family. "Warm fuzzies," in the words of one operative. Wives and other family members—children and grandchildren—became a key part of the handler's marketing strategy: the soft sell. Flashing images of himself with his family, the candidate tried to show that he cared about voters' families. Unfortunately, the family images of love and security didn't cogently connect with issues like education, jobs, or health care.

As PBS newsman Bill Moyers noted in a television documentary titled *Leading Questions*, broadcast just about a year after the presidential election, politics is now played out on the television screen. In 1988 politicians favored sentimental symbols like the family. Messages emotional enough to stir the heart. Family is easy to invoke, hard to define, and impossible to oppose. Love and togetherness can sell anything, he pointed out. Even stock.

"The monologue of television values becomes the conversation of democracy. . . . It matters not what we *do* about reality that decides the character of a nation—it's how we *feel*. Having won on flags, furloughs, and family, Bush's standing depends on the continuing confession of emotions."

Moyers referred to an interview the Bushes gave to David Frost for broadcast from their summer home in Kennebunkport. Moyers's editors excerpted from that tape a string of snippets of Bush "emoting" at length. "As a country we are emotional," the president said. "We Bushes cry easily." "We feel in our heart." "It was so moving." Moyers ended here.

When it was Mrs. Bush's turn to talk interviewer David Frost spoke with the first lady about her popularity. He gushed, "Don't you feel a real, a tidal wave of love coming your way?" She seemed to. And the explanation she gave was that people liked her because "I don't make any big decisions. I'm trying to say this nicely so I don't hurt my own feelings, but I mean, no Marilyn Monroe am I."

Ceremony and historical precedent aside, this is where first ladies today play their most important public role. Barbara Bush is an image maker for her husband. Bar has developed her own public following, one that has eclipsed her husband's. She is admired for her warmth, caring, and puppies, and not for her political ideas, values, or judgment. Because of that she is a West Wing asset.

Why is Barbara Bush so well liked? In contrast to Kitty Dukakis, who, like so many American women, appeared to be constantly battling with 'who she was,' Barbara Bush seems to know. Her self-image appears rock-solid, secure, and separate from the role she chose to play. Unlike Kitty and several other wives in the 1988 race—Barbara Bush knows the light she basks in is reflected light. She stood out as a woman sure of her place in the political arena and content with it. Of that generation of women who never considered it an effort to wait on, wait for, or wait alongside their husbands, Bar never seemed even to notice her role was limited.

In the midst of her environment, Bar exudes steadfastness and strength. "We've all heard repeatedly of the trials of being a political wife—the lack of privacy, the pressure to be the ideal spouse. Some women—like Nancy Reagan—thrive on it. Others—like Kitty Dukakis—learn to survive it. Bush seems to have risen above it. Being a political spouse hasn't undermined her sense of who she essentially is and likes to be—a mother and a grandmother," Illinois writer Joanne Cleaver wrote in an essay published in the *Chicago Tribune*.

She is funny and she has spunk. In the prescribed banality of public life, Mrs. Bush injects a few hilarious sparks. She kissed back the hand of the man who kissed hers, staid Denis Thatcher's, outside 10 Downing Street. She told New York's Cardinal O'Connor, as his robes became entangled at a formal dinner, "I've got to teach you how to lift your skirt."

She appears genuine and her own person. "Her charm is not that she is concerned about literacy, or that she looks like the mother most of us never had," John Duka wrote in *Vogue* magazine, "Or that, unlike the Dukakises, she abhors public displays of affection, which she calls 'fake.' Barbara Bush just doesn't let herself get pushed around. One could call it a style."

Her "I am who I am" attitude could even be called feminist, after a fashion.

Barbara Bush has taken on her role as professional homemaker to a nation, as Mrs. Thousand Points of Light. She regularly re-enacts the model of the ladies' charity. This kind of hands-on volunteer work does good. But more important, it is politically pragmatic, easy to get on TV, and much less expensive than tax-supported social justice. She is lauded for her photo opportunities at a homeless kitchen, or with an AIDS baby. At the same time her husband's administration nixes pamphlets promoting condom use for reducing AIDS, and budgets $100 million less for education than Ronald Reagan did. On the nation's domestic problems, Mrs. Bush at times has seemed to be a victim of *her* class.

In her interview with NPR's Susan Stamberg, Mrs. Bush seemed unaware of the economic pressures most women face. Mrs. Bush said that she had never spent her time as well as when she was home with her children. "I never have been more grateful for the fact that I was lucky enough and fortunate enough to be able to stay home with my children."

Stamberg agreed. "There was a lot of luck and so few now . . . I mean, given inflation and what prices are like . . ."

Mrs. Bush responded, "Well, no, given what we want. We don't want one TV set," referring, she said, not to the single mother who has to work, but women who "choose" to work.

Stamberg came back: "Most people that I hear about where both [partners] work, work because they *must*, simply to pay the rent in a not extravagant house with *one* television set."

"Yes," Mrs. Bush responded. "And that I would say, you have to do. But I know a lot of young women who are *very* successful who opt to work, too."

Though she is admired for her warmth and caring and her grandmotherly ways, Bar's real strength lies in her political know-how, her toughmindedness, her charisma, and her formidable ambition—and in the facade she maintains that politics is a hardball business that mere "wives" sensibly shun. Like many political wives, Bar has in a way been almost smuggled into power alongside her elected husband. Publicly, she carries out her purely decorative, symbolic role, but behind the scenes, as her children and friends say, she's a full partner in the family business of politics.

An ambitious political wife, she appears to be just along for the ride. When questions of policy arise, she deflects them or keeps quiet. "She has plenty of opinions," a former aide says, "but even within the confines of the campaign plane, she'd keep her mouth shut. Because she knows she'll read about it. She'll tell someone who will tell someone and she'll read about it."

Mrs. Bush acknowledges that she is "very candid" with her husband in private about issues that concern her, as well as staff who trouble her. "I tell him what I think, and he tells me what he thinks, and then we are united."

"She is influential. Obviously. If you have a good relationship," Sheila Tate has said.

Using the same kind of logic she applied when not talking about redecorating the White House, or closeting her top-drawer wardrobe, Mrs. Bush correctly points out that she is "not the elected official."

Because she is neither docile nor unintelligent, Barbara Bush has to be especially careful, deceptive perhaps. "I don't mess with George's office and he doesn't mess with my house," she frequently says in an unconvincing self-effacing display. In truth the first lady is a political pro. Few in Washington doubt that Barbara Bush has enormous influence with the president, despite her *pro forma* disclaimers.

Barbara Bush's strength is that of the classic political wife. She has but one goal: getting her husband into office and keeping him happy while there. Hers is a simple "mission," as the Bush family calls their devotion to George Bush's career. There is no room for moral ambiguity or inner confusion with that purpose in mind. Bar's way of life is spun out of Yankee stock, and honed by years in political life. Even the smallest of her efforts and thoughts appears to be directed to that end. When asked about what she put into her published campaign diary, she said, "I'm not going to lie to you; I think about whether it will help him or hurt him politically." She did the same when it came to making her key staff choice: selecting a black woman as her press secretary, the most visible member of her staff. "It is important because George has asked for years in this office to please get minorities and since my office is really *his* office—I mean, we all work for George—I decided I could do what he asked," she explained.

To advance George's career, Bar masks a steely determination behind a self-deprecating wit and self-effacing modesty. She is not an activist, but a volunteer. Like her husband, she has no "vision thing." Accepting the rightness of "the mission," Barbara Bush also accepts without apparent question the limits political life places on wives. Fortunately for her, the American political system is one that rewards appearance rather than reality. As long as Barbara Bush appears to be making Oatmeal Lace Cookies, not public policy, she'll remain an asset to the Oval Office.

The world around Barbara Bush has changed. As one Republican woman said, an outspoken woman is "a problem in our Party." Playing it close to the vest enables Barbara Bush to avoid controversy. By taking a low-key stance Bar can function where it

counts, beyond the realm of the media, and keep her privacy, like
Bess Truman, whom she admires—and who entered into almost
every decision Harry Truman ever made.

★   ★   ★

Traditionally the press has taken a hands-off attitude toward the
president's wife and family. But as 1988 showed, these women are
players in the presidential sweepstakes. Observers like William
Safire, *New York Times* columnist, argue that the most serious
question the first lady raises, one he directed to Nancy Reagan,
was "Did she, without the knowledge of the President but with
her derivative authority, actively interfere with the political workings of the Administration?"

The question is more basic than that: The first lady answers to
her husband, but does she ever answer to his electorate?

Though publicly shunning politics and refusing to talk issues on
the campaign trail, Mrs. Bush confessed in interviews, "I talk privately about it." Her posture affords her a much-needed private
life, yet puts her on a tightrope. She admits to advising her husband in certain areas, but when asked about it she insists such
matters are private. Uncertain of where to find guidelines when
questioning the president's family about their influence, reporters
back off.

In her 1975 book, *The Power Lovers,* reporter Myra MacPherson of *The Washington Post* questioned such behavior. She wondered: "The question is should we have different regulations for
different types of political wives? Should a wife who acts as a lieutenant or auxiliary politician for her husband and has untold private influence in his decision making be as liable to criticism as the
officeholder? Can a wife and family of a political leader skip back
and forth between a public figure one day and private citizen the
next?"

The first lady's is an ill-defined role, without constitutional
power. But as Carolyn Heilbrun pointed out in her book *Writing a
Woman's Life:* "The true representation of power is not of a big
man beating a smaller man or a woman. Power is the ability to
take one's place in whatever discourse is essential to action and the
right to have one's part matter. This is true in the Pentagon, in
marriage, in friendship, and in politics."

In the end the American public may never know if they elected a team into the White House. Ultimately, as Barbara Bush shows, private influence or power so far remains unaccountable.

Barbara Bush may also be the last first lady of her kind: a throwback. An old-fashioned woman playing a role in a way very much at odds with how most American women live their lives. Paradoxically, by taking such a low-key profile Mrs. Bush may open the way for another woman to go another way. "Can't you just see a Hattie Babbitt or a Liddy Dole leaving the White House each morning with her briefcase?" Irene Natividad said with a grin when the 1988 race kicked off.

After she left the White House, Nancy Reagan said she thought it would be a shame to give up the opportunity to be first lady. "I believe if a future first lady thinks she can have a career outside the White House, she will be shortchanging her husband and herself. She would miss so much of the experience and joy and the satisfaction of the job. It would be a terrible personal loss to pass that up . . . because you might think you have something else better to do."

Natividad didn't quite agree with that analysis but conceded that it might be difficult for the first lady to continue with a professional career while in the White House. She told a reporter at the beginning of the race: "If they aren't going to allow her to have her own career, then they ought to pay her. The traditional role of the first lady has to be rethought; I think the American public should be aware of what they exact from these women."

Given the rigors of presidential campaigning, it's hard to imagine a spouse sustaining a professional career all the way to the White House door. But there are spouses of potential presidential contenders—the economist wife of Texas Senator Phil Gramm or New Jersey Senator Bill Bradley's wife, a university professor—who may have to make the choice. Regardless, it is likely the public will see more issue-talking professional surrogates on the trail and a growing recognition of these women as the political partners that many are and always have been—a fact more and more historians are beginning to document. The difficulty today, as 1988 painfully showed, is that some women are still "in between." They yearn to be recognized as full partners in the political process yet find themselves confined to the realm of political image-making.

Kitty Dukakis once said, "If I wanted to be taken seriously, then I had to be serious about the work I was doing."

But for a political wife to be taken seriously means the public has to recognize her as a player and hold her accountable for whatever influence she wields. It means recognizing overt, not covert, power. Barbara Bush may not be willing to accept that new definition of first lady. Kitty Dukakis wasn't quite ready. But with more Liddy Doles and Jim Schroeders on the campaign trail, the phenomenon of "first partner" is unavoidably on the horizon.

Index